PSAT/NMSQT®

STRATEGIES, PRACTICE & REVIEW

2015 Edition

Kaplan offers resources and options to help you prepare for the PSAT, SAT, ACT, AP exams, and other high-stakes exams. Go to www.kaptest.com or scan this code below with your phone (you will need to download a QR code reader) for free events and promotions.

snap.vu/m87n

PSAT/NMSQT®

STRATEGIES, PRACTICE & REVIEW

2015 Edition

By the Staff of Kaplan Test Prep and Admissions

PUBLISHING

New York

© 2014 by Kaplan, Inc.

Published by Kaplan Publishing, a division of Kaplan, Inc.
395 Hudson Street
New York, NY 10014

Printed in the United States of America

10 9 8 7 6 5 4 3 2 1

ISBN-13: 978-1-61865-577-6

Kaplan Publishing books are available at special quantity discounts to use for sales promotions, employee premiums, or educational purposes. For more information or to purchase books, please call the Simon & Schuster special sales department at 866-506-1949.

Table of Contents

AVAILABLE ONLINE

ADDITIONAL PRACTICE

kaptest.com/PSATbooksonline

As an owner of this quide, you are entitled to get more practice and help online. Log on to **kaptest.com/PSATbooksonline** to access additional practice. Kaplan's online PSAT practice is free of charge to purchasers of this book. You'll be prompted for a password that can be found in this book, so have your book handy when you log on.

FOR ANY TEST CHANGES OR LATE-BREAKING DEVELOPMENTS

kaptest.com/publishing

The material in this book is up-to-date at the time of publication. However, the College Board may have instituted changes in the test after this book was published. Be sure to carefully read the materials you receive when you register for the test. If there are any important late-breaking developments—or any changes or corrections to the Kaplan test preparation materials in this book—we will post that information online at **kaptest.com/publishing**.

For customer service, please contact us at **booksupport@kaplan.com**.

HOW TO USE THIS BOOK

Welcome to *PSAT/NMSQT Strategies, Practice & Review 2015*!

In this section, we'll walk you through everything you'll need to know to take advantage of the book and online resources.

HERE'S A HANDY CHECKLIST TO GET YOUR STUDYING ON TRACK:

☐ **Register your online companion** for extra practice, Live Online classroom events, Fast Fact videos, and more.

☐ **Take the online diagnostic quiz** to figure out your strong and weak areas. You should also **take the full-length Diagnostic Test in the book,** which will help further guide your study.

☐ **Figure out which chapters you need to study the most** and review those chapters first. As needed, refer to the Fast Fact videos online.

☐ When you've learned all of Kaplan's proven score-raising strategies, you can **practice, practice, practice with three full-length tests in the book and one online**.

Knowing the PSAT inside and out will gain you points on *every section*. So, **Part One: Getting Ready for Test Day** covers basic information on the PSAT, and Kaplan's overall strategies for approaching the test. These are the fundamentals you need to be ready for the exam and to get a great score.

Part Two: Diagnostic Test is your first opportunity to take a full-length practice test. Take the Diagnostic Test and use your results to see how you would do if you took the test today without any additional preparation. Then, use the detailed answer explanations to understand what questions you missed and why. You should also use your score to figure out which chapters of the book you need to review most.

After you take the diagnostic test, proceed to **Part Three: PSAT Strategies** which will guide you through improving your score on the three sections of the PSAT. The three chapters in Part Three break down the three sections of the test and give you clear strategies on how to succeed on each. At the end of each chapter, you will have an opportunity to test your newly improved skills on a brief practice section.

First, **Chapter 5: How to Attack the Critical Reading Sections,** covers the two Critical Reading question types: Sentence Completion and Reading Comprehension. You will also learn specific strategies to use for decoding tough vocabulary, completing one- and two-blank sentences, and answering various reading comprehension questions. Chapter 5 also gives you specific tips and strategies for improving your vocabulary—something that will help you earn points on test day.

Next, **Chapter 6: How to Attack the Math Sections** switches gears to math skills. This chapter covers SAT math strategies and short cuts and offers a review of both basic and advanced math concepts that you will need to know for the exam.

If you struggled with the Writing section, or you just need more review, turn to **Chapter Seven: How to Attack the Writing Section,** which covers the Writing section of the PSAT in depth. You'll learn strategies to help you answer the three types of writing questions on the PSAT: Sentence Errors, Improving Sentences, and Improving Paragraphs.

When you are ready to apply everything you've learned in the review chapters, **Part Four: Practice Tests** offers three additional full-length practice tests. Again, you should use the detailed answer explanations to understand what you missed, and to learn more about the score-raising strategies that could help you answer similar questions on test day.

As test day approaches, explore the information in **Part Five: PSAT Resources**, which includes additional items that can help you improve your score on the PSAT. This part also includes an SAT Essay Preview that may help you if you plan to take the SAT later in your high school career. Additional essay practice can be found online in the online companion's syllabus.

USING YOUR SAT ONLINE COMPANION

REGISTER YOUR ONLINE COMPANION

Register your online companion using these simple steps:

1. **Go to Kaptest.com/booksonline.**
2. Follow the on-screen instructions. Please have a copy of your book available.

GET A MOBILE VERSION OF THIS BOOK

Sign up for your online companion and learn how to get a mobile version of this book.

After you register for your online companion and set up a Kaplan ID and password, you will receive an email explaining how to get a mobile version of the *Kaplan PSAT/NMSQT Strategies, Practice & Review 2015*.

JOIN A LIVE ONLINE EVENT

Kaplan's PSAT Live Online sessions are interactive, instructor-led SAT prep lessons that you can participate in from anywhere you can access the Internet.

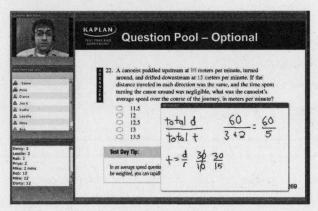

PSAT Live Online sessions are held in a state-of-the-art virtual classroom—actual lessons in real time, just like a physical classroom experience. Interact with your teacher and other classmates using audio, instant chat, whiteboard, polling, and screen-sharing functionality. And just like courses at Kaplan centers, PSAT Live Online sessions are led by experienced Kaplan instructors.

TO REGISTER FOR A PSAT LIVE ONLINE EVENT:

1. Once you've signed in to your student home page, open your Syllabus.

2. In the Syllabus window, go to the "Live Online Registration" menu option.

3. Click on the link. A separate window will appear with registration instructions.

PSAT Live Online events are scheduled to take place throughout 2014. Please check your online companion for dates and times!

Please note: Registration begins one month before the session date. Be sure to sign up early because spaces are reserved on a first-come, first-served basis.

WATCH THE FAST FACT VIDEOS

In Fast Fact videos, one of Kaplan's highly rated SAT tutors explains and reinforces the most important concepts from each chapter.

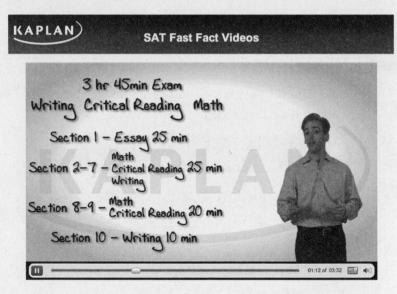

Fast Fact videos can only be accessed through your online companion. Here's how:

1. Once you've signed into your student home page, open your Syllabus.

2. In the Syllabus window, go to the "Fast Fact Videos" menu option.

3. Click on the link for the video you'd like to see. A separate window will appear with your video.

BUT WAIT, THERE'S MORE ...

In addition to a practice test and Fast Fact videos, the PSAT/NMSQT online companion offers study sheets, flashcards, and access to other items that will help you prepare for test day.

GOOD LUCK!

PSAT STUDY GROUP GUIDE

PSAT STUDY GROUP GUIDE

WHAT

What is the PSAT? An opportunity—that's what it is! It is an opportunity to break out of the mold of teacher and student, classes in public, and study in private. It is an opportunity to improve your understanding of the PSAT in a personal, supportive, motivational, and . . . dare we say . . . even fun environment. Preparing for the PSAT in small groups—if done correctly—has been proven to be extremely effective in demystifying the test and improving both a student's confidence and score.

WHY

Have you ever tried to run a marathon alone? (And that means no iPod, too.) Ever wonder why bicyclists in the Tour de France train and ride in packs? Did you know that even a professional singles tennis player has a coach and multiple hitting partners? It took more than one person to design and construct the PSAT, so it's going to take more than one person to ace it as well.

Good news—you already have hundreds of Kaplan test prep experts on your side, but a few more wouldn't hurt. That is where your PSAT study buddies come in.

The structure and built-in support of a regularly scheduled study group can also provide the motivation you need to avoid procrastinating. When a group of peers is depending on you, it's much harder to bail on them. It's one thing to skip out on a trip to the movies, but another to miss your turn explaining (or getting an explanation for) planar geometry.

If two heads are better than one, then four to five should be even better! Take advantage of your study buddies' various strengths and let them take advantage of yours. Together, you can shore up each other's academic weaknesses as you learn from each other.

Some students who are more reserved Monday to Friday in class may have an easier time asking questions, or providing insight, to peers rather than authority figures. After all, it will be you, not the teachers, who will be on the spot on test day. Who else has more of a vested interest in doing well besides your fellow test takers?

Study groups also allow members to play teacher for the day. Ever hear the old medical adage: "See One. Do One. Teach One"? Teaching concepts requires a higher level of understanding of the material; consequently, that actually makes it a great learning tool.

Study buddies are also extremely useful in helping to simulate accurate testing conditions—no small issue for a test that can be somewhat nerve-racking. There is a significant difference between five students working their way through the same diagnostic test at the same time, with a parent minding the clock, and sitting at your own kitchen table with a cup of hot cocoa, your older sister clicking through her Facebook page in the other room, your cell phone beeping with every text message, and your dad's football game in the background.

And finally, this actually can be fun. Yes, seriously. We all know that studying and work can be deathly boring, but we also know getting a good score on the PSAT is important. Fortunately, fun and productivity need not be exclusive. Even though misery loves company, studying does not mean there cannot be breaks, food, or some kind of enjoyable diversion immediately following.

Just make sure that everyone understands that acing the PSAT is the most enjoyable of all.

WHO

Just who should be invited to help cram for the PSAT, and how many is too many? As for the latter question, the group's number is completely a personal preference. If you work best with only one friend/study partner, that's fine. However, be careful of backsliding from work to gossip or chitchat too quickly.

For many people, a group of three to five study buddies is the ideal number. It is small enough to organize and be manageable, yet large enough to share a variety of expertise and viewpoints.

When you get more than five or six people and your group goes from small to medium, however, things can get a bit more unwieldy. A larger group requires a stricter guiding hand . . . say a teacher . . . and that is what you're trying to avoid in a small, self-driven study group. If you've ever tried to organize six or more people to go to the movies or for a weekend outing, you're already familiar with the frustration of meshing numerous personalities and desires. Plus, when a group gets too large, you also run the risk of forming individual cliques, or mini-groups, that can detract from your study sessions. So do yourself a favor and stay small and manageable.

Now, on to the question of exactly who would make a great study buddy. You may be tempted to invite your closest friends because you know them well and feel comfortable around them. This could seriously backfire, however, if it becomes a social gathering. Save that for Saturday nights or the summertime. Furthermore, close friends are much easier to blow off and let slide in terms of work . . . and vice versa. You're actually more likely to work better and more seriously with a friend whose biggest connection to you is a shared desire to increase your scores. Someone similarly motivated to get a great score will help you stay focused.

Also keep in mind the relative strengths and weaknesses of the members of your group. While it's often best to study with people who are around the same score range as you, it's also worth considering whether you want to target people who are strong in areas where you are weak, and vice-versa, so you can peer-tutor each other and use each other's strengths. People who will either make you feel insecure about your weaknesses or whom you will wind up helping on every topic while not really building your own score are not the best study partners. Choose partners with an eye to building everyone's scores.

Try to find some motivated and serious students who are interested in performing well on the PSAT. Hopefully, they will have decent work habits and a better attitude about spending some R&R time on optional PSAT study. And if they have a similar schedule to yours, all the better.

If possible, try to assemble a dream team of study buddies with complementary fortes. Make sure you have at least one whiz in the math department and one budding English major to handle Reading Comprehension and Writing. That way, you can help each other as you take turns both learning and teaching.

HOW

How a study group goes about preparing for the PSAT is limited only by the imaginations of its members, but here are a few suggestions to get you started:

- *Play Stump the Group.* Have members bring in five vocabulary words that they find particularly difficult, and see who else shares that view. Talk about the words and turn them into catchy statements. "You're so not *perspicacious*, John, for thinking this word has anything to do with perspiration." "I'm, like, totally *enervated* in science class—I can hardly keep my eyes open."

- Have everyone maintain a growing pile of vocabulary flashcards, and take turns quizzing one another.

- *Play vocabulary Memory.* Make two index cards for every word: one with the word and one with the definition. Jumble the cards on the floor upside down and try to match them up. Whoever matches up the most wins.

- *Write a practice essay.* Have everyone write the same practice essay for "homework," and then critique (and praise) them one by one. This may seem scary because until now only your teachers and maybe family have seen your writing, but keep in mind, these are your friends and they have every reason to be fair and help you out. After all, you'll be doing the same for them.

- *Take timed quizzes together.* When you're finished, take turns puzzling over, and then explaining, the questions people got wrong. Make the quizzes as testlike as possible, with no talking and someone "proctoring" and watching the clock.

- *Set up a rotation of group leaders to determine the agenda for each session.* Let each leader teach his strength. One day Jill could go over the intricacies of coordinate geometry; the next week Malcolm can relate how he gets to the bottom of the Critical Reading passages so quickly.

- *Brainstorm a "cheat sheet" of math formulas.* With a group of you contributing, it is much more likely nothing will be missed. Have the cheat sheet out for the group to see when you are covering math, but then make it disappear as you get closer to test day.

- *Develop quizzes.* Use this and other test prep books to develop your own quizzes.

- *Talk to others who have already taken this type of exam.* Invite older friends or siblings to stop in once in a while to talk about the SAT and college application process. After all, the PSAT isn't an end in itself.

- *Play PSAT Jeopardy.* Divide the group into two teams, and have the group leader act as Alex Trebek as you play your own version of PSAT Jeopardy.

- *Break up the monotony with logic puzzles and brainteasers.* This is great for some of those trickier math problems. Try Sudoku, crosswords, and Mensa-type games and puzzles. You may not see these exact questions on test day, but they will stretch your brain and teach you to think flexibly and quickly.

- *Substitute in PSAT questions as you play Trivial Pursuit* (or any other competitive board game).

- *Play vocabulary-building games.* Hand out a list of difficult vocabulary words at the beginning of the session, and see who can work them into normal conversation first. Earn one point for using the word properly in a sentence and one point for creativity! Once a word is used, everyone has to cross it off his or her list and no one else can score off of it. The day's group leader can judge whether the word is used with accuracy and comic style.

- *Practice spotting grammatical and stylistic errors in each other's school assignments.* Bonus—your grades in school will improve as well.

WHEN

The frequency of your group's meetings is entirely up to your mutual schedules. Ideally, you should be getting together as much as possible; however, regularly is more important than periodically. Once a week would be fantastic, once every two weeks works very well, even monthly would be okay if you start early enough and also practice on your own. The important thing is to pick a mutually convenient schedule and then stick to it.

Ideally, you should aim to spend between two and three hours together at each session. One hour is too short to accomplish much, and more than three hours would be tedious. Try two to three hours with at least one break built in.

WHERE

Sometimes schools will encourage study groups by opening up classrooms for student use. See if your favorite teacher wouldn't mind setting one up for you. Occasionally, that teacher might even donate some time and guide a session or two. Hooray for guest speakers!

More likely, however, is the prospect of spending some quality time in your or someone else's home. All that is required is a decent space to work (a dining room, study, basement) and some quiet. If one locale fits the bill, then use it. Or you could rotate the group's meeting place from home to home. See if the host of that week's study session would provide some tasty refreshments. (To any parents reading this section: You do want to encourage your child to study, right?) It's PSAT studying but that doesn't mean it can't be any fun at all . . . or taste good.

THE PROS AND CONS

If you've made it this far, you know that there are a ton of pros to group study and very few cons if you select your group well and stay focused. When partnered with individual work, a reputable test prep book, and a good attitude, small-group studying can be an effective and enjoyable way to become familiar with the topics and form of the PSAT. It may not be a night out, but group study is almost always effective and, if you let it, might even be fun.

PARENTS' GUIDE TO SURVIVING THE PSAT

PARENTS' GUIDE TO SURVIVING THE PSAT

SO SOON?

I know. It feels like only yesterday Junior was learning how to ride a bicycle and taking his first swing in little league. Now, he is halfway through high school, and it's time to begin the long and winding road that is the college application process, if he hasn't already. Maybe you remember your own experience with the test junior and/or sophomore year in high school? Whether that memory is happy, sad, or maybe more than a little fuzzy, it's time to begin indoctrinating your child into the somewhat intimidating world of PSATs and SATs.

DOESN'T THE "P" IN PSAT STAND FOR PRELIMINARY? THAT MEANS IT'S UNIMPORTANT, RIGHT?

Yes . . . and no. Though the admissions staff of your colleges of choice will certainly not be looking too closely at your child's PSAT scores, the test does play an important role in transitioning your student from the insular comfort of the classroom to a nationally competitive test. Acing the PSAT also holds the possibility of netting some sizeable (and likely helpful) monetary rewards for college. There is real money on the line here. National Merit program and scholarships aside, however, the PSAT more importantly offers a prime opportunity for you and your child to begin building fruitful standardized test study habits that can lead to success on the all-important SAT.

Furthermore, the PSAT (especially if taken as a sophomore) can provide an accurate read on where your child's strengths and weaknesses lie, which is invaluable information for developing a course of study for the months to come.

On the complimentary PSAT score report, the College Board will provide a detailed and personalized breakdown of which questions your child struggled with, how that compares to students across the country, and how to improve those scores for the next go-round.

If a student takes the test "cold," that score is much less likely to be indicative of where the student could be scoring with 12 months' time of targeted study. There's little use in being told you need to bone up on elementary algebra or verb tenses when you actually just spent too much time reading the directions or stressing over Grid-in problems . . . or simply weren't prepared the day of.

Very few students simply wake up one morning, waltz into the testing center, and snag a 240 on the PSAT (equivalent to 2400 on the SAT). However, thousands and thousands of students do learn about the topics and structure of the test and work their way to their goal score. Kaplan was founded on this very prospect. The earlier you and your child begin the process, the more time you will have to push the goal score higher and higher and higher . . .

Outside of scores and test prep, the PSAT also has the benefit of providing test takers with perhaps their first taste of college recruitment. The College Board's Student Search Service offers test takers the chance to connect with thousands of colleges looking for students just like your daughter or son. If you do not want to give your post office delivery person a workout, simply decline to enroll in the program; however, many students find it exciting to begin prospecting for their future collegiate home through the mail and online.

Finally, you really have nothing to lose. This is an opportunity to get your feet wet in the SAT pool with exactly zero consequences and several benefits: SAT preparation, free scholarship money, improving study habits—what a deal! Where can you sign up, you ask?

HOW CAN I HELP?

First, you can familiarize yourself with the PSAT and this book. In particular, take a look at chapter 1, PSAT Basics. Talk it over with your child and make sure everyone is on the same page with this test. Next, make sure your future coed takes the Diagnostic Test, located on page 23, under relatively realistic testing conditions. There's no need to pilfer one of those tiny classroom desks with the palette-shaped workspace from the local high school, but accurate timekeeping and a general absence of distractions would be nice. They may not like it, but this is the only way to get a decent read on where to start in the book.

From there, the path to PSAT greatness varies greatly depending on your child's personal preferences, needs, and desires and your willingness to accommodate them. Some children can be very proactive and require little academic wrangling. Others might . . . how should we say . . . benefit from a bit more structure. If your child falls somewhere in the middle of the spectrum, fear not, we have some general tips to help you help them get the most out of this book and the PSAT.

START EARLY!

Though only high school juniors are eligible to win college scholarships through the National Merit program, students of all ages are eligible to reap the benefits of taking the test multiple times. Studies have shown that students exposed to the PSAT at an early age (usually seventh or eighth grade) post significant improvements when they take it again "for real" during the autumn of their junior year. Additionally, those students are much more comfortable handling the SAT their junior and/or senior year.

Thus, we highly recommend starting the PSAT prep process as soon as possible.

In terms of timing the test with this textbook, we recommend roughly two and a half months as the ideal time period to gear up for the PSAT. Of course, this time frame only works if you and your child are . . .

. . . Staying on Track

Practice does make perfect, but regular practice makes being perfect a regular occasion. This is where you as the parent can have a tremendous impact. You may not need to hang over your child's shoulder while she tackles Pythagorean triangles, but it definitely would be helpful to check in once and a while to make sure she is making significant and regular progress through the book. Don't stress, but make it clear that this is important, because, well, it is.

Amidst all the task mastering, however, don't forget to . . .

. . . Empathize

Your child may not actually believe this, but you have seen a thing or two in life (probably including the PSAT), and know what it means to work and struggle toward a goal. It's okay to let your guard down and let your child know that it's okay to feel some anxiety over this test, the inevitable tests to come in the future, or the entire college application process. Fear is a perfectly natural and beneficial aspect of life. The sooner your child understands that, and that you are completely and absolutely on his side, the better off everyone will be.

IF YOU CAN'T BE THE STUDY BUDDY, FIND SOMEONE (OR TWO) WHO WILL

If you now (or still) find the PSAT somewhat mystifying, there's no need to leave all of the teaching to Kaplan (although we are completely prepared for that possibility). Study buddies or small study groups are a fantastic way to get students immersed in the material and learning from each other. If you haven't already done so, take a look at PSAT Study Group Guide on page xv, particularly the section on providing tasty snacks for your hardworking test takers.

In addition to group study, many schools offer optional PSAT/SAT classes after hours and on weekends. See if your school is offering any such programs. An even better option might be your local Kaplan Center where we can provide a classroom or private tutoring course that will complement and expand upon the contents of this book.

But don't worry; there's plenty you can do on your own, including the following:

ENCOURAGE EXTRA READING

One of the hardest things PSAT/SAT teachers and tutors have to deal with when prepping students for standardized tests is a general lack of reading skills and familiarity with good writing. The PSAT and SAT can be gamed only so much with strategy and guile, but if a test taker simply has not read enough quality material, achieving upper-level scores can be extremely difficult.

Reading really is fundamental and not just for life: over three-fifths of the PSAT is based on reading and grammar skills. The sooner you start bringing those skills up to speed, the better. They build vocabulary, communication skills, persuasive writing skills, and reading comprehension—all of which are tested heavily on the PSAT and are pretty useful in college and in life as well.

So get those kids reading! Obviously, high-caliber newspapers and periodicals are ideal. The *New York Times, Wall Street Journal, Newsweek, Washington Post, New Yorker, Time, Popular Science,* and *National Geographic* are all wonderful choices. However, don't downplay the benefits of reading regularly, no matter the material. *Sports Illustrated* actually has decent articles, and there's nothing particularly childish about the Harry Potter series. The important thing is that your child is exposed to new ideas, arguments, and words . . . and enjoys dealing with them.

REWARD THE EFFORT

Once you (ideally) have your child dutifully preparing for the PSAT and college application process, it is not the time to become Machiavellian. Of course, the ends are important, but don't forget to reward and praise the serious effort your child is putting in. Let's face it—test prep really isn't that much fun, so your child should be reminded and rewarded for her hard work. (For all you students sneaking a look at this section, no, this doesn't mean your parents are going to start paying you!) It hopefully does mean, however, that you are being as supportive as possible as your child enters a particularly stressful period of life. Try to make sure your expectations and those of your child are 1) the same and 2) realistic. Also keep in mind that while pressure can create a diamond, it also can crush the coal into dust.

With that in mind, try to support your child to the best of your ability. After the goal score has been determined, try to not harp on it too much. Focus on what can be managed now—the effort and diligence your child is going to need to work through the practice tests, chapters, and numerous passages and problems this book provides.

BE AVAILABLE

Whether it means running vocabulary flashcards nightly with your son, working through each test question three different ways with your daughter, minding the egg timer, or simply driving your child to his weekly study group, be available for your test taker. The PSAT and the prospect of taking the SAT in the near future can be scary things, and your child is likely going to need you—whether he is willing to admit it or not.

Among you, this book, and your child, you have the means and material to prepare for any challenge the PSAT could possibly pose. Your challenge now is to provide the support, guidance, and love your child needs to succeed.

Good luck and thank you for choosing Kaplan.

| Part One |

GETTING READY FOR TEST DAY

CHAPTER 1: PSAT BASICS

IF YOU ONLY LEARN TWO THINGS IN THIS CHAPTER . . .

1. You need to learn about the exam before you can start preparing for it so you'll know what to expect on test day.

2. The PSAT gives you practice for the SAT and offers you the opportunity to earn scholarships to pay for college.

CHAPTER 1 OVERVIEW

The first step to PSAT success is to learn the structure of the test and why it's so important for your future.

Almost everyone prepares for the SAT. The same cannot be said for the PSAT. This is great news for you because you are one of the students who are preparing, and that means you have a really good chance of scoring higher than the kids who aren't.

Think about it: if you prep for the PSAT, *you have an advantage*. You will be the one running downhill, the one swimming downstream, and the one with the wind at your back.

PSAT STRUCTURE

The PSAT is 2 hours and 10 minutes long and is made up of mostly multiple-choice questions that test three subject areas: Critical Reading, Math, and Writing Skills. These areas are broken down into five sections on the exam.

Sections 1 and 3—Critical Reading	
Length	Content
25 minutes each	13 Sentence Completion and 35 Reading Comprehension multiple-choice questions (short and long passages)

Sections 2 and 4—Math	
Length	Content
25 minutes each	28 Regular math multiple-choice questions and 10 Grid-in questions

Section 5—Writing Skills	
Length	Content
30 minutes	14 Identifying Sentence Errors, 20 Improving Sentences, and 5 Improving Paragraphs questions

You get a five-minute break between Sections 2 and 3 and a one-minute break between Sections 4 and 5.

PSAT SCORING

Here's how the PSAT is scored:

Correct answer	1 point
Unanswered question	0 points
Incorrect answer to a Math grid-in	0 points
Incorrect answer to a multiple-choice question	–1/4 point

You gain one point for each correct answer on the PSAT and lose a fraction of a point (1/4) for every wrong answer. The exception is Math Grid-ins, for which you lose nothing for a wrong answer. You do not lose any points for questions you leave blank. This is important, so we'll repeat it: *You do not lose any points for questions you leave blank.*

RAW SCORES

The totals for the Critical Reading, Math, and Writing Skills sections are added up to produce three separate raw scores. These raw scores equal the number you got right minus a fraction of the number you got wrong.

Raw score = number right – 1/4 of the number wrong

SCALED SCORES

Each of your raw scores is converted to a scaled score between 20 and 80. The exact formula for how this is done is not made public. In 2009, the average scaled score for a grade 11 student on the Critical Reading, Math, and Writing Skills components was approximately 47, 48, and 46 respectively.

SELECTION INDEX

When you add the three scaled scores together, you get your Selection Index, which ranges from 60 to 240. The average Selection Index for a grade 11 student is approximately 141.

PERCENTILE

The PSAT also gives you a percentile, which allows you to compare your scores with those of other juniors applying to college. A student with a percentile of 63 has earned a score better than 63 of every 100 college-bound juniors who took the test.

WHERE AND WHEN TO TAKE THE PSAT

The PSAT is offered every year in mid-October. It is administered at your high school, not at a testing center. Home-schooled students can sign up at the nearest local high school. Most high schools administer the exam on a Saturday; some offer it on a Tuesday.

Some high schools recommend that their sophomores take the test for additional practice.

Sophomores who take the PSAT are not eligible to qualify for the National Merit Scholarship unless they are in an accelerated program and are preparing to graduate the following year. However, some schools will administer the test to their students only once, in the beginning of their junior year; thus, students wanting to take it as sophomores would have to get permission from their guidance counselors.

WHY TO TAKE THE PSAT

The PSAT/NMSQT stands for the Preliminary SAT/National Merit Scholarship Qualifying Test. It has two main functions:

FUNCTION 1

The PSAT gives you practice for the SAT. Although shorter than the SAT (2 hours, 10 minutes compared with 3 hours, 45 minutes), it contains the same types of math, reading, and writing questions, except it does not have a written essay, which the SAT has. The PSAT also measures your score against your classmates and peers across the country, just as the SAT does.

FUNCTION 2

Taking the PSAT also gives you a chance to qualify for several scholarship programs, most notably the National Merit Scholarship Program. Aside from the possibility of receiving tuition for college, recognition by the National Merit Scholarship program is an impressive addition to your college applications.

The top 50,000 scorers on the PSAT are recognized by the National Merit program and sent letters of commendation. More than 10,000 of these students share more than $47 million in National Merit Scholarship money.

SCHOLARSHIPS OFFERED

The most well-known scholarship offered, of course, is the National Merit Scholarship. As noted, only juniors who take the PSAT are eligible for National Merit Scholarships. The top 16,000 scorers become semifinalists, and approximately 15,000 semifinalists become finalists. Finally, almost 8,500 National Merit finalists actually receive National Merit Scholarships, with each award up to $2,500 a year toward a college education. Many high scorers who don't receive National Merit Scholarships may still be awarded merit scholarships from the schools to which they apply based on their high scores. Whether you qualify as a Commended Student, a Semi-Finalist, a Finalist, or a full-fledged National Merit Scholar, it's definitely worth noting this achievement on your college applications.

Note, also, that if you do receive a letter of commendation but do not qualify to become a National Merit finalist, you could still be eligible for a Special Scholarship. To be considered for Special Scholarships, students who meet a corporate or business sponsor's criteria must file entry forms directly with that organization, which then forwards the entry forms back to the National Merit Scholarship Corporation (NMSC). A list of corporate organizations that sponsor

Special Scholarships is given in the PSAT/NMSQT Student Bulletin. The NMSC subsequently contacts high-scoring candidates through their high schools, and the students and their school officials then submit detailed scholarship applications. Finally, these applications are evaluated, and approximately 1,300 students are awarded Special Scholarships.

For more information on the National Merit Scholarships and Special Scholarships, visit www.nationalmerit.org or write to:

National Merit Scholarship Corporation
1560 Sherman Avenue, Suite 200
Evanston, IL 60201-4897

THE NATIONAL HISPANIC SCHOLAR RECOGNITION PROGRAM

Hispanic students may qualify for aid from the National Hispanic Scholar Recognition Program, which sends the names of 4,000 high-scoring Hispanic students to colleges to promote recruitment efforts and offers of financial aid.

For more information, write to:

National Hispanic Scholar Recognition Program
c/o The College Board
1233 20th Street, NW
Washington, DC 20036

NATIONAL SCHOLARSHIP SERVICE

African American students who plan to attend two- or four-year colleges may qualify for the National Scholarship Service. This program offers a college advisory and recruitment service at no charge.

For more information, email info@nationalscholarshipservice.com or write to:

National Scholarship Service
980 Martin Luther King Drive, SW
PO BOX 11409
Atlanta, GA 30310

THE TELLURIDE ASSOCIATION

The Telluride Association offers scholarships to gifted juniors for summer seminars in the humanities and social sciences.

For more information, email telluride@cornell.edu, visit www.tellurideassociation.org, or write to:

Telluride Association
217 West Avenue
Ithaca, NY 14850

SUMMARY

- There are five sections on the PSAT. They appear in the following order:

Critical Reading	25 min.
Math	25 min.
Critical Reading	25 min.
Math	25 min.
Writing	30 min.

- You get 1 point for every right answer, and you lose 1/4 point for every wrong answer (except for Grid-ins, where you lose nothing for a wrong answer).

- The PSAT can help you get two things:

  1. Scholarship money

  2. SAT practice

CHAPTER 2: BASIC PSAT STRATEGIES

IF YOU ONLY LEARN TWO THINGS IN THIS CHAPTER . . .

1. You can use the PSAT's particular structure to your scoring advantage.

2. The nine basic strategies in this chapter can help you succeed on test day.

CHAPTER 2 OVERVIEW

The material in this chapter will help you understand specific strategies for critical reading, math, and writing presented later in this book. Be sure you understand the basics in this chapter before moving on to specific review chapters.

Now that you know what the test is all about and why to take it, let's get into how to attack the PSAT.

The PSAT is different from the tests you are used to taking in school. The good news is you can use the PSAT's particular structure to your scoring advantage.

Here's an example. On a school test, you probably go through the problems in order. You spend more time on the hard questions than on the easy ones because harder questions are usually worth more points. You often show your work because the teacher tells you that how you approach a problem is as important as getting the answer right.

None of this works on the PSAT. If you use the same approach on the PSAT, your score will suffer. On the PSAT, you benefit from moving around within a section if you come across hard questions because the hard questions are worth the same point value as the easy ones. It doesn't matter how you answer the questions—only that you get them right.

The PSAT is *special*. To succeed on the PSAT, you need to know its quirks and how to use them to your advantage. Once you fully understand the PSAT's personality, you may even find yourself wishing tests at school were more like it.

BASIC STRATEGY 1

KNOW THE TEST

The key to success on the PSAT is knowing what to expect. The PSAT format—that is, the directions, the types of questions, and the traps that the test makers put in the questions—is almost identical from test to test. The only things the test makers change are the questions themselves.

This means one of the easiest things you can do to improve your performance on the PSAT is to know its format *before* you take the test. For example, if you learn the PSAT directions as you read this book, you can spend all of your time during the test answering the questions and getting your highest score possible instead of reading the directions, which you already know, because they never change.

BASIC STRATEGY 2

USE ORDER OF DIFFICULTY TO YOUR ADVANTAGE

Many of the PSAT sections are arranged so that the questions get more difficult as you work through a question set. In a question set that goes from 1 to 9, question 2 will be fairly easy, question 5 will be moderately more difficult, and question 9 will be really hard.

This is true of both Math question types (regular math and Grid-ins) and the Sentence Completion questions in the Critical Reading sections. The Reading Comprehension portion of the Critical Reading sections and the Writing Skills section questions are *not* arranged in any particular order of difficulty.

You can use this knowledge to your scoring advantage. As you work, always be aware of where you are in the set. When working on the easy problems, you can generally trust your first impulse—the obvious answer is likely to be right. As you get to the end of the set, you need to become more suspicious. The answers probably shouldn't come easily. If they do, look at the problem again because the obvious answer is likely to be wrong. Watch out for the answer that just *looks right*. It might be a distracter or a trap—a wrong answer choice meant to entice you. (We'll go into detail on the PSAT's favorite kinds of distracters later.)

BASIC STRATEGY 3

DON'T GET STUCK, MOVE ON

You're not allowed to work on other sections during the test, but you are allowed to skip around within each section of the PSAT. High scorers know this. They move through the test efficiently. They don't dwell on any one question, even a hard one, until they've tried every question at least once.

The key is to be systematic: When you run into questions that look tough, circle them in your test booklet and skip them. Go back and try again after you have answered the easier ones. Remember, you don't get more points for answering hard questions. If you get two easy ones right in the time it would have taken you to get one hard one right, you just gained points.

There's another benefit to coming back to hard ones later. On their second look, troublesome questions can turn out to be simple. By answering some easier questions first, you can come back to a harder question with fresh eyes, a fresh perspective, and more confidence.

BASIC STRATEGY 4

KNOW WHEN TO GUESS

There is no penalty for guessing on the PSAT. There is only a penalty for getting a wrong answer. If you can determine that one or more answers are definitely wrong, then you should probably guess from the remaining choices. Even if you aren't sure which one of them is absolutely correct, you've increased your chances of success by paring the selection down.

EXPERT TUTOR TIP

" Circling and returning to difficult questions can pay huge dividends—especially if that difficult question resides in the first half of the question set. Chances are you simply missed a shortcut; some time away from the problem will likely allow you to look at it with a fresh perspective. "

EXPERT TUTOR TIP

" Though it is in your best interest to guess when you can eliminate even one wrong answer, don't stop there! If you can knock off one, chances are you can cross out another, which increases your guessing advantage significantly. Intelligent guessing is just as important as intelligence itself on the PSAT. "

Here's why: If you get an answer wrong on any multiple-choice question on the PSAT, you lose 1/4 point. These fractional points you lose are supposed to offset the points you might earn accidentally by guessing the correct answer, and here's where our techniques really help you out. By learning Kaplan's techniques, you can eliminate wrong answer choices on almost all PSAT questions, even if you have no idea what the actual right answer is. By eliminating wrong answer choices, you are creating a *guessing advantage*.

The PSAT has one question type that is not affected by this strategy, the Grid-in. Remember, if you get an answer wrong on a Grid-in math question, for which you write in your own answers, you lose nothing. So you should *write in an answer for every Grid-in.* The worst that can happen is that you get zero points for the questions you guessed on and got wrong.

BASIC STRATEGY 5

RESPECT YOUR ANSWER SHEET

It sounds simple, but it's extremely important: Don't make mistakes filling out your answer grid. When time is short, it's easy to get confused going back and forth between your test book and your answer grid. If you know the answer, but misgrid it, you won't get the points. To avoid mistakes on the answer grid, try some of the following methods.

CIRCLE THE QUESTIONS YOU SKIP

Perhaps the most common PSAT disaster is filling in all of the questions with the right answers in the wrong spots. Every time you skip a question, put a big circle in your test booklet around the question you skipped to help you locate these questions when you are ready to go back to them. Also, if you accidentally skip a box on the grid, you can always check your grid against your book to see where you went wrong.

CIRCLE THE ANSWERS YOU CHOOSE

Circling your answers in the test book makes it easier to check your grid against your book. It also makes the next grid strategy possible.

GRID FIVE OR MORE ANSWERS AT ONCE

Time is of the essence on this exam. To save time and make sure you are marking your answers in the correct bubbles, circle your answer choices in the test booklet and then transfer your answers to the answer grid after every five questions or at the end of each reading passage, rather than after each question. That way, you won't keep breaking your concentration to mark the grid. You'll end up with more time and fewer chances to make a mistake on your answer sheet.

BASIC STRATEGY 6

THINK ABOUT THE QUESTION BEFORE YOU CHECK THE ANSWER CHOICES

The people who make the test love to put distracters among the answer choices. Distracters are answer choices that look right but aren't, and they are easy to choose if you haven't read the question carefully. If you jump right into the answer choices without thinking first about exactly what you're looking for, you're much more likely to fall for these traps.

BASIC STRATEGY 7

USE SHORTCUTS IF YOU HAVE TO

There are usually a number of ways to get to the right answer on a PSAT question. Most of the questions on the PSAT are multiple-choice questions. That means the answer is right in front of you—you just have to find it. This makes PSAT questions open to several different ways of finding the answer.

If you can't figure out the answer the straightforward way, try other techniques. We'll explore these approaches in detail in the following chapters.

BASIC STRATEGY 8

PAY ATTENTION TO WHERE YOU ARE IN A QUESTION SET

As we noted earlier, many of the question sets (except for Reading Comprehension and the Writing Skills section) start out easy and gradually get harder. Therefore, if an early question seems hard, make sure to take a second look; you're bound to be missing something obvious. If a hard question seems easy, watch out! You may be falling into a trap.

Finally, don't be upset if you have to skip a couple of the hard questions altogether; by spending your time elsewhere, you'll probably do better on the questions you did answer. You don't have to answer every single question, even if you're aiming for a National Merit Scholarship.

BASIC STRATEGY 9

LOOK FOR QUICK POINTS WHEN YOU'RE RUNNING OUT OF TIME

Some questions can be done quickly. For instance, some Critical Reading questions will ask you to identify the meaning of a particular word in the passage. These can be done at the last minute, even

EXPERT TUTOR TIP

❝ Other places for quick points (these will be covered later in the text):

- Geometric figures that can be eyeballed

- Reading Comprehension detail questions with specific line numbers

- Reading Comprehension main idea questions, after reading the first paragraph of the passage and topic sentences of the subsequent paragraphs

- Math problems with numbers in the answer choices that can be backsolved ❞

if you haven't read the passage. When you start to run out of time, try to locate and answer the questions that can earn you quick points. When you take the PSAT, you should have one clear objective in mind—to score as many points as you can. It's that simple. The rest of this book will help you do that.

SUMMARY

- Know when a question set is arranged easiest to hardest and approach it accordingly.

- Don't spend too much time on any one question. Move around in a section, answering the questions you know you can do easily and saving the hard ones for last.

- If you can eliminate at least one wrong answer choice, you should guess.

- Be careful transferring your answers from your booklet to your answer sheet.

- Think about the question before you look at the answers.

- Look for quick points when you are running out of time.

CHAPTER 3: STRATEGIES FOR TEST DAY SUCCESS

IF YOU ONLY LEARN THREE THINGS IN THIS CHAPTER . . .

1. The week before the PSAT you should:

   —Take a Practice Test.

   —Review chapters 3 through 7 and any PSAT resources you feel will help.

2. Don't cram the night before the PSAT.

3. When you are taking the PSAT, plow ahead, don't pay attention to other test takers, breathe, and take time out to relax if you feel yourself getting tired or stressed.

CHAPTER 3 OVERVIEW

This chapter is all about getting your head on straight. It goes over what you can do before the test to make sure you are as ready as you can be and what you can do during the test to make sure you perform as well as possible.

The PSAT can only help you, so there's no real reason for you to get stressed out as your test date approaches. However, some students will still get nervous before a test, whether it counts or not and whether they are prepared or not. This is understandable. For others, having to use their brain for any extended period of time is reason enough to worry. With that in mind, this chapter provides a game plan for the week heading into the test and arms you with strategies for stifling any pretest jitters.

ONE WEEK TO PSAT GREATNESS

SEVEN DAYS BEFORE THE TEST

Take a full-length PSAT Practice Test. Score your test and see what areas still need work.

THREE TO SIX DAYS BEFORE THE TEST

Review one to two chapters a day from this book. Focus primarily on the areas where you want to improve your score, but don't overload your brain. Cramming generally doesn't help on the PSAT. Continue to solidify and expand your PSAT vocabulary knowledge by reading through the vocabulary lists in the PSAT Resources.

TWO DAYS BEFORE THE TEST

Do your final studying—a few more practice problems, a few more vocabulary words, and whatever strategies you want to read one last time, and then put the study materials down. Do some good reading, work out, or do other things to stay sharp and focused, but leave the practice books closed. It's time to get ready for Test Day.

THE DAY BEFORE THE TEST

Our first piece of advice: Do not cram! Cramming only causes undue stress and doesn't allow the information you are taking in to settle and take shape.

Give yourself the night off the evening before the exam. By that time, if you've studied well, everything you need to know will be firmly stored in your memory bank. If you haven't studied well, it's pretty much too late by that point anyway. What do you think is better: to be relaxed and unprepared or panicked and unprepared? Of course the best way to achieve being relaxed *and* prepared is to get your act together sooner rather than later. That's why you bought this book.

THE NIGHT BEFORE THE TEST

Don't study. Eat a healthy dinner. Get together the following items:

- A comfortable outfit, with different layers for different temperatures
- A familiar calculator with fresh batteries
- A few sharpened No. 2 pencils
- Erasers
- A snack—there's a break between Sections 2 and 3, and you'll probably get hungry; a banana or an energy bar makes for an especially good brain snack.

EXPERT TUTOR TIP

" In studies of athletes before big games, scientists have shown that sleeping well the night before is actually less important than getting a good night's sleep two nights before. Make sure you get at least eight hours of sleep two nights before the test. Then, if you sleep well on PSAT-eve, so much the better, but if you don't because of nerves, at least you'll have some currency in your sleep bank to withdraw. "

Most likely you'll be taking the test on Saturday morning in your own high school. If you're not taking the test in your own high school, make sure you know how to get to where your test will be given.

After you've done all of this, try to keep the upcoming test out of your consciousness the night before. Go to a movie, take a long walk, play your favorite computer game, or just simply relax.

Get plenty of rest the night before the test. Just don't go to bed too early. It's hard to fall asleep earlier than you're used to, and you don't want to lie there thinking about the test. In fact, don't do anything that drastically changes from your everyday behavior. You don't need any weird surprises the day of the test as a result of a change in behavior.

Note: if you're not much of a weekend-morning person and you're taking the test on Saturday, try taking a practice test at 8:00 AM on the Saturday before the test to get the most realistic practice before Test Day.

THE MORNING OF THE TEST

Eat breakfast. Make it substantial, but don't veer too far from your normal breakfast eating habits. Stay away from heavy or greasy food. Also, try to not drink a lot of coffee if you're not used to it; bathroom breaks can eat into valuable test time, and the caffeine could make you jumpy. Dress in layers so that you can adjust to the temperature of the test room. Read a newspaper or magazine article to warm up your brain. Don't let the PSAT be the first thing you read that day.

DURING THE TEST

Not everyone feels stress when taking standardized tests, but for some students, all the test preparation in the world won't keep their food in their stomachs. If you know from experience that you are likely to feel test-day jitters, the first thing you should realize is that jitters are not necessarily a bad thing. That edgy feeling simply means that your body is pumping adrenaline into your system, and a little adrenaline can actually help you to think more quickly (and get a higher score). Here are some strategies for managing your stress during the test.

> **EXPERT TUTOR TIP**
>
> " Energize your body and wake up your mind! Get that blood flowing with some simple exercises. Test day is not the day to hit your stride on Section 4. Hit the ground running! "

> **EXPERT TUTOR TIP**
>
> " Watch your time. Test proctors can be very helpful or no help at all. Take them out of the equation by making sure you have a timepiece (cell phones do not count). One easy way to ensure you are staying on track is to figure out where the halfway point is in a section, and then make sure you are somewhere near there after roughly 12 minutes have elapsed (15 minutes for Writing Skills). This way, you can adjust your approach with plenty of time to spare. "

PLOW AHEAD

Remember to keep moving forward. You don't have to get everything right to get a great score or a National Merit Scholarship. Don't linger on a question that is going nowhere, even if you've spent a lot of time on it, which you should never do in the first place. The best test takers skip difficult material temporarily in search of the easier material. They mark the questions that require extra time and thought, and then return to them after they have answered all of the easy questions. This strategy also builds confidence so you can handle the tough questions later.

WEAR BLINDERS

Don't be thrown if other test takers seem to be working more busily and furiously than you are. In fact, don't even pay attention to the other students at all. Work at the pace we've told you to work at. Take the test the right way. It's going to lead to higher-quality test taking and better results. Don't mistake the intense scribbling of others for signs of progress and superiority. Your points are on your page, so keep your focus there.

BREATHE IN, BREATHE OUT

Oxygen comes in, carbon dioxide goes out. It's the natural process that keeps you alive and helps your PSAT score. Weak test takers tend to forget to breathe properly as the test proceeds. They start holding their breath without realizing it, or they breathe erratically or arrhythmically. Improper breathing interferes with clear thinking—especially if you black out. It's really hard to fill in the right bubble when you're unconscious.

GET FUNKY

Don't be afraid to take a 20-second break now and then. Performing some quick isometrics during the test—especially if your concentration is wandering or your energy is waning—can put you back in test-taking mode. Try this one: Put your palms together and press intensely for a few seconds. Concentrate on the tension you feel through your palms, wrists, forearms, and up into your biceps and shoulders. Then, quickly release the pressure. Feel the difference as you let go. Focus on the warm relaxation that flows through the muscles. As long as you're quiet about it and don't disturb your neighbor, no one cares what relaxation methods you use.

REMIND YOURSELF HOW WELL YOU'VE PREPARED

You know the feel and structure of the test. You don't have to waste time on the instructions. You've studied every question type. You know where to find the tough questions and what to do with a question that gives you trouble.

If something goes wrong, don't panic. The proctor is there to help you if there's a defect in your test booklet or a problem with your desk. If you accidentally misgrid your answer sheet or put the answers in the wrong section, again, don't panic. Raise your hand, and tell the proctor so you can know what your options are.

You're armed and ready to do your best on the test. This book—and all that you have learned in school—have given you the information you'll need to answer the questions. You've learned everything you need to tame your test anxiety and stress. You're going to get a great score.

AFTER THE TEST

Once the test is over, congratulate yourself and put it out of your mind. You did your best, and you should feel great about that.

When you get your score results, we hope you will be pleased.

SUMMARY

- Cramming won't help you.
- Don't study the day before the test.
- After you've gotten together everything you will need, spend the night before the test just relaxing.
- Get a good night's sleep and eat right.
- Celebrate after the test is over!

EXPERT TUTOR TIP

" Bring some snacks and drinks to the test. You can't have them while you work, but you do get a five-minute break after Section 2. This is a great time to boost your blood sugar and energy. "

Part Two

DIAGNOSTIC TEST

CHAPTER 4: DIAGNOSTIC TEST

The Diagnostic Test is a full-length PSAT test designed to help you identify your strengths and weaknesses as you prepare for the actual exam. The goal is to help you determine the areas that you should focus on while studying. The questions on the Diagnostic Test cover all of the areas you will encounter on the actual exam.

Score your Diagnostic Test once you have completed the exam. If you score well, you are in terrific shape. Keep doing what you're doing. If you don't score as well as you'd like, you have some studying to do.

PSAT DIAGNOSTIC TEST ANSWER SHEET

Remove (or photocopy) this answer sheet and use it to complete the test. See the answer key following the test when finished. Chapter 11 will show you how to find your score.

Start with number 1 for each section. If a section has fewer questions than answer spaces, leave the extra spaces blank.

SECTION 1

1. Ⓐ Ⓑ Ⓒ Ⓓ Ⓔ   7. Ⓐ Ⓑ Ⓒ Ⓓ Ⓔ   13. Ⓐ Ⓑ Ⓒ Ⓓ Ⓔ   19. Ⓐ Ⓑ Ⓒ Ⓓ Ⓔ
2. Ⓐ Ⓑ Ⓒ Ⓓ Ⓔ   8. Ⓐ Ⓑ Ⓒ Ⓓ Ⓔ   14. Ⓐ Ⓑ Ⓒ Ⓓ Ⓔ   20. Ⓐ Ⓑ Ⓒ Ⓓ Ⓔ
3. Ⓐ Ⓑ Ⓒ Ⓓ Ⓔ   9. Ⓐ Ⓑ Ⓒ Ⓓ Ⓔ   15. Ⓐ Ⓑ Ⓒ Ⓓ Ⓔ   21. Ⓐ Ⓑ Ⓒ Ⓓ Ⓔ
4. Ⓐ Ⓑ Ⓒ Ⓓ Ⓔ   10. Ⓐ Ⓑ Ⓒ Ⓓ Ⓔ   16. Ⓐ Ⓑ Ⓒ Ⓓ Ⓔ   22. Ⓐ Ⓑ Ⓒ Ⓓ Ⓔ
5. Ⓐ Ⓑ Ⓒ Ⓓ Ⓔ   11. Ⓐ Ⓑ Ⓒ Ⓓ Ⓔ   17. Ⓐ Ⓑ Ⓒ Ⓓ Ⓔ   23. Ⓐ Ⓑ Ⓒ Ⓓ Ⓔ
6. Ⓐ Ⓑ Ⓒ Ⓓ Ⓔ   12. Ⓐ Ⓑ Ⓒ Ⓓ Ⓔ   18. Ⓐ Ⓑ Ⓒ Ⓓ Ⓔ   24. Ⓐ Ⓑ Ⓒ Ⓓ Ⓔ

☐ # right in Section 1

☐ # wrong in Section 1

SECTION 2

1. Ⓐ Ⓑ Ⓒ Ⓓ Ⓔ   6. Ⓐ Ⓑ Ⓒ Ⓓ Ⓔ   11. Ⓐ Ⓑ Ⓒ Ⓓ Ⓔ   16. Ⓐ Ⓑ Ⓒ Ⓓ Ⓔ
2. Ⓐ Ⓑ Ⓒ Ⓓ Ⓔ   7. Ⓐ Ⓑ Ⓒ Ⓓ Ⓔ   12. Ⓐ Ⓑ Ⓒ Ⓓ Ⓔ   17. Ⓐ Ⓑ Ⓒ Ⓓ Ⓔ
3. Ⓐ Ⓑ Ⓒ Ⓓ Ⓔ   8. Ⓐ Ⓑ Ⓒ Ⓓ Ⓔ   13. Ⓐ Ⓑ Ⓒ Ⓓ Ⓔ   18. Ⓐ Ⓑ Ⓒ Ⓓ Ⓔ
4. Ⓐ Ⓑ Ⓒ Ⓓ Ⓔ   9. Ⓐ Ⓑ Ⓒ Ⓓ Ⓔ   14. Ⓐ Ⓑ Ⓒ Ⓓ Ⓔ
5. Ⓐ Ⓑ Ⓒ Ⓓ Ⓔ   10. Ⓐ Ⓑ Ⓒ Ⓓ Ⓔ   15. Ⓐ Ⓑ Ⓒ Ⓓ Ⓔ

☐ # right in Section 2

☐ # wrong in Section 2

SECTION 3

25. Ⓐ Ⓑ Ⓒ Ⓓ Ⓔ   31. Ⓐ Ⓑ Ⓒ Ⓓ Ⓔ   37. Ⓐ Ⓑ Ⓒ Ⓓ Ⓔ   43. Ⓐ Ⓑ Ⓒ Ⓓ Ⓔ
26. Ⓐ Ⓑ Ⓒ Ⓓ Ⓔ   32. Ⓐ Ⓑ Ⓒ Ⓓ Ⓔ   38. Ⓐ Ⓑ Ⓒ Ⓓ Ⓔ   44. Ⓐ Ⓑ Ⓒ Ⓓ Ⓔ
27. Ⓐ Ⓑ Ⓒ Ⓓ Ⓔ   33. Ⓐ Ⓑ Ⓒ Ⓓ Ⓔ   39. Ⓐ Ⓑ Ⓒ Ⓓ Ⓔ   45. Ⓐ Ⓑ Ⓒ Ⓓ Ⓔ
28. Ⓐ Ⓑ Ⓒ Ⓓ Ⓔ   34. Ⓐ Ⓑ Ⓒ Ⓓ Ⓔ   40. Ⓐ Ⓑ Ⓒ Ⓓ Ⓔ   46. Ⓐ Ⓑ Ⓒ Ⓓ Ⓔ
29. Ⓐ Ⓑ Ⓒ Ⓓ Ⓔ   35. Ⓐ Ⓑ Ⓒ Ⓓ Ⓔ   41. Ⓐ Ⓑ Ⓒ Ⓓ Ⓔ   47. Ⓐ Ⓑ Ⓒ Ⓓ Ⓔ
30. Ⓐ Ⓑ Ⓒ Ⓓ Ⓔ   36. Ⓐ Ⓑ Ⓒ Ⓓ Ⓔ   42. Ⓐ Ⓑ Ⓒ Ⓓ Ⓔ   48. Ⓐ Ⓑ Ⓒ Ⓓ Ⓔ

☐ # right in Section 3

☐ # wrong in Section 3

SECTION 4

19. Ⓐ Ⓑ Ⓒ Ⓓ Ⓔ	24. Ⓐ Ⓑ Ⓒ Ⓓ Ⓔ	29. Ⓐ Ⓑ Ⓒ Ⓓ Ⓔ	34. Ⓐ Ⓑ Ⓒ Ⓓ Ⓔ	
20. Ⓐ Ⓑ Ⓒ Ⓓ Ⓔ	25. Ⓐ Ⓑ Ⓒ Ⓓ Ⓔ	30. Ⓐ Ⓑ Ⓒ Ⓓ Ⓔ	35. Ⓐ Ⓑ Ⓒ Ⓓ Ⓔ	# right in Section 4
21. Ⓐ Ⓑ Ⓒ Ⓓ Ⓔ	26. Ⓐ Ⓑ Ⓒ Ⓓ Ⓔ	31. Ⓐ Ⓑ Ⓒ Ⓓ Ⓔ	36. Ⓐ Ⓑ Ⓒ Ⓓ Ⓔ	
22. Ⓐ Ⓑ Ⓒ Ⓓ Ⓔ	27. Ⓐ Ⓑ Ⓒ Ⓓ Ⓔ	32. Ⓐ Ⓑ Ⓒ Ⓓ Ⓔ	37. Ⓐ Ⓑ Ⓒ Ⓓ Ⓔ	# wrong in Section 4
23. Ⓐ Ⓑ Ⓒ Ⓓ Ⓔ	28. Ⓐ Ⓑ Ⓒ Ⓓ Ⓔ	33. Ⓐ Ⓑ Ⓒ Ⓓ Ⓔ	38. Ⓐ Ⓑ Ⓒ Ⓓ Ⓔ	

If Section 4 of your test book contains math questions that are not multiple-choice, continue to item 29 below. Otherwise, continue to item 29 above.

29. 30. 31. 32. 33.

34. 35. 36. 37. 38.

SECTION 5

1. Ⓐ Ⓑ Ⓒ Ⓓ Ⓔ	11. Ⓐ Ⓑ Ⓒ Ⓓ Ⓔ	21. Ⓐ Ⓑ Ⓒ Ⓓ Ⓔ	31. Ⓐ Ⓑ Ⓒ Ⓓ Ⓔ	
2. Ⓐ Ⓑ Ⓒ Ⓓ Ⓔ	12. Ⓐ Ⓑ Ⓒ Ⓓ Ⓔ	22. Ⓐ Ⓑ Ⓒ Ⓓ Ⓔ	32. Ⓐ Ⓑ Ⓒ Ⓓ Ⓔ	
3. Ⓐ Ⓑ Ⓒ Ⓓ Ⓔ	13. Ⓐ Ⓑ Ⓒ Ⓓ Ⓔ	23. Ⓐ Ⓑ Ⓒ Ⓓ Ⓔ	33. Ⓐ Ⓑ Ⓒ Ⓓ Ⓔ	
4. Ⓐ Ⓑ Ⓒ Ⓓ Ⓔ	14. Ⓐ Ⓑ Ⓒ Ⓓ Ⓔ	24. Ⓐ Ⓑ Ⓒ Ⓓ Ⓔ	34. Ⓐ Ⓑ Ⓒ Ⓓ Ⓔ	# right in Section 5
5. Ⓐ Ⓑ Ⓒ Ⓓ Ⓔ	15. Ⓐ Ⓑ Ⓒ Ⓓ Ⓔ	25. Ⓐ Ⓑ Ⓒ Ⓓ Ⓔ	35. Ⓐ Ⓑ Ⓒ Ⓓ Ⓔ	
6. Ⓐ Ⓑ Ⓒ Ⓓ Ⓔ	16. Ⓐ Ⓑ Ⓒ Ⓓ Ⓔ	26. Ⓐ Ⓑ Ⓒ Ⓓ Ⓔ	36. Ⓐ Ⓑ Ⓒ Ⓓ Ⓔ	
7. Ⓐ Ⓑ Ⓒ Ⓓ Ⓔ	17. Ⓐ Ⓑ Ⓒ Ⓓ Ⓔ	27. Ⓐ Ⓑ Ⓒ Ⓓ Ⓔ	37. Ⓐ Ⓑ Ⓒ Ⓓ Ⓔ	
8. Ⓐ Ⓑ Ⓒ Ⓓ Ⓔ	18. Ⓐ Ⓑ Ⓒ Ⓓ Ⓔ	28. Ⓐ Ⓑ Ⓒ Ⓓ Ⓔ	38. Ⓐ Ⓑ Ⓒ Ⓓ Ⓔ	
9. Ⓐ Ⓑ Ⓒ Ⓓ Ⓔ	19. Ⓐ Ⓑ Ⓒ Ⓓ Ⓔ	29. Ⓐ Ⓑ Ⓒ Ⓓ Ⓔ	39. Ⓐ Ⓑ Ⓒ Ⓓ Ⓔ	
10. Ⓐ Ⓑ Ⓒ Ⓓ Ⓔ	20. Ⓐ Ⓑ Ⓒ Ⓓ Ⓔ	30. Ⓐ Ⓑ Ⓒ Ⓓ Ⓔ	40. Ⓐ Ⓑ Ⓒ Ⓓ Ⓔ	# wrong in Section 5

DIAGNOSTIC TEST

SECTION 1

Time—25 Minutes
24 Questions

For each of the following questions, choose the best answer and darken the corresponding oval on the answer sheet.

Select the lettered word or set of words that best completes the sentence.

Example:

Today's small, portable computers contrast markedly with the earliest electronic computers, which were ----.

(A) effective
(B) invented
(C) useful
(D) destructive
(E) enormous   Ⓐ Ⓑ Ⓒ Ⓓ ●

1. After having a really bad day, the ---- sailor tried to pick a fight by ---- the obnoxious man.

(A) violent . . . praising
(B) talkative . . . helping
(C) angry . . . attacking
(D) ferocious . . . ignoring
(E) peaceful . . . goading

2. When Joe made the finals, he was so ---- that he was jumping for joy.

(A) quizzical
(B) crestfallen
(C) ambivalent
(D) excited
(E) perplexed

3. The castle gate is designed to ---- the welfare of its citizens by ---- entry by invaders.

(A) maintain . . . allowing
(B) protect . . . preventing
(C) guard . . . encouraging
(D) uphold . . . commending
(E) destroy . . . prohibiting

4. The noble hoped to ---- the local official by offering her a sack of gold as a sign of good faith.

(A) appease
(B) sully
(C) belittle
(D) harass
(E) mock

5. The new government aid programs were introduced without much ----, but they had a ---- effect on the struggling organizations that benefited, substantially reducing their operating expenses.

(A) fanfare . . . monumental
(B) concealment . . . cursory
(C) alarm . . . negotiable
(D) debate . . . specious
(E) hesitation . . . incredible

GO ON TO THE NEXT PAGE ⇨

> Answer the questions below based on the information in the accompanying passages.

Questions 6–11 are based on the following passage.

The following passage explores advantages of the modern supermarket.

Many people today do not enjoy grocery shopping, but the experience we have is still many times better than that of the past. Supermarkets have done much to alleviate
(5) the problems that plagued traditional grocery stores. Gone are the days when consumers paid higher prices for the "privilege" of an excruciatingly slow shopping experience. In addition to lower prices, supermarkets also
(10) offer shoppers added convenience and much quicker service.

In the old days, grocery shopping was even more of a chore. Consumer-sized packages did not yet exist, so unless you were stocking
(15) up for a hurricane, a clerk had to measure out the precise amount you needed of everything you bought. This system was incredibly labor-intensive and very expensive. On top of that, the entire experience was extremely time-con-
(20) suming as, much like buying meat at a butch-er shop, the number of shoppers that a store could service simultaneously was limited by the size of its staff. The higher labor costs and poor efficiency were quite a problem for both
(25) the industry and its price-conscious public—a problem that needed a solution.

The supermarket is a large departmental-ized retail store, offering "one-stop shop" convenience with housewares, magazines,
(30) beauty products, and much more in addi-tion to the food items sold by traditional stores. Need soap to go with your newspaper and bread? The supermarket saves you time by providing all three items under one roof.
(35) Along with added convenience came added efficiency. Shoppers could now fetch their own products from shelves instead of waiting for service. This in turn reduced the need for

additional staff, helping owners to cut costs
(40) considerably and to pass the savings back to the consumer. In fact, supermarkets pass so much of the savings back that their margins are razor-thin—only 1 to 3 percent—so they must rely on extremely high turnover
(45) rates and keeping operating expenses low (by not offering delivery for one) to make a prof-it. The result is a quick and painless shopping experience with very reasonable prices.

6. The main purpose of this passage is to

   (A) discuss the disadvantages of the tradi-tional grocery store

   (B) explain why the general public hates gro-cery shopping

   (C) give reasons for the razor-thin margins of supermarkets

   (D) trace the history of the supermarket's origin

   (E) outline the advantages that supermarkets have over traditional grocery stores

7. Each of the following is listed as a disadvantage of traditional grocery stores EXCEPT

   (A) higher prices

   (B) slower service

   (C) the need to hire more staff

   (D) lower profit margins

   (E) lower variety of products for sale

GO ON TO THE NEXT PAGE →

8. According to the passage, supermarkets do not offer delivery because

    (A) they want to keep costs down
    (B) it is a good marketing strategy
    (C) there would be no demand for such a service
    (D) it was the primary cause for the inefficiency of traditional grocery stores
    (E) they are departmentalized

9. As used in the passage, "margins" (line 42) most nearly means

    (A) borders
    (B) gaps
    (C) profits
    (D) expenses
    (E) variety

10. The passage implies that, compared with the modern supermarket, traditional grocery stores

    (A) employed higher quality staff
    (B) had lower operating expenses
    (C) had higher operating expenses
    (D) offered better prices
    (E) offered a delivery service

11. Which of the following statements best expresses the main idea of paragraph 2?

    (A) Traditional grocery stores could only serve as many customers as they had staff for.
    (B) Traditional grocery stores carried a lower variety of goods than supermarkets.
    (C) Traditional grocery stores were an excellent choice when stocking up for a hurricane.
    (D) Traditional grocery stores were very inefficiently run.
    (E) Traditional grocery stores had very high labor expenses.

Questions 12–13 are based on the following passage.

Some psychologists believe that humans have developed special nervous systems capable of recognizing subtle expressions out of necessity, due to the weight of such recogni-
(5) tion in human communication. To test this theory, researchers showed photographs of people displaying emotions of joy, anger, and surprise to a group of trained pigeons. The birds were not only able to distinguish
(10) between expressions, they could even match each correctly to the same expression displayed by photographs with different faces. While the experiment results do not conclusively prove that the pigeons can comprehend the
(15) meaning of the tested expressions, it does cast doubt upon the theory proposed by the psychologists.

12. The passage implies that the ability to recognize facial expressions

    (A) can only be taught to pigeons
    (B) is not limited to humans
    (C) is important to all forms of communication
    (D) suggests that pigeons are capable of higher brain functions
    (E) is not at all difficult to test

13. The word "weight" in line 4 mostly nearly means

    (A) heaviness
    (B) strength
    (C) significance
    (D) pound
    (E) necessity

GO ON TO THE NEXT PAGE ⇒

Questions 14–17 refer to the following passages.

Passage 1

The American Civil War was an enormous tragedy in the history of the United States. To prevent a secession by the Southern states, the American public found itself fighting its own
(5) people rather than foreign invaders. Sparked in 1861, this terrible war included many bloody battles with severe casualties. In fact, the body count was so high that the South started running out of manpower when the
(10) war finally ended four years later in 1865. While the war did unite America, was it truly worth the price?

Passage 2

The Civil War rapidly accelerated the manufacture of materials, especially in the North. After the fighting stopped, America shifted into a period of dramatic economic growth.
(5) The federal government was extremely accommodating toward industrial expansion during this period. It established tariff barriers and did not interfere with private enterprise. Production taxes from the war largely
(10) vanished and the few taxes that remained were not directed upon businesses.

14. Which of the following best expresses the main idea of Passage 1?

(A) The Civil War was one of the bloodiest wars in history.

(B) The South lost the war due to a shortage of manpower.

(C) It is better to fight foreign invaders than your own people.

(D) The American public fought its own people to prevent secession.

(E) The Civil War was a tragic historic event.

15. With which of the following statements regarding the Civil War would the author of Passage 2 most likely agree?

(A) It was a tragic period in American history.

(B) It caused the federal government to realize the importance of industry.

(C) It was very bloody and claimed many lives.

(D) Its impact was primarily positive.

(E) It helped to strengthen America's economy.

16. Which of the following best describes the main difference between the two passages?

(A) Passage 1 considers the war tragic while Passage 2 does not.

(B) Passage 1 focuses on the negative aspects of the war while Passage 2 examines some of its positive aftereffects.

(C) Passage 1 presents the war as a necessary evil while Passage 2 does not.

(D) Passage 1 shows how the nation benefited from the war while Passage 2 focuses on its toll.

(E) Passage 1 is indifferent about the war while Passage 2 is for it.

17. The authors of both passages would most likely agree with which of the following statements?

(A) The Civil War was an extremely tragic event.

(B) The Civil War had a positive effect on American industry.

(C) The Civil War is an important part of American history.

(D) The Civil War was not worth its price.

(E) The Civil War was inevitable.

GO ON TO THE NEXT PAGE

Questions 18–24 are based on the following passage.

The following passage gives a comparison between two types of business entities.

Take a stroll through the business sector of New York City and you may find yourself surrounded by skyscrapers as tall as the eye can see. Each day, giant corporations conduct
(5) their business in these colossal towers, overlooking the busy streets. But what about the individual? What about the individual who wants to operate a business, yet doesn't want to be subject to the whims of corporate share-
(10) holders? How can such an individual realize her dreams to own a business, perhaps not the equal in size of large corporations but at least their rival in ambition? All is not lost, for the eager entrepreneur starting out small has
(15) two distinct options.

For the confident entrepreneur looking to succeed on her own, there is the sole proprietorship. In a sole proprietorship, there is one owner who is "solely" responsible for
(20) the business and any decisions regarding its operation. Want to run a business *exactly* as you see fit without compromise? Then a sole proprietorship may be the answer you're looking for. Of course, as with all choices in
(25) life, this does not come without its share of disadvantages. Sole proprietorships aren't seen as separate from their owners so credit may be a problem, especially if you don't have a lot of financial assets on hand. You're fine
(30) if the business is lucrative, but running in the red is a scary proposition since being the only boss also means taking on any and all debt that your business incurs. And the bigger your business becomes, the deeper the ditch
(35) that awaits you.

If our entrepreneur is lucky enough to have a group of like-minded acquaintances to start her company with, she and her associates might instead opt to form a partnership.

(40) A partnership sacrifices some of the operational freedom that comes with a sole proprietorship, as you now have a bunch of "friends" to convince before you can have things your way on any business decisions that need to be made, but these same indi-
(45) viduals will also be chipping in on expenses and sharing responsibility for any debt that the business may incur. Profits are shared with your partners on payday but the extra sup-
(50) port that they can provide if the business goes under helps to make up for that.

While the partnership seems to alleviate many of the problems that plague the sole proprietorship, it does have its share
(55) of disadvantages. In a sole proprietorship, the business could be sold if you the owner desire it, but the partnership requires consent from your partners before this can take place. Moreover, unlike corporations, which come
(60) with limited liability for their shareholders, if the business runs really deep into the red, you are still responsible for your complete share of the debt, even if you do have others to share that debt with. When viewed in this
(65) light, the "evil corporations" surrounding us may in fact be a necessary evil indeed.

18. Which of the following would make the best title for the passage?

(A) The Evils of Corporations
(B) How to Start Your Own Partnership
(C) The Advantages of Being a Sole Proprietor
(D) Two Alternatives to Forming a Corporation
(E) Corporate America: A Case Study

GO ON TO THE NEXT PAGE

19. The phrase "running in the red" (lines 30–31) most likely means

(A) losing money

(B) growing too quickly

(C) getting too ambitious

(D) not being able to pay the rent

(E) falling into a ditch

20. Based on the passage, which of the following best expresses the author's opinion of partnerships?

(A) They have no drawbacks compared to sole proprietorships.

(B) They have no drawbacks compared to corporations.

(C) They may be a necessary evil.

(D) They are the best choice for first-time entrepreneurs.

(E) They are not as risky as sole proprietorships.

21. Which of the following is an advantage unique to sole proprietorships?

(A) Not being subject to the whims of share-holders

(B) Having partners who are jointly responsible for debts

(C) Being able to run the business exactly as you see fit

(D) Being seen as separate from its owner when applying for credit

(E) Earning larger profits than partnerships due to not having to share

22. The fourth paragraph's purpose is to

(A) recommend partnerships

(B) recommend corporations

(C) discuss the advantages of partnerships

(D) discuss the disadvantages of partnerships

(E) discuss the advantages of sole proprietorships

23. The word "credit" in line 27 most probably refers to

(A) recognition for a job well done

(B) the ability to get a loan

(C) an honorable reputation

(D) the financial assets that one has on hand

(E) a way to measure a business's growth

24. Which of the following individuals would benefit most from a sole proprietorship?

(A) A high school dropout with limited funds

(B) A retired widow who can't afford to lose more than her investment

(C) A wealthy businesswoman who is tired of doing things someone else's way

(D) A middle-aged man with no business experience

(E) A recent college graduate who doesn't like taking risks

IF YOU FINISH BEFORE TIME IS CALLED, YOU MAY CHECK YOUR WORK ON THIS SECTION ONLY. DO NOT TURN TO ANY OTHER SECTION IN THE TEST. **STOP**

SECTION 2

Time—25 Minutes
18 Questions

Solve each of the following problems, decide which is the best answer choice, and darken the corresponding oval on the answer sheet.

Notes:

(1) Calculator use is permitted.

(2) All numbers used are real numbers.

(3) Figures are provided for some problems. All figures are drawn to scale and lie in a plane UNLESS otherwise indicated.

(4) Unless otherwise specified, the domain of any function f is assumed to be the set of all real numbers x for which $f(x)$ is a real number.

Reference Information

$A = \frac{1}{2}bh$ $c^2 = a^2 + b^2$ Special right triangles $A = \pi r^2$ $V = \ell wh$ $V = \pi r^2 h$ $A = \ell w$
                                                              $C = 2\pi r$

The sum of the degree measures of the angles in a triangle is 180.
The number of degrees of arc in a circle is 360.
A straight angle has a degree measure of 180.

1. The digit 4 has a value of $\frac{4}{10}$ in which one of the following?

    .4

    (A) 5.0427
    (B) 4.6817
    (C) 3.4029
    (D) 2.0147
    (E) 1.3704

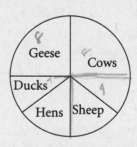

2. The graph above shows all the animals at a local farm. If there are 8 geese at the farm, about how many cows are there?

    (A) 10
    (B) 12
    (C) 14
    (D) 15
    (E) 18

    $8 = 25 \%$

    $8 \times 4 = 32$

GO ON TO THE NEXT PAGE

3. If j is odd and k is even, which of the following must be even?

   (A) $j + k$
   (B) $j + 2k$
   (C) $j - k$
   (D) $\dfrac{jk}{2}$
   (E) jk

Yearly Profits
(in millions of dollars)

4. The graph above shows the yearly profits of Cod Enterprises. If the company's profits continue to grow at the same rate, in which year will Cod Enterprises have a yearly profit of $100 million?

   (A) 2011
   (B) 2012
   (C) 2013
   (D) 2014
   (E) 2015

5. The price of a grill dropped from $48.00 to $38.40. What was the percent decrease in price?

   (A) 9.6%
   (B) 12%
   (C) 15%
   (D) 18%
   (E) 20%

6. Lana's Linoleum Luxuries makes rectangular kitchen tiles with an area of t square inches. Lana's new line, The Tile, is $\dfrac{3}{4}$ as long and three times as wide as her kitchen tiles. What is the area, in square inches, of The Tile?

   (A) $\dfrac{9}{4}t$
   (B) $2t$
   (C) t
   (D) $\dfrac{3}{4}t$
   (E) $\dfrac{1}{3}t$

7. If q is a negative integer, which of the following has the greatest value?

   (A) $-q$
   (B) $|q|$
   (C) $2q^4$
   (D) $5q^{15}$
   (E) $8q^{23}$

8. During spring break, Ian studied 3 hours on the first day, 6 hours on the second day, and 4 hours on the third day. How many hours must he study on the fourth day if he wants to spend an average (arithmetic mean) of 5 hours each day?

   (A) 6
   (B) 7
   (C) 8
   (D) 9
   (E) 10

GO ON TO THE NEXT PAGE

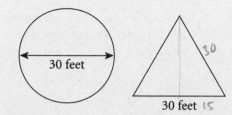

30 feet

30 feet

9. Farmer Sanders has a plot of land that she wants to put a fence around. She can either choose a circular field that's 30 feet wide or a triangular field that's 30 feet wide on each side. If she chose the circular field over the triangular field, how much more fencing, in feet, would Farmer Sanders need?

(A) $30\pi - 90$

(B) $30\pi - 30$

(C) $225\pi - 450$

(D) $225\pi - 90$

(E) $225\pi - 30$

10. A jeweler uses $\dfrac{3}{8}$ of a 6-foot chain to make accessories. If each accessory is 3 inches long, how many accessories can the jeweler make?

(A) 3

(B) 6

(C) 8

(D) 9

(E) 12

11. Betsy owns a pair of cows that drink water proportional to their weight. One of her cows weighs 600 pounds and drinks 200 cups of water a day. If the other cow drinks 225 cups of water a day, how much does it weigh?

(A) 75 pounds

(B) 200 pounds

(C) 520 pounds

(D) 585 pounds

(E) 675 pounds

12. If y and z are negative, which of the following is positive?

(A) $2y^6z^3$

(B) $3y^7z^4$

(C) $4y^8z^7$

(D) $5y^9z^{11}$

(E) $8y^{10}z^{13}$

House 1	House 2	House 3
12	15	20
$h = 12$	$h = 30$	$h = 60$

13. A construction company plans to build a long row of houses, each with a certain number of brown shingles on its roof. The company wants to assign an h-value to each house, where h is the product of the house number and its number of brown shingles, as shown in the figure above. If this pattern continues and only whole brown shingles are used, which of the following is the h-value for the seventh house?

(A) 390

(B) 420

(C) 450

(D) 480

(E) 540

GO ON TO THE NEXT PAGE

14. In the figure above, a rectangle has a diagonal of length d. What is the value of d in terms of m?

    (A) $m\sqrt{5}$
    (B) $m\sqrt{13}$
    (C) m
    (D) $13m$
    (E) $13m^2$

15. The floor plan to Suzanne's house has a scale of 1 inch = 4 feet. If the actual living room is 12 feet long and the actual bedroom is 16 feet long, how much longer, in inches, is the bedroom than the living room on the floor plan?

    (A) 1
    (B) 4
    (C) 12
    (D) 24
    (E) 48

16. In the figure above, what is the area of $\triangle ABC$?

    (A) 24
    (B) 48
    (C) 70
    (D) 96
    (E) 140

17. Lines L, M, and N are parallel lines cut by transversal O as shown below. If $t = 130$, what is the value of $t + u + v + w$?

    (A) 180
    (B) 200
    (C) 230
    (D) 320
    (E) 360

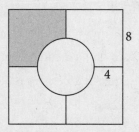

18. In the figure above, a circle sits in the middle of four identical squares. What is the area of the shaded region?

    (A) $256 - 64\pi$
    (B) $256 - 16\pi$
    (C) $256 - 4\pi$
    (D) $64 - 16\pi$
    (E) $64 - 4\pi$

19. In the second round of the local Coin Draw
    competition, Shelly drew 7 quarters, 11 dimes,
    and 6 nickels out of a pouch. If she needs to
    draw 15 more coins and there are no dimes left
    in the pouch, what is the GREATEST number
    of quarters Shelly can draw this round without
    going over $5?

    (A) 2
    (B) 3
    (C) 4
    (D) 5
    (E) 6

20. A circle with diameter 8 is cut into 4 equal
    pieces along the dotted lines shown below.
    What is the total perimeter of the four pieces?

    (A) $16 + 8\pi$
    (B) $32 + 8\pi$
    (C) $64 + 8\pi$
    (D) $32 + 16\pi$
    (E) $64 + 16\pi$

SECTION 3

Time—25 Minutes
24 Questions

For each of the following questions, choose the best answer and darken the corresponding oval on the answer sheet.

Select the lettered word or set of words that best completes the sentence.

Example:

Today's small, portable computers contrast markedly with the earliest electronic computers, which were ----.

(A) effective
(B) invented
(C) useful
(D) destructive
(E) enormous

25. The ---- of *Star Trek*—the vast reaches of outer space—was a refreshing change from the earthly scenery that was common in other shows of its time.

(A) appeal
(B) plot
(C) mood
(D) setting
(E) rehearsal

26. Paradoxically, a settlement that is ---- did not always have a(n) ---- of supplies.

(A) adapting . . . lavishness
(B) thriving . . . overabundance
(C) vexing . . . corpulence
(D) awakening . . . practicality
(E) abounding . . . commonness

27. Patients who suffered from lower back pain purchased the luxury bed because of its ---- qualities.

(A) succulent
(B) redolent
(C) cerebral
(D) mandatory
(E) therapeutic

28. After two decades of in-depth study, Adele's ---- finally resulted in technological breakthroughs that ---- the foundation for her later inventions.

(A) advancements . . . undermined
(B) debacles . . . prepared
(C) investigations . . . provided
(D) experiments . . . dissolved
(E) misconceptions . . . reinforced

29. The sudden avalanche completely sealed off the mountain pass, ---- any attempts to rescue the trapped survivors for several hours.

(A) thwarting
(B) forfeiting
(C) implementing
(D) discharging
(E) redoubling

GO ON TO THE NEXT PAGE

30. The masses were angered by the politician's
---- speech and reciprocated in a(n) ----
manner.

    (A) commendable . . . flattering

    (B) intemperate . . . haranguing

    (C) radical . . . praising

    (D) conciliatory . . . enraging

    (E) indulgent . . . accommodating

31. Having injured his foot, Matt walked with
a ---- gait, hobbling slowly down the trail.

    (A) halting

    (B) robust

    (C) constant

    (D) prompt

    (E) facile

32. Desiring attention, Klassa exaggerated her
injury by being ----; for example, she'd make a
big show of clutching her knee and wailing in
pain whenever anyone walked by.

    (A) imperious

    (B) inscrutable

    (C) pretentious

    (D) melodramatic

    (E) solicitous

Answer the questions below based on the information in the accompanying passages.

Questions 33–34 refer to the following passage.

When a mammal is young, it resembles a
miniature version of an adult. However, the
same cannot be said of animals that undergo
metamorphosis. The larvae of these animals
(5) bear little resemblance to their mature form
and lead very different lives. Caterpillars, for
one, are wingless creatures with plenty of legs.
They move by crawling and feed on leaves.
A caterpillar that undergoes metamorphosis
(10) transforms itself into a winged, six-legged
creature that feeds on the nectar of flowers.
When the transformation is complete, the
newly formed butterfly soars into the skies,
ready to mate and begin the process all over
(15) again.

33. The caterpillars mentioned in line 6 are an
example of

    (A) mammals

    (B) mature forms

    (C) six-legged creatures

    (D) animals that undergo
metamorphosis

    (E) creatures that feed on the nectar
of plants

34. The tone of the passage can best be
described as

    (A) informational

    (B) biased

    (C) admiring

    (D) condescending

    (E) subjective

GO ON TO THE NEXT PAGE

Questions 35–46 refer to the following passages.

The two passages discuss the role of computers in our lives. Passage 1 focuses on the technological advancements while Passage 2 takes a closer look at the impact on society.

Passage 1

Of all the great inventions of modern times, none can compare to that of the personal computer. Once deemed a toy only for the wealthy, the personal computer is now
(5) ubiquitous in homes across America. While most things in the world appreciate in value, advances in computer technology have actually served to continually decrease the price of computers as time went on. In their early
(10) years, computers were too expensive to be anything but a niche product. Thanks to technological advances, the modern computer has penetrated the mainstream and left its mark.

While a great number of things as mun-
(15) dane as looms and abacuses were called computers in the past, the Electronic Numerical Integrator and Computer (ENIAC) is generally regarded as the first electronic computer. Built for the U.S. Army in 1943, the ENIAC
(20) became operational in the following year. The 30-ton behemoth looked nothing like the computers we see today. At nearly half a million dollars in cost, a colossal 1,800 square feet in size, and requiring a staggering 174
(25) kilowatts to operate, it's not surprising that the ENIAC didn't find its way into the average American home. Those who had the pleasure of working with the beast may remember the punch cards used to feed it input and the
(30) vacuum tubes that transported this input throughout.

I can still remember the day when I bought my first computer. The year was 1980 and, for the bargain basement price of $4,000, I
(35) was the proud owner of a brand new Apple II. The technological marvel sported a 1 megahertz processor, 4 kilobytes of memory, and a tape drive for input and storage. In comparison, a $5 digital watch pur-
(40) chased today could run laps around it. But I didn't care. I had the bragging rights in town because I got the premium model, so my Apple II was also capable of color. Grinning from ear to ear, I would turn it on before
(45) heading down to the corner café while I waited for the software to load up. The café owner must have been thrilled with the sudden influx of business from the neighborhood!

Today, computers have penetrated deep into
(50) the mainstream. As technology has advanced, its focus has been to make computers smaller, easier to use, and more affordable. Businesses depend on them for productivity, schools use them for educational purposes, and families
(55) use them for entertainment. Not only have personal computers, once luxuries owned by a select few, become commonplace, but powerful computers are now integrated into hundreds of everyday devices, from cars to
(60) telephones to home appliances. Computers have certainly had an enormous impact on our lives, and today it would be difficult to imagine our world without them.

Passage 2

Seated at their desks, the restless children nervously await their math test. At the teacher's signal, an intelligent student turns over his test paper to reveal the first question, a
(5) multiplication problem that reads "6 × 7 =" along with a blank for the answer. But does he wrack his brain to find the solution? No. He simply takes out his calculator, and a glance around the classroom reveals that the
(10) other children are doing the same.

Computers have become an unmistakable part of our lives. From the workstation in the public library to the portable music player in our pocket, their existence has penetrated

(15) every facet of our society. Oftentimes, their
presence is a great boon as they can greatly
improve our productivity both in the work-
place and at home. They serve as our traffic
lights, our bank tellers, and even our security
(20) systems. Chores that used to take hours can
now be handled in minutes, with less physical
exertion from us. Cooking, for example, used
to take the better part of a day chopping
wood for fuel, but now with a simple push
(25) of a button a machine will happily cook
your food for you. Despite all these benefits,
however, the advent of computers and our
increasing dependence upon them has its disadvantages as well.

(30)   As computers become an increasingly
important aspect of our lives, children are
exposed to them at younger and younger
ages. And rightfully so, as they are better
able to learn and master things introduced
(35) to them at an earlier age. Since the optimal
window for learning is all too short, earlier
is usually better. Unfortunately, there is such
a thing as "too early" in this case—when
knowledge of the use of a seemingly harmless
(40) electronic assistant starts competing with the
necessity to master basic fundamentals that
are no less important to know.

As part of this early push toward familiar-
izing children with computers at a young age,
(45) our public school system encourages the use
of calculators on tests. Since we will always be
within reach of some device capable of performing most calculations, there is no longer
a need for children to be tested on the ability
(50) to actually work out problems by hand.
But how far will this go? How much
longer before we have a generation that
knows no math, that is completely lost on
any calculation, no matter how simple,
(55) without a calculator? The current trend is
indeed a frightening one but it is only the
beginning. Today, the need to know basic
math has been removed. Years from now,

I have no doubt that this will extend to
(60) complex math, and even science. In fact,
proper spelling and grammar have already
taken a step back in importance on the
Internet! How long will it be before the
human race is but a mindless hive, incapable
(65) of anything beyond pushing a button?

The advent of computers has indeed made
a significant impact upon our lives. These
marvelous machines have made life easier by
reducing the amount of work required for
(70) menial tasks. But is their coming a beneficial
thing?

35. The word "appreciate" in Passage 1, line 6
is closest in meaning to

(A) relish

(B) abate

(C) fathom

(D) increase

(E) praise

36. The "$5 digital watch" (line 39) in Passage 1 is
used to

(A) provide an example of an affordable
electronic device

(B) support the fact that smaller devices are
more powerful

(C) show how advancements in technology
can greatly impact their popularity

(D) depict the effects of inflation

(E) illustrate the rate at which technology
has improved

GO ON TO THE NEXT PAGE

37. Which of the following statements would the author of Passage 1 most likely agree with?

    (A) Society has become overly dependant on computers.

    (B) Computers have made the world a better place.

    (C) A steady decline in price was the primary reason for the growing popularity of computers.

    (D) Computers should not replace the need to learn basic fundamentals.

    (E) The use of calculators in the classroom is not detrimental.

38. In Passage 1, the author's attitude toward computers is

    (A) admiring

    (B) cryptic

    (C) aloof

    (D) suspicious

    (E) reserved

39. According to Passage 1, each of the following is true of the ENIAC EXCEPT

    (A) it is generally regarded as the first computer

    (B) it required a lot of power to operate

    (C) it was not affordable for the general public

    (D) it received input from punch cards

    (E) it is much larger than the modern computer

40. The author in Passage 2 mentions traffic lights, bank tellers, and security systems in order to support the fact that

    (A) our society is becoming overly dependent on computers

    (B) computer technology has made great strides

    (C) computers are beneficial to society

    (D) modern electronic equipment is mainstream

    (E) depending on computers can have disadvantages

41. The word "window" in Passage 2, line 36 is closest in meaning to

    (A) glass viewing surface

    (B) location

    (C) time frame

    (D) transparent surface

    (E) pane

42. With which of the following statements would the author of Passage 2 most likely agree?

    (A) Children should never be allowed to use calculators.

    (B) Automated bank tellers are a problem for society.

    (C) Chopping wood is a basic fundamental skill that should not be neglected.

    (D) Children should be introduced to computers as early as possible.

    (E) Society should employ computers as a tool rather than a crutch.

GO ON TO THE NEXT PAGE

43. In Passage 2, the student in the first paragraph is most likely

    (A) an example of a widespread problem

    (B) someone who only studies the night before a test

    (C) a smart test taker

    (D) an example of how computers can improve society's efficiency

    (E) cheating

44. The reference to "proper spelling and grammar" (Passage 2, line 61) serves to

    (A) give an example of society's emerging needs

    (B) show how computers have made such a menial task obsolete

    (C) indicate another trend stemming from the overdependence on computers

    (D) compare the importance of proper writing skills with proper math skills

    (E) explain the sudden burst in popularity of computers in recent years

45. The authors of both passages would most likely agree that

    (A) computers can be a benefit to our society

    (B) society is becoming overly dependent on computers

    (C) price is a major part of the computer's growing popularity

    (D) computers have made society a much better place

    (E) computers can harm productivity

46. The author of Passage 2 would most likely agree with which of the following statements about lines 62–63 of Passage 1 ("it would be difficult to imagine our world without them")?

    (A) Such a world would be far less productive.

    (B) Such a world might be preferable to the overly dependent society that we've become.

    (C) Such a world is not difficult to imagine at all.

    (D) Such a world is possible if society realizes the dangers of computers.

    (E) Such a world would be a far better place.

GO ON TO THE NEXT PAGE

Questions 47–48 refer to the following passage.

It has long been believed that the best system of government is one where everyone in a given society would vote on each and every law. Such a system of referendum
(5) would prevent corrupt politicians from serving their own self-interests when voting on a law. In the past, such a system could only be considered for small communities as it would be impossible to execute efficiently
(10) on a large scale. However, the existence of modern technology renders this objection moot. If our society so desires it, all of us may one day cast votes on individual laws from the comfort of our homes.

47. Information concerning the "corrupt politicians" (line 5) would most likely be used to

   (A) support the argument advanced by those who oppose a system of referendum

   (B) justify the need for the existence of modern technology

   (C) persuade the masses that a system of referendum would not be possible

   (D) argue that small communities would not benefit from modern technology

   (E) provide a reason for replacing the current system of government with a system of referendum

48. The passage implies which one of the following?

   (A) Corrupt politicians will only serve their own self-interests.

   (B) Modern technology would not benefit small communities.

   (C) Society might not want a system of referendum.

   (D) Home is the most comfortable place to vote.

   (E) The lack of efficiency is society's only objection to a system of referendum.

SECTION 4

Time—25 Minutes
20 Questions

Solve each of the following problems, decide which is the best answer choice, and darken the corresponding oval on the answer sheet.

Notes:

(1) Calculator use is permitted.

(2) All numbers used are real numbers.

(3) Figures are provided for some problems. All figures are drawn to scale and lie in a plane UNLESS otherwise indicated.

(4) Unless otherwise specified, the domain of any function f is assumed to be the set of all real numbers x for which $f(x)$ is a real number.

Reference Information

$A = \frac{1}{2}bh$ $c^2 = a^2 + b^2$ Special right triangles $A = \pi r^2$ $V = \ell wh$ $V = \pi r^2 h$ $A = \ell w$
$C = 2\pi r$

The sum of the degree measures of the angles in a triangle is 180.
The number of degrees of arc in a circle is 360.
A straight angle has a degree measure of 180.

21. $4x^3 + 3y^3 - 9x^3 - 16 + 5x^3 + 7 =$

    (A) $3x^3 - 16$

    (B) $3x^3 - 9$

    (C) $3y^3 - 9$

    (D) $3y^3 - 18x^3 - 16$

    (E) $3y^3 - 18x^3 - 9$

22. On Monday morning, Sarah sold 14 boxes of Girl Scout cookies before lunch. If the cookies are \$3.25 a box and Sarah needs to sell at least \$80 worth for the day, how many more boxes must Sarah sell after lunch in order to meet her goal?

    (A) 11

    (B) 14

    (C) 17

    (D) 21

    (E) 25

GO ON TO THE NEXT PAGE

23. The figure below shows a ladder propped against the side of a building. If the base of the ladder is 17 feet from the building, how long, in feet, is the ladder?

   17 feet

   (A) 17

   (B) $17\sqrt{2}$

   (C) $17\sqrt{3}$

   (D) 34

   (E) $17\sqrt{5}$

24. What is the value of $2a + b$ if
    $4a^2 + 6ab + 2b^2 = 36$ and $a + b = 3$?

   (A) 3

   (B) 4

   (C) 5

   (D) 6

   (E) 7

25. Foggy the Frog is trying to climb out of a well. He climbs 6 inches the first day, 9 inches the second day, and 7 inches the third day. Unfortunately, it rained on the fourth day and Foggy slid down 6 inches. How many inches did Foggy average on each of the 4 days?

   (A) 1

   (B) 3

   (C) 4

   (D) 7

   (E) 8

26. The area of circle Q is 16π. If $\overline{FC}$ is a diameter of circle Q and F corresponds to point $(4, 7)$ on the standard (x, y) coordinate plane, which one of the following coordinates could be point C?

   (A) $(0, 7)$

   (B) $(4, -1)$

   (C) $(4, 3)$

   (D) $(8, 7)$

   (E) $(12, 15)$

27. If $x = 2$ and $y = 3$, what is the value of $2x^3y^2 - 4x^3y^3$?

   (A) -720

   (B) 124

   (C) 336

   (D) 648

   (E) 1,008

28. When is the statement $\dfrac{c}{f} = \dfrac{f}{c}$ true?

   (A) always

   (B) only when c and f are both 1

   (C) only when $c = f$

   (D) only when $|c| = |f|$

   (E) never

GO ON TO THE NEXT PAGE

DIRECTIONS FOR STUDENT-PRODUCED RESPONSE QUESTIONS

For each of the questions below (29–38), solve the problem and indicate your answer by darkening the ovals in the special grid. For example:

Answer: 1.25 or $\frac{5}{4}$ or 5/4

Write answer → in boxes.

Grid-in result. →

Fraction line
Decimal point

Either position is correct.

You may start your answers in any column, space permitting. Columns not needed should be left blank.

- It is recommended, though not required, that you write your answer in the boxes at the top of the columns. However, you will receive credit only for darkening the ovals correctly.

- Grid only one answer to a question, even though some problems have more than one correct answer.

- Darken no more than one oval in a column.

- No answers are negative.

- Mixed numbers cannot be gridded. For example: the number $1\frac{1}{4}$ must be gridded as 1.25 or 5/4.

  (If ☐1☐1☐/☐4☐ is gridded, it will be interpreted as $\frac{11}{4}$, not $1\frac{1}{4}$.)

- Decimal Accuracy: Decimal answers must be entered as accurately as possible. For example, if you obtain an answer such as 0.1666…, you should record the result as .166 or .167. **Less accurate values such as .16 or .17 are not acceptable.**

Acceptable ways to grid $\frac{1}{6}$ = .1666 …

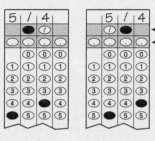

29. If $3a^2 + 6ab + 2b^2 = 13$ and $a^2 + 3ab + b^2 = 2$, then what is a possible value of a?

30. What is the sum of all the positive odd integers less than 64?

GO ON TO THE NEXT PAGE

31. Mario has a crate of 400 cherries that weighs 22 pounds. If the empty crate weighs 2 pounds and he gives 150 cherries away to his friend Sandra, how many pounds do the remaining cherries weigh?

33. A baker wants to cut a 24-inch piece of dough into three smaller pieces, such that the first piece is 2 inches shorter than the second piece and the second piece is 2 inches shorter than the third piece. If she used all 24 inches on the three pieces, what would be the length, in inches, of the longest piece?

32. Andrea drove 3 miles south to the grocery store, then 6 miles west to the library, then 5 miles south to the gym. How many miles shorter would her trip be if she went straight to the gym from the beginning?

34. The average of a set of 7 consecutive whole numbers is 14. What is the sum of the largest and smallest numbers in the set?

GO ON TO THE NEXT PAGE

35. Wally Wilk's marshmallow factory cuts marshmallow squares that are 2 inches on each side from a giant marshmallow sheet that's 24 inches long and 36 inches wide. How many marshmallow squares can the Wally Wilk's factory cut from four of these giant sheets?

37. In the figure above, what is the value of $c + d$?

36. At a birthday party, $\frac{2}{5}$ of the children are boys. If there are six more girls than boys, how many children total are at this party?

38. If the median of the set of consecutive integers from -87 to x, inclusive, is 1, what is the value of x?

SECTION 5

Time—25 Minutes
39 Questions

For each of the following questions, choose the best answer and darken the corresponding oval on the answer sheet.

Directions: The following sentences test your knowledge of grammar, usage, diction (choice of words), and idioms.

Some sentences are correct.

No sentence contains more than one error.

You will find that the error, if there is one, is underlined and lettered. Elements of the sentence that are not underlined will not be changed. In choosing answers, follow the requirements of standard written English.

If there is an error, select the <u>one underlined part</u> that must be changed to make the sentence correct, and fill in the corresponding oval on your answer sheet.

If there is no error, fill in answer oval (E).

1. The team <u>assembled</u> by Mike <u>done</u> most
                  A   B
    of the <u>painting</u> for <u>the new garden shed</u>.
              C   D
    <u>No error</u>
      E

2. Susan failed <u>asking</u> for help, <u>but</u> as <u>it turns</u>
                    A   B   C
    out, it wasn't <u>exactly</u> needed. <u>No error</u>
    C   D   E

3. The detective <u>reluctantly admitted</u> that
                      A
    the series of crimes <u>were</u> <u>likely to</u> continue
                          B   C
    <u>for some time</u>. <u>No error</u>
        D   E

4. <u>Only after</u> confirming the shot five times
        A
    <u>were</u> the judges <u>able to declare</u> that the
      B   C
    former champion <u>had been defeated</u>. <u>No error</u>
                        D   E

5. Nathan <u>was scolded</u> by his mother, <u>but</u> the
                A   B
    misdeed to which <u>she inferred</u> was <u>not one that</u>
                        C   D
    he was guilty of. <u>No error</u>
                        E

GO ON TO THE NEXT PAGE

6. <u>Having not eaten</u> for days, my <u>younger</u>
      A   B

brother and <u>me</u> <u>hungrily devoured</u> the
          C   D

cookies. <u>No error</u>
        E

7. When <u>given</u> a choice between new and used
       A

books, students usually choose <u>the latter</u> as
                             B

<u>they</u> tend to be <u>cheapest</u>. <u>No error</u>
 C   D   E

8. My friend James <u>decided to buy</u> a collection
               A

of paintings similar <u>with the few</u> <u>bought by</u>
                 B   C

me <u>on Tuesday</u>. <u>No error</u>
    D   E

9. Many people <u>recommend</u> a nice, interesting
         A

novel <u>for</u> travelers who <u>are forced</u> to spend
    B   C

four hours <u>in</u> an uncomfortable position.
        D

<u>No error</u>
  E

10. Sugar-free candy, though not <u>as healthy as</u>
                      A

fruit, <u>are</u> the snack <u>of choice</u> for people
     B   C

<u>on a diet</u>. <u>No error</u>
  D   E

11. The mighty sailor <u>related</u> tales <u>of grandeur</u>,
               A   B

but the boy was <u>clearly noninterested</u>,
             C

<u>nodding off</u> as the sailor spoke. <u>No error</u>
  D   E

12. Molly gave Marie a hug when <u>she</u> was
                   A

<u>selected</u> to represent <u>their</u> school <u>in the race</u>.
 B   C   D

<u>No error</u>
  E

13. Due to <u>unusually strong</u> winds, <u>tonight's</u>
       A   B

hurricane will be <u>twice as strong</u> as <u>last year</u>.
             C   D

<u>No error</u>
  E

14. <u>That</u> <u>diamonds are</u> a form of carbon <u>has</u>
  A   B   C

<u>been established</u> for <u>a couple of centuries</u>.
     C   D

<u>No error</u>
  E

GO ON TO THE NEXT PAGE

Directions: The following sentences test correctness and effectiveness of expression. In choosing answers, follow the requirements of standard written English; that is, pay attention to grammar, choice of words, sentence construction, and punctuation.

In each of the following sentences, part of the sentence or the entire sentence is underlined. Beneath each sentence, you will find five ways of phrasing the underlined part. Choice (A) repeats the original; the other four are different.

Choose the answer that best expresses the meaning of the original sentence. If you think the original is better than any of the alternatives, choose it; otherwise, choose one of the others. Your choice should produce the most effective sentence—clear and precise, without awkwardness or ambiguity.

15. Kaitlyn was <u>nearly as talented a painter as she was at singing</u>.

   (A) nearly as talented a painter as she was at singing
   (B) nearly as talented a painter as she was a singer
   (C) nearly as talented a painter as at singing
   (D) nearly as talented at painting and singing
   (E) nearly talented as a painter and a singer

16. Professor Samson <u>wrote short stories, they speak of</u> very interesting events.

   (A) wrote short stories, they speak of
   (B) writing short stories, they speaking of
   (C) wrote short stories, and speaking of
   (D) writing short stories, and they speak of
   (E) wrote short stories that speak of

17. Global warming issues could be alleviated if everyone insulated their homes, <u>invested in energy-efficient appliances</u>, and carpooled to work.

   (A) invested in energy-efficient appliances
   (B) investing in energy-efficient appliances
   (C) and invested in energy-efficient appliances
   (D) invested in appliances that are energy-efficient
   (E) and investing in energy-efficient appliances

18. <u>Aside from them we addressed during the final club meeting</u>, no other issues remained.

   (A) Aside from them we addressed during the final club meeting
   (B) Other than them we had addressed at the final club meeting
   (C) Aside from those we addressed during the final club meeting
   (D) Besides them we addressed during the club's final meeting
   (E) Aside from them that we addressed during the final club meeting

19. Reaching an internal temperature of 250°, the firefighters scrambled to put out the blazing inferno with buckets of water.

   (A) the firefighters scrambled to put out the blazing inferno
   (B) the firefighters scrambled the blazing inferno
   (C) the firefighters had scrambled to put out the blazing inferno
   (D) the blazing inferno was put out by the scrambling firefighters
   (E) the blazing inferno put out the scrambled firefighters

20. Many adults prefer going to the movies over renting a DVD, another preference is that adults prefer eating out over cooking.

   (A) movies over renting a DVD, another preference is that adults prefer eating out over
   (B) movies over renting a DVD; another preference is that adults prefer eating out over
   (C) movies over renting a DVD; another adult preference is for eating out over
   (D) movies over renting a DVD, another adult preference is eating out over
   (E) movies over renting a DVD, which also is a preference for eating out over

21. Suzanne scolded her disobedient son, which was covered with mud.

   (A) son, which was covered with mud
   (B) son, who was covered with mud
   (C) son, whom was covered with mud
   (D) son, who covers mud
   (E) son, that was covered with mud

22. Dependent upon its services, Mount Nittany Medical Center is a hospital that many people visit.

   (A) Dependent upon its services, Mount Nittany Medical Center is a hospital that many people visit.
   (B) A hospital visited by many people dependent upon their services is Mount Nittany Medical Center.
   (C) Dependent upon its services, the hospital Mount Nittany Medical Center is a place that many people visit.
   (D) Dependent upon its services, many people visit the Mount Nittany Medical Center hospital.
   (E) Many people dependent on Mount Nittany Medical Center and visiting it.

23. The exquisite texture of fine Italian cuisine can be experienced in either Bell's or Beagleman's pizza.

   (A) in either Bell's or Beagleman's
   (B) either Bell's or Beagleman's
   (C) either in Bell's or in Beagleman's
   (D) in Bell's or Beagleman's
   (E) either in Bell's nor in Beagleman's

24. Professor Epstein spent many years researching the theory of genetic mutation, which he was fascinated by, and these are his results that are included in his latest scientific journal.

   (A) these are his results that are included in
   (B) the inclusion of these, his results is in
   (C) his results having been included in
   (D) his inclusion of these results in
   (E) included his results in

GO ON TO THE NEXT PAGE

25. The topic we discussed <u>that was whether or not our club should take a field trip</u> later this month.

    (A) that was whether or not our club should take a field trip
    (B) was the decision of whether or not a field trip should be taken by our club
    (C) was whether or not a field trip should be taken by our club
    (D) was whether our club should take a field trip
    (E) whether our club should take a field trip

26. You could have lunch at a fast-food <u>restaurant, you could have dinner</u> at the local diner.

    (A) restaurant, you could have dinner
    (B) restaurant, you could also have dinner
    (C) restaurant, however, you could have dinner
    (D) restaurant; you could also have dinner
    (E) restaurant; you could also have decided to have dinner

27. The small <u>island, once a thriving community, is now a barren area</u> completely devoid of life.

    (A) island, once a thriving community, is now a barren area
    (B) island, because it was once a thriving community, is now a barren area
    (C) island, once a thriving community, is now an area that is barren and
    (D) island was once a thriving community, it is now a barren area
    (E) island was once a thriving community, and it is now a barren area

28. The longer I interact with society, the more I realize <u>that one's success in life is not related to your outward appearance</u>.

    (A) that one's success in life is not related to your outward appearance
    (B) that one's success in life is not related to one's outward appearance
    (C) that your success in life is not related to one's outward appearance
    (D) that one's success in life is not related to their outward appearance
    (E) one's success in life is not related to your outward appearance

29. Having a good work <u>ethic allows painters to become a better artist</u>.

    (A) ethic allows painters to become a better artist
    (B) ethically allows painters to become a better artist
    (C) ethic allows painters to become better artists
    (D) ethic allowing painters to become a better artist
    (E) ethic is allowing painters who dream of becoming better artists

GO ON TO THE NEXT PAGE

30. Claire rescued the unconscious man from the fire, but she <u>accepted neither acknowledge for the deed or the reward that the city offered her for</u> the heroic act.

(A) accepted neither acknowledge for the deed or the reward that the city offered her for

(B) accepted neither acknowledgement for the deed or the city's reward for

(C) accepted neither acknowledge for the deed nor

(D) accepted neither acknowledgement or

(E) accepted neither acknowledgement for the deed nor the city's reward for

31. For many a successful orator, <u>having style is more important than</u> having substance.

(A) having style is more important than

(B) stylishness has more importance than

(C) to be stylish is more important than

(D) being stylish is more important than

(E) it is more important to have stylishness than

32. <u>One of the symptoms of the flu is when you</u> develop a splitting headache.

(A) One of the symptoms of the flu is when you

(B) One of the symptoms of the flu is that you

(C) One of the symptoms of the flu includes when you

(D) Symptoms of the flu including that

(E) Symptoms of the flu including when

33. Some obsessed fans insist that <u>Elvis's not being discovered alive, this has to do with his not wanting to be found</u>.

(A) Elvis's not being discovered alive, this has to do with his not wanting to be found

(B) the failure to discover Elvis alive, it is because he does not want to be found

(C) for Elvis who has not been discovered alive, this has to do with his not wanting to be found

(D) Elvis has not been discovered alive because he doesn't want to be found

(E) when denying that Elvis is alive, this has to do with his not wanting to be found

34. <u>Being friendlier and more playful compared with the other dogs</u>, Bailee was easily the office favorite.

(A) Being friendlier and more playful compared with the other dogs

(B) By being more playful and more friendlier than the other dogs

(C) Both friendlier and more playful compared to the other dogs

(D) Friendlier and more playful, unlike the other dogs

(E) Friendlier and more playful than the other dogs

GO ON TO THE NEXT PAGE

Directions: The passage below is an early draft of an essay. Parts of the passage need to be rewritten.

Read the passage, and answer the questions that follow. Some questions are about individual sentences or parts of sentences; in these questions, you are asked to select the choice that will improve sentence structure and word choice. Other questions refer to parts of the essay or the entire essay and ask you to consider the organization and development. You should follow the conventions of standard written English in answering the questions. After you have chosen your answer, fill in the corresponding oval on your answer sheet.

Questions 35–39 are based on the following passage.

(1) *Last summer, my dad and I went fishing.* (2) *We caught a very big fish.* (3) *It weighed nearly five pounds.* (4) *But my dad wouldn't let me.* (5) "*The fish would be happier if we throw it back in.*" (6) *I really liked it so threw it back in the water.*

(7) *Whenever we go fishing, I can feel nature's affect on me.* (8) *With the gentle wind upon my back, the riverbank is a great place for me to relieve stress.* (9) *Fishing can be very relaxing after a long day's work.* (10) *They always swim in groups, making them easy to catch.*

(11) *A lot of people say it's boring.* (12) *They think, "What's so interesting about sitting in a boat for hours doing nothing?"* (13) *They just don't understand.* (14) *Fishing takes a lot of patients but it is worth the effort when you catch one.*

35. Which of the following would be the most suitable sentence to insert immediately after sentence 3?

(A) I thought it weighed six pounds.

(B) I wanted to go home.

(C) It was a trout.

(D) I wanted to smoke it for lunch.

(E) I was about to sing a song.

36. In context, which of the following words are the most logical to insert at the beginning of sentence 5 (reproduced below)?

"*The fish would be happier if we throw it back in.*"

(A) He tells me,

(B) He insists,

(C) My father tells me,

(D) Since he tells me,

(E) He told me,

37. In context, which of the following is the best version of the underlined portion of sentence 7 (reproduced below)?

Whenever <u>we go fishing, I can feel nature's affect on</u> me.

(A) (As it is now)

(B) we go fishing, we can feel nature's affect on

(C) I go fishing, I can feel nature's affect on

(D) we go fishing, I can feel nature's effect on

(E) I go fishing, we can feel nature's effect on

GO ON TO THE NEXT PAGE

38. Which of the following is the best way to combine sentences 11 and 13 (reproduced below)?

    A lot of people say it's boring. They just don't understand.

    (A) A lot of people say it's boring, but they just don't understand.

    (B) A lot of people just don't understand, but they say it's boring.

    (C) A lot of people say they just don't understand because it's boring.

    (D) A lot of people say it's boring; for example, they just don't understand it.

    (E) A lot of people say it's boring, and they don't understand it.

39. Which of the following words are the most logical to insert at the beginning of sentence 8 (reproduced below)?

    With the gentle wind upon my back, the riverbank is a great place for me to relieve stress.

    (A) Because

    (B) In contrast,

    (C) For example,

    (D) Did you know that

    (E) In the same way,

DIAGNOSTIC TEST: ANSWER KEY

SECTION 1

1. C	10. C	19. A
2. D	11. D	20. E
3. B	12. B	21. C
4. A	13. C	22. D
5. A	14. E	23. B
6. E	15. E	24. C
7. D	16. B	
8. A	17. C	
9. C	18. D	

SECTION 2

1. C	9. A	17. E
2. B	10. D	18. E
3. E	11. E	19. D
4. C	12. D	20. A
5. E	13. B	
6. A	14. B	
7. C	15. A	
8. B	16. C	

SECTION 3

25. D	34. A	43. A
26. B	35. D	44. C
27. E	36. E	45. A
28. C	37. B	46. B
29. A	38. A	47. E
30. B	39. A	48. C
31. A	40. C	
32. D	41. C	
33. D	42. E	

SECTION 4

21. C	29. 3
22. A	30. 1,024
23. D	31. 12.5
24. D	32. 4
25. C	33. 10
26. B	34. 28
27. A	35. 864
28. D	36. 30
	37. 219
	38. 89

SECTION 5

1. B	16. E	31. A
2. A	17. A	32. B
3. B	18. C	33. D
4. E	19. D	34. E
5. C	20. C	35. D
6. C	21. B	36. E
7. D	22. D	37. D
8. B	23. A	38. A
9. E	24. E	39. C
10. B	25. D	
11. C	26. D	
12. A	27. A	
13. D	28. B	
14. E	29. C	
15. B	30. E	

DIAGNOSTIC TEST: ASSESS YOUR STRENGTHS

Use the following tables to determine which question types you need to review most.

Question Type	Section and Question
Sentence Completion	Section 1, 1–5
	Section 3, 25–32
Reading Comprehension	Section 1, 6–24
	Section 3, 33–48
Regular Math	Section 2, 1–18
	Section 4, 19–28
Grid-in Math	Section 4, 29–38
Identifying Sentence Errors	Section 5, 1–14
Improving Sentences	Section 5, 15–34
Improving Paragraphs	Section 5, 35–39

Question Type	Number of Questions on Test	Number Correct
Sentence Completion	13	
Reading Comprehension	35	
Regular Math	28	
Grid-in Math	10	
Identifying Sentence Errors	14	
Improving Sentences	20	
Improving Paragraphs	5	

ANSWERS AND EXPLANATIONS

SECTION 1

1. C

The sailor had a bad day and is trying to pick a fight. Such a person would be *angry* and might pick fights by *attacking* others. Choice (A) has *goading*, which means urging or provoking in the second blank. *Goading* someone is a way to pick a fight, but (A) can't be the right answer, because the first blank has *peaceful*. (C) is the only answer that is a good match for both blanks.

2. D

Joe made the cut and is jumping for joy, which shows that he is happy. Only (D), *excited*, makes sense as a way to describe someone having a positive response to good news. *Quizzical* (A) means puzzled. *Crestfallen* (B) means disappointed. *Ambivalent* (C) means having mixed feelings. *Perplexed* (E) means confused.

3. B

Start with the second part of the sentence. Castle gates usually keep invaders out, so look for a word that describes keeping them from entering, such as *preventing* (B) or *prohibiting* (E). Invaders threaten the welfare of citizens, so the first blank of the sentence should describe how gates are meant to keep the citizens safe. *Protect* matches that prediction.

4. A

First, read the sentence and decide whether the blank will be a positive or a negative word. A person most likely wouldn't give someone gold in a negative way, so you can eliminate any of the answer choices that you know mean something negative. That leaves just *appease* (A), which means to satisfy or to placate. *Sully* (B) means to soil or to taint. *Belittle* (C) means

to express a low opinion of something. *Harass* (D) means to annoy. *Mock* (E) means to ridicule.

5. A

The word *but* is a clue that the sentence contains a contrast. Start with the second part of the sentence because it offers more clues to what the missing word should be. A substantial cut in operating expenses is a major, positive effect. That rules out *cursory* (B), which means superficial; *specious* (D), which means deceptive; and *negotiable* (C), which means open to modification. The first blank will contrast with the major benefits the groups received. The programs were probably introduced quietly, or without *fanfare*. Choice (A) fits both blanks.

THE MODERN SUPERMARKET

The passage begins with a paragraph that labels traditional grocery stores as a problem and supermarkets as the solution to that problem. Paragraph 2 details the problems with traditional stores. Paragraph 3 then shows us how supermarkets address the problems mentioned in the previous paragraph. While the passage is informational in nature, the author's regard for the superiority of supermarkets is clear.

6. E

Main purpose questions require you to look at the passage as a whole. Choices (B) and (D) are way outside of the scope while (C) is a detail in the passage. Choice (A) may be tempting, but talk of the disadvantages of traditional grocery stores constitutes only half of the passage.

The passage's purpose is really to help show the advantages that supermarkets have over traditional stores. Choice (E) is correct.

7. D

Choices (A) and (B) are mentioned as early as lines 8–10, (C) is implied through lines 37–40, and (E) can be found in lines 29–30. While the passage does mention the razor-thin margins of supermarkets, it never actually discusses the margins of traditional stores, making (D) the correct choice.

8. A

Choices (B) and (C) are never mentioned in the passage. Choice (D) *may* be a cause for inefficiency, but there's no way to tell from this passage if it was the *primary* cause. Choice (E) would not affect delivery. In lines 46–47, not offering delivery is given as an example of a means of keeping operating expenses low: that's (A).

9. C

Margins are razor-thin is given as a reason for having to keep expenses low, so margins must be referring to profits. Choice (C) is correct.

10. C

Given the tone of the passage, you may have predicted something negative for the answer, which eliminates (A) and (D). While supermarkets did not offer delivery, there's no mention as to whether or not traditional shops did, so (E) is out as well. The passage mentions that traditional grocery stores were expensive to run in lines 17–19, so (C) is the answer.

11. D

The second paragraph details the problems with traditional stores. Choices (A), (B), and (E) are all specific problems mentioned in that paragraph, but they don't make up the overall main idea. Choice (C) has nothing to do with problems with traditional stores. Choice (D) is the answer.

PIGEON RECOGNITION

This short passage presents a theory by psychologists that humans have developed a special ability to recognize facial expressions. This theory may have been discounted by researchers, who found that trained pigeons were able to distinguish between expressions.

12. B

The question is a bit vague, so you may have found it easier to go straight to the choices. Choice (A) goes too far as the passage never says that *only* pigeons could be taught. Higher brain functions in (D) and the difficulty of testing in (E) are never mentioned. Choice (C) might be tempting but the passage only mentions recognition as a part of *human* communication. Only (B) remains, and it works as the pigeons in the experiment have proven.

13. C

The author gives the *weight of such recognition* as a reason for why humans developed recognition out of necessity, so *weight* must mean *significance*. Choice (C) is correct.

THE AMERICAN CIVIL WAR

These two short passages present two views of the Civil War. Passage 1 looks at how the war was tragic because of the large number of Americans killed or wounded. The writer questions whether the war, despite the fact that it reunited the country, was worth the casualties. Passage 2 looks at the positive results of the war, including the expansion of manufacturing and industry and economic growth.

14. E

Bloody battles are mentioned, but there's no reason to believe that (A) is true. The shortage of manpower in (B) was not mentioned as the cause for defeat. The opinion given in (C) is never discussed. While (D) is mentioned in the passage, it is not the overarching theme. The true purpose of the passage is to convey how tragic the war was. That's (E).

15. E

The prevalent tone of Passage 2 is that of hope, so eliminate (A) and (C). Choice (D) is a bit too strong as the author never gives a definitive opinion in this regard. While the government *is* accommodating, we can't be certain that it was due to (B). Choice (E), however, works as the passage focuses on the economy-strengthening aspects of the war's aftermath.

16. B

Look at the main idea of each passage. You already know, from question 14, that the writer of Passage 1 sees the war as tragic. And question 15 established that the writer of Passage 2 thinks that the war had a positive aspect. Choice (B) is the answer.

17. C

The correct answer to an author agreement question for paired passages is usually very general, and this one is no different. While the two authors cannot seem to agree on much, one thing that neither should dispute is the fact that the war was important to America's history (for better or for worse). That's (C).

SOLE PROPRIETORSHIPS AND PARTNERSHIPS

The passage begins by introducing corporations and reasons why entrepreneurs may want an alternative. The second paragraph discusses the advantages and disadvantages of sole proprietorships. Paragraph 3 continues by exploring the advantages of partnerships while paragraph 4 discusses some of their disadvantages as well as hinting that corporations have their benefits as well. While

the passage is mainly informational in nature, the author's opinion that none of the three options seems to be the winner in every situation is clear.

18. D

The passage is about corporations and two alternatives to them. Choice (D) fits that perfectly.

19. A

Reread the sentence in which the phrase appears and the lines surrounding it. It says that sole proprietorships are good if they are successful. The *but* indicates a contrast. The second part of the sentence says that whatever *running in the red* is, it is *scary* because you, the boss, would have to take on all the debt. That's a clue that the answer will be about being low on money. Choice (A) is your answer.

20. E

Find the paragraph in which the author talks about partnerships. The author says that a partnership *sacrifices some of the operational freedom that comes with a sole proprietorship … but [the partners] will also be chipping in on expenses and sharing responsibility for any debt.* This is paraphrased in (E). Choices (A) and (B) are discounted in the last paragraph. Choice (C) is wrong because the author says in the last line that corporations, not partnerships, may be a necessary evil. Choice (D) is not mentioned in the passage.

21. C

Sole proprietorships seem to have a lot of negatives (being solely responsible for debts, funding the business all by yourself, etc.), but one clear advantage they have is the ability to run things as you like (since you own it by yourself), so (C) has it right. Choice (A) is tempting, but this advantage is shared by partnerships as well. Choice (E) is also tempting, but sharing profits in a partnership does not necessarily mean that these shares are smaller than the profits of a sole proprietorship, especially because a partnership would likely be a much larger business. Choice (B) is an advantage for partnerships, and (D) is not mentioned.

22. D

The fourth paragraph discusses some of the disadvantages of partnerships and hints that corporations have their benefits, too. That's (D). Although the author ends the passage by saying that corporations may be a necessary evil, that is not the same as recommending corporations, so don't be thrown off by (B).

23. B

Credit is listed as a problem *especially if you don't have a lot of financial assets on hand.* Therefore, it must refer to your ability to get these needed financial assets. Choice (B) has it right.

24. C

The person who benefits the most from a sole proprietorship would be the one who values its strengths and can cope with its weaknesses. Sole proprietorships shine for those who like total control of their business, but they take more money to start up than the other two options and can potentially put you into financial ruin. These criteria immediately eliminate (A), (B), and (E) as possible candidates. Choice (D) may or may not be better off than his eliminated rivals, but the businesswoman in (C) is the clear winner of the bunch.

SECTION 2

1. C

Begin by converting the fraction: $\frac{4}{10} = 0.4$, with the 4 one spot to the right of the decimal point. The only choice that has a 4 there is (C).

2. B

You are given the number of geese and asked to find the approximate number of cows. The geese portion of the pie chart is roughly 25 percent of the chart, so there are $8 \times 4 = 32$ total animals at the farm. Subtract the 8 geese and you have $32 - 8 = 24$ animals remaining. Cows represent roughly half of this number, or $\frac{24}{2} = 12$.

3. E

Whenever you see variables in both the question stem and the answer choices, pick numbers. For this problem, pick 3 for j and 2 for k. Plug these values into each of the choices and look for an even number:

(A) $3 + 2 = 5$

(B) $3 + 2(2) = 3 + 4 = 7$

(C) $3 - 2 = 1$

(D) $\frac{3 \times 2}{2} = 3$

(E) $3 \times 2 = 6$

Only (E) is even, so it must be correct.

4. C

Cod Enterprises had a yearly profit of $40 million in 2007 and has been growing by $10 million annually. To reach $100 million, it would need $100 million − $40 million = $60 million more in profits. At $10 million more per year, it would take $\frac{\$60,000,000}{\$10,000,000} = 6$ more years. Therefore, Cod Enterprises will reach an annual profit of $100 million in $2007 + 6 = 2013$.

5. E

The original price was $48.00 and the new price is $38.40, so the drop in price is $48.00 − $38.40 = $9.60. The percent decrease is therefore $\frac{\$9.60}{\$48.00} = \frac{1}{5} = 20\%$. Choice (E) is correct.

6. A

Because you're not given the original length and width, pick a value to make the calculation more concrete. If the original length and width are each 1, then t would be 1 as well. The new length would be $\frac{3}{4}$, and the new width would be 3. The new area is then $\frac{3}{4} \times 3 = \frac{9}{4} \times 1$. Plug t back in place of 1, and the new area is $\frac{9}{4}t$.

7. C

Picking numbers is often the quickest way to the correct answer. Because q is a negative integer and quite a few of the choices have large exponents, pick -1 for q. Plug this into the choices and look for the choice with the greatest value:

(A) $-(-1) = 1$
(B) $|-1| = 1$
(C) $2(-1)^4 = 2 \times 1 = 2$
(D) $5(-1)^{15} = 5(-1) = -5$
(E) $8(-1)^{23} = 8(-1) = -8$

(C) is therefore correct.

8. B

Understanding how averages and sums are connected is the key to solving a problem like this. So far, Ian has studied for $3 + 6 + 4 = 13$ hours in the first three days. To average 5 hours per day for four days, he needs to study for a total of $5 \times 4 = 20$ hours. Therefore, Ian needs to study for $20 - 13 = 7$ hours on the fourth day.

9. A

To fence in the circular field, Farmer Sanders will need its circumference in fencing. The circumference of this circle is its diameter times π, or 30π feet. The triangle is 30 feet on each side, so its perimeter is

$30 \times 3 = 90$ feet. The difference, in feet, is $30\pi - 90$. Choice (A) is correct.

10. D

When a problem uses multiple units of measure, convert them into a single unit before doing the math. A 6-foot chain is $6 \times 12 = 72$ inches long. The jeweler uses $\frac{3}{8} \times 72 = \frac{3}{1} \times 9$ inches for accessories. Each accessory is 3 inches long, so $\frac{27}{3} = 9$ accessories can be made.

11. E

It often pays to consider critical thinking opportunities before diving straight into the math. The first cow drinks 200 cups and weighs 600 pounds. Because the second cow drinks more, it must also weigh more. Of the choices, only (E) is greater than 600.

You could also solve this problem by setting up a proportion. Call x the number of pounds that the second cow weighs. Set up a proportion and solve for x:

$$\frac{200}{600} = \frac{225}{x}$$
$$\frac{1}{3} = \frac{225}{x}$$
$$x = 675$$

12. D

Because y and z are both negative and the coefficient of each choice is positive, the correct choice will have either two even powers (making both positive) or two odd powers (making both negative). That's (D).

13. B

You could try to figure out the h-values of the first seven houses using the pattern, but it's much quicker to think about the nature of a house's *h*-value. Each *h*-value is the product of the house number and some other whole number, so the *h*-value of the seventh house must have 7 as one of its factors. The only choice that is divisible by 7 is (B).

14. B

The sides $2m$, $3m$, and d form a right triangle, so plug these values into the Pythagorean theorem, then solve for d:

$$a^2 + b^2 = c^2$$
$$(2m)^2 + (3m)^2 = d^2$$
$$4m^2 + 9m^2 = d^2$$
$$13m^2 = d^2$$
$$\sqrt{13m^2} = d$$
$$m\sqrt{13} = d$$

That's (B).

15. A

The actual bedroom is $16 - 12 = 4$ feet longer than the living room. Because the scale is 1 inch = 4 feet, the bedroom is 1 inch longer than the living room on the floor plan.

16. C

Begin by figuring out the dimensions of the triangle. Point B has the same x-coordinate as A and the same y-coordinate as C, so its coordinates are $(-6, -4)$. The length of AB is $6 - (-4) = 6 + 4 = 10$ and the length of BC is $8 - (-6) = 8 + 6 = 14$. The area of ΔABC is $\frac{1}{2} \times 14 \times 10 = 70$.

17. E

When a pair of parallel lines is cut by a transversal, every acute angle equals every other acute angle, every obtuse angle equals every other obtuse angle, and any acute angle is supplementary to any obtuse angle.

In the figure, t and u correspond to obtuse angles while v and w correspond to acute angles. There are a total of two obtuse angles and two acute angles, or two pairs of supplementary angles. A pair of supplementary angles sums to 180°, so the total value of the four angles is $180 \times 2 = 360$.

18. E

When a geometry figure contains multiple shapes, transfer information from one shape to another. Each of the smaller squares has a side of length 8. The circle sits in the middle and the portion of each square that isn't touching it has a length of 4, so the circle's radius is $8 - 4 = 4$. The area of a small square is $8 \times 8 = 64$. The area of the circle is $(4^2)\pi = 16\pi$. Only $\frac{1}{4}$ of the circle is covering the shaded square, so the area of the shaded region is $64 - \frac{16\pi}{4} = 64 - 4\pi$.

19. D

Shelly already has 7 quarters ($1.75), 11 dimes ($1.10), and 6 nickels ($0.30) for a total of $1.75 + $1.10 + $0.30 = $3.15. She needs to draw 15 more coins and not go over $5, so the value of the 15 coins cannot exceed $5.00 - $3.15 = $1.85. Backsolve this problem beginning with (E): Because there are no dimes left in the pouch, if Shelly drew 6 quarters ($1.50), she would need to draw $15 - 6 = 9$ nickels ($0.45) for a total of $1.50 + $0.45 = $1.95. That's too much, so eliminate (E). Now try (D): If Shelly drew 5 quarters ($1.25), she would need to draw $15 - 5 = 10$ nickels ($0.50) for a total of $1.25 + $0.50 = $1.75. You know $1.75 is less than $1.85, so this is the correct answer.

20. A

When cut along the dotted lines, the perimeter of each quarter of the circle will be $\frac{1}{4}$ of the circle's total circumference plus two radii. The total perimeter would be the circumference of the whole circle plus

$4 \times 2 = 8$ radii. Because the diameter is 8, the radius is $\frac{8}{2} = 4$, and the circumference of the circle is $2 \times 4 \times \pi = 8\pi$. The total perimeter is then $4 \times 4 + 8\pi = 16 + 8\pi$. That's (A).

SECTION 3

25. D

Two clues are present in this sentence: *The vast reaches of outer space* serves as a definition of the blank, and the comparison to *earthly scenery* means the blank must be parallel to it. Choice (D) fits both clues.

26. B

The word *paradoxically* is a clue that there is a contrast in this sentence. So a good guess is that the sentence will say either that a settlement that is flourishing has few supplies or that a settlement that isn't flourishing has many supplies. This rules out (A), (C), (D), and (E). Choice (B) reflects your guess, so that's the answer.

27. E

Purchased…because of tells you that the blank is the primary reason for buying the bed. *Patients with lower back pain* would primarily be interested in *therapeutic* qualities. Choice (E) matches our prediction.

28. C

Technological breakthroughs is a clue that something Adele studied had a positive result and allowed her to create her inventions. The positive tone means (A), (B), (D), and (E) are wrong. Choice (C) fits and is your answer.

29. A

Because the mountain pass is completely sealed, rescue attempts would be difficult if not downright impossible. Only (A) fits this prediction.

30. B

Start with the second blank. A crowd of angry people would react in a negative manner. That rules out (A), (C), and (E). Would a speech that is *intemperate* (showing no signs of being under control) or *conciliatory* (appeasing or disarming) be more likely to anger a crowd? The former, (B), is your answer.

31. A

The blank is describing the manner in which Matt walks. A person with an *injured foot* who is *hobbling* would find walking difficult. Only (A), *halting*, makes sense here.

32. D

This straight definition blank is a tough one due to the difficult vocabulary in the choices. The example, *making a big show of*, is a clue that the blank has to do with *acting* or *theatricality*. Only (D) fits this prediction.

METAMORPHOSIS

This short passage discusses caterpillars, which undergo metamorphosis, meaning the young creatures don't look or act as they do as adults.

33. D

The same caterpillars in line 6 are described in line 9 as creatures that undergo metamorphosis. That's (D). Although the other choices are mentioned in the passage, they do not apply to caterpillars.

34. A

There is no hint of the author's views on anything in the passage as the passage is purely a recounting of facts, so you should predict a neutral choice. Only (A) works.

THE IMPACT OF COMPUTER TECHNOLOGY

PASSAGE 1

Passage 1 is informative and provides a brief history of the modern computer. Paragraph 1 mentions how computers began as a niche product too expensive for the masses that eventually broke into the mainstream. Paragraph 2 provides background information on the ENIAC, the first electronic computer. The third paragraph takes a look at the author's past, including information concerning the author's first computer purchase and how that computer stacks up to a modern device. The final paragraph explores some of the uses of computers in today's society. Throughout the passage, the author's tone is a positive one, praising the computer as a boon to society.

PASSAGE 2

Passage 2 is of the persuasive nature. Its first paragraph opens with a scenario inside a classroom—one that foreshadows the argument to be made. The second paragraph focuses on the merits of computers, but the author's true opinion of computers is revealed at the end of the paragraph. Paragraph 3 continues the trend of praising computers, but the paragraph ends with a clear reason for the author's concern—the fact that society can become overly dependent on computers to a point that is detrimental. The fourth paragraph reexamines the scenario introduced in the first in much greater detail and presents its implications for the future. Finally, the last paragraph ends by questioning the merit of computers. While the author of Passage 2 does not hold the same view as the author of Passage 1, they are not in complete disagreement as both do recognize the benefits of computer technology.

35. D

While most things in the world appreciate in value is a clue that the meaning of *appreciate* has something to do with what something is worth, and *advances in computer technology have actually served to continually decrease the price of computers as time went on* signals that *appreciate* is the opposite of *decrease*. Choice (D) is your answer.

36. E

Choices (A) and (C) sound plausible, but neither happens to be the purpose of this particular example. (B) and (D) are outside the scope of the passage. The $5 watch (a cheap modern computer) is being compared to the author's first computer (an expensive computer of the past) to emphasize the difference in technology of the two time periods. That's (E).

37. B

Choices (A) and (D) happen to be the second author's opinion. The primary reason in (C) and the use of calculators in (E) are not mentioned in Passage 1. The author of the first passage implies that the world is a better place because of computers by focusing only on their positive effects. Choice (B) is correct.

38. A

This question can be answered by first deciding whether the tone of the passage is positive or negative. In the first line of the passage, the author writes that *none [of all the modern inventions] can compare to that of the personal computer*. This means that the author has a positive attitude toward computers, ruling out (B), (C), (D), and (E). Choice (A) is your answer.

39. A

To find the answer to this question, simply go back to the passage and find each of the answer choices. The one you cannot verify will be your answer. Choice (B) is in lines 25–26. Choice (C) is in lines 23–24. Choice (D) is in line 30. Choice (E) is in lines 24–25. Choice (A) is tricky. Read it carefully, and compare it with the passage. The passage says that the ENIAC was the first *electronic* computer, not just the first computer. Choice (A) is the answer.

40. C

Read the sentences that come before and after where traffic lights, bank tellers, and security systems are mentioned. The passage says they *greatly improve our productivity*, which is a benefit, therefore (C) is correct.

41. C

The *optimal window for learning* is described as being short, with *earlier is usually better* as the recommendation, so *window* must refer to *a period of time* rather than *a physical object*. That's (C).

42. E

Passage 2's issue with computers is an overly dependent society that's helpless without them, not with the use of computers as an aid or a convenience, and (E) sums this up quite nicely. Choices (A) and (B) are far too extreme, (C) is never mentioned, and (D) goes counter to the author's statements.

43. A

The student isn't even given a name, much less any useful background information, so we cannot conclude anything too specific about him. Eliminate (B), (C), and (E). The example is definitely used to

introduce a problem rather than an improvement in efficiency, so (A) is correct.

44. C

When the question concerns a detail, be sure to consider the context as well as the content. *In fact* shows that the sentence will continue along the same vein as the rest of the paragraph, which is an assault on the overly dependent society, or (C). Choices (A) and (D) are not within the scope of the passage, and (B) and (E) are too positive to be correct.

45. A

In questions that ask for agreement between authors, expect some choices that only agree with one author and expect the answer to be general. Choice (B) is a view held by Author 2, (D) is held by Author 1, and (C) and (E) are not mentioned by either. While the second author has some reservations on the matter, neither author disputes (A).

46. B

The author of Passage 2 explores advantages and disadvantages without clearly choosing a side, so expect the correct answer to be just as uncertain. Choices (A) and (E) are far too strong, and (C) and (D) aren't mentioned at all. Only (B) matches in tone and language.

SYSTEM OF REFERENDUM

The author of this short passage says that the best system of government is one in which everybody votes for each and every law. The author believes that modern technology will make that possible one day.

47. E

The corrupt politicians are presented as a problem with our current system, making it ideal for (E). Choice (A) goes counter to its purpose, and (B), (C), and (D) have nothing to do with the example.

48. C

The phrase *If our society so desires it* suggests (C). While (A) and (E) are both tempting, the word *only* ruins both of them. Choices (B) and (D) are not mentioned at all.

SECTION 4

21. C

Begin by rewriting the expression as $3y^3 + 4x^3 + 5x^3 - 9x^3 - 16 + 7$. Since $4 + 5 - 9 = 0$, the x^3 terms cancel each other out, leaving you with $3y^3 - 16 + 7 = 3y^3 - 9$. That's (C).

22. A

Sarah has already sold $14 \times \$3.25 = \$45.50$ worth of cookies, so she needs to sell another $\$80 - \$45.50 = \$34.50$ after lunch. Ten more boxes would net her $\$3.25 \times 10 = \$32.50$, which is less than a full box short of her goal. The 11th box brings the total to $\$32.50 + \$3.25 = \$35.75$, enough to meet that goal.

23. D

The sides of a 30-60-90 triangle are in the proportion $x : x\sqrt{3} : 2x$. Because 17 feet is opposite the 30° angle, the hypotenuse will be twice its length, or $17 \times 2 = 34$ feet.

24. D

You are given the value of $a + b$. To make use of it, reverse FOIL the equation $4a^2 + 6ab + 2b^2 = 36$, and try to factor out an $a + b$:

$$4a^2 + 6ab + 2b^2 = 36$$
$$(2a + 2b)(2a + b) = 36$$
$$2(a + b)(2a + b) = 36$$

Now substitute 3 for $a + b$ and solve for $2a + b$:

$$2(3)(2a + b) = 36$$
$$6(2a + b) = 36$$
$$2a + b = 6$$

Therefore, (D) is correct.

25. C

Foggy climbed $6 + 9 + 7 = 22$ inches on the first three days. On the fourth day, he lost 6 inches due to the rain, for a total climb of $22 - 6 = 16$ inches for the four days. The average climb per day is $\dfrac{16}{4} = 4$ inches. That's (C).

26. B

The area of circle Q is 16π so its radius is 4. $\overline{FC}$ is a diameter so its length must be $4 \times 2 = 8$. You could backsolve by plugging $(4, 7)$ along with each choice into the distance formula to see which one gives you 8, but it's quicker to first check for a choice that is 8 away on either the x-axis or the y-axis but not both. $(4, -1)$ is exactly 8 units away from $(4, 7)$ on the y-axis, so (B) is correct.

27. A

When the gap between choices is fairly large, estimation can be more efficient than calculation. Since x and y are both positive integers, $2x^3y^2$ is less than $4x^3y^3$. A smaller quantity subtracting a larger quantity will always result in a negative value. The only choice that's negative is (A).

You could also solve this problem by plugging in the values for x and y and calculating:

$$2x^3y^2 - 4x^3y^3$$
$$2(2^3)(3^2) - 4(2^3)(3^3)$$
$$2(8)(9) - 4(8)(27)$$
$$144 - 864 = -720$$

28. D

This problem looks complicated but it can be quite manageable if you remember to pick numbers. Pick 3 for c and 4 for f. Because $\frac{3}{4} \neq \frac{4}{3}$, so eliminate (A). Next pick 3 for both c and f. $\frac{3}{3} = \frac{3}{3}$ is true, so eliminate (B) and (E). To determine whether the answer is (C) or (D), pick 3 for c and -3 for f. $\frac{3}{-3} = \frac{-3}{3}$ is also true, so (D) is correct.

29. 3

Multiply the second equation by 2, use combination to simplify the system of equations, then solve for a:

$$2(a^2 + 3ab + b^2 = 2) = 2a^2 + 6ab + 2b^2 = 4$$

$$\begin{aligned} 3a^2 + 6ab + 2b^2 &= 13 \\ -(2a^2 + 6ab + 2b^2 &= 4) \\ \hline a^2 &= 9 \\ a &= \pm 3 \end{aligned}$$

Grid-ins can't be negative, so the answer is 3.

30. 1,024

Don't try to add them all up as that would take forever. There are 32 positive odd integers less than 64. Because the integers are consecutive odd integers, their average is the average of the first and last terms, or $\frac{1+63}{2} = 32$. Multiply this 32 by the 32 terms and you have $32 \times 32 = 1,024$.

31. 12.5

Mario's crate of cherries weighs 22 pounds. The crate itself is 2 pounds, so the 400 cherries weigh $22 - 2 = 20$ pounds. If he gives 150 cherries away, he'll have $400 - 150 = 250$ cherries left. Call c the

weight of 250 cherries. Set up a proportion and solve for c:

$$\frac{20}{400} = \frac{c}{250}$$
$$\frac{1}{20} = \frac{c}{250}$$
$$20c = 250$$
$$c = \frac{250}{20} = \frac{25}{2} = 12.5$$

32. 4

Begin by sketching out Andrea's trip:

To find the length of the dotted line, add the following two lines to form a right triangle:

The newly formed right triangle has sides of 6 and 8, so its hypotenuse is 10. The original trip was $3 + 6 + 5 = 14$ miles, so Andrea's trip would be $14 - 10 = 4$ miles shorter. Grid in 4.

33. 10

The lengths of the second and third pieces are given in relation to the first, so call the first piece x. The second piece is 2 inches longer than the first, or $x + 2$. The third piece is 2 inches longer than the second, or $(x + 2) + 2 = x + 4$. Set up the equation and solve for x:

$$x + (x + 2) + (x + 4) = 24$$
$$3x + 6 = 24$$
$$3x = 18$$
$$x = 6$$

The longest piece is $6 + 4 = 10$ inches long.

34. 28

The average of an odd number of consecutive whole numbers is always equal to the middle number in the set. In a set of seven consecutive whole numbers, the largest number will be 3 more than the middle number, and the smallest will be 3 less than the middle number. In this set, the largest number is $14 + 3 = 17$ and the smallest is $14 - 3 = 11$. Their sum is therefore $11 + 17 = 28$.

35. 864

Begin by finding out how many squares Wally Wilk's can cut from just one sheet. If the squares are 2 inches long and 2 inches wide, the sheet can cut $\frac{24}{2} = 12$ squares across the length and $\frac{36}{2} = 18$ squares across the width. Each sheet can be cut into $18 \times 12 = 216$ squares. With four sheets, the factory can cut $216 \times 4 = 864$ squares.

36. 30

If $\frac{2}{5}$ of the children are boys, then the other $\frac{3}{5}$ must be girls. There are six more girls than boys at this party, and this number represents $\frac{3}{5} - \frac{2}{5} = \frac{1}{5}$ of the total number of children. Therefore, the total number of children is $6 \times 5 = 30$.

37. 219

While you do not know what c and d are individually, you do know that $c + d + 71 + 70 = 360$. $71 + 70 = 141$, so $c + d$ must be $360 - 141 = 219$.

38. 89

The median of a set of numbers is the middle term. The median of this set of consecutive integers is 1, and there are 88 terms less than the median (-87 to 0). Therefore, there must also be 88 terms greater than the median. Add 88 to 1 (because they are consecutive integers) and you have 89.

SECTION 5

1. B

Done, the past participle form of the irregular verb *to do*, is used incorrectly and should be replaced with the simple past tense *did*. Choices (A) and (C) are both correct verb forms. Choice (D) correctly serves as the object of the sentence.

2. A

The sentence shows that Susan did not ask for help. She didn't fail asking for help. She failed *to* ask for help. Choice (B) correctly identifies the contrast in the sentence. Choice (C) is correct idiomatic usage. Choice (D) correctly uses an adverb to modify a verb.

3. B

Series refers to something plural but the noun itself is singular, so the correct verb would be *was*. Choice (A) correctly uses an adverb to modify a verb. Choices (C) and (D) are correct idiomatic usage.

4. E

This sentence is correct as written. Choice (A) is proper idiomatic usage. Choice (B) agrees with its subject *the judges*. Choice (C) is correct in idiom and tense. Choice (D) is correct use of the past perfect tense.

5. C

Watch out for words with different meanings that sound the same. *Infer* means to deduce by reasoning. The correct verb is *refer*, which in this context, means to direct attention. Choice (A) is in the correct tense. Choice (B) correctly identifies the contrast in the sentence. Choice (D) correctly uses *one* as a pronoun and *that* as a conjunction.

6. C

This sentence incorrectly uses the objective pronoun *me* as the subject of the verb *devour*, instead of the subjective pronoun *I*. This mistake is easier to see if you remove the first part of the sentence, leaving *me hungrily devoured*, which is not grammatically correct. It should read *I hungrily devoured*. Choice (A) is correct idiomatic usage. Only two people are mentioned, so (B) correctly uses the comparative. Choice (D) properly modifies a verb with an adverb.

7. D

Use the comparative to compare two things. Here, the superlative *cheapest* should be *cheaper*. Choice (A) is in the correct tense. Choice (B) correctly refers to the second of two things. Choice (C) is correct in quantity and type.

8. B

The problem with this sentence is idiomatic, meaning it most likely has to do with the sentence's prepositions. Reread the sentence, and listen for a prepositional phrase that doesn't sound right. *Similar with* should be *similar to*. Choice (A) correctly

follows the simple past tense with an infinitive. Choices (C) and (D) are correct prepositional usage.

9. E

This sentence is correctly written. Choices (A) and (C) are correct verb tenses. Choices (B) and (D) are proper uses for their respective prepositions.

10. B

Whenever you see a verb, check to see if it agrees with the subject. In this case, the subject is *sugar-free candy*, which is singular, so the verb *are* should be *is*. Choices (A) and (C) are idiomatically correct. Choice (D) uses the correct preposition.

11. C

Watch out for similar-sounding words that can have very different meanings (or no meaning at all). The prefix *non-* is incorrectly used in this instance. *Uninterested* is the correct choice, while *disinterested* could mean not biased or not interested. Choice (A) is the correct verb tense. Choice (B) uses the correct preposition. Choice (D) is idiomatically correct.

12. A

She is ambiguous because this pronoun can refer to either Molly or Marie. Choice (B) is the proper verb tense. Choice (C) isn't ambiguous as it refers to both Molly and Marie. Choice (D) is correct idiomatic usage.

13. D

When a sentence contains a comparison, make sure that the two things being compared are parallel. Here, *tonight's hurricane* is being compared to *last year*. *Last year's* would be parallel. Choice (A) correctly uses an adverb to modify an adjective. Choice (B) is proper use of the possessive form. Choice (C) is idiomatically correct.

14. E

Be wary when a late question seems to have an obvious "error." When you read this sentence in its entirety, it is clear that (A) is a correct use of *that* as a conjunction rather than an incorrect use as an adjective modifying *diamonds*, as it might appear at first glance. Choice (B) correctly pairs a plural subject with a plural verb. Choice (C) is the correct verb tense. Choice (D) is idiomatically correct.

15. B

Whenever a sentence compares two things, check to see if they are parallel. In this sentence, Kaitlyn's talent as a painter (a person noun) is being compared to her talent at singing (a gerund). Choices (B), (D), and (E) address this problem, but (E) changes the meaning of the sentence and (D) results in a sentence fragment. Therefore, (B) is correct.

16. E

This sentence contains two independent clauses that are improperly joined, creating a run-on. The correct choice needs to either join the clauses properly, (*wrote short stories, and they speak of* or *wrote short stories; they speak of*) or make the sentence less wordy. Choice (E) does both by deleting the comma and replacing *they* with *that*. The clause *that speak of very interesting events* correctly modifies *short stories*. Choices (B), (C), and (D) all introduce new errors.

17. A

When a sentence contains a list of two or more things, check to see if the items are parallel. In this case, the three things *are* parallel (they are all *-ed* verbs) so (A) is correct. Choices (B) and (E) distort the parallel. Choices (C) and (D) are unnecessarily wordy.

18. C

You may have heard *them* and *those* used interchangeably, but they in fact mean different things. *Them* is the objective form of *they* while *those* is the plural form of *that*. A relative pronoun is needed here, so (C) correctly changes *them* to *those*. Choices (B) and (D) merely reword the underlined phrase. Choice (E) makes the phrase wordier without addressing the issue.

19. D

This sentence contains a modifier issue as the subject of an introductory phrase must come right after the comma. In this case, it's the *blazing inferno* that reaches an *internal temperature of 250°*, not the *scrambling firefighters* (unless they were boiling mad at something). This narrows it down to (D) and (E). Choice (E) has the inferno putting the firefighters out with buckets of water, which wouldn't make sense, so (D) is correct.

20. C

The main issue with this sentence is the comma splice, creating a run-on. Only (B) and (C) address this issue, but (B) is overly wordy and awkward, making (C) the correct choice.

21. B

This sentence incorrectly uses the pronoun *which* to refer to a person. Choice (E) incorrectly uses *that* to refer to a person. Choices (B) and (D) correctly use *who,* but (D) changes the meaning, so (B) is correct. Choice (C) incorrectly uses *whom* instead of *who*.

22. D

Whenever you see an introductory phrase, make sure that it modifies the correct noun. The people are dependent upon the services, so the correct choice must place the people right after the comma. Choice (D) does this, so it is correct. Choice (B) is unnecessarily wordy and awkward. Choice (C) does not address the issue. Choice (E) is a sentence fragment.

23. A

This sentence is correct as written. Choice (B) incorrectly omits *in*. Choice (C) is also correct grammatically, but it is wordier. Choice (D) incorrectly omits *either*. Choice (E) incorrectly pairs *either* with *nor*.

24. E

The sentence is grammatically correct, but its wordiness makes it awkward. Choice (E) offers the most concise rewrite by turning the second clause into a dependent clause, so it is correct. Choice (B) seems to say that the *inclusion* is in the journal rather than the *results*. Choices (C) and (D) each lack a verb.

25. D

The use of the word *that* implies an additional clause, which isn't present in the sentence. Choice (D) correctly omits *that*. Choice (B) is excessively wordy. Choice (C) unnecessarily uses the passive voice. Choice (E) creates a sentence fragment by omitting *was*.

26. D

The sentence is a run-on so the correct choice will either replace the comma with a semicolon or make one of the clauses subordinate. Only (D) and (E) address this issue, but (E) is unnecessarily wordy, so (D) is correct.

27. A

This sentence is correct as written. Choices (B) and (E) add a cause and effect relationship that was not in the original sentence. Choice (C) is unnecessarily wordy. Choice (D) contains a comma splice.

28. B

Pronoun use in a sentence must be consistent. Only (B) addresses this issue by replacing *your* with *one's*.

Each of the incorrect choices contains a mismatched pair of pronouns.

29. C

Painters (plural) cannot become *a better artist* (singular) as the nouns must agree in quantity. Only (C) and (E) address this issue, but (E) creates a sentence fragment, so (C) is correct.

30. E

This difficult sentence contains two problems: Claire is receiving the action, so *acknowledge* should be *acknowledgement*, and *neither* must be paired with *nor*. Choice (C) does not address the first problem. Choices (B) and (D) fail to address the second problem. Choice (E) is correct.

31. A

When two things are being compared, they should have parallel structures. Only (A) does this so it is correct as written. The remaining choices all deviate from the structure.

32. B

The problem with this sentence is idiomatic. Reread the sentence, and listen for what doesn't sound right. The problem isn't with *One of the symptoms of the flu* because you can turn the sentence around— Developing a splitting headache is *one of the symptoms of the flu*—so the problem must be with *is when you*. Simplify the sentence to say *One symptom is _____ you develop a headache*. Does *when* sound right? No, but *that* does.

33. D

This sentence features a comma splice. Only (D) corrects this, so it is correct. Aside from not addressing the issue, each of the remaining choices is unnecessarily wordy and awkward.

34. E

To correctly compare two things with *more*, *than* must be used. Only (B) and (E) address this issue, but (B) uses *more friendlier*, which is idiomatically incorrect.

35. D

The author's father forbids an action claiming that the fish would be happier in the water, so the correct choice will reference an action that contradicts this. Given this context, only (D) makes sense.

36. E

The events in this story happened *last summer*, so the correct choice needs to use the past tense. Only (E) does this.

37. D

Be wary of words that sound the same but mean different things. *Affect* is a verb and should be replaced with *effect* (a noun). Choices (D) and (E) address this, but (E) creates a pronoun issue (*we* cannot feel the effect on *me* if only *I* go fishing), so (D) is correct.

38. A

We are given two short sentences and asked to combine them. First, we must determine their relationship to each other and the passage. Sentence 11 states that a lot of people say fishing is boring. Sentence 13 says that these people don't understand the things that the author believes make fishing interesting. Choice (A) correctly combines the sentences with the word *but*. Choices (B) and (C) switch the order of the sentences, which changes their intended meaning. Choice (D) sets up the second sentence as an example of why people say it's boring, but that's not what the author intended. Choice (E) changes the original meaning of the two sentences.

39. C

Adding a phrase at the beginning of sentence 8 will probably set up its relationship to sentence 7. Choice (C) signals that sentence 8 shows one way in which nature has an effect on the author and that sentence 8 should definitely follow sentence 7. Adding (A) makes the sentence a fragment. Choice (B) signals that sentence 8 is the opposite of sentence 7, which is incorrect. Choice (D) would require the period to be changed to a question mark. In addition, the author would then be addressing the reader, which he or she does not do throughout the piece. Choice (E) sets up a comparison between what is said in sentence 8 and what is said in sentence 7, and that doesn't make sense.

Part Three

PSAT STRATEGIES

CHAPTER 5: HOW TO ATTACK THE CRITICAL READING SECTIONS

IF YOU LEARN ONLY FIVE THINGS IN THIS CHAPTER . . .

1. The two Critical Reading sections each have the following types of questions: Sentence Completion questions and Reading Comprehension questions. They test reading, reasoning, and vocabulary.

2. Sentence Completion questions are faster reads than Reading Comprehension questions.

3. It's important to read the passages strategically—especially the long passages. Make a passage map as you read.

4. Reading Comprehension questions can be divided into four categories:

    —Big Picture questions

    —Little Picture questions

    —Inference questions

    —Vocabulary-in-Context questions

5. Reading Comprehension questions include both short and long passages. The strategy for each passage is the same.

CHAPTER 5 OVERVIEW

This chapter explains the Critical Reading question types (Sentence Completion and Reading Comprehension) and gives you specific strategies for approaching each. Once you feel comfortable with the material, work through the practice set at the end of the section.

The two PSAT Critical Reading sections are pretty predictable. They don't test your knowledge of Shakespeare or Hemingway. They don't test your grammar knowledge, either. (The Writing section takes care of that.) Instead, they test a fixed set of skills in three areas: reading, reasoning, and vocabulary.

So no matter what kind of English student you are, we can help you improve your skills and score on the PSAT's Critical Reading section.

CRITICAL READING BASICS

The Critical Reading portion of the PSAT is comprised of two scored sections that last 25 minutes each. In total, the two sections are made up of two main question types:

- 13 Sentence Completion questions
- 35 Reading Comprehension questions (short and long passages)

SENTENCE COMPLETION

Sentence Completion questions can be answered fairly quickly, leaving you time to concentrate on the more demanding Reading Comprehension questions. The Sentence Completion question sets start off easy and increase in difficulty, so it's important to always pay attention to where you are in the set. Early and late questions call for different approaches: Early questions in a set should be straightforward and easier to handle, whereas later questions contain more traps and trickier vocabulary.

READING COMPREHENSION

Reading Comprehension question sets follow no particular order. The first question could be the hardest, or the last could be the easiest. Like many things in life, the questions in this area are random and unpredictable.

The PSAT includes both long and short passages. Although the subject matter for reading comprehension varies widely, expect to see one science passage and one passage in the form of a first-person narrative, which could be either fiction or nonfiction. Other common PSAT passage topics include history, literature, and art. You'll also see one or two paired-passage sets that present two different passages on the same topic.

Long Reading Comprehension passages begin with italicized introductions. Read these carefully—they provide helpful information for understanding the passage: where it comes from, what it's about, when it was written, and so on.

VOCABULARY AND CONTEXT

The PSAT Critical Reading section, as we've noted, tests your reading and thinking skills and, to a smaller extent, your vocabulary. In this book, we will help you to develop a good PSAT-friendly vocabulary between now and test day. It's simply a matter of knowing how to make the most of your time so you can learn words quickly and achieve the score you're looking for. Take the quiz in the Vocabulary Building section at the end of this chapter to find out how much you need to focus on actually increasing your word knowledge, and use the tips there to personalize your vocabulary study.

The ability to decipher the meaning of unfamiliar words is just as important as having a good vocabulary. When you come across a strange word in a book you are reading, do you look it up? Most times, probably not. Often, you don't really need to look up the meaning because the manner in which it is used clues you in to the meaning of the word.

This is called understanding vocabulary through context, and it's an essential Critical Reading skill. The PSAT Critical Reading section always provides some sort of context for tough vocabulary words. Our strategies show you how to squeeze the most out of these context clues.

DECODING TOUGH VOCABULARY

No matter how much time you spend studying, you're bound to face some mystery words on your PSAT. No big deal. Fortunately, there are ways of dealing with unfamiliar vocabulary on the PSAT.

TRUST YOUR HUNCHES

Vocabulary knowledge is not an all-or-nothing proposition. Don't write off a word you see on the PSAT just because you can't recite its definition. If you feel like you've

---

EXPERT TUTOR TIP

" Reading Comprehension questions are not arranged in order of difficulty, but rather by the general order of the passage. This means that Little Picture and vocabulary questions pertaining to the first paragraph of the passage are much more likely to be found early in the question set. However, Big Picture questions could be found in the beginning, middle, or end. If you are in a time crunch, knowing how the questions are arranged can snag you a few more points on test day. "

seen or heard the word before but are not sure what the exact definition is, look through the answer choices, and trust your gut. Don't be afraid to take a risk.

TRY TO RECALL WHERE YOU'VE HEARD THE WORD BEFORE

If you can recall a phrase in which the word appears, that may be enough to get you to the correct answer. Take a look at the following example. Remember that you don't need to know the dictionary definition to solve a question like this one. A sense of where you've heard a word before may be all you need.

> After the military government banned the opposing political party, its members continued to meet in ---- groups.
>
> (A) amicable
> (B) elaborate
> (C) clandestine
> (D) auspicious
> (E) sanctioned

Looking through the answer choices, you may not know the definition of *clandestine*, but you may have heard the word used in phrases like *clandestine operations* or *clandestine meetings* on the news or in spy movies. If you remembered clandestine in this context, you could have gleaned the meaning of the word. *Clandestine* means "done in secret." Choice (C) is correct.

BREAK IT DOWN

Don't be intimidated by a long and unfamiliar word. If you break it down into smaller parts, you will often find pieces that seem familiar. Studying the Root List in the PSAT Resources is a good way to prepare for this, but you can also make informed guesses based on similar words you already know. For example, you may not be sure about the meaning of the word *impoverished*, but if you break it into parts—im-pover-ished—you might notice that -*pover*- looks a lot like *poverty*. *Impoverished* means "poor" or "poverty-stricken," so that connection could help you choose the right answer.

THINK POSITIVE/NEGATIVE

Sometimes just knowing the charge of a word—that is, whether a word has a positive or negative sense—is enough to get a question correct. Take the word *felicitous*. Let's assume you don't know its dictionary definition. Ask yourself: Does *felicitous* sound positive or negative? How about *vituperative*? Negative words sometimes have ugly or harsh sounds that enhance their sense of negativity, whereas positive words often sound more friendly. If you thought *felicitous* sounded positive, you're right. It means fortunate or well suited. Likewise, if you thought *vituperative* sounded negative, you're right again. *Vituperative* means critical and abusive. You can also use prefixes to help determine a word's charge. *Pro-*, *ben-*, *magn-*, and *eu-* often indicate a positive, whereas *mal-*, *de-*, *dis-*, *dys-*, *un-*, *in-*, *im-*, and *mis-* are often negative words.

These strategies for making the most of your vocabulary knowledge will pay off in both Sentence Completion and Reading Comprehension questions. Now let's look at specific strategies to help you master each of the PSAT's Critical Reading question types.

SENTENCE COMPLETION QUESTIONS

Sentence Completion questions test your knowledge of PSAT vocabulary and your ability to follow the logical flow of a sentence. Lots of students like Sentence Completion questions because you can work through them faster and gain points more quickly than with Reading Comprehension questions. Also, unlike Reading Comprehension questions, you only have to deal with one sentence at a time. With practice, you should be able to handle this question type with speed and confidence.

It's important to remember that Sentence Completion question sets are arranged in increasing order of difficulty. The first few Sentence Completion questions in a set should be the easiest, and the last few should be the hardest. By becoming an expert in this question type, you'll be well on your way to a great Critical Reading score.

Let's take a look at the Sentence Completion directions and a sample question.

<u>Directions:</u> Select the lettered word or set of words that best completes the sentence.

> Rain is traditionally viewed as an ---- sign; many believe that
> if it rains on the day of your wedding, you will enjoy financial
> prosperity.
>
> (A) unfortunate
> (B) oblique
> (C) auspicious
> (D) original
> (E) indifferent

So you're looking for the answer that fits the meaning of the rest of the sentence. In this example, the second half of the sentence states that many people believe rain can predict financial prosperity. This is considered a good thing, so rain must be viewed as a positive sign. Whether or not you know what all of the words mean, this information can help you eliminate wrong answers. We're looking for something that means "good," so we can get rid of "unfortunate," "oblique," "original," and "indifferent." Thus, (C), *auspicious*, meaning favorable, is correct.

As you can see, the key to answering a Sentence Completion question is to locate clues in the rest of the sentence that will allow you to predict the meaning of the missing word. Let's take a look at our strategy for Sentence Completion questions.

KAPLAN'S FOUR-STEP METHOD

Step 1. Read the sentence for clues.

Step 2. Predict an answer.

Step 3. Scan the answer choices for a match.

Step 4. Read your selected answer choice back into the sentence.

STEP 1. READ THE SENTENCE FOR CLUES

Don't look at the answer choices before you've read through and thought about the sentence. Each Sentence Completion question contains clues that lead you directly to the correct answer. With practice, and with our help, you'll learn to spot these clues.

STEP 2. PREDICT AN ANSWER

Once you've spotted the clues within the sentence, think of a word that would fit in the blank. This will save you valuable time when you go through the answer choices. You generally don't have to make an exact prediction. Sometimes it's enough simply to predict whether the word is positive or negative.

STEP 3. SCAN THE ANSWER CHOICES FOR A MATCH

Quickly eliminate choices that do not match your prediction, and zero in on the answer choice that is the closest to your word. Make sure to read *every answer choice* before deciding.

STEP 4. READ YOUR SELECTED ANSWER CHOICE BACK INTO THE SENTENCE

Confirm your answer choice by reading it back into the sentence. Learn to trust your ear on Sentence Completion questions. If something doesn't sound right, it probably isn't.

Okay, buckle up. Let's take the strategy for a test drive.

> Although some of the revelations in the movie star's memoirs will
> surprise even his most ardent fans, much of his story is quite ----.
>
> (A) significant
> (B) familiar
> (C) impressive
> (D) explicit
> (E) thorough

Read the sentence carefully, looking for clues. The word *although* is a major clue here. It tells you that the sentence switches direction midstream. Another clue is *some . . . revelations . . . will surprise*. So although some revelations will surprise the fans, the rest of his story must be the opposite of surprising.

You're ready to predict an answer. Here you might predict something such as *unsurprising*. Scan the answer choices for a match. The only answer choice that comes close to our prediction is (B), *familiar*. Something that is familiar is not surprising at all.

You still want to check your answer by reading the selected choice back into the sentence: *Although some of the revelations in the movie star's memoirs will surprise even his most ardent fans, much of his story is quite familiar.* That sounds fine, so (B) is the correct answer.

Let's work through another example.

> As different schools of thought on child rearing go in and out of vogue, parents who at one time were esteemed for imposing strict rules and strong discipline upon their children may find themselves marginalized, decried for being ----.
>
> (A) despotic
> (B) controversial
> (C) effective
> (D) pragmatic
> (E) erratic

There are no obvious structural clues in this sentence, but there are clues to tell you that the sentence contains a contrast. Given that attitudes *go in and out of vogue*, if the parents were at one time seen as good disciplinarians, they were later seen as bad examples of how to discipline children. Clearly, you can predict that a negative word will fill in the blank. From that alone, you can get rid of *effective* (C) and *pragmatic* (D), which are positive in charge.

You're looking for a negative take on *imposing strict rules and strong discipline*. A good prediction would be *overly disciplinarian* (you don't have to come up with a perfect one-word prediction). The best match for this prediction is (A), *despotic*, which means repressive and authoritarian.

Even if you didn't know the meaning of *despotic*, by the process of elimination, you would still get the correct answer; neither *controversial* (B) nor *erratic* (E) matches our prediction. Once again, if you read (A) back into the sentence, it sounds right, which means you're done.

GET A CLUE

Structural clues help you to get a fix on whether the sentence will continue along in the same line or shift directions and contrast with the rest of the sentence.

BE ON THE LOOKOUT FOR STRUCTURAL CLUES SUCH AS THE FOLLOWING:

Continuations:	Contrasts:
• ; (a semicolon)	• but
• and	• however
• because	• although
• also	• despite
• consequently	• yet
• similarly	• on the other hand
• : (a colon)	• though
• likewise	• different from
• since	• compared to
• both	• instead of
• alike	• in contrast

TWO-BLANK SENTENCE COMPLETION QUESTIONS

Think two-blank Sentence Completion questions must be twice as hard as one-blank questions? Think again. With two-blank Sentence Completion questions, you have twice as many opportunities to zero in on the correct answer, so these questions can actually be easier than those with just one blank. However, to handle two-blank questions in the most efficient manner possible, we have to alter our approach ever so slightly.

Step 1. Read the sentence for clues.

Step 2. Decide which blank is easier to predict. Predict an answer for that blank.

Step 3. Scan the answer choices, and eliminate those that don't match the prediction.

Step 4. Read the remaining answer choices back into the sentence. Keep the one that works for both blanks.

Notice that with this type of question, you need to decide which blank will be easier to make a prediction for. By focusing on one blank at a time and eliminating answer choices based on that blank, your job becomes much easier. Take a look:

> Jazz developed as a style of music that was uniquely characterized by its heavy reliance on improvisation and on ---- musical boundaries; yet today, a lot of jazz has become so ---- that many listeners cannot stand to hear one of their favorite "jazz standards" played in a novel manner.
>
> (A) respecting . . . fixed
> (B) expanding . . . ambiguous
> (C) expanding . . . standardized
> (D) sustaining . . . particularized
> (E) transgressing . . . universal

The structural clue *yet* lets you know that there is a contrast in this sentence. The first half discusses the origins of jazz, which are based in improvisation. The second half discusses its current state, which avoids anything *novel*, or original.

It might be easier to predict the second blank here. We want a word that means the opposite of *original*; a good prediction might be *rigid* or *formulaic*.

The only answer choices that match this prediction for the second blank are *fixed* (A) and *standardized* (C). We could go ahead and try to make a prediction for the first blank now, but we've narrowed down the field so much that we can also just try out the remaining choices. First, try (A).

> Jazz developed as a style of music that was uniquely characterized by its heavy reliance on improvisation and on *respecting* musical boundaries; yet today, a lot of jazz has become so *fixed* that many listeners cannot stand to hear one of their favorite "jazz standards" played in a novel manner.

Respecting musical boundaries? That doesn't sound right—the early musicians were innovators. Trust your ear, eliminate, and move on. But we should make sure that (C) works before we start to celebrate.

> Jazz developed as a style of music that was uniquely characterized by its heavy reliance on improvisation and on *expanding* musical boundaries; yet today, a lot of jazz has become so *standardized* that many listeners cannot stand to hear one of their favorite "jazz standards" played in a novel manner.

Now that makes sense. Choice (C) is the correct answer.

EXPERT TUTOR TIP

" If you are stumped by a two-blank Sentence Completion, word charge can be especially useful. Think of how the two blanks relate to each other. Are they the same? Opposites? Share a cause and effect relationship? Even if you are unfamiliar with the answer choice words, sometimes you can determine if a pair of answers has the same relationship you are looking for in the question stem. "

GUESSING TIPS

If a Sentence Completion question on the PSAT has you stumped—you don't know a lot of the words in the sentence or in the answer choices—do not panic. You should almost always be able to eliminate a few wrong-sounding answer choices, and then guess. Here are a few things to remember about eliminating and guessing on Sentence Completion questions:

- Don't forget to use our strategies for decoding unfamiliar words on the test. Try to recall where you've seen the word before; see if you can break the word apart, and try to get a sense of the word's charge.

- If an answer sounds wrong to your ear for any reason, trust your instincts, and get rid of that clunker. Your ear often does know best on Sentence Completion questions.

- If you're completely stumped on the very last Sentence Completion question (the toughest question in the set), try picking the answer choice that contains the very weirdest and toughest vocabulary word. Use this strategy only if you otherwise don't have a clue.

Sometimes it can be very difficult to make a prediction for either blank on a two-blank Sentence Completion question. Take a stab at the tough question below.

> Sanders was blind to his own double standards, which were so apparent to all those who knew him; he was unable to tolerate even the slightest hint of ---- in others, and yet he regularly offended his colleagues with his own ---- conduct.
>
> (A) snobbery . . . boorish
> (B) timidity . . . impudent
> (C) conceit . . . supercilious
> (D) impropriety . . . prudish
> (E) duplicity . . . moralistic

You probably figured out that we're looking for negative words here. But that doesn't help much because all the words in the answer choices are somewhat negative. So what kind of negative behavior are we looking for? Unfortunately, the sentence doesn't contain any solid clues. When you find that none of your question-busting techniques is working, try the following *if-all-else-fails* technique.

If you can't make exact predictions on a two-blank Sentence Completion question, determine the relationship between the blanks. Are the missing words opposites? Are they very similar in meaning?

You know that Sanders operates with a double standard. Therefore, you can predict that he engages in the very behavior that he cannot tolerate in others. You don't know what the missing words are, but you know that they should be practically synonymous. Now let's check out the answer choices.

(A)   Is *snobbery* a synonym for *boorish*? No, *boorish* means crude or unrefined, which is nothing like being a snob.

(B)   Is *timidity* a synonym for *impudent*? No, someone who is timid is shy, whereas someone who is impudent is offensively bold—in other words, they are antonyms.

(C)   Is *conceit* a synonym for *supercilious*? Why yes, it is! Both mean arrogance. Let's keep checking the other choices to be sure, though.

(D)   Is *impropriety* a synonym for *prudish*? No, *impropriety* is the state of being improper, whereas *prudish* means overly proper—here's another case of antonyms.

(E)   Is *duplicity* a synonym for *moralistic*? No, *duplicity* means deceit, whereas *moralistic* means self-righteous.

So (C) is, in fact, the answer.

If you thought that the vocabulary was starting to get a bit tough on the last example, you haven't seen anything yet. Some of the Sentence Completion questions in the practice set at the end of the chapter reach the PSAT's maximum level of difficulty. Sentence Completion questions definitely make serious demands on your vocabulary skills. So if you want to do well on this question type, it really pays to study the PSAT word lists in the back of this book.

READING COMPREHENSION QUESTIONS

The Reading Comprehension question sets combine to make up 35 of the 48 Critical Reading section questions. Just like with all of the other question types, we have several strategies for maximizing your points on Reading Comprehension questions. Let's get right to them.

KNOW THE DIRECTIONS

The same directions apply to each passage, with a few important differences for paired passages. There are a couple of things to notice about these directions.

First, note that every question is based strictly on the content of the passage. This means that you should be careful not to apply outside knowledge when answering the questions. This is actually good news. No matter how unfamiliar the subject matter may be to you, the information to answer the question is right there in front of you.

Next, notice the italicized introductions to the long passages. (Short passages don't have these introductions.) These introductions provide helpful *and important* context about the author and the passage.

LONG VERSUS SHORT PASSAGES

We mentioned at the beginning of this chapter that the Reading Comprehension sections are composed of two types: long and short passages. What's the difference? The short passages are single paragraphs, approximately 100 words long. The longer passages usually have several paragraphs and range from 450 to 800 words.

The passages and questions are predictable because the test makers use a formula to write them. The topics are drawn from the arts, humanities, social sciences, natural sciences, and fiction. Both passage types use the same kinds of questions that test the same skills. When we get to our strategy for Reading Comprehension questions, you'll see that the method works for short *and* long Reading Comprehension passages.

WHAT DO READING COMPREHENSION QUESTIONS TEST?

Reading Comprehension questions do not test your ability to read thoroughly and understand every facet of what you just read. They do not test your ability to relate what you read to outside knowledge. They also do not test your ability to offer a creative or original interpretation of what you just read.

In the Reading Comprehension section, you'll be asked about the overall tone and content of a passage, specific details from the text, and what the author suggests or implies in the passage. The paired passages we've mentioned will consist of two related excerpts with questions that ask you to compare and contrast the texts.

READING STRATEGICALLY

Many students have trouble approaching a Reading Comprehension passage with confidence. They may ask themselves, "How am I ever going to get through this long passage and get to all those questions in such a short period of time?" Good question.

Time management is critical on the PSAT Reading Comprehension section. Students often spend too much time meticulously reading the passage. They should instead:

- Read through the passage once
- Attack the answer choices with the information you've absorbed, only returning to the passage later if needed for specific questions.
- Choose the best response

EXPERT TUTOR TIP

" Do NOT look at questions first unless you are simply seeing how many there are. Marking up a passage may seem like a waste of time, but it will actually save you time (and points!) in the long run. "

As you read through a passage, you don't want to get bogged down by details. Focusing on details can hurt your score. Why? Most of the passage's details *will not* be referenced in the questions, so reading and remembering useless details will waste your valuable time.

We're going to teach you how to read these passages strategically. You will focus on getting a sense of the passage as a whole. The main ideas of the passages offer the most bang for the buck—often these ideas relate to the most questions and, therefore, give you the most points.

MAKING A PASSAGE MAP

Longer passages cover many different aspects of a topic. For example, the first paragraph might introduce the subject, the second paragraph might present one viewpoint, and the third paragraph might argue for a different viewpoint. Within each of these paragraphs, there are several details that help the author convey a message.

Because there is a lot to keep track of, you need to mark up long passages as follows:

- Write simple notes in the margin as you read.

- Write down the purpose of each paragraph.

- Underline key points.

- Concentrate especially on places where the author expresses an opinion. Most Reading Comprehension questions hinge on opinions and viewpoints, not facts.

These notes are your *passage map*. The passage map helps you find the part of the passage that contains the information you need. The process of creating your passage map also forces you to read actively. Because you are constantly trying to identify the author's viewpoint and the purpose of each sentence and paragraph, you will be working hard to understand what's happening in the passage. This translates into points on the test.

PASSAGE MAP

A good passage map should:

- Contain single words or short phrases (e.g., "what author now thinks"), rather than whole sentences

- Include markings in the passage such as underlined and circled words

- Concentrate on viewpoints and opinions

- Note places where opinions other than the author's are expressed

- Avoid specific details

EXPERT TUTOR TIP

❝ Note when an author (especially in a nonfiction passage) employs key words such as *because, not only, though, similarly, however,* etc. That means the passage is about to take a logical turn, and you want to turn with it. The PSAT test makers have a tendency to generate questions around these key words. *Hint*: Circle or box them as you go. ❞

STRATEGIC READING PRACTICE

Try out your passage map skills on the passage below. Remember to read for the main idea, and identify the author's point of view. After you read, fill out the questions about the main idea and the purpose of each paragraph.

This passage is from a book on classical art and architecture.

Some places are so beautiful that it's hard to believe they are real, and not some glimpse into another world or paradise. Lying on the bank of the Yamuna River in northern India is one such place, one of the world's most
(5) famous and beautiful buildings. The Taj Mahal was built by the Mughal emperor Shah Jahan as a mausoleum for his favorite consort, Arjumand Banu Bagam. She was known as Mumtaz Mahal, "the Elect of the Palace." Construction began soon after her death in 1631. The
(10) mausoleum was completed by about 1643, and the surrounding complex of buildings and gardens was completed about ten years later.

The Taj Mahal is much more than an expression of love and loss, though. Its architect employed centuries of
(15) Iranian and Central Asian mausoleum design to construct a breathtakingly symmetrical representation of heaven. The mausoleum is set within a square garden 1,002 feet on each side. The garden is bounded by red sandstone walls. Canals divide the garden into four smaller squares, each of
(20) which contains fountains, flower beds, and cypress trees—Mughal symbols of death. The canals converge on a large, rectangular pool in which the white marble mausoleum appears to float. Flanking the mausoleum are two identical red sandstone buildings.

(25) One of these buildings is a mosque; the other is a replica (Jawab, or "answer") of the mosque placed there to preserve the complex's unearthly proportionality. One can see this proportionality in the design of the mausoleum's exterior. The mausoleum is essentially a cube
(30) set upon a raised, marble platform of approximately 313 square feet. Minarets (towers) jut skyward from the platform's corners. The mausoleum has four identical façades, each of which contains a large, recessed, pointed arch 108 feet in height. On top of the cube rests
(35) a 240-foot-high onion dome. Four smaller domes lie next to this dome. They are situated along the diagonal axes formed by the top square face of the mausoleum, thus mirroring the placement of the minarets on the square platform. A sense of serene majesty pervades

(40) the mausoleum's interior. Sunlight enters the octagonal hall through delicately carved, jewel-studded marble screens. Mumtaz Mahal's gem-encrusted tomb lies in the center. Her beloved's equally opulent crypt lies at its side.

The Taj Mahal complex is one of the supreme human achievements. As *(45)* an architectural representation of the afterlife, it is unmatched. The heaven it portrays is one of serenity and symmetry. A perfect balance is struck between the mausoleum's curves and straight lines, between its bulges and recesses—even between the solidity of its marble and the form that marble gives to the empty space around it. This equilibrium pervades the *(50)* surrounding gardens, where the constant, gentle flow of water mixes with the aroma of flowers to produce the sense of peace after death yearned for by all cultures.

What's the topic of the passage? _____

PASSAGE MAP

Paragraph 1 (in 2–6 words): _____

Paragraph 2 (in 2–6 words): _____

Paragraph 3 (in 2–6 words): _____

Paragraph 4 (in 2–6 words): _____

What's the main idea of the passage (in no more than 15 words)? _____

_____

TYPES OF READING COMPREHENSION QUESTIONS

When you read passages on the PSAT, you're reading for a specific purpose: to be able to correctly answer as many questions as possible. Fortunately, the PSAT tends to use the same kinds of Reading Comprehension questions over and over again, so whatever the passage is about and however long it may be, you can expect the same four basic question types:

- Big Picture
- Little Picture
- Inference
- Vocabulary-in-Context

EXPERT TUTOR TIP

" A good passage map includes the answer to the biggest Big Picture question: What is this passage about? If you can't answer that after reading the passage, keep your guard up as you work through the questions. Better yet, if you have time, skim the first and last paragraphs of the passage as well as the topic sentences of the middle paragraphs. That should be enough to give you the main idea. "

You can expect slightly more than half of the questions to be Little Picture and Inference questions; fewer (approximately 30–40 percent) will be Big Picture questions and Vocabulary-in-Context questions.

BIG PICTURE QUESTIONS

Big Picture questions test how well you understand the passage as a whole. They ask about:

- The main point or purpose of a passage or individual paragraphs
- The author's overall attitude or tone
- The logic underlying the author's argument
- How ideas relate to each other in the passage

If you're still stumped on a Big Picture question after reading the passage, do the Little Picture questions first. They can help you fill in the Big Picture. Big Picture questions will usually be at the end of the question set anyway, so you can often use the question order to help you get a deeper understanding of the whole passage.

Here's a Big Picture question based on the long passage you read earlier.

> The author's primary purpose in the passage is to describe
>
> (A) the Taj Mahal as an expression of love and loss
>
> (B) the relationship between Shah Jahan and Mumtaz Mahal
>
> (C) the Taj Mahal as an architectural representation of heaven
>
> (D) the balance between the mosque and the mausoleum in the Taj Mahal complex
>
> (E) the size and dimensions of the Taj Mahal complex

This is a little tricky because the main idea is in the first third of the passage but not in the first paragraph. If you identified the big idea and thought about the passage before looking at the question, this shouldn't have been too hard. The first paragraph gives you a hint at the main idea and describes one reason for the Taj Mahal's construction. The rest of the passage—as indicated by the first two sentences of the second paragraph—shows that the main idea is that *the Taj Mahal is an architectural representation of heaven*, (C).

Of the wrong answers, (A) and (B) say more or less the same thing, and both are directly contradicted by the first sentence of paragraph 2. Many wrong answers to Big Picture questions can be eliminated because they are too specific, referring to only one part of the passage. In this case, (D) and (E) are also just details from the passage.

LITTLE PICTURE QUESTIONS

About a third of Reading Comprehension questions are Little Picture questions that ask about localized bits of information—usually specific facts or details from the passage. These questions usually give you a line reference—a clue to where in the passage you'll find your answer. Beware of answer choices that provide a reasonable answer to the question stem but don't make sense in the context of the passage or that are true but refer to a different section of the text.

Little Picture questions often test:

- Whether you understand significant information that's stated in the passage

- Your ability to locate information within a text

- Your ability to differentiate between main ideas and specific details

Sometimes the answer to a Little Picture question will be directly in the line or lines that are referenced. Other times, you might need to read a few sentences before or after the referenced line(s) to find the correct answer. When in doubt, use the context (surrounding sentences) to confirm the right choice.

Answer the following Little Picture question, still based on the previous passage.

> According to the passage, the Jawab (line 26) was placed across from the mosque in order to
>
> (A) provide more white marble to complement the red sandstone walls
>
> (B) maintain the perfect balance among the various architectural elements in the complex
>
> (C) introduce an element of disproportion to the complex
>
> (D) divide the garden into four equal squares
>
> (E) provide support for the onion dome

Go directly to line 26. The passage states that the Jawab was placed across from the mosque for the sake of proportionality. Choice (B) is a paraphrase of this idea.

Choice (A) is wrong because the Jawab was made of red sandstone. Choice (C) contradicts the passage. Choice (D) is a distortion—the canals divide the garden into four equal squares. Choice (E) is also a distortion. The Jawab is a freestanding building—it can't support the mausoleum's onion dome. Notice how the correct answer to this question is consistent with the answer to the Big Picture we looked at earlier.

EXPERT TUTOR TIP

" Little Picture, or detail, questions do not require memory, thought, or analysis. Think of them as "go fetch" questions and easy points. You know you're dealing with a Little Picture question when you see "according to the passage," "the author cites," "in line 52," "the author states," etc. You should be able to put your finger on the answer. Detail questions often are written out word for word (or a close facsimile) in the text. Your job? Go fetch! No guessing required. "

INFERENCE QUESTIONS

If you've done any practice exams, you probably noticed that many Reading Comprehension questions begin as follows: "It can be inferred that the author..." To *infer* is to draw a conclusion based on reasoning or evidence. For example, if you wake up in the morning and there are three feet of fresh snow on the ground, you can safely infer that school will be canceled.

Often, writers will use suggestion or inference rather than stating ideas directly. But they will also leave you plenty of clues so you can figure out just what they are trying to convey. Inference clues include word choice (diction), tone, and specific details. For example, say a passage states that a particular idea "was perceived as revolutionary." You might infer from the use of the word *perceived* that the author believes the idea was not truly revolutionary but only *perceived* that way.

Thus, Inference questions test your ability to use the information in the passage to come to a logical conclusion. The key to Inference questions is to stick to the evidence in the text. Most Inference questions have pretty strong clues, so avoid any answer choices that seem far-fetched. If you can't find any evidence in the passage, then it probably isn't the right answer.

Take a shot at the Inference question below. Like the previous questions, it refers to the passage you read earlier.

> What does the passage suggest about the long history of Iranian and Central Asian mausoleum design?
>
> (A) It had little to do with the design of the Taj Mahal complex.
>
> (B) It stipulated that only white marble be used for mausoleums.
>
> (C) It was the proper architectural tradition to use to express the loss of a loved one.
>
> (D) It constituted the architectural tradition of which the Taj Mahal was the culmination.
>
> (E) It emphasized a balance between curves and straight lines.

Scan the passage for *Iranian*. You'll find it in the sentence at the beginning of paragraph 2, which states that the architect *employed centuries of Iranian and Central Asian design*, so you can definitely eliminate (A). You can also eliminate any choice that refers to any paragraph other than the second one, so (E) is out. *White marble* and *love and loss* are in the second paragraph, but both are wrong—the *white marble* reference, (B), is a distortion; the *love and loss* choice, (C), goes against the main idea of the passage. Only (D) is consistent with the passage as a whole and the language of paragraph 2 in particular.

VOCABULARY-IN-CONTEXT QUESTIONS

Vocabulary-in-Context questions ask about the usage of a single word. These questions do not test your ability to define hard words like *archipelago* and *garrulous*. Instead, they test your ability to infer the meaning of a word from the context in which it is used.

The words tested in this type of question on the PSAT will probably be familiar to you—they are usually fairly common words with more than one definition. But that's the trick! Many of the answer choices will be different definitions of the tested word, but only one will work in context. Vocabulary-in-Context questions almost always have a line reference, and you should always use it!

Sometimes one of the answer choices will jump out at you. It'll be the most common meaning of the word in question—but it's RARELY right. You can think of this as the *obvious* choice. For example, say *curious* is the word being tested. The obvious choice is *inquisitive*. But curious also means *odd*, and that's more likely to be the answer.

Using context to find the answer will help prevent you from falling into this trap. But you can also use these obvious choices to your advantage. If you get stuck on a Vocabulary-in-Context question, you can eliminate the *obvious* choice and guess from the remaining answers.

Here's our strategy for Vocabulary-in-Context questions: Once you find the tested word in the passage, treat the question like a Sentence Completion question. Pretend the word is a blank in the sentence. Read a line or two around the imaginary blank if you need to. Then predict a word for that blank. Check the answer choices for a word that comes close to your prediction. Now, use this knowledge to work through the following Vocabulary-in-Context question, which refers to the Taj Mahal passage.

As used in the passage, "unmatched" (line 45) most nearly means which of the following

(A) uneven
(B) solitary
(C) outmoded
(D) noncompeting
(E) supreme

Go to line 45 and read the sentence: *As an architectural representation of the afterlife, it is unmatched.* This sentence refers to the Taj Mahal, so even if you were unsure of

> **EXPERT TUTOR TIP**
>
> " If stuck on a Vocabulary-in-Context question, don't forget to read your top choices back into the sentence in the passage. Your ear can sometimes be "smarter" than your head. "

the meaning of *unmatched*, you should be able to tell from this sentence, as well as from the passage as a whole, that its meaning must be positive. Thus, the only answer that makes sense is (E), *supreme*. When you read this choice back into the sentence, it still makes sense.

KAPLAN'S FIVE-STEP METHOD

Once you've read a passage strategically and created a passage map, you're ready to attack the questions. Here's Kaplan's Five-Step Method for Reading Comprehension questions:

Step 1. Read the question stem.

Step 2. Locate the material you need.

Step 3. Predict the answer.

Step 4. Scan the answer choices.

Step 5. Select your answer.

STEP 1. READ THE QUESTION STEM

This is the place to really read carefully. Make sure you understand exactly what the question is asking. Is it a Big Picture question? Little Picture? Inference? Vocabulary-in-Context? Are you looking for an overall main idea or a specific piece of information? Are you trying to determine the author's attitude or the meaning of a particular word?

STEP 2. LOCATE THE MATERIAL YOU NEED

If you are given a line reference, read the material surrounding the line mentioned. It will clarify exactly what the question is asking and provide you with the context you need to answer the question correctly.

If you're not given a line reference, scan the text to find the place where the question applies, and quickly reread those few sentences. Keep the main point of the passage in mind.

STEP 3. PREDICT THE ANSWER

Don't spend time making up a precise answer. You need only a general sense of what you're after so you can recognize the correct answer quickly when you read the choices.

EXPERT TUTOR TIP

By researching and predicting the answer, you are making sure that it is untainted by opinion or assumption (because it comes right from the passage) AND you are avoiding possible traps in the answer choices. The PSAT test makers really earn their pay here!

STEP 4. SCAN THE ANSWER CHOICES

Scan the choices, looking for one that fits your idea of the right answer. If you don't find an ideal answer, quickly eliminate wrong choices by checking back to the passage. Rule out choices that are too extreme or go against common sense. Get rid of answers that sound reasonable but don't make sense in the context of the passage or the question. Don't pick far-fetched inferences, and make sure there is evidence for your inference in the passage. Remember, PSAT inferences tend to be strongly implied in the passage.

STEP 5. SELECT YOUR ANSWER

You've eliminated the obvious wrong answers. One of the remaining answers should fit your ideal. If you're left with more than one contender, consider the passage's main idea, and make an educated guess.

BEWARE AND BE AWARE OF WRONG ANSWER TYPES

Opposite—180 degrees from what you are looking for, but it also can be oddly tempting if you are reading quickly and haphazardly.

Extreme—Answer choices that go too far. Watch out for absolutes such as *always*, *never*, and the extreme forms of adjectives.

Out of Context—The answer comes from left field. It either doesn't answer the question at all or brings in information not found in the passage.

Misused Detail—This is when the answer cites a detail from another part of the passage; it's true but that doesn't mean it answers the question, right?

Distortion—This answer warps the information in an illogical way, trying to confuse you into picking it.

Next time you find yourself eliminating down to an answer, try putting some labels on the wrong answers. It may help you arrive at the correct answer faster.

THE FIVE-STEP METHOD IN ACTION

Let's see how the method works on a typical short Reading Comprehension passage.

> I cannot remember my first train ride, but by the time
> I was six, trains were a serious hobby. Not for me were the
> swept-back fins of gas-guzzling 1950s sedans. No, my vision
> of the ultimate was the rise and fall of a train's melancholy
> (5) whistle. The very names of long-distance trains resonated
> with adventure: the *Yankee Clipper*, the *Silver Meteor*, and the
> *Twentieth-Century Limited*. By my tenth birthday, my col-
> lection of railroad timetables filled three large scrapbooks.
> I knew the stops on entire routes by heart, and my after-
> (10) school playground was Grand Central Station in New York.

For the author, the names of his favorite long-distance trains served to

(A) aid in locating the schedules of particular trains in the timetables

(B) indicate the originating points and destinations of the trains

(C) create an aura of adventure and excitement

(D) remind the author of exciting train journeys he had taken

(E) make the trains more compelling than automobiles for the author

STEP 1. READ THE QUESTION STEM

This question has a very narrow focus—the names of the trains.

STEP 2. LOCATE THE MATERIAL YOU NEED

Here's the sentence you need: "The very names of long-distance trains resonated with adventure: the *Yankee Clipper*, the *Silver Meteor*, and the *Twentieth-Century Limited*."

STEP 3. PREDICT THE ANSWER

The author seems very fond of the names. He also notes that they *resonated with adventure*. Look for an answer choice that talks about this sense of adventure or excitement.

STEP 4. SCAN THE ANSWER CHOICES

Choices (C) and (D) both mention excitement. Choices (A) and (B) are too mundane and functional—they don't allude to the sense of adventure from your prediction. Choice (E) is a distortion of ideas from the passage; the author does prefer trains to cars but not simply because of the trains' names.

STEP 5. SELECT YOUR ANSWER

Choose between (C) and (D). On closer inspection, (D) doesn't quite work—the author never says that train names remind him of trips. In fact, he hardly mentions actually getting on a train at all. Choice (C), however, works well.

VOCABULARY BUILDING

We've shown you tips for making the most of your vocabulary with strategies to avoid getting stumped by tough words in both kinds of Critical Reading questions. Nevertheless, if a lot of the words in the examples were unfamiliar to you, you'll want to put some time into increasing your vocabulary knowledge, too.

BOOSTING YOUR VOCABULARY

There are two distinct types of tough PSAT vocabulary words:

- Unfamiliar words
- Familiar words with unfamiliar secondary meanings

Some words will be hard simply because you have never seen them before. There's a good chance you've never come across words like *redoubtable* or *expiate*, but these words could easily appear on the PSAT.

Other common words, such as *appropriate* and *flag*, could also pose some problems because the test makers will most likely be testing their secondary, less familiar definitions. Watch for this, especially on Reading Comprehension questions; this section almost always contains Vocabulary-in-Context questions that will test your knowledge of unfamiliar meanings to familiar words.

To get a sense of your vocabulary strength, take a few minutes to go through the following list of typical PSAT vocabulary words and see how many you know. Write your definition to the right of each word, and then score yourself. Give yourself one point for every word you know. (You'll find answers and study advice based on your score following the quiz.)

chafe _____

veracity _____

vanquish _____

ardor _____

lethargic _____

eradicate _____

pensive _____

legible _____

vex _____

stoic (adj.) _____

adept (adj.) _____

exculpate _____

guile _____

disinterested _____

pine (v.) _____

din _____

covert _____

wag (n.) _____

censure (n.) _____

loquacious _____

temper (v.) _____

acumen _____

diffident _____

lachrymose _____

toady _____

lumber (v.) _____

latent _____

admonish _____

foible _____

specious _____

Here are the definitions:

chafe	to wear away or irritate by rubbing
veracity	truthfulness
vanquish	to defeat or conquer in battle
ardor	fiery intensity; zeal
lethargic	sluggish, inactive, apathetic
eradicate	to remove or eliminate
pensive	thoughtful
legible	possible to read or decipher
vex	to irritate or annoy
stoic (adj.)	indifferent; impassive
adept (adj.)	skilled
exculpate	to remove guilt or blame
guile	skillful deceit; treacherous cunning
disinterested	impartial; unbiased
pine (v.)	to long for

din	loud noise; clamor
covert	hidden; secret
wag (n.)	a humorous person, a wit
censure	strong disapproval or harsh criticism
loquacious	extremely talkative
temper (v.)	to moderate, reduce
acumen	accuracy and keenness of judgment or insight
diffident	shy and timid
lachrymose	tearful
toady	a flatterer; a sycophant
lumber (v.)	to walk with heavy clumsiness
latent	present but inactive; dormant
admonish	to scold or reprove gently
foible	a minor weakness or failing of character
specious	seemingly true but actually false; misleading

If you got 10 definitions or fewer right, you should start working on building your vocabulary. The techniques and tools in this chapter will teach you ways to improve your word base and make the most out of what you do know about words.

If you got between 11 and 20 correct, your vocabulary is about average. If you're willing to put in the time, using these techniques and tools can help you improve your vocabulary and your score on the exam.

If you knew the definitions to more than 20 words, your vocabulary is in great shape. You can polish it further, particularly if you are aiming for a National Merit Scholarship, but you don't have to. If your time is short, learn the strategies in the "Decoding Tough Vocabulary" part of this chapter first, and concentrate on other aspects of the PSAT that you find difficult.

A VOCABULARY-BUILDING PLAN

A great vocabulary can't be built overnight, but you can develop a better PSAT vocabulary in a relatively short period of time with a minimum amount of pain. You need to study wisely. Be strategic. How well you use your time between now and the day of the test is just as important as how much time you spend prepping.

LEARN WORDS STRATEGICALLY

The best words to learn are words that have appeared often on the PSAT and SAT. Fortunately, the test makers are not very creative in their choice of words for each test, so words that have appeared frequently are likely bets to show up again.

Start with the PSAT Word List in the PSAT Resources at the back of this book. This list contains words that have been seen on previous PSATs (and SATs). You probably already know a lot of the words on this list. We suggest you learn ten words a day from this list by using the techniques discussed in this chapter. You'll want to continue to review those words until you know their definitions as well as you know the class schedule of the intriguing new transfer student!

STUDY WORD ROOTS

Most PSAT words are made up of prefixes and roots that can get you at least partway to a definition. Thankfully, on the PSAT, partway is often far enough to get you points.

For instance, if you know that the prefix *circum* means around or that *locution* means talk or speech, you might be able to decode the definition of *circumlocution*, which means talking around, as when someone avoids talking about a particular subject. Use the Root List in the PSAT Resources appendixes to pick up the most valuable PSAT roots. Target these words in your vocabulary review. Many of these word roots—including *circum* and *locution*, in this case—may already be familiar if you've studied a foreign language, particularly a Romance language such as French, Spanish, or Latin.

PERSONALIZE YOUR VOCABULARY STUDY

There's not just one right way to study vocabulary. Figure out a study method that works best for you, and stick to it. Here are some of our proven strategies:

- Use flashcards. Write down new words or word groups on one side of a 3 × 5 index card and a short definition on the back. Run through the flashcards whenever you have some spare time.

- Create a vocabulary notebook. List words in one column and their meaning in another. Cover up the meanings or fold the page to test yourself, and see what words you can define from memory. Make a sample sentence using each word in context.

- Record yourself reading the unfamiliar words and their definitions. Pause for a moment before you read the definition. This will give you time to define the

> **EXPERT TUTOR TIP**
>
> " Try to work the new words you are studying into your essays and comments at school. It's a great way to add some points to your GPA *and* PSAT! "

word in your head when you play the recording back. Quiz yourself. Listen to your recording on your mp3 player. Play it when you're in the car, on the bus, or whenever you have some free time.

- Try to come up with hooks to lodge a new word in your mind: Create visual images of words to build associations between them and their definitions.

- Use rhymes and other devices that help you remember the words. For example, you might remember that a *verbose* person uses a lot of verbs.

It doesn't matter which techniques you use, as long as you learn words steadily and methodically. Doing so over several months with regular reviews is ideal. If you are short on time, though, don't panic! Increasing your word knowledge can be a big help, but the PSAT Critical Reading section tests a lot more than just vocabulary. If you learn the strategies in the earlier parts of this chapter and do the practice tests, you'll be ready to tackle most Critical Reading questions even if they do contain unfamiliar words.

PRACTICE

The following practice set should give you some sense of your areas of strength and weakness on the PSAT Critical Reading sections. Be sure to keep in mind the strategies you have learned in this chapter.

When you finish the practice set, take time to thoroughly review the answers, *even for the questions you got right*. You may find that you got the right answer for the wrong reason or that you missed a more efficient way to tackle the problem.

Finally, be sure to take advantage of the PSAT Resources at the end of this book to help you build your vocabulary and Critical Reading skills for test day.

Select the lettered word or set of words that best completes the sentence.

Example:

Today's small, portable computers contrast markedly with the earliest electronic computers, which were ----.

(A) effective

(B) invented

(C) useful

(D) destructive

(E) enormous

1. Except for specific, solitary life stages, wolves act as ---- animals, generally living in packs with strong bonds and clear hierarchies.

(A) carnivorous

(B) fearsome

(C) social

(D) singular

(E) wild

2. Psychologists disagree about whether multiple personality is ---- disease or a shield behind which some criminals hide in order to ---- prosecution.

(A) a fallacious . . . forestall

(B) an authentic . . . ensure

(C) a genuine . . . evade

(D) an invalid . . . elude

(E) a diagnosable . . . guarantee

3. Despite its stated goals of fostering productivity and hard work, the company promotes many unproductive and ---- employees.

(A) creative

(B) discontented

(C) independent

(D) lackadaisical

(E) meritorious

4. Despite his ---- beginnings as the son of a minor tribal chieftain, the conqueror Tamerlane became one of the greatest ---- in Asia.

(A) impoverished . . . nuisances

(B) auspicious . . . failures

(C) famed . . . enigmas

(D) obscure . . . rulers

(E) luxuriant . . . monarchs

5. Winston Churchill's ---- speeches boosted British morale during World War II.

(A) stolid

(B) ignoble

(C) farcical

(D) resolute

(E) tremulous

6. Because of her ----, Elizabeth Bishop was not a ---- writer, but she won critical acclaim for the hundred or so poems she allowed to be published during her lifetime.

    (A) notoriety . . . creative
    (B) perfectionism . . . prolific
    (C) affluence . . . renowned
    (D) allusiveness . . . poetic
    (E) aphasia . . . contemplative

7. President Calvin Coolidge was notoriously ----, usually saying no more than was absolutely necessary.

    (A) abstemious
    (B) clairvoyant
    (C) nefarious
    (D) parsimonious
    (E) taciturn

Answer the questions below based on the information in the accompanying passages.

Questions 8–9 refer to the following passage.

In the early 1990s, commuter railroads expanded greatly, effectively doubling in number in the United States. This incredible expansion was largely in response to a complex,
(5) interrelated set of factors: suburban population growth, increasing traffic on crowded roads and highways caused by a growing workforce, governmental and private concern over air pollution, and escalating fuel costs.
(10) Many state governments saw in commuter rails a remedy to these growing pains, and established programs to finance and manage commuter railroads to service metropolitan areas. Despite the great expense involved,
(15) most governments also chose to partially subsidize the cost of the tickets, rather than transfer the entire burden of the cost of the system to its users.

8. The author gives all of the following as reasons for the expansion of commuter railroads in the United States EXCEPT

    (A) growing congestion and traffic due to automobiles
    (B) an increase of population in suburbs
    (C) the extreme expense involved in such an expansion
    (D) the rise in the price of fuel
    (E) concerns about unclean air due to cars

9. The information in the passage suggests that government funding of commuter railroads

    (A) was seen primarily as a response to environmental pollution
    (B) failed to achieve its primary goals
    (C) was an effective alternative to subsidizing rapidly rising fuel costs
    (D) succeeded in reducing traffic congestion and air pollution
    (E) was chosen as an alternative to relying solely on ticket prices to provide funding

Question 10 refers to the following passage.

While studying Sanskrit, linguist Sir William Jones made a surprising discovery. He found that this ancient language of India bore some striking similarities to Latin and Greek. This
(5) caused scholars to posit that both Sanskrit and Latin had a common source, which likely originated in north-central Europe. It was further hypothesized that this root language then developed into dozens of different languages,
(10) leaving traces of common lineage. For example, we see that the English word "three" is quite similar to "tre" in Albanian, "tri" in Russian, "trois" in French, "drei" in German, and even "tri" in Sanskrit.

10. The similar words for the number 3 in various languages, listed in lines 12–14, serve as

    (A) an illustration of the development of an ancient central European root language

    (B) a citation of the similarities of Greek and Latin

    (C) proof that Greek and Latin evolved into the cited modern languages

    (D) evidence that several different languages likely originated from a common source

    (E) partial proof that modern languages influence one another to at least a minor extent

Questions 11–17 refer to the following passage.

The following passage analyzes one of the best known works of Younghill Kang (1903–1972), a Korean writer who came to the United States as an immigrant in 1921.

East Goes West, published in 1937, is one of two important books written by Younghill Kang over a period of seven years. It has been described as a travelogue, a record of
(5) an Asian immigrant's experiences in America during the early decades of this century. But it is much more than a mere catalogue of experiences. It chronicles a journey of disillusionment and despair, for Kang discovered that
(10) the utopian image of America which he had constructed in his own mind before departing his native Korea bore little resemblance to the actual conditions he found upon arriving at America's shores.
(15) *East Goes West* is written in the form of an autobiographical novel. It is the fervent personal expression of an immigrant who longed to be accepted into American society. The protagonist Chungpa Han, a slightly fic-
(20) tionalized representation of Kang, comes to America from Korea not for a temporary sojourn but to establish a new life. Han's

attempts to find a doorway into American society prove to be largely futile, however.
(25) Searching for the Western civilization to which he has been introduced in his reading of Shakespeare, he receives an education of another sort altogether as he is ridiculed and exploited by employers and rejected by those
(30) he would befriend. Han's hopes and expectations clash continually with the loneliness and alienation with which he must contend. He is gradually forced to give up his dream of finding the place for himself in America
(35) that he had envisioned.

No doubt because it painted a less than flattering picture of life in America for Asian immigrants, *East Goes West* was not well received by contemporary literary critics.
(40) According to them, the novel displayed a curious lack of insight regarding the American effort to accommodate those who had come over from Korea. The facet of the novel the reviewers did find praiseworthy was Han's per-
(45) severance and sustained optimism in the face of adversity. This was, in their opinion, a model that Asian Americans should use in overcoming the obstacles of racism and discrimination.
(50) *East Goes West* is a precious part of America's cultural heritage. It has given subsequent generations of Asian Americans a rare glimpse into the trials and tribulations undergone by their immigrant ancestors. Although Kang can-
(55) not be considered representative of the Korean American community of his time, whose members generally were not concerned with immersing themselves in American life, his novel contains many bits and pieces of their collective
(60) experience.

Furthermore, *East Goes West* was an important literary event because Kang broke new ground in his description of his experiences in America. One finds neither the superficial
(65) commentary of the casual tourist nor the polite observations of the visiting dignitary, both of

which were characteristic of the works of Asian authors prior to Kang. Kang differed from those who had come to America before him in that
(70) he did not consider himself to be a guest in someone else's country; he wanted to forge an American identity for himself.

11. The primary focus of the passage is on the

(A) terrible plight of Asian immigrants in the early decades of the last century

(B) failure of Chungpa Han to assimilate into American society

(C) significance that *East Goes West* had as an innovative literary form

(D) literary expression of an Asian immigrant's effort to create an American identity

(E) response of the critics to Younghill Kang's depiction of America in *East Goes West*

12. The statement "…he receives an education of another sort altogether…" (lines 27–28) conveys a sense of

(A) irony regarding the difference between Han's expectations and reality

(B) disdain for Han's hopelessly idealistic aspirations

(C) dismay that Han was the victim of such horrible treatment

(D) amusement that Han was so misinformed about life in America

(E) surprise that Han did not find what he was looking for

13. In line 32, "contend" most likely means

(A) argue

(B) believe

(C) discuss

(D) struggle

(E) accept

14. In lines 40–41, the word "curious" most nearly means

(A) engrossed

(B) inquisitive

(C) odd

(D) unfamiliar

(E) interested

15. Paragraph 3 indicates that the response of critics to the publication of *East Goes West* was one of

(A) outright rejection of the novel as a one-sided account of historical events

(B) admiration of the courage and creativity Kang showed in breaking from literary tradition

(C) confusion about the motivation of the protagonist

(D) qualified disapproval of Kang's perception of his adopted homeland

(E) anger that Kang had so viciously attacked American society

16. The author indicates that Kang "cannot be considered representative of the Korean American community of his time" (lines 54–56) primarily because

(A) few Korean Americans wrote novels about their experiences

(B) most Korean Americans were involved in diplomatic relations

(C) few Korean Americans tried to assimilate into the American way of life

(D) only part of Kang's novel relates to the immigrant experience

(E) few Korean Americans were knowledgeable about Western civilization

17. The casual tourist and the visiting dignitary are presented primarily as examples of people who

    (A) became disillusioned with America
    (B) struggled against racism and discrimination
    (C) wrote about America as outsiders
    (D) influenced Kang in his work
    (E) tried to forge American identities

Questions 18–19 refer to the following passage.

Today, it's a widely held belief that James Watson and Francis Crick "discovered" DNA—deoxyribonucleic acid—the transmitter of genetic information from parent to offspring.
(5) However, it would be more accurate to consider their discovery of DNA's structure as a single milestone in a long history leading up to and continuing after the breakthrough. For example, in 1869, Johann Friedrich Miescher identified
(10) an acidic substance (later named DNA) in the nuclei of human cells, though its function remained obscure. In 1949, a biochemist named Erwin Chargaff found that the amount of DNA in a cell varies from one species to
(15) another, marking it as a likely carrier of genetic information.

18. The author would most likely describe the belief cited in lines 1–2 as a

    (A) dangerously incomplete notion
    (B) vitally important milestone
    (C) somewhat inaccurate simplification
    (D) sound, though complex, impression
    (E) simplistic and naive conception

19. In line 15, the word "marking" most nearly means

    (A) indicating
    (B) transmitting
    (C) writing
    (D) commemorating
    (E) assessing

Questions 20–27 refer to the following passages.

The following passages present two views of the current state of professions in America. Passage 1 discusses professions from a historical point of view. Passage 2 presents a defense of the legal profession.

Passage 1

Despite the honor accorded them by society and the usually substantial monetary rewards they enjoy for their work, many modern professionals complain that they feel demoralized.
(5) They don't command the respect of the public or enjoy special privileges as members of exclusive groups to the extent that professionals once did. This decline in the status of the professions is difficult for them to bear because, they vehe-
(10) mently maintain, the knowledge and unique skills of professionals are as vital and indispensable to society as they have ever been.

Originally, being a professional meant practicing in one of the "learned professions," a
(15) category that included only law, theology, university scholarship, and (eventually) medicine. Members of these groups distinguished themselves from the rest of society by their possession of certain special knowledge that brought
(20) with it power and abilities most others could not even fully fathom. Aspirants to a profession were required not only to devote themselves to a demanding life of learning but also to adhere to a specifically tailored system of ethics in order
(25) to prevent the misuse of professional powers. The special deference and privileges these professionals received were their reward for using

their knowledge in the service of others rather than of themselves.

(30)   Although many of today's professionals would argue that this description still applies to them, the truth of the matter is that the professional scene has changed quite a bit since the days of the "learned professions." When the members (35) of the professions began to organize themselves in the nineteenth century, establishing work standards and policing themselves in order to prevent the government from cleaning house for them, they proclaimed that they were doing (40) this for the good of the public. The professional associations that emerged from this structuring proved to be, however, far more advantageous to the professionals than to the general populace, because the associations began to function (45) as lobbies and interest groups.

A further consequence of this organizing was that the elevated position of the professional gradually eroded as members of other occupations jumped on the bandwagon. When just (50) about any group could organize itself and call itself a profession, the concept of the professional as the possessor of special knowledge and abilities didn't seem to be as valid. Thus, many professions have had to struggle to sustain the (55) notion that their members provide a critical service to society that no one else can.

Passage 2

In the past few years, numerous editorials and speeches have decried a real as well as perceived lack of ethics in various professions, often zeroing in on the profession everyone (5) now seems to love to hate. Not a lawyer myself, I feel no personal defensiveness at the charges levied against this group in the last decade. As someone who earns a living and derives a tremendous amount of job satisfaction by work- (10) ing with lawyers, however, I find the repeated attacks quite troubling.

Certainly the legal world in general and lawyers as practitioners in it are subject to charges of inequality, inefficiency, and ineffec- (15) tiveness. Examples abound. We all know the accounts of high legal fees, prolonged, acrimonious conflicts, underfunded legal services for the poor, inaccessible legal services for the middle class and an overburdened (20) system of justice for all. The backlog in civil and criminal courts, the proliferation of nuisance suits and abuses within the profession's financial base have been cited as examples of an elite group run amok.

(25)   The ills are obvious, but the maladies are frequently symptoms of more pervasive societal frailty rather than peculiar to the body—or profession—associated with the remedy. There is reason for suspicion from without and malaise, (30) even demoralization, from within the legal profession. But this very fact argues for attentiveness to and support of the profession's efforts at healing the body politic, rather than a continued obsession with the profession's ill health.

(35)   A refreshing look at ways to achieve that health is evident in the recently published work of an American Bar Association Council task force. Established by the council's section of legal education and admissions to the bar, the (40) task force devoted three years to a review of the legal profession. Its recommendations review the practice settings for which lawyers must prepare, reaffirm the principles of organization and self-regulation that must govern any profession, (45) and provide an inventory of behaviors and attitudes—labeled "skills and values"—with which any individual in the legal profession should be equipped.

The contribution such values and skills (50) make to a society in which they are disseminated is immeasurable. Certainly, many individuals, many "professionals"—both lawyers and otherwise—fall short of the marks set out in such reports. That doesn't mean that

(55) professional credos are not worth articulating. Neither does it mean that the individuals who enter a profession, but fail to embody the ideal of skills and values, are hateful, nor the profession itself dispensable.

20. Passage 1 indicates that the response of professionals to the "decline in the status of the professions" (line 8) has been one of

(A) understanding that this is due to the rise of professional organizations

(B) denial that the professions command less respect from the public than in the past

(C) insistence that their monetary rewards should be greater

(D) dejection over the lack of appreciation of their work

(E) urgent desire to regain public respect by reorganizing the professions

21. In Passage 1, line 17, the word "distinguished" most nearly means

(A) isolated

(B) differentiated

(C) recognized

(D) honored

(E) discerned

22. In lines 5–11 of Passage 2, the author most likely describes herself in order to

(A) emphasize that she cannot be accused of a lack of ethics

(B) indicate that people should empathize with the plight of lawyers

(C) admit that she cannot offer an expert opinion on law matters

(D) state her impartiality toward the issue discussed

(E) explain the position from which she will argue

23. The author of Passage 2 uses the example of the work of the American Bar Association Council task force (lines 37–41) primarily to illustrate the

(A) number of areas in which the legal profession needs improvement

(B) difficulty encountered when reform of a profession is undertaken

(C) endeavor on the part of the legal profession to improve its condition

(D) result of the legal profession's obsession with its failings

(E) changes that have been effected in the legal profession

24. The tone the author uses when describing the recommended "behaviors and attitudes" (Passage 2, lines 45–46) of lawyers is

(A) laudatory

(B) disparaging

(C) indifferent

(D) cynical

(E) hesitant

25. In the last paragraph of Passage 2, the author acknowledges which flaw in the legal profession?

(A) the ineffectiveness of professional credos

(B) the poor quality of most aspiring lawyers

(C) the lack of respect for the task force's work

(D) the presence of professionals with inadequate skills

(E) the rigidity of the code of skills and values

26. How would the author of Passage 1 respond to the affirmation of the American Bar Association task force that "principles of organization and self-regulation must govern any profession" (Passage 2, lines 43–44)?

    (A) A group's ability to organize and regulate itself develops as its members acquire knowledge.

    (B) Only a few of the professions should be organized and regulated.

    (C) The government should regulate the professions in order to prevent abuses.

    (D) The American Bar Association is merely seeking to extend its political influence.

    (E) The professions have been hurt as well as helped by organization and self-regulation.

27. The view expressed in lines 28–34 shows the author of Passage 2 to be different from the author of Passage 1 in that she

    (A) considers the possibility of future improvement in the professions

    (B) refuses to admit that professionals are demoralized

    (C) maintains that professionals are at odds with the rest of society

    (D) investigates the relationship between professionals and the public

    (E) believes there are legitimate reasons for professionals to be demoralized

ANSWERS AND EXPLANATIONS

1. C

The phrase *generally living in packs with strong bonds and clear hierarchies* virtually defines the missing word. Animals like wolves that live in such groups are (C), *social* animals, in contrast to the "lone wolf" stereotype alluded to in the sentence's opening phrase. While wolves are (A) *carnivorous*, or meat-eating, the topic of the sentence is their social habits, not their eating habits. The words *wild* (E) and *singular* (D) both miss the sentence's point—that wolves live in packs. *Fearsome* (B) can have two nearly opposite meanings: frightening or timid.

2. C

The sentence sets up a contrast between two differing views of multiple personality; either *it's a ---- disease* or *it's a shield that some criminals use to ---- prosecution.* Because it's a safe bet that criminals don't want to be prosecuted, or tried for their crimes, the second blank should be filled by a word like *escape.* To provide the necessary contrast, the first word must be something like *genuine. Genuine . . . evade* is the best match for this prediction. *Authentic* (genuine) and *diagnosable* (capable of having its cause determined) might fit in the first blank, but the second words in (B) and (E)—*ensure* and *guarantee*, respectively—contrast sharply with our prediction for the second blank. In (A) and (D), the second words are possibilities, but the first words don't fit. In (A), *forestall* means prevent, but *fallacious* means false, just the opposite of what's needed in the first blank. Likewise, in (D), *elude* fits the second blank, but *invalid* (not legitimate) doesn't work in the first blank.

3. D

The sentence sets up a contrast between the company's goal of *fostering* (encouraging) *productivity and hard work* and the fact it *promotes . . . unproductive and ---- workers. Unproductive* obviously contrasts with *productivity*, so it's logical to assume that the correct answer should be something that contrasts with *hard work*—perhaps something like *lazy. Lackadaisical*, which means indifferent, lazy, or apathetic, comes closest to this prediction. The workers may well be *discontented* (B), but discontented doesn't complete the sentence's implied contrast with hard work. The remaining choices all have a positive charge, which wouldn't make sense here. *Meritorious* (E) means deserving of praise or reward.

4. D

The clue word, *despite*, sets up a contrast between the conqueror Tamerlane's beginnings and his later life. A word like *humble* would fit the first blank, and something like *general* or *conqueror* would fit logically in the second. *Obscure . . . rulers* is the best match; *obscure* means not well-known. In (A), *impoverished*, which means very poor, might work for the first blank, but *nuisances* doesn't create the necessary contrast or enhance the idea of a conqueror. Choice (B) has a contrast, but with the opposite meaning to your prediction: *auspicious* means promising or having good prospects. In (C), *famed* doesn't make sense for the son of a minor chieftain, and *enigmas* means puzzles. *Monarchs* in (E) is a synonym of *rulers* in the correct choice, but the first word, *luxuriant* (meaning lush or profuse, not necessarily luxurious) doesn't fit the first blank.

5. D

To boost morale or make people feel better during a war, you'd want speeches that were courageous, emotionally stirring, fiercely determined, or something along those lines. *Resolute* fits best—it means resolved and determined, with a strong sense of purpose. None of the other choices fits the meaning of the sentence. *Stolid* means having or showing little emotion, but you'd want an emotional speech to boost morale. *Ignoble* means dishonorable. *Farcical*, which comes from the noun *farce*, means laughably absurd. And *tremulous* means timid and fearful or shaking or quivering—certainly not a quality that would make people feel better in times of war.

6. B

The *but* is a clue that the sentence contains a contrast. The second part of the sentence indicates that she was a great writer who didn't allow many of her poems to be published. Take that into consideration when you're deciding what the blanks should say. Start with the blank that is easier to fill, which is more likely the second one. You can rule out (A), (C), and (D) because the second part of the sentence indicates she must have been *creative*, *renowned*, and *poetic*. That leaves (B) and (E). Plug each of the choices into the sentence to see which makes more sense. Choice (B) fits better because a perfectionist would be extremely picky about which works are published, meaning she was not a *prolific*, or productive, writer.

7. E

You don't have to know that Coolidge was nicknamed "Silent" Cal to answer this vocabulary question correctly. But you do have to see that the missing word is defined by the phrase *usually saying no more than was absolutely necessary*. The only choice that fits is *taciturn*, which means uncommunicative or not inclined to speak much. A writer might describe a taciturn person as being *parsimonious with words*, but by itself, *parsimonious* means miserly, stingy, or ungenerous with money, not with words. *Abstemious* means moderate in appetite. *Clairvoyant* means able to see the future. And *nefarious* means evil.

COMMUTER RAILROADS PASSAGE

This short passage looks at the expansion of commuter railroads in the early 1990s. The author cites several reasons for the expansion and states that governments helped to fund and manage the railroads.

8. C

To find the answer to this Little Picture question, simply go back to the passage and find each of the answer choices. The one you cannot verify will be your answer. Lines 5–10 contain (A), (B), (D), and (E). That leaves (C).

9. E

The last sentence indicates that the burden of paying for the railroads was not transferred entirely to the railroad users. Instead, the state governments subsidized ticket prices. That matches (E). Choice (A) is too extreme, because there were many factors besides pollution that lead to the railroad expansion. Choices (B), (C), and (D) all deal with the success of the program. Since the passage never says whether the railroads actually dealt with the problems listed, you can rule out all three of these answer choices.

LANGUAGE PASSAGE

This short passage looks at how Sanskrit, an ancient language of India, is similar to Latin and Greek and says that it is believed that the languages all had a common root language. The writer cites the word *three* as an example of how a word can be similar in different languages.

10. D

Why would the author bother to list the number 3 in five other languages? In order to show that apparently different languages actually have a lot in common.

Why is this important? To help prove that these languages came from the same root language (D). The author doesn't spend too much time talking about the root language itself (A), or the specifics of Greek and Latin (B). Choice (C) is a tempting distortion— it was the root language that evolved into so many languages, not Greek and Latin. Choice (E) would be a feasible explanation for the similarities, but it's not an explanation that the author endorses.

IMMIGRANT PASSAGE

The italicized introduction tells us that the passage looks at the works of a Korean immigrant to the United States. The author looks at the autobiographical novel *East Goes West* about a Korean who finds that America is not what he had imagined it to be. The author says the novel was not well received by critics, except for the fact that the character continues to remain optimistic, which they said should be a model for all Asian Americans. The book provides Asian Americans who have come after the character a look at what their ancestors went through in America. The author of the passage says the book is different from books by other Asian writers in that the author sought to become American, not just to be a guest in another country.

11. D

This is a Big Picture question. The right answer will cover the entire passage, not just a paragraph or two. Step back for a second and you'll see that the passage focuses primarily on the book *East Goes West*; in fact, you knew that it would before you read the passage because you wisely read the introduction. Choice (D) states the correct answer, Kang's book, in a slightly fancy way. All of the other choices are wrong because they home in on various details of the passage rather than taking in the big picture.

12. A

When you go back and reread the lines in which this reference appears as well as a couple of lines before and after it, you get a feel for the author's tone. It is the difference between what Han expects (the world of Shakespeare) and what Han experiences (ridicule and rejection) that creates the cruel irony of the statement *he receives an education of another sort altogether.* Choice (A) captures the tone nicely. The author is definitely not expressing disdain for Han (B); if anything, we feel sorry for him. In (C), however, *dismay* is much too strong a word to be the correct answer. Neither the author nor anyone else is very likely to be amused by what happens to Han, so (D) is wrong, but you also aren't surprised that he doesn't find the world of Shakespeare, so (E) can be eliminated as well.

13. D

This is a Vocabulary-in-Context question. Depending on the context, the word *contend* can mean a variety of things. Here, the author is using it in a sense that means "combat" or (D), *struggle*—the character discussed has to contend with *loneliness and alienation* in a foreign country. Wrong choices (A) through (C) are possible definitions of *contend* that don't fit here— you can't *argue, believe,* or *discuss* with loneliness. Choice (E), *accept,* isn't a possible definition, and it doesn't fit the passage either—there's no indication that Kang's hero has to accept his fate.

14. C

The most familiar and therefore attractive definitions of *curious* are *inquisitive* (B) and *interested* (E), but neither works in the context of the passage. Tackling Vocabulary-in-Context questions means figuring out how the word is used in the context of the passage, so never choose an answer without checking back to the indicated line. In the sentence referred to by the question stem, critics think Kang's lack of insight is curious, that is, strange or *odd* (C). All of the other answer choices are synonyms of or words related to *curious*, but don't make sense in the context of the passage.

15. D

According to paragraph 3, the critics thought that *East Goes West* gave too negative a portrayal of America, but they regarded Han as a worthy model for Asian Americans due to his perseverance and optimism. This makes (D) the right answer. Both (A) and (E) are too extreme to be the right answer: the critics did not reject the book outright, nor did they see the book as an *attack* of American society. Choice (B) is misleading because it is not the critics but the author of the passage who admires Kang for breaking from literary tradition. Choice (C) is wrong simply because the passage never mentions *confusion* on the part of the critics.

16. C

Lines 54–56 explain why Kang wasn't *representative* of the Korean American community as a whole. Unlike Kang, we're told, most Korean Americans of his generation were not interested in *immersing themselves in American life.* Choice (C), *assimilating*, paraphrases this idea nicely. Choice (A)—that few Korean Americans wrote novels about their experiences—seems like a true statement looking at the passage as a whole, but it's not the specific reason that the author describes Kang as *not representative.* Similarly, (E) hits on a unique aspect of Kang's experience that isn't mentioned in paragraph 4. Choice (B) distorts paragraph 5's reference to visiting dignitaries—there's no indication that the majority of Korean Americans were diplomats. Finally, (D) is not only factually incorrect (Kang's novel is the story of an immigrant) but also doesn't fit the question,

which is about the representativeness of Kang himself, not of his novel.

17. C

This question tests your understanding of the author's logic in mentioning tourists and dignitaries in the passage. The reference appears in the fifth paragraph, so go back and skim the sentences there in order to pick up the surrounding context. Kang's literary contribution was that he wrote not as a guest in America, as had the tourists and dignitaries, but as someone trying to be American. Choice (C) is therefore correct: the author is using the tourist and the dignitary as examples of Asians who wrote about America as outsiders. Choice (E) directly contradicts (C). There is no reason to think tourists and dignitaries ever became disillusioned with America (A) as Kang did, or that they struggled against racism and discrimination (B). (You may know this is true, but the author doesn't mention tourists and dignitaries to make this point.) Finally, it's clear that Kang was not influenced by the writing of tourists and dignitaries (D), because the author stresses the fact that Kang wrote from an entirely new perspective.

DNA PASSAGE

This short passage looks at the discovery of DNA by James Watson and Francis Crick. The author says that there is a history of breakthroughs that led to Watson and Crick's discovery and cites two examples.

18. C

The author says that it would be more accurate to think of Crick and Watson's discovery as *a single milestone in a long history*, and then goes on to describe a few other discoveries that helped pave the way for Watson and Crick's work. So thinking that Watson and Crick did all the work is a *somewhat inaccurate simplification* (C). Choice (A) is too strong—there's nothing particularly dangerous going on here. Choice (B) might describe the discovery itself but doesn't cover beliefs about the discovery. The word *sound* lets you rule out (D)—the author doesn't think that the belief is sound at all. Like (A), (E) is too extreme. There's a very negative tone to the words *simplistic* and *naive*, and the author hasn't shown this negative attitude toward people who have this mistaken belief.

19. A

A scientist found that DNA depends on the species, thus *marking [DNA] as a likely carrier of genetic information.* The discovery made DNA look like such a carrier, so *marking* here means *indicating* (A). The DNA does plenty of *transmitting* (B), but the discovery about DNA did not. Choices (C), *writing,* and (D), *commemorating* (memorializing), are common meanings of *marking,* but they don't fit the context here. Choice (E) is also out, because it was the scientists, not the discoveries, that did the *assessing.*

MODERN PROFESSIONALS PASSAGES

The italicized introduction to the passages provides a good overview of what the passages are about. The author of Passage 1 looks at the history of professions and says that originally, professionals were special because they possessed knowledge that most people didn't and followed a code of ethics that benefited the general population. The author believes that because modern professionals formed professional organizations, they became more self-serving. And that led people of all sorts of occupations to organize themselves into professional groups, which meant that the original concept of "professional" was no longer so esteemed. The writer of Passage 2 looks at lawyers and finds the attacks against the profession troubling. The writer says that although it's true that the profession has problems, including high fees, long court fights, and backlogs in courts, members of the profession are trying to

fix those problems. The writer ends by saying that the societal contributions of the profession are immeasurable, but there will always be lawyers who don't possess the skills and values that ideal lawyers should.

20. D

When you read the sentence to which the line reference directs you as well as the two sentences that precede it, you know that professionals are feeling *demoralized* because they don't get the respect they deserve for the knowledge and skills they have. Take a second to get this clear in your mind and then go back to the answer choices; (D) gives you just what you're looking for. Nowhere does the author indicate that professionals see the rise of professional organizations as the cause of the decline, so (A) is out. Contrary to (B), professionals do think they command less respect than past professionals. Desire for *monetary rewards* (C) or *to regain public respect* (E) isn't mentioned in the passage at all.

21. B

As with all Vocabulary-in-Context questions, you should resist the impulse to pick an answer without checking to see how the word is used in the passage. The author is using *distinguished* here to say that members of the *learned professions* set themselves apart, or (B) *differentiated* themselves, from others by acquiring knowledge and abilities most people didn't have. All of the other choices are possible meanings of *distinguished,* but they don't make sense in the context of the passage.

22. E

In the cited lines of Passage 2, the author declares that she is not a lawyer but that she likes working with them and finds the attacks on lawyers *troubling.* She's describing herself in order to let the reader know what axe she's grinding here; in other words, she's *explaining the position from which she will argue* (E). The author is definitely not impartial on the subject of lawyers, so (D) is wrong. Choices (A) and (C) distort the author's motivation for stating that she is not a lawyer. Choice (B) may have been a tempting answer choice because the author seems to empathize with lawyers, but she does not describe herself in order to try to persuade the reader to feel the same way.

23. C

The author's purpose in bringing up the work of the ABA task force is pretty clear if you go back and read the sentence containing the line reference and the preceding sentence. She's showing how the legal profession is attempting to heal itself, or *improve its condition* (C). She talks about areas of the legal profession that need improvement primarily in the second paragraph, not the fourth, so (A) is wrong. You should have been able to eliminate (B) pretty quickly because the author doesn't discuss the difficulty of reform at all. Obsession with the legal profession's failings is just what the author wants to discourage, and she views the work of the ABA task force positively, so (D) is out. Finally, (E) is wrong because the work of the task force consisted of a review and recommendations, not changes.

24. A

The fact that the author has a high opinion of the behaviors and attitudes—the *skills and values*—of lawyers is hard to mistake: in the following sentence, she declares that the contribution they make to society is *immeasurable*. The trick here is knowing that the word *laudatory* (A) means "expressing praise." If you didn't know this, you could reach the correct choice by eliminating the others. *Disparaging* (B) means "critical" or "derogatory," which the

author definitely is not. The other choices likewise don't come close to matching the author's tone.

25. D

Go back and reread the rest of the final paragraph quickly (you already reread the first sentence in answering the last question). A quick summary: It's true that some professionals, including lawyers, don't meet the standards of their governing body, but it's still useful to have standards. Also, the author says, just because some members of a profession are below par, this doesn't mean we should do away with the whole profession. Now take a second to think. What flaw in the legal profession did the author just acknowledge? The presence of lawyers with inadequate skills (D). Choice (A) directly contradicts what the author says about the worth of professional credos. Furthermore, she never says anything about the quality of aspiring lawyers (B), lack of respect for the task force's work (C), or rigidity in the ABA's standards (E).

26. E

The remaining two questions involve relating the two passages to each other. This one requires you to figure out what the author of Passage 1 thinks about professions organizing and regulating themselves. According to his historical sketch, professions organized themselves to prevent government intervention and in so doing gained political influence, but they lost their *elevated position* at the same time. It's safe to conclude he would think that *professions have been hurt as well as helped by organization and self-regulation* (E). There is nothing in Passage 1 to indicate he would think that organization has anything to do with acquiring knowledge (A), that only a few professions should be organized (B), or that the government should regulate professions (C)—he only states that the government was on the verge of doing so in the 19th century. Nothing in the passage supports (D).

27. A

A quick reread of the third paragraph of Passage 2 reminds you that the author thinks that the problems within the legal profession indicate problems in society and that there is reason for lawyers to be demoralized but that we should support the profession's attempt to heal rather than continually criticizing it. It's the last part that sticks out the most as being different from the views of the first author, who never *considers the possibility of future improvement* (A) in any profession. Choice (B) is wrong because the author of Passage 2 does admit that professionals are demoralized. She does not, however, say that professionals are *at odds with the rest of society* (C); the wording of this choice is much more extreme than her statement that *there is reason for suspicion* from outside the legal profession. Choices (D) and (E) point out similarities, not differences, between the two authors.

CHAPTER 6: HOW TO ATTACK THE MATH SECTIONS

IF YOU LEARN ONLY FIVE THINGS IN THIS CHAPTER . . .

1. The PSAT uses multiple-choice and Grid-in questions in its Math sections. Kaplan strategies work for both question types.

2. Both Math sections are arranged easiest to hardest.

3. Kaplan has a strategy for attacking Math questions:

   —Step 1. Read through the question.

   —Step 2. Decide whether to do it now or later.

   —Step 3. Look for the fastest way to answer the question.

4. Sometimes shortcuts can save you a lot of time on a Math question. Kaplan has three good shortcuts: picking numbers, backsolving, and eyeballing.

5. A calculator is allowed on the PSAT, but you have to be careful how you use it.

CHAPTER 6 OVERVIEW

The PSAT tests a lot of math. Some of it is basic, and some of it is tough. Chapter 6 starts out by showing you Kaplan's strategies for approaching the two types of PSAT Math questions: multiple-choice and Grid-ins. After that, we go through the math concepts—easy and hard— the PSAT is likely to test. For most of the math concepts, you will see which SAT math topic (Numbers and Operations; Algebra and Functions; Geometry and Measurement; and Data Analysis, Statistics, and Probability) is covered by that concept. We cap it off with a practice quiz so you can see what skills you still need to work on when it comes to PSAT Math.

Not very good at math? Join the club. You're great at math? Good for you. Whoever you are, pay attention to this chapter because being successful at math in school is not the same as being successful at math on the PSAT. The skills you will learn in this chapter will translate into success on the PSAT. So for you, math-challenged reader, there is hope. And for you, math genius, there is always more to learn.

MATH BASICS

On math tests you take in your school classes, solving a problem by working it out and showing all of your work reaps many rewards. However, on the PSAT, solving problems that way will get you into trouble. Also, your teachers will probably still give you partial credit if you do the work properly but accidentally miss a step. On the PSAT, you will get no credit for that type of mistake.

With all of this in mind, Kaplan has developed some score-raising strategies for approaching the PSAT Math section. We'll show you how to take advantage of the PSAT's question style. Turning a good PSAT Math score into a great PSAT Math score requires learning to avoid the traps built into the questions by the PSAT writers.

One more word to those of you not crazy about math: keep an open mind. Our strategies will show you how to do the least amount of math required to still answer the questions correctly and quickly. By following our advice and by taking advantage of the PSAT standardized test format, you can get a very good score on PSAT Math, even if you're not that great at math.

The PSAT Math questions are divided into two 25-minute-long sections. There are two question types tested in the Math sections:

1. Multiple-choice questions that have five answer choices, which we call *regular math*.

2. Questions where you write your answer into a grid. We call those *Grid-ins*.

The first Math section contains 18 multiple-choice questions, and the second section is composed of 10 more multiple-choice questions as well as 10 Grid-in questions.

MULTIPLE-CHOICE QUESTIONS

The directions for multiple-choice Math questions are written below for your benefit. Learn these directions now so you won't waste time reading them on test day. That time could be spent answering one or two more questions.

Directions: Solve each of the following problems, decide which is the best answer choice, and darken the corresponding oval on the answer sheet.

Here is an example of what a multiple-choice question might look like.

If the surface area of the cube above is 96, and C is the midpoint of AB, what is the length of AC?

(A) 1

(B) 2

(C) 2.5

(D) 3

(E) 4

Don't worry about trying to answer it—you'll get plenty of practice later!

GRID-INS

The ten Grid-in questions on the PSAT are *more* like the math questions you are used to answering in math class. You don't get five answer choices to choose from. Instead, you're simply given a question and asked to figure out the answer yourself. The directions for Grid-ins appear on the following page.

When you come to a Grid-in on the PSAT test, you'll just see a question without any answer choices. Your task is to answer the question and come up with the solution yourself. Here's the catch, just finding the correct answer is not enough. You then have to write the answer into the special grid, which seems easy enough, but if you don't fill out the grid correctly, your correct answer won't be counted. Read the following discussion about filling in the grid carefully. It will be one less thing to worry about on test day.

DIRECTIONS FOR STUDENT-PRODUCED RESPONSE QUESTIONS

For each of the questions below (29–38), solve the problem and indicate your answer by darkening the ovals in the special grid. For example:

Answer: 1.25 or $\frac{5}{4}$ or 5/4

Write answer in boxes.

Fraction line
Decimal point

Grid-in result.

Either position is correct.

You may start your answers in any column, space permitting. Columns not needed should be left blank.

- It is recommended, though not required, that you write your answer in the boxes at the top of the columns. However, you will receive credit only for darkening the ovals correctly.

- Grid only one answer to a question, even though some problems have more than one correct answer.

- Darken no more than one oval in a column.

- No answers are negative.

- Mixed numbers cannot be gridded. For example: the number $1\frac{1}{4}$ must be gridded as 1.25 or 5/4.

(If [1 1 / 4] is gridded, it will be interpreted as $\frac{11}{4}$, not $1\frac{1}{4}$.)

- Decimal Accuracy: Decimal answers must be entered as accurately as possible. For example, if you obtain an answer such as 0.1666…, you should record the result as .166 or .167. **Less accurate values such as .16 or .17 are not acceptable**.

Acceptable ways to grid $\frac{1}{6}$ = .1666 . . .

FILLING IN THE GRID

Here's all you need to know about filling Grid-in grids. First of all, none of the following formats or number types will work as answers for Grid-in questions:

- Negative answers
- Answers with variables
- Answers greater than 9,999
- Answers with commas
- Mixed numbers
- Fractions with more than three digits

These restrictions sound complicated, but knowing what you can't do is just as important as knowing what you can with Grid-ins. If you come up with an answer that you determine cannot be gridded based on these restrictions, you will know your answer is wrong. For instance, if you come up with a mixed number or a fraction that won't fit, you should be able to convert it into a decimal or a fraction that does fit.

Let's say you came up with an answer of $1\frac{1}{2}$. If you tried to fill this answer into the grid without converting it, your answer would be read as the fraction $\frac{11}{2}$. Two ways to convert it are to turn the mixed number into the fraction $\frac{3}{2}$ or into its decimal equivalent 1.5. Either option, so long as you fill it in properly, is acceptable.

MORE THAN ONE RIGHT ANSWER

There can be several right ways to grid in an answer, and there may be several possible correct answers to a Grid-in question. When you get an answer in decimal form, you have to grid your answer as fully as possible, but you don't have to bother rounding up. For instance, if you wanted to fill in the decimal equivalent of $\frac{7}{9}$, which is the repeating decimal $.\overline{7}$, either .777 or .778 would be acceptable, but .77 or .78 would not.

Because you need to fill in numbers as fully as possible, we have a recommendation. Do this even if your answer has only one or two numbers. Technically, you can start in any column, but by following this rule you'll avoid mistakes: if you always start with the first column, your answers will always fit.

Of course, there is an exception to this rule: the answer 0. Because there is no oval for 0 in the first column, grid an answer of 0 in the second column.

HINT: always start your Grid-in answer in the first column box.

EXPERT TUTOR TIP

" Don't forget—never leave a Grid-in question blank. There's no penalty for a wrong answer, so take a guess. You never know... "

DIFFICULTY LEVEL: EASIEST TO HARDEST

Both PSAT Math question types are grouped into sets. These question sets start off with easy questions and gradually get harder. One of the keys for doing well on the PSAT Math section is to always know where you are in a question set. This is so important that we're going to repeat it, and we're going to add an exclamation point.

Always know where you are in a question set!

There's another important point about difficulty level. Sometimes the questions at the end of each set are hard, not because the math is a lot more complicated, but because they involve more steps and are filled with traps. We'll talk a lot about these math traps later. But first, we're going to set you up with our best strategy for attacking PSAT Math questions.

KAPLAN'S THREE-STEP METHOD

Now that you are familiar with the two questions types and understand order of difficulty, it's time to learn Kaplan's Three-Step Method for attacking PSAT Math:

Step 1. Read through the question.

Step 2. Decide whether to do it now or later.

Step 3. Look for the fastest way to answer the question.

To get your best possible math score, you need to use your time efficiently. You need to learn how to pace yourself so that you don't get bogged down and waste too much time on a single problem. That's what this strategy is all about. Here's how it works. Read the following Math question. It's the 12th question in an 18-question set.

At Fast Burger, two hamburgers and five orders of French fries cost the same as four hamburgers and two orders of French fries. If Fast Burger charges $1.50 for a single order of French fries, how much does it charge for two hamburgers?

(A) $2.25

(B) $3.00

(C) $4.50

(D) $5.00

(E) $6.00

STEP 1. READ THROUGH THE QUESTION

We suggest you never try to solve a problem before reading it all the way through. If you jump the gun, you may end up doing unnecessary work. Ask yourself: Is this question easy, medium, or hard? Because this example is question 12 from an 18-question set, you know that the test makers consider this a moderately difficult word problem.

If this was question 17, you would definitely want to watch out for math traps (more on those later on in the chapter). But even here, there's a slight twist. Notice that you're being asked to find the cost of two hamburgers, not one. Many students will get this question wrong by finding the price for one hamburger and then forgetting to double it. That's why you always have to make sure you know what's being asked.

STEP 2. DECIDE WHETHER TO DO IT NOW OR LATER

Before you try to solve the problem, decide whether you want to do it now or later. If you have no idea how to solve the problem, or if you think the problem will take a long time to solve, you should skip it and circle the question in your test booklet. Spend your time on the problems you can solve quickly, and then return to ones that give you trouble after you've finished the rest of the section.

STEP 3. LOOK FOR THE FASTEST WAY TO ANSWER THE QUESTION

Once you decide to tackle the question, it's time to look for shortcuts. Sometimes the obvious way to solve the problem is the long way. For instance, the obvious way here for many students would be to turn this word problem into two algebraic equations: $2H + 5F = 4H + 2F$, and $F = 1.50$. From there, you could substitute 1.50 for F in the first equation, solve for H, and then multiply your answer by 2.

But if you think carefully, there's often an easier approach. If two hamburgers and five orders of fries cost the same as four hamburgers and two orders of fries, take away all the items that are the same in the two orders, and you're left with three orders of fries costing the same as two hamburgers. Because one order of fries costs $1.50, three orders cost $4.50, so $4.50 must also be the cost of two hamburgers. The correct answer is (C), and you didn't even have to set up any algebraic equations.

MATH SHORTCUTS: STUDENT TESTED, KAPLAN APPROVED

Because saving time is a big part of doing well on the PSAT, shortcuts can be a really big help. Now, sometimes the textbook approach will be the best way to the answer

EXPERT TUTOR TIP

" A great habit to get into is to underline exactly what the question is asking for. (Hint: it's usually right by the question mark.) Many times the correct answer will not be the most obvious item to solve for. "

on the PSAT. However, other times, as we've just seen, shortcuts will get you to the correct answer more quickly and easily. The key is to be open to creative approaches to problem solving. On regular math questions, the answer is right in front of you—you just have to decide which answer of five is the correct one. We have three shortcuts that are extremely useful when you don't see—or would rather not use—the textbook approach to solving the question. They are as follows:

- Picking numbers
- Backsolving
- Eyeballing

Keep in mind that these shortcuts aren't *always* faster than using textbook methods, but they are always a great way to make confusing problems more concrete. If you know how to apply these shortcuts, you will get the correct answer every time you use them. Let's take a look.

PICKING NUMBERS

Here's what we mean by picking numbers to make an abstract problem concrete.

> If a, b, and c are all odd integers, which of the
> following must be odd?
>
>   I. $ab + c$
>
>   II. $c(ab + 3)$
>
> III. $2a + bc$
>
> (A) I only
>
> (B) III only
>
> (C) I and III
>
> (D) II and III
>
> (E) I, II, and III

Rather than try to think this one through abstractly, it's easier for most students to pick numbers for a, b, and c. Because a, b, and c are all odd, you could pick $a = 1$, $b = 3$, and $c = 5$. There are rules for adding, subtracting, and multiplying odd and even integers, but there's no need to memorize the rules if you pick numbers. Let's see what happens when we plug these numbers into the expressions.

>   I. $1 \times 3 + 5 = 8$ Even
>
>   II. $5(1 \times 3 + 3) = 30$ Even
>
> III. $2 \times 1 + 3 \times 5 = 17$ Odd

We can eliminate any answer choice that includes I or II: (A), (C), (D), (E).

So the correct answer must be (B).

Here's another abstract question that can be made concrete by picking numbers. It's the classic *remainder* question.

> When n is divided by 14, the remainder is 10.
> What is the remainder when n is divided by 7?
>
> (A) 2
> (B) 3
> (C) 4
> (D) 5
> (E) 6

You first have to pick a number for n. The easiest strategy is to pick $n = 24$ (because $14 + 10 = 24$). Now, try your number out: $24 \div 7 = 3$, with remainder of 3. Thus, the answer is (B).

PICKING NUMBERS: WORD PROBLEMS WITH VARIABLES

Picking numbers works great not only on odd/even and remainder problems, but also on word problems that contain variables. This is great news because these problems can be especially confusing on the PSAT. Give the following question a try.

> Four years from now, Ray will be twice as old as his sister will be then. If Ray is now R years old, how many years old is his sister now?
>
> (A) $\dfrac{R-4}{2}$
> (B) $R - 4$
> (C) $\dfrac{R+4}{2}$
> (D) $R - 2$
> (E) $2R - 4$

If you *love* to translate word problems into algebra equations, that's fine, you absolutely can if it gets you right answers! But picking numbers can be easier and safer. Here's how you do it. Begin by picking a number for R, Ray's age now. Let's make it a nice and simple round number such as $R = 10$. Now substitute 10 for R in the question and the answer choices, and you're left with the following, much simpler problem:

Four years from now, Ray will be twice as old as his sister will be then. If Ray is now 10 years old, how many years old is his sister now?

(A) $\dfrac{10-4}{2}$, or 3

(B) $10 - 4$, or 6

(C) $\dfrac{10+4}{2}$, or 7

(D) $10 - 2$, or 8

(E) $2 \times 10 - 4$, or 16

Now let's see. Ray is 10 years old, so in four years, he'll be 14, which means his sister will be 7 years old then. Because she'll be 7 in four years, that means she must be 3 years old now. The correct answer must be (A).

As we've just seen, picking numbers on word problems containing variables involves the following the steps:

THREE-STEP PICKING NUMBERS METHOD

Step 1. Pick nice, easy numbers for the variables in your question.

Step 2. Answer the question using the numbers you've picked. This answer is your target number.

Step 3. Substitute the numbers you picked for the variables in the answer choices. See which answer gives you your target number.

> **EXPERT TUTOR TIP**
>
> " Make sure to test all of the answer choices if you are picking numbers. Sometimes the number you have selected will satisfy more than one choice. When that happens, it's usually because you have chosen the most obvious number, usually 1, 2, or 0. Hint: when prompted for an odd number, try 3 instead. You'll most likely avoid a possible trap that way. "

To be safe, you should always try out all the answer choices. If more than one answer choice gives you your target number, pick different numbers to eliminate the remaining wrong answers. Don't worry. This rarely happens, and it doesn't take much time to pick numbers twice.

Not only does picking numbers make problems such as the previous one easier to understand, but when you solve a problem by picking numbers, you can be sure you got the right answer; thus, there's no need to double-check your work.

PICKING NUMBERS: WORD PROBLEMS WITH UNKNOWN VALUES + PERCENTS OR FRACTIONS

The problems we've just looked at all contain variables in the answer choices, but there are two other types of questions where picking numbers comes in handy. These are word problems that contain unknown values and either *percents* or *fractions* in the answer choices. The key to solving these problems quickly lies in knowing how to pick good numbers. Let's take a look.

The value of a certain stock rose by 30 percent from March to April and then decreased by 20 percent from April to May. The stock's value in May was what percent of its value in March?

(A) 90%

(B) 100%

(C) 104%

(D) 110%

(E) 124%

Notice that even though the question involves the value of a certain stock, that value is never given. If we pick a number for the value of the stock, we can see much more easily what is going on. On percent problems, you're almost always better off picking 100 for the unknown value. Let's say the stock originally cost $100. If it rose by 30 percent from March to April, its value in April would have been $130. If the value then decreased by 20 percent in May, 20 percent of $130 is $26, so the value drops to $104 in May. Because $104 is 104 percent of $100, the correct answer is (C).

Did you follow? Let's look at another word problem, although this time the answers are fractions.

Keiko spent $\frac{1}{4}$ of her monthly salary on a television and spent half of what was left to pay her rent and utility bills. If she spent $\frac{2}{3}$ of her remaining salary on other expenses and put what was left into her savings account, what fraction of her monthly salary went into her savings account?

(A) $\frac{1}{6}$

(B) $\frac{1}{8}$

(C) $\frac{1}{12}$

(D) $\frac{1}{24}$

(E) $\frac{1}{36}$

Our general rule for picking numbers on fraction problems is to pick the largest number from among the denominators in the answer choices. But sometimes when you start with the largest denominator in the answer choices, you quickly see that this isn't the best number. If you assume that Keiko starts with $36, she spends $\frac{1}{4}$ of that, or $9, on a television. That leaves her with $27. She is supposed to spend half of that on rent and utilities, but 27 divided by 2 does not equal a whole number. As soon as the numbers start to get ugly, you know it's time to try the next highest denominator.

Let's say that Keiko starts with $24. She spends $\frac{1}{4}$ of that, or $6, on a television. That leaves her with $18. She spends half of that on rent and utilities, so she's left with $9. She spends $\frac{2}{3}$ of that on other expenses, leaving her with $3. She puts that into her savings account, so she puts $\frac{3}{24} = \frac{1}{8}$ of her monthly salary into her savings account. The correct answer must be (B).

PICKING NUMBERS SUMMARIZED

Remember that you can pick numbers if:

- There is a variable in the answer choice. This is the most common and most important time. Remember, if there is a variable, picking numbers will always get you the right answer. Unless you have a good reason not to, you should always pick numbers if there are variables in the answer choices.

- There is a percent or fraction in the answer choice. Remember to think about what number you should pick—some numbers work much better than others.

- There is an unknown value in the problem. Just think, this unknown value could have been represented as a variable, in which case we would be right back to where we were with variables in the answer choice.

BACKSOLVING

In the picking numbers problems, the answer choices contained variables, percents, or fractions. But some of the nastier PSAT Math problems have numbers in the answer choices, so picking numbers won't work. On these questions, try backsolving instead.

When you backsolve, you simply plug the answers back into the question until you find one that works. If you do it systematically, it shouldn't take you too much time. Here's the system.

THREE-STEP BACKSOLVING METHOD

Step 1. Start with choice (C).

Step 2. Eliminate choices you know are too big or too small.

Step 3. Keep going until you find the choice that works.

Watch and learn.

> In a certain school, the ratio of boys to girls is 3:7. If there are 84 more girls than boys, how many boys are there?
>
> (A) 36
> (B) 48
> (C) 63
> (D) 84
> (E) 147

The correct answer should yield a ratio of boys to girls of 3:7, so try out (C).

If there are 63 boys, there are $63 + 84 = 147$ girls, so the ratio of boys to girls is $\frac{63}{147} = \frac{9}{21} = \frac{3}{7}$, which is just what we are looking for. That means we're done.

Okay, so that was kind of easy. The answer isn't *always* (C). But usually, when you start with (C) and it doesn't work, you'll know which direction to go. Either (C) will be too big or too small, leaving you with only two answers that could possibly be correct. Let's try the example from earlier in the chapter.

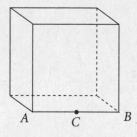

> If the surface area of the cube above is 96, and *C* is the midpoint of *AB*, what is the length of *AC*?
>
> (A) 1
> (B) 2
> (C) 2.5
> (D) 3
> (E) 4

For some reason, when the problem involves geometry, many students completely forget that there are shortcuts to the answer. On a confusing geometry problem with numbers in the answer choices, backsolving is definitely the way to go.

Start with (C): If $AC = 2.5$, the edge length of the cube is 5, so each face of the cube is $5^2 = 25$ square inches. There are six faces to a cube, so the entire surface area would be $25 \times 6 = 150$ square inches. This is too large, so (C), (D), and (E) are all out.

Try (B): If $AC = 2$, the edge length of the cube is 4, so each face of the cube is 4^2 square inches. There are six faces to a cube, so the entire surface area would be 96 square inches. The answer is (B).

BACKSOLVING SUMMARIZED

Remember that you can backsolve if:

- You see the phrase "What is the value of x?" or "How many ...?" There are a few exceptions, but in general, when you see one of these phrases you can (and should) backsolve.
- There is an equation in the problem and numbers in the answer choices. The numbers normally stand for a single part of a larger equation or expression, so more than likely you can backsolve.

Now let's take a look at one last shortcut that can help you out in a pinch on tough geometry problems.

EYEBALLING

One of the nice things about PSAT geometry problems is that, according to the test maker's own rules, the figure will always be drawn to scale unless you are told it is not: "Note: Figure not drawn to scale."

Why is this such a nice thing? It means when you're in doubt, you can always trust your eyes. On about half of all diagram questions, you can get a reasonable answer without solving anything. This technique works especially well on difficult geometry problems.

Here's a tough one that you might just want to answer by eyeballing:

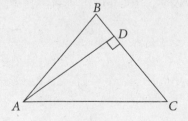

If $AB = 5$, $BC = 5$, and $AC = 6$, what is the length of AD ?

(A) $4\sqrt{3}$

(B) $4\frac{4}{5}$

(C) 4

(D) $2\sqrt{3}$

(E) $2\frac{2}{5}$

You can eliminate at least three of the five answer choices by estimating roughly. Eyeballing should tell you that AD is slightly smaller than AB, so it's just slightly less than 5. Going to the answer choices:

(A) $4\sqrt{3} \approx 6.93$. This is too big. Eliminate.

(B) $4\frac{4}{5}$

(C) 4

(D) $2\sqrt{3} \approx 3.46$. This is too small. Eliminate.

(E) $2\frac{2}{5}$ is too small. Eliminate.

But you can do even better than that. If you take the edge of a piece of paper and mark it to make a ruler, you'll see that AB is only very slightly longer than AD. Choice (B) is therefore the best answer.

THE THREE TECHNIQUES SUMMARIZED

While eyeballing is a fairly straightforward technique, picking numbers and backsolving can take some effort to master. In order to save time with these techniques, you need to know exactly *how* and *when* to use them. Therefore, it is important to practice these techniques whenever the problem can be solved with one of them.

In order to help you with this, we have identified every problem in the book that can be solved with one of these techniques. If you look in the Answers and Explanations sections of the practice problems and Practice Tests, you will see symbols for backsolving, picking numbers, or eyeballing next to the answer choices. These symbols mean that the problems can be solved with one of these techniques. Since the techniques are explained in their own sections, we normally avoid using them in the actual explanations of the answers. Just know that any problem that has one of these symbols can be solved with those techniques, and it is a great idea to explore these different methods in your practice.

Okay, you have been very patient. We know you have been reading through this stage with one question gnawing at your gut:

What about calculators?

CALCULATORS AND THE PSAT

On the PSAT, just like on the SAT, students are allowed to use calculators on the Math sections. Does this mean a perfect score is now within your grasp? Probably not, unless you were really close to begin with.

The best calculator in the world is not going to improve your PSAT Math score dramatically. In fact, since students were first allowed to use calculators on the PSAT, the test makers have made it their mission to write math problems that offer no advantage to using a calculator. The nerve! In fact, you can easily be tempted to waste a lot of time using the calculator on questions that don't actually require lengthy computations. Remember, you don't need to use a calculator to answer any math question on the PSAT.

The more familiar you become with the PSAT Math problems and the best ways to solve them, the less tempted you'll be to automatically pull out your calculator on every question. We do not, however, recommend that you avoid using a calculator altogether. Research has shown that students who use calculators on the PSAT perform slightly better than students who do not.

It's just that you have to know how to use a calculator, when to use a calculator, and when not to use a calculator. That's where we come in.

WHEN TO USE ONE

Calculators are most helpful on Grid-ins. Grid-ins require you to be especially careful with your calculations because there are no answer choices to help you out. But you still have to know how to use your calculator selectively. Consider this problem:

> If a gallon of fertilizer covers an area of 300 square feet and costs $4.75, what is the cost in dollars to fertilize a level rectangular field that measures 160 feet by 750 feet? (Disregard $ sign when gridding in your answer.)

This word problem has two steps. First, you have to set up a proportion:

$$\frac{\$4.75}{300 \text{ sq ft}} = \frac{x}{160 \text{ ft} \times 750 \text{ ft}}$$

After a bit of manipulating, you're ready to whip out the calculator:

$$\frac{4.75 \times 160 \times 750}{300} = x, \text{ so } x = 1,900$$

WHEN NOT TO USE ONE

The rule is pretty simple. Any time a question involves a ton of calculating, there's bound to be an easier approach. For instance, try the following:

$2(9 - 6)^2 + 56 \div 4 =$

(A)   18.5

(B)   32

(C)   50

(D)   95

(E)   158

Simply plugging the numbers and operations into the calculator will just create trouble. You must follow PEMDAS: $2(9 - 6)^2 + 56 \div 4 = 2(3)^2 + 56 \div 4 = 18 + 14 = 32$. The correct answer is (B).

If you don't know the order of operations PEMDAS (or its helpful mnemonic: Please Excuse My Dear Aunt Sally), many calculators will get this question wrong. Some graphing calculators will resolve complex equations if you plug the whole thing in correctly, but not always, and that's no replacement for knowing the rules. What PEMDAS means is: first you do all the stuff inside Parentheses, then all the Exponents, then all the Multiplication and Division (together, going from left to right), and then all the Addition and Subtraction (likewise). So with the calculator, do not make these following steps your first:

- Grab calculator.

- Punch in all the numbers.

- Put down an answer and hope you didn't screw up.

Instead, try this approach:

- Think first.

- Decide on the best way to solve it.

- Then—and only then—use your calculator.

> **EXPERT TUTOR TIP**
>
> " Remember, you should always do as much work as you can with paper and pencil, only using the calculator when you come to arithmetic that would take a long time to do by hand. "

BASIC MATH AND HOW TO ATTACK IT

It's impossible to cover every problem-solving technique that can help you on the PSAT Math section. If you find yourself struggling with the practice set at the end of the chapter or on any of the Practice Tests in this book, you should spend some time studying the 100 Essential Math Concepts at the back of this book. It reviews the recommended approaches to almost any kind of math question that could appear on the PSAT.

That said, there are some problems that appear on just about every PSAT and deserve special mention. It's time now to take a look at them, along with Kaplan's techniques for solving them.

SYMBOLS

NUMBERS AND OPERATIONS; ALGEBRA AND FUNCTIONS

You can count on having at least one symbol question on the PSAT. Symbol questions can be scary because they contain weird-looking symbols that you've never seen before. Take a look:

> If $a \star b = a^2 b + a - b$ for all integers a and b, then
> $4 \star 3 =$
>
> (A) 12
> (B) 16
> (C) 37
> (D) 49
> (E) 111

No, they did not teach the star symbol on that day you were absent from algebra class. The PSAT writers like to put strange symbols in questions to confuse or unnerve you. Don't let them. Symbol questions really just test your ability to understand and follow directions. In fact, symbol problems look really hard, but often have the easiest math of any of the problems on the test.

For the above question, you just have to plug in 4 for a and 3 for b into the expression $a^2 b + a - b$. You should get $4 \star 3 = (4)^2(3) + 4 - 3 = 16 \times 3 + 4 - 3 = 48 + 4 - 3 = 49$. So (D) is the correct answer. It also deserves mention that sometimes symbol questions come in pairs. When this happens, the second question is almost always more difficult than the first, requiring more steps to solve it. But we still think you can handle it.

If $a \star b = a^2b + a - b$ for all integers a and b, then
$5 \star 3 =$

(A) $3 \star 5$

(B) $6 \star 2$

(C) $15 \star 1$

(D) $4 \star 4$

(E) $2 \star 25$

First, you have to figure out the value of $5 \star 3$.

$$5 \star 3 = (5)^2(3) + 5 - 3 = 25 \times 3 + 5 - 3 = 75 + 5 - 3 = 77$$

Now you have to go to the answer choices and find one that equals 77. You're likely to save time if you realize that answer choices with numbers that remind you of the original numbers in the question are usually traps:

(A) $3 \star 5$. Probable trap, so ignore for now.

(B) $6 \star 2 = 6^2(2) + 6 - 2 = 36 \times 2 + 6 - 2 = 72 + 6 - 2 = 76$. Eliminate.

(C) $15 \star 1$. Possible trap, so ignore for now.

(D) $4 \star 4 = 4^2(4) + 4 - 4 = 16 \times 4 + 4 - 4 = 64 + 4 - 4 = 64$. Eliminate.

(E) $2 \star 25 = 2^2(25) + 2 - 25 = 4 \times 25 + 2 - 25 = 100 + 2 - 25 = 77$. Bingo!

BEWARE!

Symbol answer choices that remind you too much of the *numbers* you're given (ignoring the *equation* you're given) are often traps. If you have to check out the answer choices, try those answer choices last.

AVERAGES

NUMBERS AND OPERATIONS; ALGEBRA AND FUNCTIONS

You're bound to see at least one average problem on the PSAT. There's not much to fear here because you just have to know the formula for solving average questions, i.e.,

$$\text{Average} = \frac{\text{Sum of terms}}{\text{Number of terms}}$$

EXPERT TUTOR TIP

Jot the average formula down when you are dealing with an average problem. However complicated the problem seems, it always comes back to this simple formula where if you know two parts of it, you can find the third.

Of course, PSAT average problems often put a slight spin on the formula. Take a look:

> The average age of the members in a five-person choir
> is 34. If the ages of four of the members are 47, 31, 27,
> and 36, what is the fifth member's age?
>
> (A) 29
>
> (B) 32
>
> (C) 34
>
> (D) 37
>
> (E) 41

HINT: Work with the sum.

Note that the average formula involves three elements: the average, the sum, and the number of terms. Thus, any time you are given two of the elements in the formula, you can automatically calculate the third element.

For instance, here you're told that the average age of the members in a five-person choir is 34. So that means you can calculate the sum of their ages: $34 = \dfrac{\text{Sum}}{5}$; therefore, the sum of their ages is 170. If we call the fifth member's age x, then $47 + 31 + 27 + 36 + x = 170$, so $x = 170 - 141 = 29$. The answer is (A).

Sometimes you may be asked to find the average of a large group of evenly spaced numbers. These questions would seem to require a lot of calculating.

But as you know, whenever it seems that you need to pull out a calculator and start punching away, there's got to be an easier approach. Try this one:

> What is the average (arithmetic mean) of all the even
> integers greater than 25 and less than 347?
>
> (A) 167
>
> (B) 175
>
> (C) 186
>
> (D) 206
>
> (E) 212

In case you never learned it, here's the trick. Whenever you're dealing with evenly spaced numbers, the average is equal to the average of the two outer numbers.

So in this case: $\text{Average} = \dfrac{26 + 346}{2} = \dfrac{372}{2} = 186$

EXPERT TUTOR TIP

If you use common sense, you can often ballpark the answer to an averages problem. If most of the given terms are more than the given average, then the unknown term must be less than the average to balance them out. Likewise, if adding a new term increases the average of a group, then the new term must be larger than the original average.

RATES

NUMBERS AND OPERATIONS; ALGEBRA AND FUNCTIONS

A rate is simply a word fraction. A rate compares *distance* over *time* or *amount* over *time* or *cost* over *units*. In other words:

$$\text{Rate} = \frac{\text{Distance}}{\text{Time}} \text{ or } \frac{\text{Amount}}{\text{Time}} \text{ or } \frac{\text{Cost}}{\text{Units}}$$

To solve a rate problem, you just have to set up a proportion, convert units if necessary, and solve. Try the following out for size:

> It takes Cameron 1 hour and 30 minutes to drive to work at an average speed of 40 miles per hour. If she returns home along the same route at an average speed of 45 miles per hour, how long, in minutes, does the return trip take?
>
> (A) 75
> (B) 80
> (C) 85
> (D) 90
> (E) 95

It takes Cameron 1 hour and 30 minutes (i.e., 1.5 hours) to travel at a rate of 40 miles per hour, so first figure out the distance from Cameron's home to work:

$\dfrac{40 \text{ miles}}{1 \text{ hour}} = \dfrac{\text{Distance}}{1.5 \text{ hours}}$, so the distance is $40 \times 1.5 = 60$ miles.

Furthermore, if she travels at a new rate of 45 mph, her new traveling time would be:

$\dfrac{45 \text{ miles}}{1 \text{ hour}} = \dfrac{60 \text{ miles}}{x \text{ hour}}$, so $x = \dfrac{60}{45} = \dfrac{4}{3}$ hours, which equals $\dfrac{4}{3} \times 60 = 80$ minutes.

(B) is the correct answer.

SPECIAL TRIANGLES

GEOMETRY AND MEASUREMENT

Take it from people who've spent way too much time looking at PSAT: if there's one thing the PSAT Math test makers love, it's a triangle. And if there's one kind of triangle they really can't get enough of, it's a special triangle.

Just what are these special triangles? Take a look.

EXPERT TUTOR TIP

" Watch your units when faced with a rate problem. Sometimes the problem will force you to make a common conversion, such as hours to minutes or years to days. Many rate problems on the PSAT use variables rather than numbers. On these, we strongly recommend that you pick numbers! "

Note: Figure not drawn to scale.

In $\triangle ABC$ above, $AB = 5$ and $AC = 8$. If $\triangle ABC$ is isosceles and $BC <$ AC, what is the area of this triangle?

(A) 10

(B) 12

(C) 16

(D) 18

(E) 24

Special triangles are triangles that convey a lot of information. For instance, if you know the length of one side of a 30-60-90 triangle, you can easily work out the lengths of the other sides.

Special triangles allow you to transfer one piece of information around the whole figure. Before we solve the above problem, here are all the special triangles that you should look out for on the PSAT. It's a good idea to memorize the ratios, although many of them are listed in the instructions. But even more important, you should be familiar enough with the triangles to recognize them when you see them.

EQUILATERAL TRIANGLE

All interior angles are 60°, and all the sides are the same length. You may want to memorize the area formula for an equilateral triangle, which is Area $= \dfrac{\sqrt{3}}{4}(\text{side})^2$.

ISOSCELES TRIANGLE

Two sides are the same length, and the angles opposite these sides are equal.

RIGHT TRIANGLES

These contain a 90° angle. The sides are related by the Pythagorean theorem: $a^2 + b^2 = c^2$, where a and b are the legs and c is the hypotenuse.

THE *SPECIAL* RIGHT TRIANGLES

GEOMETRY AND MEASUREMENT

Many triangle problems contain *special* right triangles whose lengths always come in predefined ratios. If you recognize them, you won't have to use the Pythagorean theorem to find the value of a missing side.

THE ISOSCELES RIGHT TRIANGLE

Note the side ratio: 1 to 1 to $\sqrt{2}$. Also note that this triangle is half a square divided diagonally.

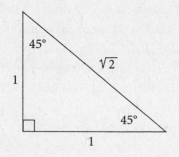

THE 30-60-90 RIGHT TRIANGLE

Note the side ratio: 1 to $\sqrt{3}$ to 2. Also note that this triangle is half an equilateral triangle divided along its height.

THE 3-4-5 AND 5-12-13 RIGHT TRIANGLES

Be on the lookout for multiples of 3-4-5 and 5-12-13 as well.

Now let's get back to our previous example. If you drop a vertical line from B to line AC, the triangle divides into two 3-4-5 right triangles. Now it's easy to find the area.

Area $= \dfrac{1}{2}bh$.

The base is 8, and the height is 3, so Area $= \dfrac{1}{2}(8 \times 3) = \dfrac{1}{2}(24) = 12$.

The correct answer is (B).

ADVANCED MATH AND HOW TO ATTACK IT

SETS

ALGEBRA AND FUNCTIONS

The things in a set are called *elements*, or *members*. The PSAT will likely ask a question about the union or intersection of two sets. The union of Set A and Set B, sometimes expressed as $A \cup B$, is the set of elements that are in either or both of Set A and Set B. If Set $A = \{1, 2\}$ and Set $B = \{3, 4\}$, then $A \cup B = \{1, 2, 3, 4\}$. The intersection of Set A and Set B, sometimes expressed as $A \cap B$, is the set of elements common to both Set A and Set B. If Set $A = \{1, 2, 3\}$ and Set $B = \{3, 4, 5\}$, then $A \cap B = \{3\}$. Here's a sample question:

> Set A consists of all the even integers greater than 5. Set B consists of all the numbers greater than 2 and less than 7. Which of the following numbers is in the union, but not the intersection, of Sets A and B?
>
> (A) 1
> (B) 2
> (C) 4
> (D) 6
> (E) 9

The union of two sets consists of all the elements that are in either set. The intersection consists of all the elements that are in *both* sets. You need to find a number that is in one set but not in both sets. (A), (B), and (E) are not in either set. (D) is in both sets. So (C) is the answer. Let's do another.

> Set K consists of all the negative integers greater than or equal to −100. Set L consists of all the numbers which have an absolute value equal to or less than 5. How many elements are in the intersection of sets K and L?
>
> (A) 5
> (B) 6
> (C) 10
> (D) 12
> (E) infinitely many

(A) is the answer. The intersection of two sets consists of the elements found in both sets. How many numbers are in both set K and set L? Set L consists of all numbers between −5 and 5, including the endpoints. Set K contains 5 of these numbers: −5, −4, −3, −2, and −1. Thus, (A) is the correct answer.

SEQUENCES INVOLVING EXPONENTIAL GROWTH

ALGEBRA AND FUNCTIONS

In a geometric sequence, if r is the ratio between consecutive terms, a_1 is the first term, and a_n is the nth term, then $a_n = a_1 r^{n-1}$. Here's an example:

If the fourth term in a geometric sequence is 81, and the ratio between terms is 3, what is the first term?

(A) 3

(B) 6

(C) 9

(D) 18

(E) 27

Use $a_n = a_1 r^{n-1}$ to solve for the first term:

$$81 = a_1 3^3$$
$$81 = a_1 27$$
$$a_1 = 3$$

So the answer is (A).

ABSOLUTE VALUE

ALGEBRA AND FUNCTIONS

The absolute value of a number is the distance of the number from zero on the number line. Because absolute value is a distance, *it is always positive*. So the absolute value of 7 is 7; this is expressed $|7| = 7$. Similarly, the absolute value of -7 is 7: $|-7| = 7$. Every positive number (like 7) is the absolute value of two numbers: itself (7) and its negative (-7).

If $|b - 7| = 0$, which of the following must be true?

(A) $|b^2 - 7| = 0$

(B) $|b + 7| = 0$

(C) $b = 7$

(D) $b = -7$

(E) $|b + 7| = 7$

If $|b - 7| = 0$, that means the distance on the number line between b and 7 is 0. Therefore, b must equal 7. None of the answer choices other than (C) is true when $b = 7$.

Ready for another one? Wonderful.

EXPERT TUTOR TIP

Don't forget:

If solving for x in |x|, the answer could be x or –x.

Which of the following inequalities best describes the indicated values on the number line above?

(A) $|x + 5| \le 3$

(B) $|x - 3| \le 5$

(C) $|x - 3| \le 0$

(D) $|x + 1| \le 3$

(E) $|x + 1| \le 4$

(E) is the answer. The easiest way to solve this problem is probably to plug the largest and smallest values given into the answer choices to see if they fit. For example, $|3 + 5| = 8$, which is not less than or equal to 3, so (A) is incorrect. You could also note that the center of the highlighted values is -1. The endpoints are each 4 units away. Therefore, the difference between any highlighted value x and -1 must be less than or equal to 4. This can be written as $|x - (-1)| = |x + 1| \le 4$.

RATIONAL EQUATIONS

ALGEBRA AND FUNCTIONS

Your first goal when solving for a variable is to isolate that variable on one side of the equation. If you have a quadratic equation, try to factor it. If it can't be factored easily, you can use the quadratic formula $\left(x = \dfrac{-b \pm \sqrt{b^2 - 4ac}}{2a} \right)$, but most quadratic equations on the PSAT can be factored. Try one:

If $\dfrac{x^2 - 4x + 4}{x - 2} = 2$, what is the value of x?

(A) -4

(B) -2

(C) 0

(D) 2

(E) 4

The quadratic expression in the numerator can be factored, which allows you to simplify the problem considerably:

$\dfrac{x^2 - 4x + 4}{x - 2} = \dfrac{(x - 2)(x - 2)}{x - 2} = x - 2$. Since $x - 2 = 2$, $x = 4$.

> **EXPERT TUTOR TIP**
>
> " Become familiar with the classic quadratic expressions. The PSAT test makers aren't too imaginative and return to them frequently.
>
> $x^2 - y^2 = (x + y)(x - y)$
>
> $x^2 + 2xy + y^2 = (x + y)(x + y)$
>
> $x^2 - 2xy + y^2 = (x - y)(x - y)$ "

(E) is your answer. Let's try another.

If $\dfrac{a+4}{a^2+a+3} = 1$, what are the possible values of a?

(A) -1 and 0

(B) -1 and 1

(C) 0 and 1

(D) 0 and 3

(E) 1 and 2

(B) is the answer. Here's how we got it.

$$\frac{a+4}{a^2+a+3} = 1$$
$$a+4 = a^2+a+3$$
$$0 = a^2-1$$
$$0 = (a+1)(a-1)$$
$$a = 1 \text{ or } a = -1$$

RADICAL EQUATIONS

ALGEBRA AND FUNCTIONS

A radical equation contains at least one radical expression. Solve radical equations by using standard rules of algebra. If $5\sqrt{x} - 2 = 13$, then $5\sqrt{x} = 15$ and $\sqrt{x} = 3$, so $x = 9$.

If $2\sqrt{x} + 3 = 9$, what is the value of x?

(A) 1

(B) $\sqrt{3}$

(C) 3

(D) $\sqrt{6}$

(E) 9

Isolate $\sqrt{x}$ on one side of the equation, then square both sides:

$$2\sqrt{x} + 3 = 9$$
$$2\sqrt{x} = 6$$
$$\sqrt{x} = 3$$
$$x = 9$$

(E) is the correct answer.

Okay, again.

> **EXPERT TUTOR TIP**
>
> " Be careful when you are working through a problem with a radical to not let a rogue number "slide" under your radical sign. It's a very common error to make. "

If $4p = 8\sqrt{p}$ and $p \neq 0$, what is the value of p?

(A) 8

(B) 4

(C) 2

(D) $\sqrt{2}$

(E) $\dfrac{1}{\sqrt{2}}$

Again, isolate the radical term first, then square both sides of the equation:

$$4p = 8\sqrt{p}$$
$$p = 2\sqrt{p}$$
$$(p)^2 = (2\sqrt{p})^2$$
$$p^2 = 4p$$
$$p^2 - 4p = 0$$
$$p(p - 4) = 0$$
$$p = 0 \text{ or } p = 4$$

Eliminate $p = 0$, because you're given that $p \neq 0$; you're then left with $p = 4$.

(B) is the correct answer.

MANIPULATION WITH INTEGER AND RATIONAL EXPONENTS

ALGEBRA AND FUNCTIONS

To find the value of a number raised to a negative power, simply rewrite the number, without the negative sign, as the bottom of a fraction with 1 as the numerator of the fraction: $3^{-2} = \dfrac{1}{3^2} = \dfrac{1}{9}$. If x is a positive real number and a is a nonzero integer, then $x^{\frac{1}{a}} = \sqrt[a]{n}$. So $4^{\frac{1}{2}} = \sqrt[2]{4} = 2$. If p and q are integers, then $x^{\frac{p}{q}} = \sqrt[q]{x^p}$. So $4^{\frac{3}{2}} = \sqrt[2]{4^3} = \sqrt{64} = 8$.

If $m^{\frac{3}{2}}$ and $n^{\frac{4}{3}}$ are both greater than zero, which of the following must be true?

  I. $m > 0$

  II. $n > 0$

  III. $n \neq 0$

(A) I only

(B) III only

(C) I and III only

(D) II and III only

(E) I, II, and III

If you have trouble remembering the rules of exponents, try picking numbers for m and n to see which of the following answers could be correct. First off, you can think of $m^{\frac{3}{2}}$ as $(\sqrt{m})^3$. You can't take the square root of a negative number, so m has to be positive. Likewise, you can rewrite $n^{\frac{4}{3}}$ as $(\sqrt[3]{n})^4$. Whether n is positive or negative, a number raised to an even power is always positive, so n does not have to be positive. However, n cannot equal zero, because if $n = 0$, $n^{\frac{4}{3}}$ must also equal zero. So options I and III must be correct, but option II does not have to be true. Choice (C) is the answer. Let's try another one:

$$\text{If } q^{-\frac{1}{2}} > 1, q > 0, \text{ and } r^2 < 1, \text{ what is one possible value of } q + r?$$

Find the range of possible values for q and r, and then add them together: $q^{\frac{-1}{2}} > 1$

$$\frac{1}{\sqrt{q}} > 1$$
$$1 > \sqrt{q}$$
$$1 > q$$

So $0 < q < 1$

$$r^2 < 1$$
$$-1 < r < 1$$
$$-1 < q + r < 2, \text{ but you can't grid negative numbers,}$$
$$\text{so grid 0 or a number between 0 and 2.}$$

DIRECT AND INVERSE VARIATION

ALGEBRA AND FUNCTIONS

In direct variation, $y = kx$, where k is a nonzero constant. In direct variation, the variable y changes directly as x does. For example, if a unit of Currency A is worth 2 units of Currency B, then $A = 2B$. If the number of units of B were to double, the number of units of A would double, and so on for halving, tripling, etc. In inverse variation, $y = k/x$, where x and y are variables and k is a constant. A famous inverse relationship is *rate × time = distance*. Imagine having to cover a distance of 24 miles. If you were to travel at 12 miles per hour, you'd need two hours. But if you were to halve your rate, you would have to double your time. This is just another way of saying that rate and time vary inversely. Try this Grid-in:

> The number of pigeons and squirrels in Davies Park is described by the equation $ps = 1,000$, where p is the number of pigeons and s is the number of squirrels. If there are 100 pigeons in the park, how many squirrels are there?

This is really just a simple substitution problem—plug the given value of p into the equation and solve for s:

$$100s = 1,000$$
$$s = 10$$

Now let's do a multiple-choice question.

> The time Dave spends working on homework each week is directly proportional to the number of pages his teachers assign. One week, Dave's teachers assigned ten pages of homework, and he spent two hours working on it. Another week, Dave spent four hours and 24 minutes working on homework. How many pages did his teachers assign that week?
>
> (A) 10
> (B) 20
> (C) 22
> (D) 24
> (E) 26

> **EXPERT TUTOR TIP**
>
> " Remember:
> Direct Variation
> $y = kx$
> one goes up, the other goes up
>
> Inverse Variation
> $y = k/x$
> one goes up, the other goes down "

If the time Dave spends on homework is directly proportional to the number of pages assigned, the relationship between time spent (t) and pages assigned (n) can be expressed as $t = kn$, where k is a constant. You can use the first week's data to find k, then plug that in with the time spent in the second week to find the number of pages assigned that week.

$$120 \text{ minutes} = k(10 \text{ pages})$$

$$\frac{12 \text{ minutes}}{\text{page}} = k$$

$$264 \text{ minutes} = \frac{12 \text{ minutes}}{\text{page}} \times n$$

$$22 \text{ pages} = n$$

The answer is (C).

FUNCTIONS AS MODELS

ALGEBRA AND FUNCTIONS

The PSAT will likely ask you to glean and use information from tables like these.

	Number of plants		
	Bushes	Pine trees	Maple trees
Smith family	2	2	1
Jones family	3	2	4
Harris family	1	3	3

	Fertilizer needed each year (in liters)		
	Bush	Pine tree	Maple tree
In good soil	0.1	0	0.7
In poor soil	0.2	0.5	1.2

The tables above show the number of plants each of three families has around their houses and the amount of fertilizer each plant requires each year. The amount of fertilizer needed depends on whether the plant is in good soil or poor soil. If all the plants around the Jones family's house are in good soil, how much fertilizer does the Jones family need to apply each year?

(A) 1.4 L

(B) 2.2 L

(C) 3.1 L

(D) 5.2 L

(E) 6.4 L

You only need to use one line from each table. In this case, you need to know how many plants of each type the Jones family has and how much fertilizer each of those plants will need in good soil:

$$3(0.1) + 2(0) + 4(0.7) = 0.3 + 2.8 = 3.1$$

The answer is (C).

> If all the plants around the Harris family's house are in poor soil, how much fertilizer will the Harris family have to apply each year?
>
> (A) 1.2 L
>
> (B) 2.4 L
>
> (C) 3.1 L
>
> (D) 5.3 L
>
> (E) 6.4 L

Now you need to know how many plants of each type the Harris family has and how much fertilizer they need in poor soil:

$$1(0.2) + 3(0.5) + 3(1.2) = 0.2 + 1.5 + 3.6 = 5.3$$

(D) is the answer.

> The amount of time it takes for a company to produce a new software product can be represented by the equation $t = 140 - 6\sqrt{p}$, where t is the number of days it takes to produce the software and p is the number of programmers working on the project. This relationship holds as long as there is at least one programmer working on the project. How many programmers would the company need to complete a new product in 80 days?
>
> (A) 2
>
> (B) 5
>
> (C) 10
>
> (D) 100
>
> (E) 1,000

The answer is (D). This problem looks a little complicated, but all you have to do is solve the equation $t = 140 - 6\sqrt{p}$ when t equals 80:

$$80 = 140 - 6\sqrt{p}$$
$$6\sqrt{p} = 60$$

$$\sqrt{p} = 10$$
$$p = 100$$

(Backsolving would also work well here.)

LINEAR FUNCTIONS—EQUATIONS AND GRAPHS

ALGEBRA AND FUNCTIONS; GEOMETRY AND MEASUREMENT

EXPERT TUTOR TIP

❝ Remember:

Slope = m

m = change in y ÷ change in x

rise/run

$y_2 - y_1 / x_2 - x_1$ ❞

Which of the following equations represents a line parallel to line l above?

(A) $y = \dfrac{1}{2}x + 5$

(B) $y = \dfrac{2}{3}x + 2$

(C) $y = x - 2$

(D) $y = \dfrac{3}{2}x + 2$

(E) $y = 2x - 4$

Parallel lines have the same slope. First, calculate the slope of line l, then find the answer choice with that slope. Recall that slope is change in y over change in x: use the points (–4, 0) and (0, 2) on the line and the slope formula.

$$\frac{2 - 0}{0 - (-4)} = \frac{2}{4} = \frac{1}{2}$$

So the answer is (A). Let's do another.

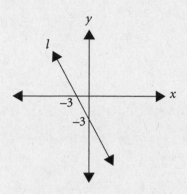

Note: Figure not drawn to scale.

Which of the following points is on line *l* in the graph above?

(A) $(-2, -5)$

(B) $(-1, -4)$

(C) $(-4, 5)$

(D) $(2, -5)$

(E) $(5, -2)$

When in doubt, use logic and eliminate answer choices that are obviously wrong. This makes your odds of guessing the right answer increase.

Use the given points, $(-3, 0)$ and $(0, -3)$, to determine the equation of line *l*:

$$y = mx + b$$
$$(-3) = m(0) + b$$
$$-3 = b$$
$$(0) = m(-3) + (-3)$$
$$3 = m(-3)$$
$$m = -1$$

So the equation of our line is $y = -x - 3$. Now we just plug in the points in the answer choices and see which one works:

$$y = -x - 3$$
$$(-5) = -(-2) - 3$$
$$-5 = -1$$

Choice (A) does not work.

$$y = -x - 3$$
$$(-4) = -(-1) - 3$$
$$-4 = -2$$

Choice (B) does not work.

$$y = -x - 3$$
$$(5) = -(-4) - 3$$
$$5 = 1$$

Choice (C) does not work.

$$y = -x - 3$$
$$(-5) = -(2) - 3$$
$$-5 = -5$$

Choice (D) works!

This is also a great example of a problem where you can use eyeballing to eliminate choices.

PROPERTIES OF TANGENT LINES

GEOMETRY AND MEASUREMENT

When a line is tangent to a circle, the radius of the circle is perpendicular to the line at the point of contact. Don't forget!

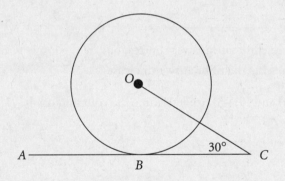

In the figure above, the center of the circle is O.
$\overline{AC}$ is tangent to the circle at its midpoint, B.
If $OC = 4\sqrt{3}$, what is the length of $\overline{AC}$?

(A) $2\sqrt{3}$

(B) 4

(C) 6

(D) $6\sqrt{3}$

(E) 12

What did we tell you not to forget? That's right—a line tangent to a circle is perpendicular to the radius of the circle. You can use this to sketch in a radius between O and B, creating a 30-60-90 special triangle. Then you can find BC, and from that AC.

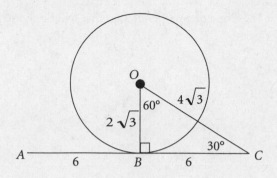

$6 + 6 = 12$

That would be (E).

COORDINATE GEOMETRY

GEOMETRY AND MEASUREMENT; ALGEBRA AND FUNCTIONS

> **EXPERT TUTOR TIP**
>
> " Remember, if a problem says *parallel* or *perpendicular*, you are going to have to find a slope. Parallel slopes are equal; perpendicular slopes are negative reciprocals. "

The figure above shows line *l*. Which of the following equations describes a line perpendicular to line *l*?

(A) $y = \dfrac{-3}{2}x + 1$

(B) $y = -3x + 2$

(C) $y = \dfrac{-2}{3}x + 4$

(D) $y = \dfrac{2}{3}x - 2$

(E) $y = \dfrac{3}{2}x + 3$

This problem is actually a little simpler than it looks. All you need to do is find the slope of line *l*, then find the slope of a line perpendicular to *l*. The slope of a line is equal to the change in *y* over the change in *x*. You can use two points from the graph, say $(0, -2)$ and $(3, 0)$, to find this. The slope of a perpendicular line will be the negative reciprocal of the slope of the other line.

Slope of l:

$$\frac{0-(-2)}{3-0} = \frac{2}{3}$$

Slope of perpendicular line:

$$\frac{-3}{2}$$

Only choice (A) has this slope. Let's try another one.

> $\overline{PQ}$ extends from $(1, 0)$ to $(5, 4)$. Which of the following equations describes a line that intersects $\overline{PQ}$ at its midpoint and is perpendicular to $\overline{PQ}$?
>
> (A) $y = -3x + 2$
> (B) $y = -2x + 3$
> (C) $y = -x$
> (D) $y = -x + 5$
> (E) $y = x + 5$

You will need to find the midpoint of $\overline{PQ}$, as well as its slope. You can then use the slope to find the slope of a line perpendicular to $\overline{PQ}$ and plug in the midpoint to find the y-intercept of the line using the equation $y = mx + b$.

Midpoint:

$$\frac{5+1}{2} = \frac{6}{2} = 3$$
$$\frac{4+0}{2} = 2$$

So the midpoint of $\overline{PQ}$ is $(3, 2)$.

Slope:

$$\frac{4-0}{5-1} = \frac{4}{4} = 1$$

So the slope of the perpendicular line is -1.

$$y = -1x + b$$
$$2 = -3 + b$$
$$5 = b$$

So the equation of the perpendicular line is $y = -x + 5$. Choice (D) is correct.

Data Interpretation, Including Scatterplots

Data Analysis, Statistics and Probability

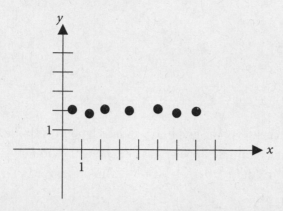

Which of the lines described by the following equations best fits these points?

(A) $y = 2x + 2$

(B) $y = 2x$

(C) $y = x + 2$

(D) $y = -x + 2$

(E) $y = 2$

Try to figure out what sort of line would fit these points. What should the slope be? What should the y-intercept be? If you think visually, you might want to try sketching the line described by each answer choice to see which one most nearly fits the points on the graph. A horizontal line has slope 0. These points are more or less horizontal, so we need to find an equation with a slope near or equal to 0. The only equation that has a slope of 0 is $y = 2$. That would be (E). Ready for another one?

Which of the lines described by the following equations best fits these points?

(A) $y = -4x$

(B) $y = -4x + 4$

(C) $y = -x - 4$

(D) $y = -x + 4$

(E) $y = x - 4$

Find the slope and y-intercept from the graph. Because each point is about as far below the previous point as it is to the right, the slope of this line should be around -1. The y-intercept is near 4. The equation that fits those criteria is $y = -x + 4$. In other words, (D).

GEOMETRIC PROBABILITY

DATA ANALYSIS, STATISTICS, AND PROBABILITY; GEOMETRY AND MEASUREMENT

Note: Figure not drawn to scale.

In the figure above, the circle is centered at O, has a radius of length one unit, and each side of the square has a length of one unit. What is the probability that a point selected randomly from inside the circle will lie within the square?

(A) $\dfrac{1}{\pi}$

(B) $\dfrac{1}{\pi^2}$

(C) $\dfrac{1}{2\pi}$

(D) $\dfrac{2}{\pi}$

(E) 2π

You'll need to find the area of the circle and the area of the square. The probability that a randomly selected point will lie within the square is the area of the square divided by the area of the circle.

Area of circle:

$$\pi(1)^2 = \pi$$

Area of square:

$$(1)^2 = 1$$

Probability:

$$\frac{1}{\pi}$$

The answer is (A).

Let's try another one using the same figure on the previous page.

If a point is selected at random from the interior of the circle, what is the probability that it will lie outside the square?

(A) $\dfrac{1}{\pi}$

(B) $\dfrac{\pi - 1}{\pi}$

(C) $\dfrac{1}{\pi}$

(D) $\pi - 1$

(E) $\pi^2 - 1$

The answer is (B), and there are two ways to get to it. First, the probability of selecting a point outside the square will equal 1 minus the probability of selecting a point inside the square, which you calculated in the last problem. Second, you could find the area of the part of the circle that is outside the square, and then divide that by the total area of the circle.

Total area of circle:	$\pi(1)^2 = \pi$
Area of square:	$(1)^2 = 1$
Area of circle outside of square:	$\pi - 1$
Probability:	$\dfrac{\pi - 1}{\pi}$

EXPERT TUTOR TIP

" In problems dealing with median and mode, sometimes the PSAT can try to trick you by presenting the list of terms out of order. Don't be fooled! A median is the middle term when the numbers are arranged in sequential order. "

MEDIAN AND MODE

DATA ANALYSIS, STATISTICS, AND PROBABILITY

In a set of numbers, the median divides the set into an upper and lower half. The median of $\{1, 2, 3, 4, 5\}$ is 3. The median of $\{-4, 0, \frac{1}{2}, \pi, 479\}$ is $\frac{1}{2}$. Note that in these two examples, the sets contained an odd number of elements. To find the median of a set with an even number of elements, simply take the average of the two middle numbers. For example, the median of $\{3, 4, 5, 6\}$ is 4.5, the average of 4 and 5. In a set of evenly spaced numbers, the median equals the average. For example, the median of $\{10, 30, 50, 70, 90\}$ is 50—the average of 10, 30, 50, 70, and 90. (For that matter, it is also the average of 90 and 10 only, as well as of 70 and 30 only.) The mode is the element that appears most frequently in a set. The mode of $\{0, 0, 1, 1, 1, 2\}$ is 1, because it appears three times—more than any other element.

What is the positive difference between the median
and mode of the set $\{-1, -1, 0, 0, 0, 4, 7, 7, 7, 7, 7\}$?

The median of the set is 4: five elements are smaller than it, and five are greater than it. The mode of the set is 7—the number that appears more than any other in the set. The positive difference between 4 and 7 is 3.

PRACTICE

Ready for a little quiz? Great, let's go.

1. If $c \neq 0$, then $\dfrac{c^5}{c^4} - \dfrac{c^3}{c^2} =$

   (A) $2c$

   (B) c

   (C) 2

   (D) 1

   (E) 0

2. The ratio of girls to boys in a class is 3:5. If there are 15 girls, how many boys must there be in the class?

   (A) 10

   (B) 18

   (C) 21

   (D) 25

   (E) 30

3. If $a^2 - 1 = (a - 1)^2$, what is the value of a?

   (A) −1

   (B) 0

   (C) 1

   (D) 2

   (E) 3

4. In a plane, lines r and s are drawn such that $r \Vert s$. If a third line t is drawn such that $t \perp s$, and a fourth line u is drawn such that $u \Vert s$, which of the following statements must be true?

   I. $t \perp r$

   II. $s \perp u$

   III. $r \Vert u$

   (A) I only

   (B) II only

   (C) III only

   (D) I and II

   (E) I and III

5. If 9 is x percent of 90, what is 50 percent of x?

   (A) 5

   (B) 9

   (C) 10

   (D) 15

   (E) 18

RANGE OF TEMPERATURES IN SELECTED
CITIES IN 1992 (IN DEGREES CELSIUS)

6. In the graph above, which city had the greatest difference between highest and lowest temperatures in 1992?

(A) Appleton
(B) Bellefield
(C) Centerville
(D) Deerwood
(E) Eastview

7. In the figure above, rectangle WXYZ is divided into six squares. If the area of each square is 2, what is the area of the shaded region?

(A) 2.5
(B) 3
(C) 4.5
(D) 5
(E) 6

8. If the average (arithmetic mean) of 20, 37, 40, and y is $y - 2$, what is the value of y?

(A) 33
(B) 34
(C) 35
(D) 36
(E) 37

Note: Figure not drawn to scale.

9. In the figure above, if the area of triangle XYZ is $4a$, what is the perimeter of triangle XYZ?

(A) 14
(B) 16
(C) 18
(D) 20
(E) 24

10. The cost of a taxi ride in a certain city is $1.25 for the first half-mile and $0.25 for each each additional $\frac{1}{8}$ of a mile. If a taxi ride costs $7.75, which of the following could be the length of the ride in miles?

(A) $3\frac{3}{8}$

(B) $3\frac{1}{2}$

(C) $3\frac{3}{4}$

(D) $3\frac{7}{8}$

(E) 4

11. Circle A has a circumference of 4π, and circle B has a circumference of 36π. If the circles intersect at exactly one point, which of the following could be the distance from the center of circle A to the center of circle B?

    (A) 10
    (B) 12
    (C) 14
    (D) 16
    (E) 18

12. A broken watch loses 15 minutes per hour. If this watch is set to the correct time at 6 o'clock, what is the least number of hours that it would take this watch to show the correct time again?

    (A) 12
    (B) 24
    (C) 36
    (D) 48
    (E) 60

13. If $|b-3| = 6$, what are the two possible values of b?

    (A) -9 and 3
    (B) -9 and 9
    (C) -6 and 6
    (D) -3 and 3
    (E) -3 and 9

14. Which of the following lines is parallel to the line $y = 4x - 6$?

    (A) $y = \dfrac{1}{4}x - 6$
    (B) $y = \dfrac{1}{2}x + 3$
    (C) $y = 2x - 6$
    (D) $y = 2x - 3$
    (E) $y = 4x + 6$

15. If $\dfrac{3}{x-6} = 3$, what is the value of x?

    (A) 3
    (B) 6
    (C) 7
    (D) 12
    (E) 14

16. If $x = \dfrac{1}{5}$, $x^{-3} =$

    (A) -25
    (B) $-\dfrac{1}{125}$
    (C) 5
    (D) $\dfrac{1}{25}$
    (E) 125

17. If $xy = k$, where k is a constant, what happens to the value of x if the value of y is halved?

    (A) It doubles.
    (B) It halves.
    (C) It increases $\sqrt{2}$ times.
    (D) It squares.
    (E) It remains the same.

Note: Figure not drawn to scale.

18. In $\overline{PS}$ above, $PQ = 3$, $RS = 10$, and $PS = 19$. What is the measure of QR?

    (A) 2
    (B) 3
    (C) 6
    (D) 9
    (E) 10

19. If P is the set of all numbers between -5.5 and 5.5, inclusive, Q is the set of all prime numbers, and R is the set of all positive odd integers, then the intersection of P, Q, and R contains how many elements?

    (A) 0
    (B) 1
    (C) 2
    (D) 3
    (E) 5

20. The initial number of elements in a certain set is p, where $p > 0$. If the number of elements in the set doubles every hour, which of the following represents the total number of elements in the set after exactly 48 hours?

    (A) $24p$
    (B) $48p$
    (C) $2p^{24}$
    (D) $(2^{48})p$
    (E) $(2p)^{48}$

21. If the price of one grapefruit is \$0.45 and the price of one orange is \$0.20, how many oranges are equal in cost to 16 grapefruit?

22. The integer p is divisible by 3, and when p is divided by 10, the remainder is 2. If p is greater than 100 and less than 200, what is one possible value of p?

23. The perimeter of a rectangle is 14. If the length of the rectangle is greater than 6, what is one possible value for the width?

25. At a certain company, the number of production employees was increased from 300 to 390. The number of clerical employees was increased by twice the percent increase of the production employees. If the final number of clerical employees was 192, what was the original number of clerical employees?

24. In the rectangular solid above, $AB = 3$, $BC = 4$, and $FC = 12$. What is the area of triangle ACF?

ANSWERS AND EXPLANATIONS

 Picking Numbers

 Backsolving

 Eyeballing

1. E

Simplify each term using rules of exponents. When dividing like bases, subtract the exponents:

$\frac{c^5}{c^4} = c^{5-4} = c^1$ which equals c;

$\frac{c^3}{c^2} = c^{3-2}$, or c^1 which also equals c.

Since $c - c = 0$, (E) is correct.

2. D

A ratio can also be written as a fraction. If the ratio of girls to boys is 3:5, then $\frac{\text{girls}}{\text{boys}} = \frac{3}{5}$. You're given that there are 15 girls, so set up a proportion to find the number of boys: let b be the number of boys. So, $\frac{3}{5} = \frac{15}{b}$. Cross-multiply and solve for b: $3b = 5 \times 15$, or 75. Divide both sides by 3 to get $b = 25$, so (D) is correct.

3. C

Using the FOIL method to expand $(a - 1)^2$, or $(a - 1)(a - 1)$, we get $a^2 - a - a + 1$, or $a^2 - 2a + 1$. So $a^2 - 1 = a^2 - 2a + 1$. Subtract a^2 from both sides: $-1 = -2a + 1$. Now subtract 1 from both sides, which gives you $-2 = -2a$, or $1 = a$. So (C) is correct.

4. E

Draw a diagram. Draw r and s parallel to each other. Then draw t perpendicular to s. Notice that t is also perpendicular to r, so (I) is true. Now draw u parallel to s. Notice that u is parallel to r and s, so (III) is true.

Since s is parallel to u, the lines cannot be perpendicular so (II) is false. Therefore, (E) is the correct answer.

5. A

If 9 is x percent of 90, then $9 = \frac{x}{100} \times 90$, or $9 = \frac{9x}{10}$. Multiply both sides by the reciprocal of $\frac{9}{10}$ to get $\frac{10}{9} \times 9 = \frac{10}{9} \times \frac{9x}{10}$, or $10 = x$. So 50% of x is 50% of 10. That is $\frac{1}{2} \times 10$, or 5. Therefore, (A) is correct.

6. B

The highest temperature in a particular town is the value corresponding to the top of that town's bar, and the lowest temperature is the value corresponding to the bottom of that bar. So the town with the longest bar will have the greatest difference in temperatures. Looking at the graph, you can see that the longest bar corresponds to Bellefield. Therefore, Bellefield has the greatest difference in temperature, so (B) is correct.

7. D

Looking at the diagram, you can see that there are 4 squares that are half shaded and 2 squares that are a quarter shaded. So 4 half squares equal 2 whole squares, and 2 quarter squares equal a half square. So the shaded part is 2.5 squares. If the area of each square is 2, then the area of the shaded part is 2.5×2, or 5. So (D) is correct.

8. C

The average formula tells us that the

Average $= \dfrac{\text{Sum of terms}}{\text{Number of terms}}$. In this case $\dfrac{20 + 37 + 40 + y}{4} = y - 2$. Multiplying both sides

by 4 gives you $97 + y = 4y - 8$. Adding 8 and

subtracting y from both sides gives you $105 = 3y$, or

$y = 35$. Choice (C) is correct.

9. C

To find the perimeter of triangle XYZ, you need
to find the length of the base XZ. You can use the
area to find the base. The formula for the area of a
triangle is area $\frac{1}{2}bh$, where b is the base and h is the
height. The area of triangle XYZ is $4a$, and the height
equals a. Therefore, $4a = \frac{1}{2}ba$. Solve for b: divide
both sides by a, which gives you $4 = \frac{1}{2}b$; multiply
both sides by 2 (the reciprocal of $\frac{1}{2}$), which gives you
$8 = b$. So $XZ = 8$, and the perimeter of the triangle is
$4 + 6 + 8 = 18$. Choice (C) is correct.

10. C

The first $\frac{1}{2}$ mile costs \$1.25. Subtract 1.25 from

7.75 to find the cost of the remaining distance: 7.75

$- 1.25 = 6.50$. Each $\frac{1}{8}$ additional mile costs \$0.25.

Divide 6.50 by 0.25 to find how many eighths of a

mile were traveled: $\dfrac{6.50}{0.25} = 26$ eighths of a mile or

$\dfrac{26}{8}$ miles, which simplifies to $\dfrac{13}{4}$ miles or $3\frac{1}{4}$ miles.

Now add the first $\frac{1}{2}$ mile to get the total distance;

$3\frac{1}{4} + \frac{1}{2} = 3\frac{3}{4}$, which is (C).

11. D

If circles A and B intersect at exactly one point,
then the circles are tangent to each other. Draw a
diagram. There are two ways that the circles can be
drawn:

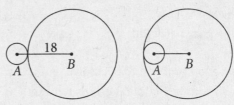

Circumference of a circle equals $2\pi r$. The
circumference of circle $A = 4\pi$, so its radius equals 2.
The circumference of circle $B = 36\pi$, so its radius
equals 18. Look at diagram #1. The distance between
the centers of the two circles is $2 + 18 = 20$. That's
not one of the choices, so look at diagram #2. The
distance between the centers of the two circles is
$18 - 2 = 16$. So (D) is correct.

12. D

A watch shows the same time every 12 hours. So the
watch will show the correct time again when it has
lost 12 hours. If the watch loses 15 minutes per hour,
then it loses 1 hour every 4 hours (or the watch loses
$\frac{1}{4}$ of the time elapsed). Let h be the least number of
hours it would take the watch to be correct again.
Therefore, $\dfrac{h}{4} = 12$, or $h = 48$. So (D) is correct.

13. E

Remember that there are two possibilities whenever
you see part of an equation inside absolute value
signs: $|b - 3| = 6$, so either $b - 3 = 6$ and $b = 9$,
or $-(b - 3) = 6$, in which case $-b + 3 = 6$ and
$-b = 3$, so $b = -3$.

14. E

Lines are parallel if they have the same slope. Remember that when an equation for a line is given in the form $y = mx + b$, m represents the slope. In this case, only $y = 4x + 6$ has the same slope as $y = 4x - 6$.

15. C

This is a good problem to backsolve, but it can also be solved algebraically. Whichever method you choose, remember to work carefully. Here's the algebraic solution:

$$\frac{3}{x-6} = 3$$
$$3 = 3(x - 6)$$
$$3 = 3x - 18$$
$$21 = 3x$$
$$7 = x$$

16. E

Be very careful when substituting given values for variables. Be sure to keep track of the sign and to write every step down as you proceed with the operation.

$$x^{-3} = \frac{1}{x^3} = \frac{1}{\left(\frac{1}{5}\right)^3} = \frac{1}{\left(\frac{1}{125}\right)} = 125$$

17. A

Pick numbers. Say $x = 4$ and $y = 6$. Then $xy = k = 24$. When y is halved to 3, x becomes 8—it doubles.

18. C

If $PS = 19$ and $PQ = 3$, then $PS - PQ = QS = 19 - 3 = 16$. Using $QS = 16$ and $RS = 10$, we can say that $QS - RS = QR$, or $16 - 10 = 6$.

19. C

The things in a set are called elements or members. The union of sets is the set of elements in one or more of the sets being united. Think of the union set as what you get when you merge sets. The symbol for set union is ∪. The intersection of sets is the set of common elements of the sets being intersected. Think of the intersection as the overlap of sets. The symbol for the intersection of sets is ∩. To be in $P \cap Q \cap R$—that is, the intersection of P, Q, and R—a number would have to be: between −5.5 and 5.5, inclusive; prime; odd and positive. Given the sets in question, the only such numbers are 3 and 5—that's two elements.

20. D

Think about the question in commonsense terms. To double is to multiply by two. The question calls for this doubling to occur 48 times. The mathematical way of expressing "doubling to occur 48 times" is 2^{48}. The answer is the total growth that occurs times the original population. Again, total growth is 2^{48}. The original population is p.

21. 36

To find out how many oranges are equal in cost to 16 grapefruit, you need to figure out how much 16 grapefruit would cost and then divide that amount by the price of one orange. If each grapefruit sells for $0.45, then 16 would cost $0.45 × 16 = $7.20. If each orange costs $0.20, you could buy $\frac{\$7.20}{\$0.20} = 36$ oranges.

22. 102, 132, 162, 192

If a number is divisible by 3, the sum of its digits must be divisible by 3. If a number is divisible by 10, its units' digit is 0—the last digit of a number represents the remainder that results when that number is divided by 10. So you need to find a number whose last digit is 2 and the sum of whose digits is divisible by 3. There are only ten numbers between 100 and 200 that end in 2, (102, 112, 122, 132, 142, 152, 162, 172, 182, and 192). The hundreds' digit of each is 1, while the units' digit is of course 2—because these digits sum to 3, in order for the entire number to be divisible by 3, the tens' digit must be divisible by 3. 102, 132, 162, and 192 are the only numbers that meet both tests.

23. 0 < width < 1

The perimeter of a rectangle is equal to 2(length + width), so $14 = 2(\ell + w)$ or $7 = \ell + w$. You are told that $\ell > 6$, so for $\ell + w$ to equal 7, w must be less than 1. If this isn't clear, manipulate the equation for perimeter to get $\ell = 7 - w$, and then substitute $7 - w$ into the inequality for ℓ. So $7 - w > 6$; adding w and subtracting 6 from both sides shows that $1 > w$. Because width must be a positive measurement, you could grid in any decimal or fraction between 0 and 1 for the width.

24. 30

This is a pretty tough visualization problem. It is helpful to label each segment with the appropriate measure. Because triangle ACF isn't clearly visible, draw in line segments AC and AF. Triangle ACF is inside this rectangular solid. One thing you need to remember about rectangular solids is that the faces,

or planes, are either perpendicular or parallel to each other. For example, plane ABC is perpendicular to plane EFC. Therefore, line segment AC, which is on plane ABC, is perpendicular to line segment FC, which is on plane EFC. This means that triangle ACF is a right triangle, where the right angle is angle ACF. To find the area of triangle ACF, we need the length of the base, AC, and the height, FC. FC is given as 12; to find AC, we need to look at triangle ABC. Although it may not look like it in the diagram, triangle ABC is a right triangle with a right angle at angle ABC, since each face of a rectangular solid is a rectangle and has right angles at the corners. So for right triangle ABC, leg AB is 3 and the other leg, BC, is 4. Right away that tells us that AC, the hypotenuse, is 5 because right triangle ABC is a 3-4-5 Pythagorean triplet. Now the area of triangle ACF is $\frac{1}{2}$(base)(height), or $\frac{1}{2}(AC)(CF)$, or $\frac{1}{2}$(5)(12), or 30.

25. 120

If the number of production employees increases from 300 to 390, that's an increase of $\frac{90}{300} = \frac{30}{100} = $ 30%. The number of clerical workers increases by twice that percent, or $2 \times 30\% = 60\%$, resulting in a total of 192 clerical workers. The question asks you to solve for the original number of clerical workers, which you can call x. You aren't told how many of the 192 are new employees, but you know that this total of 192 is equal to the original number plus 60% of the original number. Because percent × whole = part, then $160\% \times x = 192$, or $1.6 \times x = 192$. So $x = 120$.

CHAPTER 7: HOW TO ATTACK THE WRITING SECTION

IF YOU LEARN ONLY FIVE THINGS IN THIS CHAPTER . . .

1. The Writing section does not involve doing any writing.

2. The Writing questions are NOT ordered easiest to hardest.

3. There are three Writing question types:

   —Identifying Sentence Errors

   —Improving Sentences

   —Improving Paragraphs

4. There are three basic Improving Paragraphs question types:

   —Sentence revision

   —Sentence combination

   —Logic and clarity

5. All Writing questions are based on the same principle: identify the error (and, in Improving Sentences and Paragraphs questions, correct it).

CHAPTER 7 OVERVIEW

You probably haven't seen questions like the ones on the Writing section before because most of your high school classes don't teach grammar this way. We'll spend a lot of time in this chapter on the three question types used in the Writing section. We'll also show you the grammar and sentence construction errors that are most often tested on the PSAT, so you know what to look for on test day.

If you've ever read a sentence and thought, "Hmm…that doesn't look right," you've used the skills that will get you a good score on the Writing section of the PSAT. The Writing section is all about one thing—spotting mistakes in grammar and sentence construction. After you're finished working through chapter 7, you'll be able to recognize grammatical errors with the zeal and acuteness of your English teacher and will score higher on the PSAT.

WRITING BASICS

On the PSAT Writing section, you are not required to write anything. You won't have to identify words as adverbs or prepositions or past participles. You'll never see the words *ambiguous pronoun reference* or *subordinate clause*. You also won't be tested on spelling or capitalization.

What you will be required to do is demonstrate your ability to recognize the elements of good writing, including basic grammar, sentence structure, word choice, and paragraph construction.

In the days, weeks, or months that precede the PSAT, read everything—and we mean everything—with an eye toward sentence structure. Look for fragments in advertisements. Find run-on sentences in emails from your friends. Weed out misplaced modifiers in your school newspaper. Become a reader who looks for *mistakes*.

While you're training your eyes to look for writing errors, also train your ears to listen for them. Listen to how people talk. Does the English language sound different on the nightly news than it does on *Friends* reruns? Why might that be? What word choices do your friends and teachers use? Are they different? How? We're not suggesting that you start correcting people. Just listen with a more critical ear than usual. Learning to trust your ear is the best way to prepare for the PSAT Writing section.

QUESTION TYPES

Unlike the Math sections, the PSAT Writing section questions have never been designed to increase in difficulty as the section progresses. Easy, medium, and hard questions are all jumbled up. Knowing how each question type works and being familiar with the other quirks of the PSAT Writing section will save you lots of time on test day. Following is a detailed summary of the three question types:

- 14 Identifying Sentence Errors questions
- 20 Improving Sentences questions
- 5 Improving Paragraphs questions

IDENTIFYING SENTENCE ERRORS

The directions for Identifying Sentence Errors look like this:

<u>Directions:</u> The following sentences test your knowledge of grammar, usage, diction (choice of words), and idiom.

Some sentences are correct.

No sentence contains more than one error.

Several parts of the sentence will be underlined and lettered. You will find that the error, if there is one, is underlined and lettered. Elements of the sentence that are not underlined will not be changed. In choosing answers, follow the requirements of standard written English.

If there is an error, select the <u>one underlined part</u> that must be changed to make the sentence correct, and fill in the corresponding oval on your answer sheet.

If there is no error, fill in answer oval (E).

Here's an example:

<u>Even though</u> he <u>had to</u> supervise a large staff, his salary
    A   B

<u>was no greater</u> than <u>a clerk</u>. <u>No error</u>
    C   D   E

SPOT THE MISTAKE!

All Identifying Sentence Errors questions are *spot the mistake* type questions. You're given a sentence with four words and phrases underlined. The underlined parts are labeled (A) through (D). One of the underlined pieces may contain a usage error. Your task is to spot the error and fill in the corresponding oval on your grid. If the sentence is error-free, the correct answer is (E), No error. Also, you should assume that the parts of the sentence not underlined are correct.

Identifying Sentence Errors questions test your ability to catch words or phrases that high school students often use incorrectly. If you can spot these types of errors, the test makers assume that you can use the right words and phrases in your own writing.

In this example, the correct answer is (D). The current wording makes it sound as though the size of the subject's salary is being compared to the size of a clerk; in fact, the subject's salary should be compared to the size of a clerk's *salary.*

IMPROVING SENTENCES QUESTIONS

The Improving Sentences section begins with directions that look like this:

<u>Directions:</u> The following sentences test correctness and effectiveness of expression. In choosing answers, follow the requirements of standard written English; that is, pay attention to grammar, choice of words, sentence construction, and punctuation.

In each of the following sentences, part of the sentence or the entire sentence is underlined. Beneath each sentence, you will find five ways of phrasing the underlined part. Choice (A) repeats the original; the other four are different.

Choose the answer that best expresses the meaning of the original sentence. If you think the original is better than any of the alternatives, choose it; otherwise, choose one of the others. Your choice should produce the most effective sentence—clear and precise, without awkwardness or ambiguity.

Here's an example:

> To the surprise of the school's staff, the new freshman class at
> Ravenswood High <u>being larger than last year's</u>.
>
> (A) being larger than last year's
> (B) is large more so than last year
> (C) which is larger than the one last year
> (D) is larger than last year's
> (E) by far larger than the last

In Improving Sentences questions, there's just one underlined section. Your task is to decide whether the underlined section is grammatically correct. If the sentence is correct, pick (A), which is always identical to the original sentence. If the sentence is flawed, pick the answer choice that *best* corrects the error.

FIX THE MISTAKE!

Improving Sentences questions test your ability to identify and correct problems with sentence structure that often appear in students' essays. The test makers assume that if you can spot poorly constructed sentences and correct the errors, then you can probably write good sentences on your own.

In this question, the correct answer is (D). The verb *being* is in the wrong form, thus creating an incomplete sentence. Choice (D) corrects the error in a straightforward fashion.

IMPROVING PARAGRAPHS QUESTIONS

Just when you're getting great at picking apart sentences, Improving Paragraphs questions come along. In this question type, your task is to correct sentences in the context of an entire paragraph! But don't worry; these may be the easiest questions in the Writing section.

In this section, questions follow short paragraphs that can be about any topic. You do not have to know anything about the topic to answer the questions correctly. The sentences in each paragraph will be numbered. You will probably notice as you read through the passage that it is riddled with errors. Don't bother to mark them because the questions will tell you where the mistakes are located.

Most Improving Paragraphs questions ask you to clean up awkward and ambiguous sentences. The most important thing with these questions is their *context*. You can't determine the best way to repair poor or unclear sentences without knowing what comes before and after them.

A few Improving Paragraphs questions will also ask you about the overall organization of the essay. Again, context is critical. You can't, for example, decide which of five sentences best concludes an essay without knowing what the essay is all about.

There's only one Improving Paragraphs passage on the PSAT. The directions on your test will look like this:

<u>Directions:</u> The passage below is an early draft of an essay. Parts of the passage need to be rewritten.

Read the passage and answer the questions that follow. Some questions are about individual sentences or parts of sentences; in these questions, you are asked to select the choice that will improve sentence structure and word choice. Other questions refer to parts of the essay or the entire essay and ask you to consider the organization and development of the essay. You should follow the conventions of standard written English in answering the questions. After you have chosen your answer, fill in the corresponding oval on your answer sheet.

> *(1) I agree with the school board's recent decision to require high school students to complete a community service requirement before graduating. (2) As a student who has both worked and volunteered, my volunteer experience has truly enriched me as a person. (3) When I worked at a hamburger joint, all I was caring about was the money. (4) Tutoring disadvantaged children taught me to appreciate how much I have.*

> **EXPERT TUTOR TIP**
>
> " Though you are no doubt an expert at critical reading and mapping by now, the Improving Paragraphs section of the Writing test is actually no place to practice these skills. This writing is pretty bad! Read quickly for a general sense of its meaning, then let the questions direct you from there. "

Which of the following is the best way to revise the underlined portion of sentence 2 (reproduced below)?

As a student who has both worked and volunteered, <u>my volunteer experience has truly enriched me as a person</u>.

(A) my experience as a volunteer has been the thing that has truly enriched me as a person

(B) I have been truly enriched by my volunteer experience

(C) it is by volunteering that I have truly become an enriched person

(D) I will have been truly enriched by my volunteer experience

(E) that which has truly enriched me as a person is my volunteer experience

Improving Paragraphs questions test your ability to spot and correct logical flaws in a passage that contains errors often found in student essays. If you can fix the sample passage, the test makers assume you can probably do the same thing to your own writing.

In the above question, the correct answer is (B) because it clarifies that *I* and *a student* are the same person. The original wording is awkward; it sounds as though *my volunteer experience* and *a student* are the same person, which they can't be. Choice (D) uses the incorrect verb tense, and (C) and (E) are unnecessarily complicated.

IDENTIFYING SENTENCE ERRORS

Identifying Sentence Errors questions are a great place for the Writing skills test to begin because you don't have to correct the answer yourself. You simply have to point out what word or phrase is incorrect.

Kaplan's technique for tackling Writing questions helps you to rely on your instincts about what sounds right in English and to avoid pitfalls in the answer choices. For Identifying Sentence Errors questions, follow Kaplan's Three-Step Method:

Step 1. Read the sentence, *listening* for the mistake.

Step 2. Identify the error.

Step 3. If in doubt, use the process of elimination.

Let's try the Three-Step Method on the following question. First, read the sentence, *listening* for a mistake. Read silently, and listen to the voice in your head.

The <u>club members</u> are so busy <u>studying</u> for exams that
      A   B

attendance is <u>rare</u> more <u>than 50 percent.</u> <u>No error</u>
          C   D   E

Did you hear the mistake? If so, your work is done. Fill in the appropriate oval, and move on. If you didn't hear a mistake on the first reading, go back, read each underlined part, and start eliminating underlined parts that are right. There's no problem with the phrase *club members. Studying* seems fine in this context. How about *rare*? Something doesn't sound right about it. "*Rarely* more than 50 percent" would be the correct construction here. Choice (C) contains the error and is the correct answer.

This is a classic example of an adjective/adverb error. There are several different usage errors the PSAT tests over and over again. You'll learn more about the most common errors in the following pages, which offer a quick reference to the most frequently made and tested grammatical mistakes. It's much easier to spot errors when you know what to look for.

VERB TENSE ERRORS

The verb is the action part of the sentence. The verb's tense tells you in what time frame the action is taking place. You won't need to identify verb tenses by name on the test, but you will need to recognize the difference between correct and incorrect usage of verb tenses. Here's an example:

When David was in Holland, he was seeing many windmills.

EXPERT TUTOR TIP

If you don't "hear" the error after a first read, don't automatically pick (E) and move on. Writing questions require you to think like an editor, so go back and check each answer choice systematically.

If the underlined word or phrase includes a pronoun, where's the antecedent? If it's a verb, where's the subject? If it's part of a list, is that list in parallel form? If it includes a preposition, is it part of an idiom, and if so, is that idiom proper? These are the types of questions you should be asking yourself before deciding a sentence is right as written. Go through the answer choices one by one, and eliminate obvious correct answers.

Of course, don't go too crazy trying to spot the error. Roughly 20 percent of the sentences will contain no error.

You don't need to know the rules about proper use of the past tense to know that something's wrong here. Your ear should have told you that the verbs don't sound right. Try this instead:

> When David was in Holland, he saw many windmills.

That sounds better, and it's correct. Now let's look at a question with a verb tense error.

> <u>Unsatisfied</u> with the ending, the director <u>considering</u>
>   A   B
>
> <u>reshooting</u> <u>the entire film</u>. <u>No error</u>
>   C   D   E

Did this sentence make sense to you? If not, where did the confusion come in? We don't know when the director's action took place because *considering* isn't a complete verb. You could substitute *is considering* or *was considering* or even *considered*. Because (B) contains the error in this sentence, it's the right answer.

For a detailed explanation of the different verb tenses and how they are used, check out "Writing Skills" in the PSAT Resources in the back of this book.

SUBJECT-VERB AGREEMENT ERRORS

Grammar textbooks tell you that the subject and the verb of a sentence must agree in number. Put simply, this means that a singular subject takes a singular verb and a plural subject takes a plural verb. Subject and verb also have to agree in person. This means that you need to use the right form of the verb depending on whether the subject is in the first person, second person, or third person.

You most likely do this correctly a million times a day without even noticing it, and it's not as tricky as it sounds. Take a look at these sentences:

> The 4:05 train to Boston leave from the north platform.
>
> Henry's dog are brown with a white tail.
>
> The ballerinas practices for eight hours a day.
>
> You spends too much time thinking about subject-verb agreement.

Did you find the agreement errors? These are fairly basic examples of subject-verb agreement errors, and the sentences on the PSAT won't be quite this easy. But with a little practice, you'll be able to spot agreement errors in any sentence. Be on the lookout for these three classic subject-verb agreement traps:

- Collective nouns
- Intervening phrases
- Subject after the verb

TRAP 1: COLLECTIVE NOUNS

A very common trap that appears on the PSAT Writing section uses collective nouns (singular nouns describing multiple persons) to trick you. Words such as *group*, *audience*, or *committee* require a singular verb.

> The group has decided to plan a trip to a chocolate factory.
>
> The audience was moved to throw rotten vegetables at the mime.
>
> The committee votes to clean up the waterfront every year.

All of these sentences are correct. Let's try a sample question.

> That <u>particular</u> gang of pirates <u>were</u> often <u>referred to</u> as
>   A   B   C
>
> the <u>scourge of</u> the seven seas. <u>No error</u>
>   D   E

Even with advance warning, this one is tricky. The correct answer here is (B) because the subject being modified (described) is the collective singular noun *gang*. The error was harder to spot in this case because the prepositional phrase *of pirates* insinuated that the modifying verb should be plural. That phrase was thrown in the sentence just to confuse you, so be careful when deciding what the subject of a sentence is. This brings us to Trap 2.

TRAP 2: INTERVENING PHRASES

The test makers will often try to confuse the issue of subject-verb agreement by inserting an intervening phrase between the subject and verb. The following question is an example of this.

> Tax evasion, <u>a crime</u> that <u>has been documented</u> in many
>   A   B
>
> modern novels and films, <u>remain</u> a relatively <u>uncommon</u>
>   C   D
>
> <u>offense</u>. <u>No error</u>
>   D   E

Did you pick (C)? You're right. The verb *remain* goes with *evasion*, a singular noun, which requires the verb form *remains*. Don't be fooled by the plural nouns *novels* and *films*, which are part of the intervening phrase.

EXPERT TUTOR TIP

" Try breaking down complicated sentences into their rudimentary "caveman" parts—a simple subject, a verb, and maybe an object. You know… *Cavemen hunt meat*. The "caveman" version of this example problem is *Evasion remain offense*— an obvious error. "

TRAP 3: SUBJECT AFTER THE VERB

Another way the test makers try to confuse you is by placing the subject after the verb. Take a look at this example.

> <u>Although</u> nutritionists have <u>criticized pizza</u> for being
> A   B
>
> too high in fat, there <u>is</u> many people <u>who</u> continue to
>   C   D
>
> enjoy it.   <u>No error</u>
>   E

People is the subject of the verb *to be*, and it requires a plural subject. "There *are many* people" is the correct form of this sentence. Choice (C) is correct.

PRONOUN ERRORS: CASE AND NUMBER

You will see a few questions on the PSAT that test pronoun use. The key thing about pronouns is that they must agree with their antecedents in case and number. What does this mean?

Case is the form the word takes in the sentence. If the pronoun refers to the subject, it has a different case than if it refers to an object.

> Sally dances, and <u>she</u> also sings.
>
> Bob praised Sally, and he also applauded <u>her</u>.

These sentences are correct.

The number of a pronoun is just what it sounds like: singular or plural.

Give this question a try:

> A student <u>who</u> applies for a part-time job assisting
>   A
>
> Dr. Frankenstein <u>may get</u> more than <u>they</u> were <u>expecting</u>.
>   B   C   D
>
> <u>No error</u>
> E

Did you see the error here? The antecedent here is *a student* and the pronoun is *they*. To make the plural pronoun agree with its singular antecedent, you would have to use *he* or *she*, or even possibly *he or she*, so (C) is the answer here. This example demonstrates a common grammatical mistake. Many people use *they* in spoken English to refer to a single person of unknown sex. However, this is not grammatically correct in standard written English because *they* is plural. Watch out for this every time you see *they* and *them* on test day.

PRONOUN ERRORS: AMBIGUOUS REFERENCE

Another common pronoun error on the PSAT Writing section is the ambiguous reference. As we previously stated, every pronoun must have a clear antecedent.

Give this question a try:

> To expand the newspaper's <u>coverage</u> of local politics,
>   A
>
> <u>they</u> transferred a <u>popular</u> columnist <u>to</u> the City desk.
> B   C   D
>
> <u>No error</u>
>   E

This one may have been easy because you knew what you were looking for. Choice (B), *they*, is a pronoun without a clear antecedent. Who transferred the columnist? The sentence doesn't tell us. Choice (B) is correct.

Questions like this one can be tricky, because they read smoothly and do not grab the attention of your well-trained ear. Keep an eye out for ambiguous references in sentences that seem too good to be true.

IDIOMS

Idioms are hard on nonnative speakers of English because idioms are the hardest thing to learn in any foreign language. The reason for this is that idioms are simply word combinations that have become part of a language. They are correct, but there's no particular rhyme or reason for why they're correct. Most—although certainly not all—native speakers will know the proper idiom to use simply because they've heard them a thousand times. This is not so for nonnative speakers.

Prepositions are oftentimes short words—such as *by, at, among,* and *before*—that link prepositional phrases to the rest of the sentence. Most preposition questions tested on the PSAT are idiomatic. This means that you'll be listening for word combinations that often go together. Use your ear to catch prepositions that just don't sound right.

Give the following question a try.

> Many people are <u>desensitized to</u> violence on TV shows,
>   A
>
> <u>but</u> this does not mean that they are not sensitive <u>of</u> the
> B   C
>
> real-life violence around <u>them</u>. <u>No error</u>
>   D   E

There are two idiomatic uses of prepositions in this sentence. Did you spot them? *Desensitized to* and *sensitive of* are (A) and (C). *Sensitive of* simply isn't idiomatic. The proper idiomatic phrase is *sensitive to*. Choice (C) is the correct answer.

COMPARISON ERRORS

Another error that frequently shows up in the PSAT Writing section involves comparisons. This one can be sneaky because some of these sentences will sound normal to your ear. So approach comparisons slightly differently.

When you compare two or more parts of speech, like nouns or verb phrases, the parts of speech must be in the same form. Take a look at this example.

> The producer agreed that casting a drama series is harder than comedy.

If you heard this sentence, you'd probably understand what it means, although it's not grammatically correct. *Casting a drama series* is harder than…what exactly? The sentence would be clearer if it were written as follows:

> The producer agreed that casting a drama series is harder than casting a comedy series.

Both parts of the comparison are in the same form, making the sentence easier to understand and grammatically correct. See if you can spot the mistake in the next question.

> Even though <u>he</u> is a Nobel Laureate,
>   A
>
> <u>Elie Wiesel's name</u> is still <u>less well known</u> than
>   B   C
>
> <u>last year's</u> Heisman Trophy winner. <u>No error</u>
>   D   E

Did you spot the faulty comparison? The sentence compares *Elie Wiesel's name* with the *Heisman Trophy winner*. If we change (B) to read simply *Elie Wiesel*, the comparison is parallel and easier to understand.

ADJECTIVE AND ADVERB ERRORS

You probably haven't thought about adjectives and adverbs since those junior high sentence diagrams. The good news is that you probably use adjectives and adverbs correctly all the time.

> That painting is beautiful.
>
> The artist painted it skillfully.

In the first sentence, *beautiful* is an adjective modifying *painting*, a noun. In the second sentence, *skillfully* is an adverb modifying *painted*, a verb form. Now take a look at how adjectives and adverbs are often tested in the Identifying Sentence Errors questions.

> <u>Since the onset</u> of <u>his</u> blindness, the artist
>   A   B
>
> <u>has sculpted</u> more <u>slow</u> than before. <u>No error</u>
>   C   D   E

Did you hear it? Choice (D) is the correct answer because the adverb *slowly* is required to modify the verb form *has sculpted*.

DOUBLE NEGATIVES

In standard written English, it's incorrect to use two negatives in a row. Just as in math, two negatives added together create a positive.

> I don't want none of that pizza, thank you!

This sentence, if you cancel the negatives, translates to:

> I want some of that pizza, thank you!

You'll find the occasional double negative in the Identifying Sentence Errors section, although the sentences will be more difficult than the one above. Give the next example a try.

> **EXPERT TUTOR TIP**
>
> " Remember: adjectives only modify nouns and pronouns. Everything else (verbs, adjectives, adverbs) is modified by adverbs. "

The town hasn't <u>hardly any</u> money left in <u>its</u> budget
                    A   B

<u>because of</u> the unexpected snowplow <u>costs</u>. <u>No error</u>
       C   D   E

Hasn't and *hardly any* are both negative and cancel each other out, making it sound as if the town doesn't have money problems. We can figure out from the rest of the sentence that the author is trying to tell us that the town does have money problems because of the unexpected costs. Changing (A), *hardly any*, to *much* would help to eliminate one of the negatives, clearing up the meaning of the sentence.

The town hasn't much money left in its budget because of the unexpected snowplow costs.

Now that you have learned what sort of grammatical errors to look for in the Identifying Sentence Errors section, keep those rules in mind as you move into sentence corrections.

IMPROVING SENTENCES

Improving Sentences questions test the same skills as Identifying Sentence Errors questions. You'll still be using your eyes and ears to spot errors and oddities in sentences. Here's the difference: with this question type, you will be asked to correct the mistakes you find.

Each Improving Sentences question has an underlined phrase. You will be asked to decide whether the sentence is okay as is, in which case you would pick (A), or whether the underlined portion should be replaced by one of the four other answer choices.

Take a look at Kaplan's Three-Step Method for Improving Sentences. Because you have to correct the mistake, not just find it, the steps are slightly different from those for Identifying Sentence Errors questions.

Step 1. Read the sentence, *listening* for a mistake.

Step 2. Predict a correction.

Step 3. Select the answer choice that matches your prediction while eliminating clearly wrong answer choices.

Now apply the Three-Step Method to this question.

Hoping to receive a promotion, <u>the letter he received instead informed Burt</u> that he had been fired.

(A) the letter he received instead informed Burt

(B) the letter having been received, instead informed Burt

(C) Burt instead received a letter informing him

(D) information from the received letter instead told Burt

(E) Burt, instead informed by the letter he received

First, read the sentence, *listening* for a mistake. Something sounds wrong. Burt hoped to receive the promotion, but this makes it sounds as if the letter hoped to receive the promotion. Next, predict a correction. Putting *Burt* at the beginning of the second phrase seems to make the sentence sound better. Now select the choice that fits your prediction, eliminating the wrong choices. Choices (C) and (E) both put Burt at the beginning of the phrase. Choice (C) is the clearest and most concise choice, so it is the correct answer.

Any of the grammatical rules discussed in the Identifying Sentence Errors questions could also appear in the Improving Sentences question set. But with this question type, there are additional errors that need to be taken into consideration. We review those on the following pages.

SENTENCE FRAGMENTS

Sentence fragments are incomplete sentences. To be complete, a sentence requires a main subject and a main verb. Some sentences are fragments because they lack the necessary elements to make logical sense. Here are some fragments. How would you repair them?

> Stereo equipment on sale at the mall today!

Repair: _____

> The busload of tourists that wandered curiously around the ancient ruins.

Repair: _____

> Because Myrna likes the Adirondacks, frequently taking photos of them.

Repair: _____

Do you get an empty feeling when you read these fragments? Watch for that feeling on test day, and you'll be able to spot the fragments. Here are suggested repairs on each of the sample sentences above.

> Stereo equipment on sale at the mall today!

Repair: Stereo equipment <u>is</u> on sale at the mall today!

> The busload of tourists that wandered curiously around the ancient ruins.

Repair: The busload of <u>curious tourists wandered</u> around the ancient ruins.

> Because Myrna likes the Adirondacks, frequently taking photos of them.

Repair: Myrna likes the Adirondacks, <u>so she frequently takes</u> photos of them.

Give this example a try. Use Kaplan's Three-Step Method.

> Last of the world's leaders to do so, the prime minister admits that terrorist threats <u>credible enough to warrant</u> the imposition of stringent security measures.
>
> (A) credible enough to warrant
>
> (B) credible enough warrant
>
> (C) are credible enough to warrant
>
> (D) credible enough, warranting
>
> (E) are credible enough to be warranted

That empty feeling sets in right in the middle of the sentence. *Terrorist threats* are the subject, but where's the verb? *Credible* is the adjective modifying *terrorist threats*, so adding *are*, as (C) and (E) do, repairs the fragment. Choice (E), however, introduces a new problem with the phrase *to be warranted*, which is confusing. Choice (C) clearly fixes the fragment and is correct.

RUN-ON SENTENCES

A run-on sentence occurs when two complete sentences that should be separate are joined together. Here is an example:

> Jane was the preeminent scientist in her class her experiments were discussed across campus.

You can tell that this is a run-on sentence because it sounds like it should be two separate sentences. There are three ways to fix a run-on sentence.

1. Use a period.

> Jane was the preeminent scientist in her class.
> Her experiments were discussed across campus.

2. Use a conjunction, making one sentence dependent.

> Because Jane was the preeminent scientist in her class, her experiments were discussed across campus.

3. Use a semicolon.

> Jane was the preeminent scientist in her class;
> her experiments were discussed across campus.

Use the Three-Step Method and the information you just learned to fix the next sentence.

<u>Jonas Salk's vaccine for polio was introduced in 1955, the disease</u>
was one of the most feared in the United States.

(A) Jonas Salk's vaccine for polio was introduced in 1955, the disease

(B) Jonas Salk having introduced the vaccine for polio in 1955, it

(C) Before Jonas Salk's vaccine for polio was introduced in 1955, the disease

(D) Jonas Salk's vaccine for polio was introduced in 1955 the disease

(E) Prior to the introduction of the polio vaccine being by Jonas Salk, the disease

This sentence is clearly a run-on, with two complete sentences separated by a comma (called a *comma splice*). The solution must solve this problem: (C) and (E) do this by using a conjunction to make the first clause dependent on the second. Choice (E) is confusingly wordy; therefore, (C) is the right answer. Choice (B) makes a single complete sentence, but it changes the meaning. Choice (D) removes the comma, but the sentence remains a run-on.

COORDINATION AND SUBORDINATION ERRORS

Sometimes a sentence won't make sense because it contains clauses that aren't logically joined. There are two types of errors involving the improper joining of clauses in a sentence: coordination and subordination errors.

Proper coordination expresses the logical relationship between two clauses. Misused conjunctions can bring about faulty coordination and make a sentence confusing or just plain nonsensical.

Because he was very thirsty, he refused to drink the water.

This sentence doesn't make much sense (unless we're dealing with a very stubborn and confused person). What would be a better conjunction?

Although he was very thirsty, he refused to drink the water.

This is better. We still don't know why he won't drink the water, but the conjunction *although* sets up the contrast between the two clauses that helps the sentence make sense.

Problems with subordination occur when a group of words contains two or more subordinate clauses (also known as dependent clauses) but no independent clause.

> Since the advent of inexpensive portable stereos, because of a boom
> in the manufacture of headphones has occurred.

Connective words like *since, because, so that, if,* and *although* introduce subordinate clauses. As it stands, this sentence consists of two dependent clauses, with no independent clause. We can eliminate *because of* to make this a grammatically correct sentence.

> Since the advent of inexpensive portable stereos, a boom in the
> manufacture of headphones has occurred.

Try the following two questions, using Kaplan's Three-Step Method.

> New shops appeared on the <u>waterfront, however merchants</u> were
> finally able to convince customers of the area's safety.

(A) waterfront, however merchants

(B) waterfront; merchants

(C) waterfront, yet merchants

(D) waterfront, because merchants

(E) waterfront, although merchants

However is a conjunction that indicates contrast, but this sentence is about cause-and-effect. Choice (D) is correct because the use of the conjunction *because* shows the relationship between the appearance of the new shops and the merchants' ability to convince customers that the area was safe.

> Because Megan was unable to finish her tax forms before April 15,
> <u>so she filed</u> for an extension.

(A) so she filed

(B) but she was filing

(C) she filed

(D) and this led to her filing

(E) and she filed

This question tests subordination. The sentence contains two dependent clauses, each beginning with a linking word. Choice (C) eliminates the linking word and fixes the problem by creating an independent clause.

MISPLACED MODIFIERS

Modifiers are phrases that provide information about nouns and verbs in a sentence. A modifier must appear next to the word or words that it's modifying. Otherwise, things can get a bit confusing (not to mention ungrammatical).

Take a look at this example:

> Dripping on his shirt, Harvey was so eager to eat his hamburger that he didn't notice the ketchup.

As it's written, it sounds as if Harvey was dripping on his shirt, which isn't a very pleasant image. In fact, it's the ketchup that's dripping on his shirt. Misplaced modifiers are easy to fix. As long as you can spot them, these questions are usually quite easy to answer.

> Harvey was so eager to eat his hamburger that he didn't notice the ketchup dripping on his shirt.

This clears up the confusion and is a logical sentence. Now let's look at a testlike question that tests misplaced modifiers.

> <u>Flying for the first time, the roar of the jet engines intimidated the elderly man as the plane sped down the runway.</u>

(A) Flying for the first time, the roar of the jet engines intimidated the elderly man as the plane sped down the runway.

(B) The roar of the jet engines intimidated the elderly man as the plane, flying for the first time, sped down the runway.

(C) Flying for the first time, the elderly man was intimidated by the roar of the jet engines as the plane sped down the runway.

(D) The plane sped down the runway as, flying for the first time, the roar of the jet engines intimidated the elderly man.

(E) As the plane sped down the runway, flying for the first time, the elderly man was intimidated by the roar of the jet engines.

We need a choice that makes it clear that the elderly man is the one who is flying for the first time, not the roar. Choice (C) accomplishes this by placing the modifier *flying for the first time* next to *the elderly man*. Note that (E) also places the two phrases next to each other, but the modifier is sandwiched between two phrases, making it unclear which phrase it is meant to modify. Choice (C) is correct.

BAD PARALLELISM

Parallelism is very much like comparison, which we covered earlier. Essentially, whenever you list items, they must be in the same form. Take a look at the following sentence:

> On Saturday, Ingrid cleaned her apartment, bought her plane tickets for France, and was deciding to go out to dinner.

The first two verbs are parallel in the past tense, but the third verb is in a different form, thus not parallel.

> On Saturday, Ingrid cleaned her apartment, bought her plane tickets for France, and decided to go out to dinner.

In this corrected sentence, *cleaned, bought,* and *decided* are all in the past tense form, so the parallel structure is correct.

Try the next question, and see how you do.

> Changing over from a military to a peacetime economy means producing tractors rather than tanks, radios rather than rifles, and <u>producing running shoes rather than combat boots</u>.

    (A) producing running shoes rather than combat boots

    (B) the production of running shoes rather than combat boots

    (C) running shoes rather than combat boots

    (D) replacing combat boots with running shoes

    (E) running shoes instead of combat boots

Choice (C) does the trick by maintaining the parallel structure of the sentence: *tractors rather than tanks, radios rather than rifles, and running shoes rather than combat boots.*

Getting the hang of it? Good. Let's move on to the final question type in the Writing section.

IMPROVING PARAGRAPHS

Improving Paragraphs questions look a little scary because you have to read a whole paragraph. However, many students find them to be the easiest question type in the PSAT Writing section, and there are only five questions of this type on the test. The reason this type of question is tested is because test makers want to make sure you can recognize (and, in theory, write) a concise, logical, and stylistically smooth essay. The questions in this section are designed to test your skills in this area.

Lucky for you, Kaplan's Three-Step Method for Improving Paragraphs questions makes these kinds of questions a breeze.

Step 1. Before looking at any of the questions, read the essay.

This first read-through should just be a quick skim that gives you a sense of the essay's main idea.

Step 2. For each question, read the question stem and identify the error or problem.

Now you know what the question is asking you to do, and you may already be able to predict an answer, but don't commit just yet.

Step 3. Reread the relevant portion of the essay.

Look at the context of the sentence(s) in question before choosing your answer.

Try using Step 1 on the following essay. Keep your eye out for obvious errors, but don't spend time trying to repair them now. For now, just get acquainted with the passage.

> *(1) School administrators don't respect the rights of students. (2) They don't understand that many students are vegetarians. (3) I think that eating meat is unnecessary. (4) There are many delicious vegetarian dishes that all students could enjoy for lunch. (5) Students all across America have fought with administrators about this issue. (6) They may think that it's too expensive to provide a vegetarian alternative every day. (7) Many dishes can be made either with meat or meat-free. (8) For example, burritos and pizza. (9) At my school, there was a survey about whether students would like vegetarian meals or not. (10) I believe that schools should show that they respect students' needs by providing vegetarian options for lunch.*

This is a fairly typical Improving Paragraphs passage. It contains a number of errors in sentence structure and overall logic and structure. Now let's look over the various types of questions you'll see in the Improving Paragraphs section and see how to apply Steps 2 and 3. Remember, because there are only five Improving Paragraphs questions altogether, you won't see more than one or two of each of these question types on the PSAT.

SENTENCE REVISION

Step 2 is to read the question stem. Take a look at this typical sentence revision question:

> In context, which is the best revision of the underlined portion of sentence 6 (reproduced below)?
>
> *They may think that it's too expensive to provide a vegetarian alternative every day.*
>
> (A) (As it is now)
> (B) The administration may think
> (C) The students may think
> (D) The administration may have been thinking
> (E) They may have thought

This question asks you to revise a sentence in the passage. Notice that the sentence is reprinted below the question. You're given the option to keep the sentence as is, (A). This is sometimes, *but not always*, an option on revision questions.

After you've read the question stem, it's time for Step 3. Go back and reread the surrounding sentences in the passage to get a sense of the sentence's context. In sentence 6, the pronoun *they* doesn't have a clear antecedent. The sentences leading up to the sentence in question discussed the struggle between students and administration on the topic of vegetarian meals. From the preceding sentences, it's clear that students are pro vegetarian meals, and the administration is con, so we can assume that the writer would substitute *the administration* for *they* in this sentence.

Now look at the choices and see which ones match your prediction. Choices (B) and (D) both match your prediction, but (D) unnecessarily changes the verb tense. Choice (B) improves the sentence and is correct.

Did this remind you of an Improving Sentences or Identifying Sentence Errors question? It should have because the same skills are tested in Improving Paragraphs questions, with the added twist of the rest of the paragraph being included.

SENTENCE COMBINATION

This type of question asks you to combine two sentences from the passage. Sometimes you will be able to determine the best way to do this by just using the information given in the question stem itself, but it is still a good idea to check the context of the sentences within the essay before choosing your answer. Give this question a try.

> Which of the following is the best way to combine sentences 7 and 8 (reproduced below)?
>
> *Many dishes can be made with or without meat.*
> *For example, burritos and pizza.*
>
> (A) Many dishes, such as burritos and pizza, can be made with or without meat.
>
> (B) With or without meat, many dishes such as burritos and pizza can be made.
>
> (C) For example, burritos and pizza are many dishes that can be made with or without meat.
>
> (D) Burritos and pizza, for example, are among many dishes that can be made with or without meat.
>
> (E) Many dishes can be made with or without meat, for example, burritos and pizza.

Can you see why these sentences should be combined? The second sentence is a fragment. Choice (E) attempts to join the sentences with a simple comma, which won't do the trick. Choices (B), (C), and (D) are all awkward constructions that don't make sense of the sentence combination. Choice (A) smoothly combines the sentences. Checking the context within the essay confirms that (A) preserves the author's meaning, therefore this is the correct answer.

Remember that the test makers don't like wordiness, awkwardness, and redundancy. The correct answer will always be clear, concise, and grammatically correct.

LOGIC AND CLARITY

The third type of Improving Paragraphs question asks you to find and repair gaps in the author's logic and clarity.

Take a look at following question.

> The writer of the passage could best improve sentence 9 (reproduced below) by doing which of the following?
>
> *At my school, there was a survey about whether students would like vegetarian meals or not.*
>
> (A) providing data from the survey showing that students want vegetarian meals
>
> (B) profiling an individual vegetarian student
>
> (C) including vegetarian recipes
>
> (D) weakening the administration's arguments
>
> (E) providing a dictionary definition of the term *respect*

Start by rereading sentence 9 and the sentences around it in the passage. What's the problem here? Well, this sentence doesn't help the author's case very much because we know only that there was a survey. We don't know what the results of the survey showed.

Choice (A) is correct. Whereas all of the other choices provide ideas that may help the author's argument, none specifically pertains to sentence 9, which is the focus of this question.

PRACTICE

If you found the questions in this chapter to be relatively easy, you should be in pretty good shape for the Writing Skills section. If you're feeling unsure, go back and review the different question types, then try this quiz. From now until test day, remember to use your eyes and ears whenever you read. Remember to search and repair, and you'll be in good shape for the test!

DIRECTIONS: The following sentences test your knowledge of grammar, usage, diction (choice of words), and idioms.

Some sentences are correct.

No sentence contains more than one error.

You will find that the error, if there is one, is underlined and lettered. Elements of the sentence that are not underlined will not be changed. In choosing answers, follow the requirements of standard written English.

If there is an error, select the <u>one underlined part</u> that must be changed to make the sentence correct, and fill in the corresponding oval on your answer sheet.

If there is no error, fill in answer oval (E).

1. In <u>recently</u> constructed concert halls, there <u>is</u>
       A   B

   usually at least two <u>sets</u> <u>of</u> stairs at the rear of
                     C D

   the balcony. <u>No error</u>
             E

2. Whenever we <u>travel</u> abroad, a <u>sense</u> of
               A   B

   excitement and an anticipation of being in

   a foreign land <u>overtake</u> <u>you</u>. <u>No error</u>
              C   D   E

3. Many foreign electronics <u>companies</u> have
                         A

   learned <u>to build</u> machines at a lower cost by
           B

   using <u>inexpensive</u> produced <u>components</u>.
         C   D

   <u>No error</u>
    E

4. The chairwoman felt that she <u>could not</u> give
                         A

   in <u>with</u> his demands, <u>which</u> she thought were
      B   C

   <u>completely</u> unreasonable. <u>No error</u>
      D   E

5. <u>One</u> can learn more <u>about</u> new computers
     A   B

   by actually working with <u>them</u> than one can
                     C

   by <u>merely</u> reading the instruction manual.
       D

   <u>No error</u>
    E

6. The police officer <u>noticed</u> the wanted suspect
              A

   only after <u>he</u> <u>removed</u> his sunglasses and
           B   C

   <u>sat down</u> at the counter. <u>No error</u>
     D   E

7. The triathlete <u>had swam</u> three miles <u>before</u>
              A   B

   leg cramps <u>caused</u> her to <u>withdraw from</u> the
           C   D

   competition. <u>No error</u>
           E

8. The speaker <u>whom</u> the graduating class <u>chose</u>
         A   B

   to deliver their commencement address was
    C

   an <u>imminent</u> authority on international
      D

   diplomacy. <u>No error</u>
         E

9. The jazz band <u>was forced</u> <u>to return</u> the gate
               A   B

   receipts after <u>they</u> had arrived at the arena
                 C

   one hour <u>late</u>. <u>No error</u>
             D   E

10. The Soviet Union had <u>not hardly</u> developed
                        A

    a spaceship <u>suitable</u> for lunar <u>travel</u> when the
                B   C

    first U.S. astronaut <u>landed on</u> the moon in
                          D

    1969. <u>No error</u>
           E

DIRECTIONS: The following sentences test correctness and effectiveness of expression. In choosing answers, follow the requirements of standard written English; that is, pay attention to grammar, choice of words, sentence construction, and punctuation.

In each of the following sentences, part of the sentence or the entire sentence is underlined. Beneath each sentence, you will find five ways of phrasing the underlined part. Choice (A) repeats the original; the other four are different.

Choose the answer that best expresses the meaning of the original sentence. If you think the original is better than any of the alternatives, choose it; otherwise, choose one of the others. Your choice should produce the most effective sentence—clear and precise, without awkwardness or ambiguity.

11. This group of artists, masters of the short brush stroke developed by the Impressionists in the nineteenth century, did not believe in selling works of art; however, <u>some giving paintings away</u>.

    (A) some giving paintings away

    (B) giving some paintings away

    (C) paintings were given away by some of them

    (D) some having given paintings away

    (E) some gave paintings away

12. <u>Credulous people believe</u> in the existence of extraterrestrial beings, most scientists and other informed students of nature do not.

    (A) Credulous people believe

    (B) While credulous people believe

    (C) Credulous people are always believing

    (D) Since credulous people believe

    (E) Credulous people tend to believe

13. Exposed to the extremely long and severe cold spell, <u>frost soon killed the buds of the citrus trees and they did not produce fruit that season</u>.

    (A) frost soon killed the buds of the citrus trees and they did not produce fruit that season

    (B) soon the buds of the citrus trees were killed by frost, and therefore not producing fruit that season

    (C) the buds of the citrus trees were soon killed by frost, they did not produce fruit that season

    (D) fruit was not produced by the citrus trees that season because their buds had been killed by frost

    (E) the buds of the citrus trees were soon killed by frost, and the trees did not produce fruit that season

14. In the closing decades of the eighteenth century, it was believed that young women should not only <u>be obedient and soft-spoken but also master</u> such skills as needlepoint.

    (A) be obedient and soft-spoken but also master

    (B) being obedient and soft-spoken but also mastering

    (C) obey and speak softly but also to master

    (D) be obedient and soft-spoken but also to master

    (E) obeying and speaking softly but also mastering

15. Initiated in 1975, <u>sandhill cranes must unwittingly cooperate in the conservationists' project to raise</u> endangered whooping crane chicks.

(A) sandhill cranes must unwittingly cooperate in the conservationists' project to raise

(B) sandhill cranes' unwitting cooperation is required in the conservationists' project to raise

(C) the conservationists require that sandhill cranes unwittingly cooperate in their project of raising

(D) the conservationists require sandhill cranes to cooperate unwittingly in their project to raise

(E) the conservationists' project requires the unwitting cooperation of sandhill cranes in raising

16. Environmental scientists are very concerned <u>about dangerous fluorocarbons found in pressurized aerosol cans which quicken the erosion of the ozone layer when emitted</u>.

(A) about dangerous fluorocarbons found in pressurized aerosol cans which quicken the erosion of the ozone layer when emitted

(B) that, while emitting dangerous fluorocarbons, pressurized aerosol cans quicken the erosion of the ozone layer

(C) about the erosion of the ozone layer caused by pressurized aerosol cans emitting dangerous fluorocarbons

(D) that pressurized aerosol cans emitting dangerous fluorocarbons which quicken the erosion of the ozone layer

(E) when, quickening the erosion of the ozone layer, pressurized aerosol cans emit dangerous fluorocarbons

17. The characteristics of a typical Avery canvas are a purposely limited palette, a distinctive use of color for perspective, <u>and it employs obvious brushstrokes for effect</u>.

(A) and it employs obvious brushstrokes for effect

(B) and an employment of obvious brushstrokes for effect

(C) but it employs obvious brushstrokes for effect

(D) whereby, for effect, it employs obvious brushstrokes

(E) it employs obvious brushstrokes for effect

DIRECTIONS: The passage below is an early draft of an essay. Parts of the passage need to be rewritten.

Read the passage, and answer the questions that follow. Some questions are about individual sentences or parts of sentences; in these questions, you are asked to select the choice which will improve sentence structure and word choice. Other questions refer to parts of the essay or the entire essay and ask you to consider the organization and development of the essay. You should follow the conventions of standard written English in answering the questions. After you have chosen your answer, fill in the corresponding oval on your answer sheet.

Questions 18–20 are based on the following essay, which is a response to an assignment to write about an economic issue facing the United States.

(1) Recently a report came out in a science magazine that claimed the earth's protective ozone layer was being steadily depleted. (2) It named several companies that produced chemicals responsible for this situation, and consumers were advised by it to boycott these businesses.

(3) An editorial in a business magazine insisted that this report was faulty. (4) It stated that there could be other, less dangerous reasons for the changes in climate that we have been experiencing. (5) However, I believe that the scientists are right, we should all consider the effect we can have on making sure the ozone layer is not harmed more than it already has been. (6) The depletion of the ozone layer means that harmful ultraviolet rays get through to our atmosphere. (7) People who do these bad things, which contribute to this situation, should know that their actions could harm future generations.

18. Considering the essay as a whole, which is the best edit for the underlined section of sentence 2 (reproduced below)?

    It named several companies that produced chemicals responsible for this situation, and consumers were advised by it to boycott these businesses.

    (A) (As it is now)

    (B) It names several companies that produced chemicals responsible for this situation and advises consumers

    (C) Naming several companies that produce chemicals responsible for this situation, consumers are advised by the report

    (D) It is naming several companies that produce chemicals responsible for this situation and advising consumers

    (E) The report named several companies that produced chemicals responsible for this situation, and advised consumers

19. Considering the essay as a whole, which is the best way to edit and link the underlined portions of sentences 3 and 4 (reproduced below)?

    An editorial in a business magazine insisted that this report was faulty. It stated that there could be other, less dangerous reasons for the changes in climate that we've been experiencing.

    (A) The report was faulty, an editorial in a business magazine insisted, it stated

    (B) An editorial in a business magazine insisted that this report was faulty, stating

    (C) In an editorial in a business magazine was the insistence that the report was faulty and

    (D) The editorial in a business magazine insists that the consumers were faulty,

    (E) Insisting that the report was faulty, an editorial in a business magazine states

20. Sentence 7 would read more clearly in the context of the essay if the phrase *do these bad things* were replaced by which of the following?

    People who do these bad things which contribute to this situation, should know that their actions could harm future generations.

    (A) exacerbate the situations

    (B) don't participate in events

    (C) are in need of services

    (D) use the types of chemicals

    (E) consider options

ANSWERS AND EXPLANATIONS

1. B

The only verb in the sentence is the singular *is*. The subject of the sentence is *sets*, a plural noun. The word *there* preceding *is* serves to delay the subject *sets*. The subject is no longer in the position where we expect to find it: before the verb. Nevertheless, the verb should be plural—*are*—to agree with the plural subject.

2. D

We and *you* are not interchangeable in this sentence, although either one could be grammatical. But when two pronouns within one sentence refer to the same performer of actions, the pronouns should be consistent. Here, because it's underlined, *you* can change to *us* in order to match *we*.

3. C

Inexpensive seems to modify the word *produced* and to describe how the components were produced. But adverbs describe how an action is done, so the adjective *inexpensive* needs an adverbial ending. The word needed at (C) is the adverb *inexpensively*.

4. B

The idiomatic verb-preposition combination *give in to* means *submit to*, and that is the meaning of the verb in this sentence. The preposition *with* is simply unidiomatic in this usage.

5. E

There is no error in this sentence. The parallel construction in this sentence balances perfectly.

6. B

It is unclear to whom the pronoun *he* refers. Because the singular pronoun *he* could agree with either noun, *officer* or *suspect*, the pronoun's reference is unclear, and the noun should be restated.

7. A

Swam is the simple past tense of the verb *to swim*. But the required verb tense in this sentence is the past perfect because the triathlete *had swum* before *cramps caused her to withdraw*. The past perfect is formed with an auxiliary verb, *had*, and the past participle, *swum*, not *swam*.

8. D

The words *imminent* and *eminent* are easily confused. *Imminent* means "likely to occur at any moment"; it is familiar and appropriate in the phrase *imminent disaster*. But *eminent*, the word this sentence needs, means "highly regarded."

9. C

They seems to refer to the first subject, *jazz band*. But *jazz band* is a singular noun, although a band is made up of several musicians. The band must be singular because it acts as a unit, arriving late and disappointing the audience together. The pronoun referring to the band should be *it*.

10. A

Hardly is a modifier that negates the word it modifies. In this sentence, it negates *developed. Not* also negates *developed* and creates a double-negative construction where only one negation is intended. Such double negatives are substandard usage in modern English.

11. E

The underlined portion of the sentence follows a semicolon that seems to signal an independent clause, but what follows the semicolon is only a fragment. Choice (C) is an independent clause, but the passive verb, *were given (away)*, makes it wordy and roundabout. Only (E) gives the proper grammatical structure in a compact way.

12. B

The given sentence is a run-on; two independent clauses are joined only by a comma, with no proper conjunction. The run-on can be corrected by turning the first clause into a dependent clause. Only (B) creates a clause that both solves the run-on problem and expresses the logical relation of the two clauses.

13. E

This sentence contains a misplaced modifier. The introductory phrase should modify the noun immediately following the comma, but it does not in this sentence. In (E) and (C), the modified noun, *the buds*, is in the correct position following the introductory modifying phrase. But notice that (C) introduces a new error when it links the second clause to the first with only a comma, creating a run-on. Only (E) corrects the original problem without adding a new one. Of course, the modifying phrase itself cannot be rearranged in this case because it isn't underlined.

14. A

The sentence is correct as given. The wording is parallel after the correlative words *not only . . . but also.*

15. E

An introductory modifying phrase must modify the subject of the sentence. Because the introductory phrase isn't underlined, the subject must be changed. It's the *project*, not the *cranes* or the *conservationists*, that was initiated in 1975. Choice (E) gets it right.

16. C

This sentence contains a misplaced modifier, making it sound as if the cans, rather than the fluorocarbons, are emitted. Choice (C) corrects the problem and connects the facts in a logical manner.

17. B

The underlined phrase is part of a comparison and should be a grammatical match to the other items being compared: *a . . . palette* and *a . . . use of color.* These are both noun phrases. Choice (B) is the only one of the choices that matches, so it's the correct answer.

18. E

The pronoun *it* doesn't have a clear antecedent. Only (E) corrects this problem by replacing *it* with the phrase *the report*; furthermore, the rest of this sentence is grammatically consistent with the paragraph as a whole.

19. B

Choices (B) and (E) are the only ones that clearly maintain that the *editorial*, as opposed to the magazine itself, was making the statement, and they do not introduce grammatical mistakes. However, (E) is in the present tense, whereas the rest of the information surrounding the discussion of the report and the editorial is in the past tense. Therefore, (B) is correct.

20. D

The types of products that contribute to the destruction of the ozone layer are certain types of *chemicals*; therefore, (D) is the most logical and specific answer.

Part Four

PRACTICE TESTS AND EXPLANATIONS

CHAPTER 8: PRACTICE TEST ONE

HOW TO TAKE THIS PRACTICE TEST

Before taking this Practice Test, find a quiet room where you can work uninterrupted for two and a half hours. Make sure you have a comfortable desk, your calculator, and several No. 2 pencils. Use the answer sheet to record your answers. Once you start, don't stop until you've finished. Take a five-minute rest break after section two and a one-minute stretch break after section four. Remember—you may review any questions within a section, but you may not jump from one section to another.

PSAT PRACTICE TEST ONE ANSWER SHEET

Remove (or photocopy) this answer sheet and use it to complete the test. See the answer key following the test when finished. Chapter 11 will show you how to find your score.

Start with number 1 for each section. If a section has fewer questions than answer spaces, leave the extra spaces blank.

SECTION 4

19. Ⓐ Ⓑ Ⓒ Ⓓ Ⓔ	24. Ⓐ Ⓑ Ⓒ Ⓓ Ⓔ	29. Ⓐ Ⓑ Ⓒ Ⓓ Ⓔ	34. Ⓐ Ⓑ Ⓒ Ⓓ Ⓔ
20. Ⓐ Ⓑ Ⓒ Ⓓ Ⓔ	25. Ⓐ Ⓑ Ⓒ Ⓓ Ⓔ	30. Ⓐ Ⓑ Ⓒ Ⓓ Ⓔ	35. Ⓐ Ⓑ Ⓒ Ⓓ Ⓔ
21. Ⓐ Ⓑ Ⓒ Ⓓ Ⓔ	26. Ⓐ Ⓑ Ⓒ Ⓓ Ⓔ	31. Ⓐ Ⓑ Ⓒ Ⓓ Ⓔ	36. Ⓐ Ⓑ Ⓒ Ⓓ Ⓔ
22. Ⓐ Ⓑ Ⓒ Ⓓ Ⓔ	27. Ⓐ Ⓑ Ⓒ Ⓓ Ⓔ	32. Ⓐ Ⓑ Ⓒ Ⓓ Ⓔ	37. Ⓐ Ⓑ Ⓒ Ⓓ Ⓔ
23. Ⓐ Ⓑ Ⓒ Ⓓ Ⓔ	28. Ⓐ Ⓑ Ⓒ Ⓓ Ⓔ	33. Ⓐ Ⓑ Ⓒ Ⓓ Ⓔ	38. Ⓐ Ⓑ Ⓒ Ⓓ Ⓔ

right in Section 4

wrong in Section 4

If Section 4 of your test book contains math questions that are not multiple-choice, continue to item 29 below. Otherwise, continue to item 29 above.

29. 30. 31. 32. 33.

34. 35. 36. 37. 38.

SECTION 5

1. Ⓐ Ⓑ Ⓒ Ⓓ Ⓔ	11. Ⓐ Ⓑ Ⓒ Ⓓ Ⓔ	21. Ⓐ Ⓑ Ⓒ Ⓓ Ⓔ	31. Ⓐ Ⓑ Ⓒ Ⓓ Ⓔ
2. Ⓐ Ⓑ Ⓒ Ⓓ Ⓔ	12. Ⓐ Ⓑ Ⓒ Ⓓ Ⓔ	22. Ⓐ Ⓑ Ⓒ Ⓓ Ⓔ	32. Ⓐ Ⓑ Ⓒ Ⓓ Ⓔ
3. Ⓐ Ⓑ Ⓒ Ⓓ Ⓔ	13. Ⓐ Ⓑ Ⓒ Ⓓ Ⓔ	23. Ⓐ Ⓑ Ⓒ Ⓓ Ⓔ	33. Ⓐ Ⓑ Ⓒ Ⓓ Ⓔ
4. Ⓐ Ⓑ Ⓒ Ⓓ Ⓔ	14. Ⓐ Ⓑ Ⓒ Ⓓ Ⓔ	24. Ⓐ Ⓑ Ⓒ Ⓓ Ⓔ	34. Ⓐ Ⓑ Ⓒ Ⓓ Ⓔ
5. Ⓐ Ⓑ Ⓒ Ⓓ Ⓔ	15. Ⓐ Ⓑ Ⓒ Ⓓ Ⓔ	25. Ⓐ Ⓑ Ⓒ Ⓓ Ⓔ	35. Ⓐ Ⓑ Ⓒ Ⓓ Ⓔ
6. Ⓐ Ⓑ Ⓒ Ⓓ Ⓔ	16. Ⓐ Ⓑ Ⓒ Ⓓ Ⓔ	26. Ⓐ Ⓑ Ⓒ Ⓓ Ⓔ	36. Ⓐ Ⓑ Ⓒ Ⓓ Ⓔ
7. Ⓐ Ⓑ Ⓒ Ⓓ Ⓔ	17. Ⓐ Ⓑ Ⓒ Ⓓ Ⓔ	27. Ⓐ Ⓑ Ⓒ Ⓓ Ⓔ	37. Ⓐ Ⓑ Ⓒ Ⓓ Ⓔ
8. Ⓐ Ⓑ Ⓒ Ⓓ Ⓔ	18. Ⓐ Ⓑ Ⓒ Ⓓ Ⓔ	28. Ⓐ Ⓑ Ⓒ Ⓓ Ⓔ	38. Ⓐ Ⓑ Ⓒ Ⓓ Ⓔ
9. Ⓐ Ⓑ Ⓒ Ⓓ Ⓔ	19. Ⓐ Ⓑ Ⓒ Ⓓ Ⓔ	29. Ⓐ Ⓑ Ⓒ Ⓓ Ⓔ	39. Ⓐ Ⓑ Ⓒ Ⓓ Ⓔ
10. Ⓐ Ⓑ Ⓒ Ⓓ Ⓔ	20. Ⓐ Ⓑ Ⓒ Ⓓ Ⓔ	30. Ⓐ Ⓑ Ⓒ Ⓓ Ⓔ	40. Ⓐ Ⓑ Ⓒ Ⓓ Ⓔ

right in Section 5

wrong in Section 5

PRACTICE TEST ONE

SECTION 1

Time—25 Minutes
24 Questions

For each of the following questions, choose the best answer and darken the corresponding oval on the answer sheet.

Select the lettered word or set of words that best completes the sentence.

Example:

Today's small, portable computers contrast markedly with the earliest electronic computers, which were ----.

(A) effective
(B) invented
(C) useful
(D) destructive
(E) enormous

1. While the musician's biography mostly reiterates stories that many readers will find familiar, several chapters about his childhood may even be ---- to experts.

(A) surprising
(B) trivial
(C) boring
(D) unclear
(E) irrelevant

2. The chairman ---- the decision of the board members, describing it as a ---- of every worthwhile ideal that the organization stood for.

(A) defended . . . denial
(B) lamented . . . repudiation
(C) criticized . . . fulfillment
(D) endorsed . . . renunciation
(E) applauded . . . negation

3. While George Balanchine's choreography stayed within a classical context, he challenged convention by recombining the traditional idioms of ballet in ---- ways.

(A) novel
(B) familiar
(C) redundant
(D) naive
(E) awkward

GO ON TO THE NEXT PAGE

4. Despite their outward resemblance, the brothers could not be more ---- temperamentally; while one is quiet and circumspect, the other is brash and ----.

   (A) inimical . . . timid
   (B) passionate . . . superficial
   (C) dissimilar . . . audacious
   (D) different . . . forgiving
   (E) alike . . . respectful

5. Prior to the American entrance into World War I, President Woodrow Wilson strove to maintain the ---- of the United States, warning both sides against encroachments on American interests.

   (A) involvement
   (B) belligerence
   (C) versatility
   (D) munificence
   (E) neutrality

6. The movie star's ex-husband, increasingly bitter, wrote an intensely ---- memoir about her that was widely considered a betrayal of their years of ----.

   (A) hateful . . . antipathy
   (B) laconic . . . estrangement
   (C) malicious . . . intimacy
   (D) adoring . . . affection
   (E) doting . . . antagonism

7. At one time, historians spoke of ancient Greece as though its cultural and scientific achievements were wholly ----, whereas it is now generally recognized that at least some Greek science and culture was ----.

   (A) monolithic . . . homogeneous
   (B) original . . . derivative
   (C) primitive . . . simple
   (D) mistaken . . . dubious
   (E) successful . . . significant

GO ON TO THE NEXT PAGE

Answer the following questions based on the information in the accompanying passages.

Questions 8–11 are based on the following passages.

Passage 1

During the 1840s America saw a rapid expansion of its territory into the unexplored West. Politicians of the time regarded this ever-increasing westward migration and
(5) settlement as America's "Manifest Destiny." American politicians (and later American citizens) believed that it was their mission to claim all the land from the Atlantic to the Pacific. They wanted to "extend the bounda-
(10) ries of freedom" and bring democracy to all those who were capable of self-government. Despite unfortunate prejudices, the goal was just. Every nation needs a sense of purpose and destiny; every nation has a right and a
(15) duty to explore the limits of its geography and to extend its culture as far as possible.

Passage 2

From the vantage point of the 21st century, one can only look back with dismay on the expansionist fever that gripped Americans in the 1840s. Fueled by fears of English alliances
(5) with Mexico, the aftermath of two economic depressions, and a desire to expand the slave trade, Americans, egged on by the politicians of the time, pushed westward seeking their "Manifest Destiny." And what was this
(10) destiny? The settlement of the entire country, from the Atlantic to the Pacific, by white people of European descent. The tragedy, of course, is that this came at such a high price—the decimation of Native American
(15) cultures and the despoiling of the wilderness.

8. According to Passage 1, "Manifest Destiny" is best described as

(A) the desire of Americans to settle the West

(B) a form of self-government

(C) the belief that America should extend from the Atlantic to the Pacific

(D) an unfortunate prejudice held by 19th century Americans

(E) one of the Constitutional rights to which Americans are entitled

9. The phrase "egged on" in Passage 2, line 7 most nearly means

(A) urged

(B) dismissed

(C) discouraged

(D) belittled

(E) rewarded

10. The author of Passage 2 would most likely respond to the contention of the author of Passage 1 that "the goal [of Manifest Destiny] was just" (lines 12–13) by

(A) ridiculing the author of Passage 1 as naive

(B) commending the author's insight

(C) presenting a similar position

(D) defending the author's right to his opinion

(E) arguing for an alternative point of view

GO ON TO THE NEXT PAGE

11. Both authors would probably agree that

   (A) despite its drawbacks, Manifest Destiny produced good results

   (B) Americans were encouraged by their political leaders to pursue Manifest Destiny

   (C) Americans began the westward migration because they were suffering from the results of economic depression

   (D) people have no right to impose cultural values on others

   (E) Manifest Destiny was an inevitable result of the cultural climate of the time

GO ON TO THE NEXT PAGE

Questions 12–18 are based on the following passage.

The following passage is excerpted from a historian's account of the development of European classical music.

During the first half of the nineteenth century, the political and social currents in Europe in the aftermath of the French Revolution brought with them significant
(5) developments in the world of music. Patronage of the arts was no longer considered the exclusive province of the aristocracy. The increasingly prosperous middle class swelled the ranks of audiences at public
(10) concerts and music festivals. New opera houses were built to accommodate the demand, and these in turn enabled musicians to reach a larger public. Furthermore, the elevated status of the middle class increased
(15) the participation of women in the musical field, which had traditionally been associated with men. Bourgeois families encouraged their daughters to take advantage of the new-found leisure time by studying voice or piano,
(20) since this would improve their marriage possibilities and thus be an asset in the family's climb to social acceptance. Singing in particular became a focus of the woman's education, stemming from the traditional
(25) notion that a mother's singing was beneficial in nurturing a child. So many women became involved in amateur musical activities, in fact, that all the businesses that served music—piano-building, music publishing and music
(30) journalism—burgeoned.

Society was only beginning to enlarge its concept of appropriate musical education and activities for women, however. Female musical professionals were still very uncommon.
(35) Even the most competent could be forbidden by husbands and fathers to appear in public, to publish music under their own names, or to accept fees for their teaching if the men feared that these activities would have a
(40) negative impact on the family's social status. The advice and support of a man was still a necessity in the musical career of a woman no matter how talented she was.

The prevailing negative opinions that
(45) continued to constrain women musicians during this century, especially composers, can be traced back to the previous one. Many prominent eighteenth-century writers believed that women did not possess the
(50) intellectual and emotional capacity to learn or to create as artists. The influential social and educational philosopher Jean-Jacques Rousseau, for example, asserted that "women, in general, possess no artistic sensibility…
(55) nor genius." Furthermore, it was held to be unnecessary and even dangerous for women to acquire extensive musical knowledge, as such knowledge could only detract from the business of being a wife and mother. Johann
(60) Campe's opinion of female composers was representative of this view: "Among a hundred praiseworthy female composers hardly one can be found who fulfills simultaneously all the duties of a
(65) reasonable and good wife, an attentive and efficient housekeeper, and a concerned mother."

Most nineteenth-century men and women seemed to agree with these sentiments. Women who performed publicly or attempted
(70) creative work therefore suffered not only societal censure but internal conflicts about the propriety and sensibility of their own aspirations. Even the great Clara Schumann, who was exceptional in that she was
(75) encouraged both by her husband and by the musical public to compose, entertained doubts about her creative ability. In 1839 she wrote, "I once believed that I possessed creative talent, but I have given up this idea; a woman must not

GO ON TO THE NEXT PAGE

(80) desire to compose." Standard views on proper
feminine behavior were so firmly entrenched
that this mother of eight could not recognize
the significance of her own accomplishments.
   Schumann was in fact a trail-blazer—one
(85) of the very first female composers to construct a
large-scale orchestral work. In the early nineteenth century, the "art song" was
considered to be the "safe," appropriate genre
for women composers. The art song was a type
(90) of chamber music and as such fit comfortably
into a domestic environment—the woman's
domain. Women composers also gravitated
to the art song as a medium for musical
expression because its composition did not
(95) require the intensive training (often denied
to women musicians) that the more intricate
sonata or symphony did. Schumann defied
convention, however, when she composed
the "masculine" orchestral piece *Piano Concerto*
(100) *in A Minor*. Although not among those considered her finest, the work demonstrated to the
women musicians who followed Schumann
that female musical creativity could slip loose
from the bonds of society.

12. The first paragraph of the passage suggests
that for the majority of bourgeois women,
their increased participation in music in the
nineteenth century was

   (A) consistent with their traditional roles in
       the family

   (B) burdensome since they were now obliged
       to become involved

   (C) groundbreaking in that women had
       never become professional musicians
       before

   (D) discouraged by men because playing as an
       amateur was socially inappropriate

   (E) justified, considering that women had
       shown talent equal to men in music

13. The statement that the "advice and support
of a man was still a necessity" (lines 41–42)
for a woman musician no matter how talented
she was suggests primarily that women
musicians

   (A) were more emotionally fragile than their
       male counterparts

   (B) accepted the fact that they had little
       experience in making decisions

   (C) were as critical of themselves as the men
       in the family were of them

   (D) generally conformed to accepted norms of
       behavior

   (E) did not need ability so long as they were
       well connected

14. In the third paragraph (lines 44–66), the
author presents evidence to show that

   (A) the perception of women in society can
       be altered

   (B) women had an indirect influence on
       18th-century philosophy

   (C) 19th-century beliefs about women were
       long-standing and firmly rooted

   (D) chauvinism was even more rampant in
       the 18th than in later centuries

   (E) the role of great intellectuals is to point
       out society's faults

15. In line 54, "sensibility" most nearly means

   (A) aptitude

   (B) direction

   (C) thoughtfulness

   (D) practicality

   (E) knowledge

GO ON TO THE NEXT PAGE →

16. The quotation from Campe (lines 61–66) suggests that he thought women

   (A) did not have the ability to compose

   (B) had too many domestic responsibilities

   (C) could balance the demands of home and career

   (D) ought to concentrate their efforts in a single area

   (E) should not neglect domestic duties in favor of music

17. If Schumann was a trailblazing composer, why, according to the author, did she write in 1839 that she no longer thought she had creative talent?

   (A) She was compelled by her husband to do so in order to preserve the family's social status.

   (B) She was not receiving the praise that she once had.

   (C) She had not produced anything of significance by that time.

   (D) She had been influenced by society's view of women.

   (E) She felt she had exhausted her talent in the creation of *Piano Concerto in A Minor*.

18. All of the questions can be explicitly answered on the basis of the passage EXCEPT which of the following?

   (A) What were the advantages to the nineteenth-century bourgeois family of having a daughter educated in music?

   (B) What were the usual limitations imposed on nineteenth-century women regarding their musical aspirations?

   (C) What was the intellectual source of nineteenth-century beliefs regarding women's artistic ability?

   (D) What changes did Clara Schumann herself bring about in society's general attitude toward women as professional musicians?

   (E) What impact did the newfound prosperity of the middle class in the nineteenth century have on businesses associated with the music world?

GO ON TO THE NEXT PAGE

Questions 19–24 are based on the following passage.

The following passage about evolutionary science was excerpted from the writings of a well-known biologist.

There is something intrinsically fascinating about the idea of evolution. What principles govern the evolution of species? And what does evolution tell us about the place of Homo
(5) sapiens in the grand order of things? The writer George Bernard Shaw held that a mystical guiding force impels life to evolve toward eventual perfection. Modern scientists may not believe in this guiding force or in the
(10) possibility of perfection, but many would agree that life has been improving itself through evolution for billions of years. (Note that this conveniently makes Homo sapiens, a very recent product of evolution, one of
(15) the newest and most improved versions of life.) In the view of these scientists, constant competition among species is the engine that drives the process of evolution and propels life upward. In order to win one day's struggle
(20) and live to fight another day, a species always has to adapt, be a little faster, a little stronger, and a little smarter than its competitors and its predecessors.

No less an eminence than Charles Darwin
(25) put forth the idea that species were in constant competition with each other. To Darwin, nature was a surface covered with thousands of sharp wedges, all packed together and jostling for the same space.
(30) Those wedges that fared best moved toward the center of the surface, improving their position by knocking other wedges away with violent blows. The standard example that textbooks give of such competitive wedging is
(35) the interaction between the brachiopods and the clams. Clams were long held to be ancient undersea competitors with brachiopods due to the fact that the two species inhabited the same ecological niche. Clams are abundant
(40) today, whereas brachiopods (dominant in ancient times) are not. Modern clams are also physiologically more complex than brachiopods are. The standard interpretation of these facts is that the clams' physiology was
(45) an evolutionary improvement that gave them the ability to "knock away" the brachiopods.

In recent years, however, the prominent naturalists Stephen Jay Gould and C. Brad Calloway have challenged the validity of this
(50) example as well as the model it was meant to support. Gould and Calloway found that over most of geological time clams and brachiopods went their separate ways. Never did the population of brachiopods dip as that
(55) of the clams rose, or vice versa. In fact, the two populations often grew simultaneously, which belies the notion that they were fighting fiercely over the same narrow turf and resources. That there are so many more clams
(60) than brachiopods today seems rather to be a consequence of mass dyings that occurred in the Permian period. Whatever caused the mass dyings—some scientists theorize that either there were massive ecological or geological
(65) changes, or a comet crashed down from the heavens—clams were simply able to weather the storm much better than the brachiopods.

Out of these observations, Gould and Calloway drew a number of far-reaching
(70) conclusions. For instance, they suggested that direct competition between species was far less frequent than Darwin thought. Perhaps nature was really a very large surface on which there were very few wedges, and the wedges
(75) consequently did not bang incessantly against each other. Perhaps the problem facing these wedges was rather that the surface continually altered its shape, and they had to

GO ON TO THE NEXT PAGE

struggle independently to stay in a good
(80) position on the surface as it changed. In this
alternate model, competition between species is
not the impetus for evolutionary adaptation—
changes in the environment (geological and
climatic variations) are.

(85)   So where does that leave Homo sapiens
if evolution is a response to sudden,
unpredictable and sweeping changes in
the environment rather than the result of a
perpetual struggle? No longer are we the kings
(90) of the mountain who clawed our way to the
top by advancing beyond other species. We are
instead those who took to the mountains when
floods began to rage below and then discovered
that living high up has its definite advantages…
(95) so long as our mountain doesn't decide to turn
into a volcano.

19. The primary purpose of the passage is to

   (A) discuss a new alternative to an established
theory

   (B) demonstrate the usefulness of metaphors
in explaining biology ·

   (C) criticize the fundamental tenets of
evolutionary theory

   (D) examine the nature of the interaction
between two species

   (E) explain a complicated theory in
straightforward terms

20. The author uses the parenthetical statement
in lines 12–16 to make which of the following
points?

   (A) Humankind is as close to perfection as
life can hope to reach.

   (B) Scientists may be influenced by the
desire to see their own species as very
advanced.

   (C) Scientists often merely confirm our own
commonsense views.

   (D) Humankind has not had sufficient time
to improve itself through evolution.

   (E) Our species has evolved from lower forms
of life.

21. As used in the paragraph 2 (lines 24-46), the
term "wedges" refers to

   (A) an organism of a particular species

   (B) an underwater creature

   (C) an entire species

   (D) an ancient animal that has become
extinct

   (E) a group of humans

GO ON TO THE NEXT PAGE

22. In the third paragraph (lines 47–67), the author presents evidence primarily to show that

   (A) evolutionary biologists rarely agree with each other on major issues

   (B) brachiopods have never experienced a decline in population

   (C) the theories and data in antiquated text-books should not be trusted

   (D) the decline of the brachiopod was not the result of competition with clams

   (E) two competing species can undergo simultaneous increases in population

23. A "comet" is mentioned in line 65 as an example of

   (A) a possible reason that brachiopods are no longer abundant

   (B) an event that could have obscured the geological record

   (C) a phenomenon that is as infrequent as mass extinction

   (D) an occurrence that temporarily halted interspecies competition

   (E) a threat that could have had an equal impact on many different species

24. With which statement concerning Gould and Calloway's theory of evolution would the author most likely agree?

   (A) It does not allow for rapid changes in individual species.

   (B) It rules out the possibility that one species could cause the extinction of another.

   (C) It puts the status of humans in a new perspective.

   (D) It places too much importance on the effect of natural disasters.

   (E) It has not yet been tested as much as the previous model.

IF YOU FINISH BEFORE TIME IS CALLED, YOU MAY CHECK YOUR WORK ON THIS SECTION ONLY. DO NOT TURN TO ANY OTHER SECTION IN THE TEST.

STOP

SECTION 2

Time—25 Minutes
18 Questions

Solve each of the following problems, decide which is the best answer choice, and darken the corresponding oval on the answer sheet.

Notes:

(1) Calculator use is permitted.

(2) All numbers used are real numbers.

(3) Figures are provided for some problems. All figures are drawn to scale and lie in a plane UNLESS otherwise indicated.

(4) Unless otherwise specified, the domain of any function f is assumed to be the set of all real numbers x for which $f(x)$ is a real number.

Reference Information

$A = \frac{1}{2}bh$ $c^2 = a^2 + b^2$ Special right triangles $A = \pi r^2$ $C = 2\pi r$ $V = \ell w h$ $V = \pi r^2 h$ $A = \ell w$

The sum of the degree measures of the angles in a triangle is 180.
The number of degrees of arc in a circle is 360.
A straight angle has a degree measure of 180.

1. What is the hundredths' digit in the number 123,456.789?

   (A) 1
   (B) 4
   (C) 5
   (D) 8
   (E) 9

2. All of the following are equal to $9x^2$ EXCEPT

   (A) $x^2 + 8x^2$
   (B) $4x + 5x$
   (C) $(9x)(x)$
   (D) $(3x)(3x)$
   (E) $(-3x)(-3x)$

3. If $\frac{1}{3}(2x) = 30$, what is the value of x?

   (A) $3\frac{1}{3}$
   (B) 45
   (C) $5\frac{1}{3}$
   (D) 6
   (E) 10

GO ON TO THE NEXT PAGE

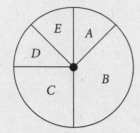

4. The circle graph above represents household expenses in dollars. If $33\frac{1}{3}$ percent of expenses go toward rent, which region on the graph best represents dollars spent on rent?

(A) A

(B) B

(C) C

(D) D

(E) E

5. A rectangle is cut in half, resulting in squares each of area 25. What is the perimeter of the original rectangle?

(A) 10

(B) 20

(C) 30

(D) 40

(E) 50

6. Driving at an average rate of 48 miles per hour, John reached his destination in exactly 2 hours and 15 minutes. To drive the same route in exactly 2 hours, John would have to average what rate of speed?

(A) 50 miles per hour

(B) 54 miles per hour

(C) 55 miles per hour

(D) 60 miles per hour

(E) 64 miles per hour

7. If $x^2 = 7$, what is the value of $(x+1)(x-1)$?

(A) 6

(B) 8

(C) 48

(D) 50

(E) It cannot be determined from the information given.

8. If x is $66\frac{2}{3}$ percent of y, then y is what percent of x?

(A) $33\frac{1}{3}\%$

(B) 75%

(C) $133\frac{1}{3}\%$

(D) 150%

(E) $166\frac{2}{3}\%$

9. A number that is divisible by 4, 6, and 10 must be divisible by all of the following EXCEPT

(A) 8

(B) 12

(C) 15

(D) 20

(E) 30

10. If the sum $\frac{1}{2}+\frac{1}{4}+\frac{1}{8}+\frac{1}{16}+\frac{1}{32}+\frac{1}{64}$ is calculated and expressed in simplest terms, what is the numerator of the sum?

(A) 1

(B) 3

(C) 6

(D) 12

(E) 63

GO ON TO THE NEXT PAGE

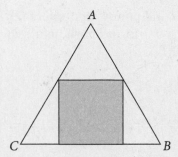

11. In the figure above, the shaded region is a square of area 3, and $\triangle ABC$ is equilateral. What is the perimeter of triangle ABC?

(A) $3\sqrt{3}$

(B) $9\sqrt{3}$

(C) $2 + \sqrt{3}$

(D) $3 + 6\sqrt{3}$

(E) $6 + 3\sqrt{3}$

12. $\sqrt{48} + \sqrt{12} + \sqrt{3} =$

(A) $\sqrt{63}$

(B) $7\sqrt{3}$

(C) $20\sqrt{3}$

(D) $4\sqrt{15} + 3$

(E) $30 + \sqrt{3}$

13. Let $x \text{ } \text{¿} \text{ } y$ be defined as $x^2 + \dfrac{y}{2}$ for all x and y. If $3 \text{ } \text{¿} \text{ } 4 = 5 \text{ } \text{¿} \text{ } n$, what is the value of n?

(A) -28

(B) -7

(C) $\dfrac{12}{5}$

(D) 6

(E) 60

14. If the average (arithmetic mean) of three distinct positive integers is 4, what is the greatest possible value for one of those integers?

(A) 5

(B) 6

(C) 9

(D) 11

(E) 12

15. If the length of one leg of a right triangle is $x + 2$, and the length of the hypotenuse is $x + 3$, where $x > -2$, what is the length of the other leg in terms of x?

(A) x

(B) $x + 1$

(C) $x + \sqrt{5}$

(D) $\sqrt{x+5}$

(E) $\sqrt{2x+5}$

16. When the positive integer n is divided by 9, the remainder is 7. What is the remainder when $5n$ is divided by 9?

(A) 4

(B) 5

(C) 6

(D) 7

(E) 8

GO ON TO THE NEXT PAGE

17. Box *A* contains 4 black marbles and 1 white marble. Box *B* contains 4 black marbles and 3 white marbles. What is the minimum number of marbles that must be moved from Box *A* to Box *B* so that the ratio of black marbles to white marbles is the same in the two boxes?

 (A) 1

 (B) 2

 (C) 3

 (D) 4

 (E) It cannot be done.

18. In the equation $V = \frac{4}{3}\pi r^3$, if the value of r is multiplied by $\frac{1}{2}$, then the value of V is multiplied by

 (A) $\frac{1}{8}$

 (B) $\frac{1}{6}$

 (C) $\frac{1}{4}$

 (D) $\frac{1}{2}$

 (E) $\frac{2}{3}$

19. If j, k, l, and m are four nonzero numbers, all of the following proportions are equivalent EXCEPT

 (A) $\frac{j}{k} = \frac{l}{m}$

 (B) $\frac{k}{m} = \frac{l}{j}$

 (C) $\frac{m}{l} = \frac{k}{j}$

 (D) $\frac{jm}{kl} = 1$

 (E) $\frac{l}{j} = \frac{m}{k}$

20. $3^{-3} + \left(\frac{1}{3}\right)^3 =$

 (A) -9

 (B) $-\frac{2}{27}$

 (C) 0

 (D) $\frac{2}{27}$

 (E) 1

IF YOU FINISH BEFORE TIME IS CALLED, YOU MAY CHECK YOUR WORK ON THIS SECTION ONLY. DO NOT TURN TO ANY OTHER SECTION IN THE TEST.

STOP

SECTION 3

Time—25 Minutes   For each of the following questions, choose the best answer and darken the
24 Questions   corresponding oval on the answer sheet.

Select the lettered word or set of words that best completes the sentence.

Example:

Today's small, portable computers contrast markedly with the earliest electronic computers, which were ----.

(A) effective
(B) invented
(C) useful
(D) destructive
(E) enormous

25. The pollution caused by mining and smelting the lead for electric car batteries may ---- the environmental benefits offered by the cars themselves.

(A) create
(B) outweigh
(C) reinforce
(D) eliminate
(E) overcome

26. The discovery of the Dead Sea Scrolls in the 1940s quickly ---- the popular imagination, but the precise significance of the scrolls is still ---- by scholars.

(A) impressed . . . understood
(B) alarmed . . . obscured
(C) troubled . . . perceived
(D) fired . . . disputed
(E) eluded . . . debated

27. Dietitians warn of the dangers of anorexia, an illness that can cause people with relatively normal physiques to starve themselves until they are too ---- to survive.

(A) glutted
(B) lachrymose
(C) emaciated
(D) superfluous
(E) satiated

28. Since the mid-18th century, there has been much ---- between the cultures of France and Germany despite the frequent ---- between those two countries.

(A communication . . . alliances
(B) hatred . . . opposition
(C) interaction . . . enmity
(D) antagonism . . . misunderstandings
(E) hostility . . . alienation

29. The downsizing of American corporations is probably not an ---- phase; it is becoming a permanent feature of American corporate management.

(A) arbitrary
(B) anticipated
(C) ephemeral
(D) administrative
(E) equivocal

GO ON TO THE NEXT PAGE

30. One theory contends that patriarchy is not ---- part of human nature, but rather it is a cultural institution that dominates in most societies because of the political and social forces that ---- it.

(A) a continuous . . . trivialize

(B) an analogous . . . effect

(C) an inherent . . . discourage

(D) an instinctive . . . promote

(E) a learned . . . underwrite

Answer the questions below based on the information in the accompanying passages.

Questions 31–32 are based on the following passage.

Are they mammals or reptiles? This was the dilemma scientists faced when they tried to classify three animals—the platypus, the short-nosed echidna, and the long-nosed
(5) echidna—that are found only in Australia and New Guinea. Scientists were perplexed since these animals have some things in common with reptiles and some things in common with mammals. For example, they lay eggs like
(10) reptiles, but they nurse their young with milk excreted from special glands, like mammals. Their eye structure is similar to that of reptiles, while their ear structure is like a mammal's. In the end, scientists,
(15) understanding that there was no perfect solution to the predicament, decided to classify them as mammals and to place them in their own order—Monotremata.

31. The opening sentence ("Are they...reptiles?") serves primarily as

(A) a summary of the information in the paragraph

(B) an indication that the question is ultimately unanswerable

(C) a challenge to prevailing scientific opinion

(D) an introduction of the paragraph's topic

(E) an attempt to rebut criticism

32. In lines 12–14, the author most likely discusses the eye and ear structure of the animals in question in order to

(A) provide an in-depth discussion of their anatomy

(B) demonstrate that the animals are more like mammals than reptiles

(C) justify their classification as mammals

(D) illustrate that the animals cannot be easily classified

(E) question the wisdom of the scientists' eventual decision

GO ON TO THE NEXT PAGE

Questions 33–38 are based on the following passage.

The following is adapted from a short story first published in 1921. The author was a Native American woman.

It was summer on the western plains, and fields of golden sunflowers, facing eastward, greeted the rising sun. Blue-Star Woman, with windshorn braids of white hair over each ear,
(5) sat in the shade of her log hut before an open fire. Lonely but unmolested, she dwelt here like the ground squirrel that took its abode near-by—both through the easy tolerance of the landowner. As the Indian woman held a
(10) skillet over the burning embers, a large round cake, with long slashes in its center, baked and crowded the capacity of the frying pan.

In deep abstraction, Blue-Star Woman prepared her morning meal. "Who am I?" had
(15) become the obsessing riddle of her life. She was no longer a young woman, being in her fifty-third year; yet now it was required of her, in the eyes of the white man's law, to give proof of her membership in the Sioux tribe in order to
(20) get her share of tribal land. The unwritten law of heart prompted her naturally to say, "I am a being. I am Blue-Star Woman. A piece of earth is my birthright."

It was taught for reasons now forgotten that
(25) an Indian should never pronounce his or her name in answer to any inquiry. It was probably a means of protection in the days of black magic; be that as it may, Blue-Star Woman lived in times when this teaching was disregarded.
(30) It gained her nothing, however, to pronounce her name to the government official to whom she applied for her share of tribal land. His persistent question was always, "Who are your parents?" Blue-Star Woman was left an orphan
(35) at a tender age, so she did not remember them.

They were long-gone to the spirit-land—and she could not understand why they should be recalled to earth on her account. It was another one of the old, old teachings of her race that the
(40) names of the dead should not be idly spoken—in fact, it was considered a sacrilege to mention carelessly the name of any departed one, especially in disputes over worldly possessions. The unfortunate circumstances of her early
(45) childhood, together with the lack of written records of a roving people, placed a formidable barrier between her and her heritage. The fact was, events of far greater importance to the tribe than her reincarnation had passed
(50) unrecorded in books. The verbal reports of the old-time men and women of the tribe were varied—some were contradictory. Blue-Star Woman was unable to find even a twig of her family tree . . .
(55) Blue-Star Woman was her individual name. For untold ages the Indian race had not used family names—a new-born child was given a brand-new name. Blue-Star Woman was proud to write her name for which she would
(60) not be required to substitute another's upon her marriage, as is the custom of civilized peoples. "The times are changed now," she muttered under her breath. "My individual name seems to mean nothing." Looking out
(65) into space, she saw the nodding sunflowers, and they acquiesced with her . . . With fried bread and black coffee she regaled herself, and once again her mind reverted to her riddle. "This also puzzles me," thought she to herself.
(70) "Once a wise leader of our people, addressing a president of this country, said: 'I am a man. You are another. The Great Spirit is our witness!' This is simple and easy to understand, but the times are changed—the white man's laws are
(75) strange."

GO ON TO THE NEXT PAGE →

33. The major purpose of the passage is to

    (A) highlight the differences between the laws of two cultures

    (B) describe the impact of a changing world on a woman

    (C) illustrate the danger of living apart from society

    (D) show the futility of preserving ancient myths in modern times

    (E) explore the challenge of establishing tribal membership

34. The author most likely mentions the "ground squirrel" (line 7) in order to

    (A) suggest Blue-Star Woman's profound relationship with nature

    (B) demonstrate Blue-Star Woman's keen observation of her surroundings

    (C) show Blue-Star Woman's adaptability to squalid living conditions

    (D) indicate Blue-Star Woman's overwhelming loneliness

    (E) reveal Blue-Star Woman's use of a stranger's land

35. In line 8, "tolerance" most nearly means

    (A) neglect

    (B) fortitude

    (C) permission

    (D) open-mindedness

    (E) limitation

36. The second paragraph suggests that the white man's law differs from the "unwritten law of heart" (lines 20–21) in that the latter

    (A) suggests that every person deserves land of his or her own

    (B) has practical consequences for Blue-Star Woman

    (C) considers each human being to be different

    (D) places restrictions on who can and cannot own land

    (E) can be explained in straightforward language

37. In the third paragraph (lines 24-35), the author conveys a feeling of tension by juxtaposing which two of the following elements?

    (A) The woman's desire for land versus her pronouncement of her name.

    (B) The assertion that the woman was an orphan versus her speculation about her parents.

    (C) The official's demand versus the woman's belief about uttering the names of the dead.

    (D) The woman's dominant presence versus the official's show of authority.

    (E) The woman's reluctance to answer questions versus her willingness to disregard beliefs.

GO ON TO THE NEXT PAGE ⇒

38. In lines 63–64, "My individual name seems to mean nothing" most nearly reflects Blue-Star Woman's

(A) gradual acceptance of the fact that she now has to change her name

(B) devastating loss of prestige and good reputation among her people

(C) sad comprehension that cherished old customs are losing their relevance

(D) great dismay that she has no children to carry on the family name

(E) unsettling realization that no member of the tribe remembers her

Questions 39–40 are based on the following passage.

Rowan couldn't believe his luck. He had proposed to Miss Ashley and she had accepted. She was such a reserved little person that he wasn't sure that she would. To be sure, they
(5) had been stepping out for the past year, but their conversations had been rather one-sided. He would recount his day or explain how his superiors could better run their business. She would nod and smile, offer a word of
(10) encouragement here, ask for clarification there. Really, she was perfect. Her father, when Rowan asked for Miss Ashley's hand, was reluctant, but when Rowan hinted that, after all, Miss Ashley was almost thirty and there wouldn't be too
(15) many other offers, Major Ashley consented. Now began the long period of engagement.

39. In the context of the passage, "stepping out for the past year" (line 5) most likely means that Rowan and Miss Ashley

(A) spent all their time together taking walks

(B) were planning to be married in a year

(C) enjoyed the sport of hiking

(D) had been dating for a year

(E) waited too long to get engaged

40. The sentence in line 11 ("Really...perfect") indicates that Rowan most likely preferred women who

(A) listened to him rather than speaking themselves

(B) were almost 30 years old

(C) enjoyed walking with him

(D) discussed business with him

(E) shared his dreams

GO ON TO THE NEXT PAGE

Questions 41–48 are based on the following passages.

The two passages, excerpted from the writings of two of America's greatest black leaders, were published just two years apart, in 1901 and 1903, respectively. Booker T. Washington, the author of Passage 1, founded Tuskegee Institute in Alabama and was an adviser to presidents. W.E.B. Du Bois, the author of Passage 2, was a pioneer in sociology and historiography.

Passage 1

My own belief is, although I have never before said so in so many words, that the time will come when the Negro in the South will be accorded all the political rights which his
(5) ability, character and material possessions entitle him to. I think, though, that the opportunity to freely exercise such political rights will not come in any large degree through outside or artificial forcing, but will
(10) be accorded to the Negro by the white people themselves, and that they will protect him in the exercise of those rights. Just as soon as the South gets over the old feeling that it is being forced by "foreigners," or "aliens" to
(15) do something which it does not want to do, I believe that the change in the direction that I have indicated is going to begin. In fact, there are indications that it is already beginning in a slight degree.
(20) Let me illustrate my meaning. Suppose that some months before the opening of the Atlanta Exposition* there had been a general demand from the press and public platform outside the South that a Negro be given a place
(25) on the opening programme, and that a Negro be placed upon the board of jurors of award. Would any such recognition of the race have taken place? I do not think so. The Atlanta officials went as far as they did because
(30) they felt it to be a pleasure, as well as a duty, to

reward what they considered merit in the Negro race. Say what we will, there is something in human nature which we cannot blot out, which makes one man, in the
(35) end, recognize and reward merit in another, regardless of colour or race.

I believe it is the duty of the Negro—as the greater part of the race is already doing—to deport himself modestly in regard to political
(40) claims, depending upon the slow but sure influences that proceed from the possession of property, intelligence, and high character for the full recognition of his political rights. I think that the according of political rights is
(45) going to be a matter of natural, slow growth, not an over-night, gourd-vine affair…

Washington was an invited speaker at the Atlanta Exposition in September of 1895.

Passage 2

… Mr. Washington represents in Negro thought the old attitude of adjustment and submission …[I]n our own land, the reaction from the sentiment of war-time has given
(5) impetus to race-prejudice against Negroes, and Mr. Washington withdraws many of the high demands of Negroes as men and American citizens. In other periods of intensified prejudice all the Negro's tendency
(10) to self-assertion has been called forth; at this period a policy of submission is advocated. In the history of nearly all other races and peoples the doctrines preached at such crises has been that manly self-respect is worth more
(15) than lands and houses, and that a people who voluntarily surrender such respect, or cease striving for it, are not worth civilizing.

In answer to this it has been claimed that the Negro can survive only through submission.
(20) Mr. Washington distinctly asks that black people give up, at least for the present, three things—First, political power; Second,

insistence on civil rights; Third, higher
education of Negro youth—and concentrate
(25) all their energies on industrial education, and
accumulation of wealth, and the conciliation of
the South. This policy has been courageously
and insistently advocated for over fifteen years,
and has been triumphant for perhaps ten years.
(30) As a result of this tender of the palm-branch,
what has been the return? In these years there
have occurred:

    1. The disfranchisement* of the Negro.

    2. The legal creation of a distinct status of
(35) civil inferiority of the Negro.

    3. The steady withdrawal of aid from
institutions for the higher training of the Negro.

    These movements are not, to be sure, direct
results of Mr. Washington's teachings; but
(40) his propaganda has, without a shadow of a
doubt, helped their speedier accomplishment.
The question then comes: Is it possible, and
probable, that nine millions of men can make
effective progress in economic lines if
(45) they are deprived of political rights, made
a servile caste, and allowed only the most
meagre chance for developing their exceptional
men? If history and reason give any distinct
answer to these questions, it is an emphatic No.
(50)   … They [who disagree with Mr. Washington]
do not expect that the free right to vote, to
enjoy civil rights and to be educated, will come
in a moment. They do not expect to see the bias
and prejudice of years disappear at the blast of
(55) a trumpet. But they are absolutely certain that
the way for a people to gain their reasonable
rights is clear. Negroes must insist continually . . . that voting is necessary to modern
[citizenship], that color discrimination is
(60) barbarism, and that black boys need education
as well as white boys.

disfranchisement: deprivation of the right to vote

41. In Passage 1, the author's attitude toward
white people in the South in his time is
primarily one of

  (A) empathy for their stoic resistance to
change

  (B) distrust of all but the most openly
humanitarian individuals in power

  (C) confidence that they cannot help but
eventually act responsibly

  (D) exasperation that their behavior so
resembles that of foreign citizens

  (E) respect for the fact that they are so
willing to heed criticism

42. The second paragraph of Passage 1
(lines 20-36) suggests that the author believes
that his being invited to speak at the Atlanta
Exposition was

  (A) a move calculated to improve the South's
image

  (B) a result of pressure from outside the
South

  (C) an indication that the South has overcome
old-fashioned views

  (D) an example of the influence already
wielded by blacks in the South

  (E) a reflection not just on himself but
on his race

GO ON TO THE NEXT PAGE

43. The phrase "slow but sure influences" (Passage 1, lines 40–41) most likely refers to the

   (A) good impressions made by wealth and accomplishments
   (B) Southern blacks' growing belief in the political system
   (C) gradual and unnoticed usurpation of power
   (D) option to move out of the South
   (E) South's adoption of Northern ways of thinking

44. The author of Passage 2 mentions "the history of nearly all other races and peoples" (lines 12–13) in order to

   (A) suggest that material possessions are an important part in a race's struggle for respect
   (B) suggest that blacks should seek equality as individuals rather than as a community
   (C) suggest that a policy of submission will never improve the status of blacks
   (D) illustrate that blacks have been the victims of prejudice throughout the world
   (E) illustrate that racism is not a problem unique to America

45. The author's tone in describing the "result of this tender of the palm-branch" (Passage 2, line 30) is

   (A) analytical and distanced
   (B) mournful and full of regret
   (C) ironic and critical
   (D) both surprised and disillusioned
   (E) alternately outraged and apathetic

46. Passage 2 suggests that Passage 1's view of "human nature" (line 33)

   (A) is naive and optimistic
   (B) may be borne out by future events
   (C) reflects the experience of an entire race
   (D) is only partially accurate
   (E) applies only to educated individuals

47. The authors of both passages would most probably agree that

   (A) the best way to gain the respect of others is to use force
   (B) accumulation of wealth does not automatically bring political power
   (C) long-standing prejudice cannot be conquered overnight
   (D) education is not as important as the possession of political rights
   (E) one should not use speculation to support an argument

48. If these two passages were found in one chapter in a collection of historical writings, the title of the chapter would most likely be

   (A) Twentieth-Century Leaders
   (B) Historical Perspectives
   (C) Conflicting Points of View
   (D) The History of the South
   (E) Viewpoints of 20th-Century Black Leaders

IF YOU FINISH BEFORE TIME IS CALLED, YOU MAY CHECK YOUR WORK ON THIS
SECTION ONLY. DO NOT TURN TO ANY OTHER SECTION IN THE TEST.

STOP

SECTION 4

Time—25 Minutes
20 Questions

Solve each of the following problems, decide which is the best answer choice, and darken the corresponding oval on the answer sheet.

Notes:

(1) Calculator use is permitted.

(2) All numbers used are real numbers.

(3) Figures are provided for some problems. All figures are drawn to scale and lie in a plane UNLESS otherwise indicated.

(4) Unless otherwise specified, the domain of any function f is assumed to be the set of all real numbers x for which $f(x)$ is a real number.

Reference Information

$A = \frac{1}{2}bh$ $c^2 = a^2 + b^2$ Special right triangles $A = \pi r^2$ $C = 2\pi r$ $V = \ell wh$ $V = \pi r^2 h$ $A = \ell w$

The sum of the degree measures of the angles in a triangle is 180.
The number of degrees of arc in a circle is 360.
A straight angle has a degree measure of 180.

21. If $x - y = 6$, $y = 5z$, and $z = 4$, what is the value of x?

   (A) −26
   (B) −14
   (C) 14
   (D) 15
   (E) 26

22. The sum of 9a and the square root of 2b is equal to the square of the sum of 3a and 3b.

   Which of the following is an expression for the statement above?

   (A) $9a + (2b)^2 = \sqrt{3a+3b}$
   (B) $9a + \sqrt{2b} = (3a + 3b)^2$
   (C) $(9a + 2b)^2 = \sqrt{3a+3b}$
   (D) $\sqrt{9a+2b} = 3a^2 + 3b^2$
   (E) $\sqrt{9a} + \sqrt{2b} = (3a + 3b)^2$

GO ON TO THE NEXT PAGE

23. One pound of spaghetti serves either 7 adults or 9 children. What is the minimum number of pounds of spaghetti needed to serve 75 people, 15 of whom are children?

(A) 7
(B) 8
(C) 9
(D) 11
(E) 13

24. If $x = \dfrac{1}{2}$, what is the value of $\dfrac{2}{x} + \dfrac{2}{(x-1)}$?

(A) −2
(B) −1
(C) 0
(D) 1
(E) 2

25. If 20 percent of J is 1,500, what is 15 percent of J?

(A) 1,125
(B) 3,000
(C) 5,125
(D) 6,000
(E) 7,500

26. Which of the following is an integer greater than 1 that has <u>only</u> itself, its square root, and 1 as its three positive integer factors?

(A) 49
(B) 81
(C) 100
(D) 144
(E) 225

27. When an integer is multiplied by itself, it can end in all of the following EXCEPT

(A) 1
(B) 3
(C) 5
(D) 6
(E) 9

28. $(-3x^5y^4)^4 =$

(A) $-3x^9y^8$
(B) $-3x^{20}y^{16}$
(C) $-81x^{20}y^{16}$
(D) $81x^9y^8$
(E) $81x^{20}y^{16}$

GO ON TO THE NEXT PAGE

DIRECTIONS FOR STUDENT-PRODUCED RESPONSE QUESTIONS

For each of the questions below (29–38), solve the problem and indicate your answer by darkening the ovals in the special grid. For example:

Answer: 1.25 or $\frac{5}{4}$ or 5/4

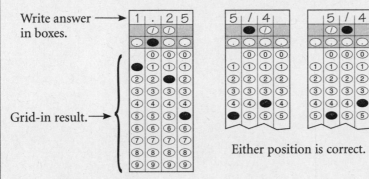

Write answer in boxes.

Grid-in result.

Fraction line
Decimal point

Either position is correct.

You may start your answers in any column, space permitting. Columns not needed should be left blank.

- It is recommended, though not required, that you write your answer in the boxes at the top of the columns. However, you will receive credit only for darkening the ovals correctly.

- Grid only one answer to a question, even though some problems have more than one correct answer.·

- Darken no more than one oval in a column.

- No answers are negative.

- Mixed numbers cannot be gridded. For example: the number $1\frac{1}{4}$ must be gridded as 1.25 or 5/4.

    (If $\boxed{1 \mid 1 \mid / \mid 4}$ is gridded, it will be interpreted as $\frac{11}{4}$, not $1\frac{1}{4}$.)

- <u>Decimal Accuracy:</u> Decimal answers must be entered as accurately as possible. For example, if you obtain an answer such as 0.1666…, you should record the result as .166 or .167. **Less accurate values such as .16 or .17 are not acceptable.**

Acceptable ways to grid $\frac{1}{6}$ = .1666 …

29. If *A* is the set of digits and *B* is the set of even numbers, then the intersection of *A* and *B* contains how many elements?

30. If $\sqrt{2-x}-1=0$, what is the value of *x*?

31. Half the product of 8 and 9 is the square root
     of what number?

33. If *A* and *B* represent distinct digits in the
     correctly worked addition problem above,
     what is the value of *A*?

32. What is the average (arithmetic mean) of $\dfrac{1}{4}$
     and $\dfrac{1}{6}$?

$$
\begin{array}{r}
AA \\
+BA \\
\hline
1B8
\end{array}
$$

34. In the figure above, *AB* is perpendicular to
     AE. If the measure of ∠*BAD* is 53 degrees,
     and the measure of ∠*CAE* is 73 degrees, what
     is the degree measure of ∠*CAD*?

GO ON TO THE NEXT PAGE

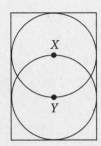

35. In the figure above, X and Y are the centers of the two circles. If each circle has circumference 9π, what is the perimeter of the rectangle?

36. Nuala baked 64 cookies for a party. After each party guest ate n cookies, there were 9 cookies left uneaten. If there were more than 9 guests at the party, and if n is an integer greater than 1, what is the value of n?

37. Boxes of candy were sold for a school fund-raiser. Small boxes cost $2 each and large boxes cost $5 each. If 150 boxes were sold for a total of $444, how many large boxes were sold?

38. What is the maximum possible area of a rectangle with perimeter 14?

SECTION 5

Time—25 Minutes
39 Questions

For each of the following questions, choose the best answer and darken the corresponding oval on the answer sheet.

Directions: The following sentences test your knowledge of grammar, usage, diction (choice of words), and idioms.

Some sentences are correct.

No sentence contains more than one error.

You will find that the error, if there is one, is underlined and lettered. Elements of the sentence that are not underlined will not be changed. In choosing answers, follow the requirements of standard written English.

If there is an error, select the one underlined part that must be changed to make the sentence correct, and fill in the corresponding oval on your answer sheet.

If there is no error, fill in answer oval (E).

1. Before <u>the advent of</u> modern surgical
   　　　　　A
   techniques, <u>bleeding patients</u> with leeches
   　　　　　　　　B
   <u>were considered</u> therapeutically <u>effective</u>.
   　　C　　　　　　　　　　　　　D
   <u>No error</u>
   　E

2. The <u>recent</u> establishment of "Crime Busters,"
   　　　A
   officially sanctioned neighborhood block-
   watching groups, <u>has</u> <u>dramatic</u> improved
   　　　　　　　　　B　　C
   relations <u>between</u> citizens and police.
   　　　　　　　D
   <u>No error</u>
   　E

3. The masterpiece auctioned so <u>successfully</u>
   　　　　　　　　　　　　　　　　　A
   today depicts a biblical scene in <u>which</u> the
   　　　　　　　　　　　　　　　　　B
   king is on his throne <u>with</u> his counselors
   　　　　　　　　　　　C
   <u>respectively</u> standing below. <u>No error</u>
   　D　　　　　　　　　　　　　　E

4. <u>During</u> the election campaign, the major
   　A
   political parties <u>have agreement</u> that
   　　　　　　　　B
   minorities must <u>be given</u> the opportunity
   　　　　　　　　C
   <u>to advance</u> in society. <u>No error</u>
   　D　　　　　　　　　E

5. Most of the delegates <u>which</u> attended the
   　　　　　　　　　　　A
   convention <u>felt</u> the resolution was <u>too</u>
   　　　　　　B　　　　　　　　　　　C
   <u>strongly</u> worded, and the majority voted
   　C
   <u>against</u> it. <u>No error</u>
   　D　　　　　E

GO ON TO THE NEXT PAGE →

6. <u>Lost in the forest</u> on a cold night, <u>the hunters</u>
    A   B
<u>built</u> a fire <u>to keep themselves</u> warm and
   B   C
<u>to frighten away</u> the wolves. <u>No error</u>
   D   E

7. The effort to <u>create appropriate</u> theatrical
               A
effects <u>often result</u> in settings that cannot
       B
be <u>effective</u> without an imaginative <u>lighting</u>
   C   D
crew. <u>No error</u>
     E

8. Every one of the shops in the town <u>were</u>
                             A
<u>closed</u> on Thursday <u>because</u> of the <u>ten-inch</u>
 A   B   C
rainfall that <u>had fallen</u> during the day.
          D
<u>No error</u>
  E

9. <u>According to</u> the directions on the package,
   A
the contents <u>are</u> intended for external use
       B
<u>only</u> and <u>should not hardly</u> be swallowed,
 C   D
even in small quantities. <u>No error</u>
                E

10. Mr. Webster's paper is <u>highly imaginary</u> and
                  A
<u>very creative</u>, <u>but</u> seems to be <u>lacking in</u>
  B   C   D
cogency. <u>No error</u>
     E

11. The late president's <u>numerous</u> memoirs now
              A
<u>about to be</u> published <u>promises</u> to be of
 B   C
special <u>historical</u> interest. <u>No error</u>
    D   E

12. The point <u>on issue</u> was whether the dock
      A
workers, <u>who</u> were <u>an extremely</u> vocal group,
     B   C
<u>would decide to</u> return to work. <u>No error</u>
   D   E

13. <u>Raising</u> living costs, <u>together</u> with escalating
  A   B
taxes, <u>have</u> proved to be a burden for
     C
everyone. <u>No error</u>
 D   E

14. A number of <u>harried</u> department store
         A
employees <u>were congregating</u> <u>around</u> the
        B   C
water cooler <u>to compare and discuss</u> their
           D
grievances. <u>No error</u>
      E

GO ON TO THE NEXT PAGE

Directions: The following sentences test correctness and effectiveness of expression. In choosing answers, follow the requirements of standard written English; that is, pay attention to grammar, choice of words, sentence construction, and punctuation.

In each of the following sentences, part of the sentence or the entire sentence is underlined. Beneath each sentence, you will find five ways of phrasing the underlined part. Choice (A) repeats the original; the other four are different.

Choose the answer that best expresses the meaning of the original sentence. If you think the original is better than any of the alternatives, choose it; otherwise, choose one of the others. Your choice should produce the most effective sentence—clear and precise, without awkwardness or ambiguity.

15. In *War and Peace*, Tolstoy presented his theories on history and underline illustrated them with a slanted account of actual historical events.

    (A) illustrated them
    (B) also illustrating them
    (C) he also was illustrating these ideas
    (D) then illustrated the theories also
    (E) then he went about illustrating them

16. In the United States, an increasing number of commuters that believe their families to be immune from the perils of city life.

    (A) that believe their families to be
    (B) that believe their families are
    (C) believes their families are
    (D) who believe their families to be
    (E) believe their families to be

17. Developed by a scientific team at his university, the president informed the reporters that the new process would facilitate the diagnosis of certain congenital diseases.

    (A) Developed by a scientific team at his university
    (B) Having been developed by a scientific team at his university
    (C) Speaking of the discovery made by a scientific team at his university
    (D) Describing the development of a scientific team at his university
    (E) As it had been developed by a scientific team at his university

18. One ecological rule of thumb states that there is opportunity for the accumulation of underground water reservoirs but in regions where vegetation remains undisturbed.

    (A) but in regions where vegetation remains undisturbed
    (B) unless vegetation being left undisturbed in some regions
    (C) only where undisturbed vegetation is in regions
    (D) only in regions where vegetation remains undisturbed
    (E) except for vegetation remaining undisturbed in some regions

GO ON TO THE NEXT PAGE

19. The Equal Rights Amendment to Islandia's constitution is dying a lingering political death, <u>many dedicated groups and individuals have attempted</u> to prevent its demise.

   (A) many dedicated groups and individuals have attempted

   (B) although many dedicated groups and individuals have attempted

   (C) many dedicated groups and persons has attempted

   (D) despite many dedications of groups and individuals to attempt

   (E) also, many dedicated groups and individuals have attempted

20. The ancient Chinese were convinced that air was composed of two kinds of particles, <u>one inactive and one active, the latter of which they called yin and we today call oxygen.</u>

   (A) one inactive and one active, the latter of which they called yin and we today call oxygen

   (B) an inactive and an active one called yin, now known as oxygen

   (C) an inactive type and the active type they called yin we now know to be oxygen

   (D) inactive and active; while they called the active type yin, today we call it oxygen

   (E) contrasting the inactive type with the active ones they named yin and we call oxygen

21. Developing a suitable environment for house plants <u>is in many ways like when you are managing</u> soil fertilization for city parks.

   (A) is in many ways like when you are managing

   (B) is in many ways similar to when you are managing

   (C) in many ways is on a par with managing your

   (D) is in many ways similar to the managing of

   (E) is in many ways like managing

22. Most students would get better grades if <u>writing were to be studied by them</u>.

   (A) writing were to be studied by them

   (B) they studied writing

   (C) writing was studied by them

   (D) they would have studied writing

   (E) they were to have studied writing

23. <u>If they do not go into bankruptcy</u>, the company will probably survive its recent setbacks.

   (A) If they do not go into bankruptcy

   (B) Unless bankruptcy cannot be avoided

   (C) If they can avoid bankruptcy

   (D) If bankruptcy will be avoided

   (E) Unless it goes bankrupt

GO ON TO THE NEXT PAGE

24. Now that I have read the works of both Henry and William James, I am convinced that Henry is <u>the best psychologist and William the best writer</u>.

    (A) the best psychologist and William the best writer

    (B) a better psychologist, William is the best writer

    (C) the best as a psychologist, William the best as a writer

    (D) the best psychologist, William the better writer

    (E) the better psychologist and William the better writer

25. When he arrived at the hospital, the doctor found that <u>several emergency cases had been admitted before</u> he went on duty.

    (A) several emergency cases had been admitted before

    (B) there were several emergency cases admitted prior to

    (C) two emergency cases were being admitted before

    (D) a couple of emergency cases were admitted before

    (E) several emergency cases was admitted before

26. The variety of Scandinavian health care services offered to residents at reduced cost <u>far exceeds low-cost health programs</u> available in the United States.

    (A) far exceeds low-cost health programs

    (B) far exceeds the number of low-cost health programs

    (C) tends to be greater than low-cost programs

    (D) far exceed the number of low-cost health programs

    (E) are greater than comparable low-cost health programs

27. The politician is benefiting from behavioral <u>research, there are new techniques for them</u> to utilize and new broadcasting methods to experiment with.

    (A) research, there are new techniques for them

    (B) research; there are new techniques for them

    (C) research; he has new techniques

    (D) research, there are new techniques for him

    (E) research; they have new techniques

28. <u>The poet Oscar Wilde was known for his aphoristic wit and brilliant conversation, he</u> wrote a number of memorable literary essays including "The Critic as Artist."

    (A) The poet Oscar Wilde was known for his aphoristic wit and brilliant conversation, he

    (B) The poet Oscar Wilde, known for his aphoristic wit and brilliant conversation; he

    (C) Known for his aphoristic wit and brilliant conversation, the poet Oscar Wilde

    (D) The poet Oscar Wilde was known for his aphoristic wit and brilliant conversation, however he

    (E) Oscar Wilde, the poet, known for his aphoristic wit and brilliant conversation, and he

GO ON TO THE NEXT PAGE

29. According to Westin's book, <u>the typical Victorian family was more interested in maintaining the appearance of propriety than in</u> securing happiness for its individual members.

    (A) the typical Victorian family was more interested in maintaining the appearance of propriety than in

    (B) the appearance of propriety was more interesting to the typical Victorian family than

    (C) the typical Victorian family, more interested in maintaining the appearance of propriety than it was in

    (D) for a Victorian family it was typical that they would be more interested in maintaining the appearance of propriety than in

    (E) the typical Victorian family was more interested in the appearance of propriety than in

30. <u>Once an enclave of privileged white males, the Wodehouse Club's directors have</u> now decided to adopt a more inclusive membership policy.

    (A) Once an enclave of privileged white males, the Wodehouse Club's directors have

    (B) The directors of the Wodehouse Club, which was once an enclave of privileged white males, have

    (C) Though once an enclave of privileged white males, the Wodehouse Club's directors

    (D) Once an enclave of privileged white males, the Wodehouse Club's directors having

    (E) The directors of the enclave of privileged white males, the Wodehouse Club, has

31. Supporters of the Eighteenth Amendment thought that banning alcohol would improve citizens' morals and enhance their quality of life by removing the temptation to drink; <u>national prohibition</u> ushered in 13 years of bootlegging, speakeasies, and violent gangster crime.

    (A) national prohibition

    (B) in fact, national prohibition

    (C) furthermore, national prohibition

    (D) but national prohibition

    (E) consequently, national prohibition

32. Though multimedia presentations have their place in the school curriculum, it is ridiculous to claim, as some do, <u>that children learn as much from watching a one-hour video as a book</u>.

    (A) that children learn as much from watching a one-hour video as a book

    (B) that children will learn as much from watching a one-hour video as they did from a book

    (C) that children learn as much from watching a one-hour video as they do from reading a book

    (D) that a one-hour video teaches more to children than book-reading

    (E) that children watching a one-hour video learn as much as reading a book

GO ON TO THE NEXT PAGE

33. Finland's national epic, the *Kalevala*, <u>based
    on an oral tradition that</u> the Balto-Finnish
    people preserved for some 2,500 years despite
    the upheavals of history and the pressures of
    foreign domination.

    (A) based on an oral tradition that

    (B) being based on an oral tradition that

    (C) is based on an oral tradition; this

    (D) basing itself on an oral tradition which

    (E) is based on an oral tradition that

34. The island of Santa Ynez was once a
    playground for wealthy American tourists; in
    recent years, however, civil unrest and a series
    of natural disasters <u>have made it so that it is
    not nearly as appealing</u> as a vacation spot.

    (A) have made it so that it is not nearly as
        appealing

    (B) are causing it to be made less appealing

    (C) greatly reducing its appeal

    (D) have greatly lessened its appeal

    (E) have not nearly made it as appealing

GO ON TO THE NEXT PAGE

Directions: The passage below is an early draft of an essay. Parts of the passage need to be rewritten.

Read the passage, and answer the questions that follow. Some questions are about individual sentences or parts of sentences; in these questions, you are asked to select the choice which will improve sentence structure and word choice. Other questions refer to parts of the essay or the entire essay and ask you to consider the organization and development. You should follow the conventions of standard written English in answering the questions. After you have chosen your answer, fill in the corresponding oval on your answer sheet.

Questions 35–39 are based on the following essay, which is a response to an assignment to write about an economic issue facing the United States.

(1) *Last year, my social studies class attended a talk given by a young woman who worked in a factory in Central America making shirts for a popular U.S. retail chain.* (2) *The working conditions she described were horrific.* (3) *She spoke of being forced to work 14-hour days and even longer on weekends.* (4) *The supervisors often hit her and the other women, most of whom were teenagers, get them to work faster.* (5) *They gave them contaminated water to drink and were only allowed to go to the bathroom twice a day.* (6) *She urged us to boycott the retail chain and to inform consumers about the conditions in their factories.*

(7) *A group of us decided to meet with a representative of the chain and we would discuss our concerns and would announce our plans to boycott.* (8) *The representative said that low wages were necessary to keep costs down.* (9) *And she claimed a boycott would never work because it would be impossible to stop people from shopping at such a popular store.* (10) *"Nobody is going to listen to a bunch of teenagers," she said.* (11) *We decided to prove her wrong.*

(12) *First, we calculated that the workers' wages accounted for less than 1 percent of the price people paid for the shirts in the United States.* (13) *We argued that if the chain were willing to make slightly lower profits, it could afford to pay*

the workers more without raising prices. (14) *And when we began informing people about the conditions under which the shirts they bought were made, they were horrified.* (15) *Many were agreeing to shop there no longer, they even wrote letters to the president of the chain in which he was urged to do something about the conditions in the factories.* (16) *Even local politicians got involved.* (17) *The winner of that year's City Council election pledged to change the conditions in the factories or shut the store down once and for all.* (18) *Finally, with business almost at a standstill, the store agreed to consumers' demands.*

35. In context, which is the best version of the underlined portion of sentence 5 (reproduced below)?

    They gave them contaminated water to drink <u>and were only allowed to go to the bathroom</u> twice a day.

    (A) (As it is now)
    (B) and were only allowing them to go to the bathroom
    (C) and allowed them to go to the bathroom only
    (D) and they were only given permission to go to the bathroom
    (E) and were allowed to only go to the bathroom

GO ON TO THE NEXT PAGE

36. In context, which of the following best replaces the word "their" in sentence 6 (reproduced below)?

She urged us to boycott the retail chain and to inform consumers about the conditions in their factories.

(A) the consumers'
(B) its
(C) the workers'
(D) the company's
(E) the students'

37. Which of the following versions of the underlined portion of sentence 7 (reproduced below) is best?

A group of us decided to meet with a representative of the chain <u>and we would discuss our concerns and would announce</u> our plans to boycott.

(A) (As it is now)
(B) to discuss our concerns and announce
(C) for the purpose of discussing our concerns and announcing
(D) where we would discuss our concerns and announce
(E) with whom we would be discussing our concerns and to whom we would announce

38. Which of the following would be the best replacement for the word "And" at the beginning of sentence 9 (reproduced below)?

And she claimed a boycott would never work because it would be impossible to stop people from shopping at such a popular store.

(A) Moreover,
(B) Rather,
(C) However,
(D) Even so,
(E) Instead,

39. In context, which of the following is the best way to revise the underlined portion of sentence 15 (reproduced below)?

<u>Many were agreeing to shop there no longer, they even wrote letters to the president of the chain in which he was urged</u> to do something about the conditions in the factories.

(A) (As it is now)
(B) Many agreed to no longer shop there and even writing letters to the president of the chain to urge him
(C) Agreeing to shop there no longer, many even wrote letters to the president of the chain urging him
(D) Many agreed to no longer shop there and also to urge the president of the chain by writing letters in which they asked him
(E) Shopping there no longer, many agreed to write letters to the president of the chain to urge him

IF YOU FINISH BEFORE TIME IS CALLED, YOU MAY CHECK YOUR WORK ON THIS SECTION ONLY. DO NOT TURN TO ANY OTHER SECTION IN THE TEST. STOP

(Answers on the next page.)

PRACTICE TEST ONE: **ANSWER KEY**

SECTION 1

1. A	9. A	17. D
2. B	10. E	18. D
3. A	11. B	19. A
4. C	12. A	20. B
5. E	13. D	21. C
6. C	14. C	22. D
7. B	15. A	23. A
8. C	16. E	24. C

SECTION 2

1. D	8. D	15. E
2. B	9. A	16. E
3. B	10. E	17. B
4. B	11. E	18. A
5. C	12. B	19. D
6. B	13. A	20. B
7. A	14. C	

SECTION 3

25. B	33. B	41. C
26. D	34. A	42. E
27. C	35. C	43. A
28. C	36. A	44. C
29. C	37. C	45. C
30. D	38. C	46. A
31. D	39. D	47. C
32. D	40. A	48. E

SECTION 4

21. E	31. 1,296
22. B	32. $\frac{5}{24}$ or 0.208
23. D	33. 9
24. C	34. 36
25. A	35. 45
26. A	36. 5
27. B	37. 48
28. E	38. $\frac{49}{4}$ or 12.25
29. 5	
30. 1	

SECTION 5

1. C	14. E	27. C
2. C	15. A	28. C
3. D	16. E	29. A
4. B	17. C	30. B
5. A	18. D	31. B
6. E	19. B	32. C
7. B	20. A	33. E
8. A	21. E	34. D
9. D	22. B	35. C
10. A	23. E	36. D
11. C	24. E	37. B
12. A	25. A	38. A
13. A	26. B	39. C

PRACTICE TEST ONE: ASSESS YOUR STRENGTHS

Use the following tables to determine which question types you need to review most.

Question Type	Section and Question
Sentence Completion	Section 1, 1–7 Section 3, 25–30
Reading Comprehension	Section 1, 8–24 Section 3, 31-48
Regular Math	Section 2, 1–18 Section 4, 19–28
Grid-in Math	Section 4, 29–38
Identifying Sentence Errors	Section 5, 1–14
Improving Sentences	Section 5, 15–34
Improving Paragraphs	Section 5, 35–39

Question Type	Number of Questions on Test	Number Correct
Sentence Completion	13	
Reading Comprehension	35	
Regular Math	28	
Grid-in Math	10	
Identifying Sentence Errors	14	
Improving Sentences	20	
Improving Paragraphs	5	

ANSWERS AND EXPLANATIONS

SECTION 1

1. A

The clue word *while* tells you that this sentence has a contrast. You need a word that will contrast with *familiar*. Choice (A) *surprising* matches this prediction.

2. B

For this straight-ahead sentence, you need a choice with either two positive words or two negative words. The chairman would either *support* the decision because it *reinforced* worthwhile ideals, or *bemoan* the decision because it *went against* worthwhile ideals. Only (B) fits the bill with two negative words, *lamented* and *repudiation*.

3. A

Since Balanchine worked *within a classical context*, he must have done something different in order to *challenge convention*. You can predict that he used traditional idioms in new ways. *Novel*, (A), matches this prediction.

4. C

Start with the second part of the sentence. One brother is *quiet*, the other *brash*. Look for a word that goes with *brash* to fit the second blank and a word that means *not alike* for the first blank. Choice (C) *dissimilar . . . audacious* does the trick.

5. E

The most important phrase in the sentence is *prior to*. Before America entered the war, Wilson couldn't maintain the *involvement* (A) or *belligerence* (B) of the United States, and (C) and (D) just don't make sense. Choice (E) *neutrality* accurately represents the prewar status.

6. C

Start with the first blank of this contrasting sentence. The movie star's ex was *bitter*, so you need a word that goes with *bitter*, like *hateful* (A) or *malicious* (C). This bitter memoir is a *betrayal* of their past, so you need a positive word for the second blank. *Intimacy* (C) matches the prediction.

7. B

The clue word *whereas* tells you that this is a contrasting sentence, so you need a choice with contrasting words. Only (B), *original . . . derivative*, provides the needed contrast.

MANIFEST DESTINY PASSAGES

These two passages present contrasting views on Americans' "Manifest Destiny," or the expansion of the country west. The writer of Passage 1 says that it was the duty of the nation to expand west in order to spread democracy. The writer of Passage 2 disagrees and says that the expansion was more to settle the country with white people of European descent. That led to tragedy—the deaths of Native Americans and the despoiling of the wild.

8. C

The author uses the phrase *Manifest Destiny* in the second sentence. Immediately following this, she goes on to say *Americans believed that it was their mission to claim all the land from the Atlantic to the Pacific.* This is the implied definition of Manifest Destiny. You need a choice that talks about the expansion of America from east to west, and (C) fits the bill. Watch out for (A)—Americans may have desired to settle the West, but they saw Manifest Destiny as a mission, not just a desire. In pursuing their Manifest Destiny, 19th century Americans operated on a prejudice, but this prejudice isn't a definition of Manifest Destiny (D).

9. A

The context here is *Fueled by fears of English alliances with Mexico, the aftermath of two economic depressions, and a desire to expand the slave trade, Americans,* egged on *by the politicians of the time, pushed westward…* A good prediction is *strongly encouraged,* and that matches (A).

10. E

The author of Passage 1 approves of Manifest Destiny and says that despite the prejudices of nineteenth-century Americans, the goal was just. The author of Passage 2 says that the pursuit of Manifest Destiny had tragic consequences—the loss of Native American culture and the ruin of the wilderness. He would most likely respond to Author 1 by reiterating his alternative point of view (E). In any case, he would not have a positive response, like (B) and (C). Choice (A) is too extreme—there's no indication that the author of Passage 1 is naive.

11. B

When answering questions about what both authors would agree with, be careful of trap answers that express the opinion of only one of the authors, and eliminate those choices that don't express the opinion of both authors. Choice (A) fits only with Passage 1, while (C) and (D) are mentioned only in Passage 2. Choice (E) talks about the inevitability of Manifest Destiny, which is not mentioned in either passage. Choice (B), however, fits with both passages—it's mentioned in the third sentence of Passage 1 and the second sentence of Passage 2.

MUSIC HISTORY PASSAGE

This passage, which focuses on the effect of societal currents on women's participation in music, is somewhat dense, so you should read through it fairly

quickly to get the gist, noting important themes in each paragraph as you go.

Paragraph 1 gives an overview of the social and political climate of the first half of the 19th century and the effect of this climate on the middle class, particularly with regard to music. In paragraph 2, the author explains that, despite the increased access to music that the middle class enjoyed at this time, women were still excluded from participation in many musical activities. Paragraph 3 explains that negative opinions about women and music can be traced to 18th-century notions. Rousseau and Campe are quoted in this paragraph. Paragraph 4 continues the idea that women were restricted from full participation in the musical world and cites the example of Clara Schumann. Paragraph 5 outlines the accomplishments of Clara Schumann and introduces the idea of the *art song*.

12. A

In the first paragraph, we learn that women's involvement with music was thought to enhance their marriageability, enhance their families' social status, and help in child-rearing. This is best characterized by (A), since all of these forms of participation are consistent with women's traditional family roles.

13. D

Reread the second paragraph, including the cited lines. If you have trouble rephrasing an answer, test each of the choices. It's most reasonable to infer that, since women at this time needed men's support and advice, they must have conformed to society's expectations. None of the other choices is supported by the passage.

14. C

As we saw in the overview preceding these answers, paragraph 3 focuses on the influence of 18th-century opinions of women. Choice (C) explains that these beliefs were long-standing, which is supported by the information in this paragraph.

15. A

Reread the lines surrounding the cited word for this Vocabulary-in-Context question. What word could you substitute for *sensibility*? *Ability* would work, and (A) *aptitude* does the trick.

16. E

Rereading the quote from Campe, you see that his focus is on the idea that music distracts women from their duties as wives, housekeepers, and mothers. This idea is paraphrased in (E).

17. D

The fourth paragraph focuses on society's negative view of women who performed music publicly or composed music. The topic of Clara Schumann is raised in this context, and the author's discussion of *societal censure* and *internal conflicts* leads us to believe that Schumann's lack of confidence was a product of society's views. This idea is paraphrased in (D).

18. D

Take the choices one by one, looking for evidence to support them in the passage. Paragraph 1 explicitly outlines the advantages of having a musically educated daughter (marriage, social status, enhanced mothering abilities), so (A) is wrong. Paragraph 2 tells us that women could be forbidden to play publicly, publish music, or accept fees, so (B) is out. Paragraph 3 is about 18th-century views of women, which was the intellectual source of nineteenth-century beliefs, knocking (C) out of the running. Choice (E) is negated by the information in the first paragraph about the burgeoning music business. Choice (D), Schumann's influence on general attitudes about women in music, is not mentioned, and it's correct.

EVOLUTION PASSAGE

This science passage is fairly straightforward and doesn't contain much scientific jargon, so you should be able to skim through it, taking note of the structure of the passage and its general themes.

Paragraph 1 introduces the concept of evolution as a process of gradual improvement whereby competition among species leads to the survival of superior species. Paragraph 2 introduces Darwin and his *wedges* model of interspecies competition, citing clams and brachiopods as examples. Paragraph 3 outlines Gould and Calloway's research into clams and brachiopods, which contradicts Darwin's theories. Paragraph 4 describes the theory of Gould and Calloway, which claims that environmental change is more important than competition in the survival of species. Paragraph 5 explores the implications for the status of Homo sapiens under Gould and Calloway's evolutionary scenario.

19. A

This is a Big Picture question, so look at the overall impression given by the passage. The general focus is on Gould and Calloway's conclusions about clams and brachiopods and the impact of their work on Darwin's theory of evolution. Choice (A) paraphrases this idea and is correct. Choice (C) is too harsh, (D) is too specific, and (B) and (E) are just off base.

20. B

The cited line shows the author poking a bit of fun at the human race's desire to see itself as superior to other species. Choice (B) gets to the heart of the quote, explaining that scientists might want to see their own species as the most advanced.

21. C

Darwin's *wedges* model, as described in the second paragraph, shows nature as a surface covered with thousands of sharp wedges jostling for the same space. These wedges represent competing species (C).

22. D

The third paragraph focuses on Gould and Calloway's evidence about clams and brachiopods, asserting that the two species never competed for the same turf and that the decline of brachiopods seems to have been caused by an environmental impact. Choices (A) and (C) are too strong; (B) directly contradicts the passage; (E) is supported, but it's not the reason that the evidence is presented. Choice (D) correctly summarizes the author's reasons for presenting the evidence.

23. A

Read the entire sentence. A comet is directly referred to as a possible cause for the decline of brachiopods (A). All the other choices are unsubstantiated or beyond the scope of the passage.

24. C

The final paragraph focuses on the status of humans in light of Gould and Calloway's new theories about evolution, and the author would most likely agree with (C). All the other choices are outside the scope of the author's possible conclusions, based on the information in the passage.

SECTION 2

 Picking Numbers

 Backsolving

Eyeballing

1. D

The hundredths' digit is the second digit after the decimal point, which, in this case, is 8.

2. B

Check out each of the choices. You can stop at choice (B), since $4x + 5x$ equals $9x$, not $9x^2$.

3. B

To simplify the equation, begin by doing the same thing to both sides. Multiply both sides by 3, and you get $2x = 90$, so $x = \dfrac{90}{2} = 45$, which is your answer.

4. B

The circle represents 100 percent of the household expenses. We need the region that represents rent, $33\frac{1}{3}$ percent of the whole. Since $33\frac{1}{3}$ is one-third of 100, you can eyeball the graph and find the region that represents one-third of the circle, region B.

5. C

Draw a diagram representing the rectangle divided into two squares. Since squares have equal sides and each square has an area of 25, each side of a square must be 5. Add $5 + 5$ for the short sides of the rectangle, and $10 + 10$ for the long sides, and you get your answer, 30.

6. B

Start by using the average rate formula to calculate the distance that John drove. Distance = Rate × Time. Distance = 48 miles per hour × 2.25 hours, so the distance is 108 miles. For John to drive the same distance in 2 hours, set up the equation: 108 (distance traveled) Rate × 2 (number of hours). Your answer is 54, (B).

7. A

In order to solve for x, replace x in the equation with its value, $\sqrt{7}$. You get $(\sqrt{7} + 1)(\sqrt{7} - 1)$. Use FOIL (**f**irst, **o**uter, **i**nner, **l**ast) and you get $7 - \sqrt{7} + \sqrt{7} - 1$. The square roots of 7 cancel each other out, and you have $7 - 1 = 6$, (A).

8. D ①②③

First, let's convert from percent to fractions by dividing $66\frac{2}{3}$ by 100. You get $x = \frac{2}{3}y$. You can then solve for y by multiplying both sides by $\frac{3}{2}$, and your result is $\frac{3}{2}x = y$. You can then change back to percents by multiplying $\frac{3}{2}$ by 100 and find that y is 150 percent of x, (D).

9. A ①②③

Start by finding the least common multiple of 4, 6, and 10. It's 60. You can then check each of the choices to see if it's a factor of 60. Choice (A), 8, is the correct answer since it's not a factor of 60.

10. E

You may have been able to pick out the right answer without doing the calculation by realizing that the final sum is just $\frac{1}{64}$ shy of 1, or $\frac{63}{64}$. Otherwise, you would begin by finding the least common denominator for all the fractions, which is 64, and add them up. 63 is your final numerator.

11. E

Start with what you know about the shaded square. Since its area is 3, each side must be $\sqrt{3}$. The two vertical sides of the square each form a leg of a 30-60-90 right triangle, making the short legs 1 each. You now have the length of the base of the large equilateral triangle: $1 + \sqrt{3} + 1 = 2 + \sqrt{3}$. Therefore, each side of the large equilateral triangle is $2 + \sqrt{3}$. Multiply by three and you get $6 + 3\sqrt{3}$, (E).

12. B

In order to add these square roots, you need to simplify them. $\sqrt{48}$ simplifies to $\sqrt{16} \times \sqrt{3}$, or $4\sqrt{3}$. $\sqrt{12}$ simplifies to $\sqrt{4} \times \sqrt{3}$, or $2\sqrt{3}$. So you now have $4\sqrt{3} + 2\sqrt{3} + \sqrt{3} = (4 + 2 + 1)\sqrt{3} = 7\sqrt{3}$, (B).

If you hate simplifying square roots, you could instead guesstimate your way to the answer (but you still have to know that $\sqrt{3}$ is close to 1.7). For instance, $\sqrt{48}$ is slightly less than 7, $\sqrt{12}$ is a bit more than 3, and $\sqrt{3}$ is slightly less than 2, so a good guesstimate for $\sqrt{48} + \sqrt{12} + \sqrt{3}$ is around $7 + 3 + 2$, or about 12. Of the answer choices, only (B), $7\sqrt{3} \approx 7 \times 1.7 \approx 12$, comes even close.

13. A ↩

Set up an equation, replacing x and y in the symbol definition with the numbers and variables in the question stem:

So, $3^2 + \frac{4}{2} = 5^2 + \frac{n}{2}$. Now solve for n: $11 = 25 + \frac{n}{2}$, so $11 - 25 = \frac{n}{2}$. Thus, $n = 2(-14) = -28$, choice (A).

14. C

Average × Number of Items = Sum. We know the average, 4, and the number of items, 3, so the sum is $4 \times 3 = 12$. Because the numbers are both positive and distinct, the two smallest values we could use are 1 and 2. Subtracting 1 and 2 from 12 gives us 9 (C), the largest possible value.

15. E

Because this is a right triangle, you can use the Pythagorean theorem to find the length of the second leg: $a^2 + b^2 = c^2$. Your equation will look like this: $(x + 2)^2 + b^2 = (x + 3)^2$. Multiplying out both sides, you get $x^2 + 4x + 4 + b^2 = x^2 + 6x + 9$. To isolate b^2 on the left side, subtract $x^2 + 4x + 4$ from both sides, leaving $b^2 = 2x + 5$. Your answer for the value of b, then, is the square root of $2x + 5$, (E).

16. E

For remainder questions like this one, begin by picking a number for n. Because the remainder when n is divided by 9 is 7, pick any multiple of 9 and add 7. The easiest multiple is 9, so $9 + 7 = 16$. Plug 16 into the question and see what happens. $5 \times 16 = 80$; $80 \div 9 = 8$ remainder 8. Bingo! It's (E).

17. B

You may want to do a quick sketch to set this one up. Be sure as well to read the question carefully. Box A contains 4 black marbles and 1 white marble, for a ratio of 4:1. Box B contains 4 black marbles and 3 white marbles, for a ratio of 4:3. You want to move the minimum number of marbles from Box A to Box B, so start with 1 *black* marble (since Box A has the higher ratio of black to white marbles). You're left with 3:1 in Box A, and 5:3 in Box B. No luck, so move another marble. After a second black marble is moved, you're left with 2:1 in Box A and 6:3 in Box B. 2:1 and 6:3 are the same ratio, so (B), 2 marbles moved, is the correct answer.

18. A

Because r is cubed, if its value is multiplied by $\frac{1}{2}$, the value of V must be multiplied by $\left(\frac{1}{2}\right)^3 = \frac{1}{8}$. To prove this, pick a number for r. If $r = 2$, $r^3 = 8$; $2 \times \frac{1}{2} = 1$, and $1^3 = 1$, which is $\frac{1}{8}$ of 8. Choice (A) is correct.

19. D

The trickiest part of this question is realizing that 3^{-3} is the same as $\frac{1}{3^3}$, so:

$$3^{-3} + \left(\frac{1}{3}\right)^3 = \frac{1}{3^3} + \frac{1^3}{3^3} = \frac{1}{27} + \frac{1}{27} = \frac{2}{27}$$

20. B

Cross-multiply each choice. You will find that (A), (C), (D), and (E) are equivalent to $jm = kl$. Only (B) cross-multiplies to $jk = ml$.

SECTION 3

25. B

The key words here are *pollution* and *environmental benefits*. You need a word that explains that the negative pollution may offset the benefits of the cars. Only (B), *outweigh*, matches this prediction.

26. D

The key word *but* tells you that this is a contrasting sentence. Look for a positive word for the first blank, like *impressed* (A) or *fired* (D). Note that the word *fired* could seem negative in a job context, but here it's positive, because the popular imagination was *set on fire*. *Disputed*, a negative word, provides the contrast you need for the second blank, making (D) correct.

27. C

This question tests your vocabulary. Look among the choices for a word that goes with *starve*. *Emaciated* (C) means extremely thin and is the correct answer.

28. C

Despite is the key word that tips you off that this is a contrasting sentence. Look for a choice that provides two contrasting words. Only (C) gives you the contrast that you need, since the concepts of *interaction* (communication) and *enmity* (hostility) are in opposition to one another.

29. C

This contrasting sentence is a little confusing because of the word *not*. Rephrasing the sentence, *downsizing* is *becoming a permanent feature*, so downsizing is probably not temporary. *Ephemeral* (C) matches this prediction and is correct.

30. D

This is a long sentence, so focus first on the second part. Rephrasing, you see that patriarchy dominates because political and social forces do something with it. This must be a positive word, like *support*. You can eliminate (A) and (C). Looking back at the whole sentence, you see that if these *social forces* are what is supporting patriarchy, patriarchy must not be a natural instinct for humans. *Instinctive* (D) matches this prediction and is correct.

ANIMALS PASSAGE

This short passage is about scientists' problem in classifying three animals. The animals have characteristics of both mammals and reptiles. The scientists' solution is to create an order just for them under mammals.

31. D

For function questions like this one, put yourself in the author's shoes—why would she write such a sentence? The author starts with this question to let you know what the topic of the passage is (A). She could have done it the conventional way; something like: "Scientists couldn't decide whether platypuses and echidnas were mammals or reptiles." Instead, she chose a more dramatic beginning—asking the same question that the scientists she discusses were asking.

32. D

When you back up a couple of lines from the discussion of eyes and ears, you see the phrase *for example*. So what are the eyes and ears examples of? *These animals have some things in common with reptiles and some things in common with mammals.* That fits (D) pretty well. Watch out for (B). It looks reasonable (it's about the differences between the two types of animals), but it doesn't quite work, because the author doesn't make such a definitive statement.

BLUE-STAR WOMAN PASSAGE

This fiction passage tells the story of a Native American woman's struggle for identity as she tries to reconcile her lost culture with the laws of the country in which she lives. Read through the passage, focusing on the themes of names and laws that are repeated in the text.

33. B

The author's focus is on Blue-Star Woman and the effect of a changing world on her identity. Only (B) accurately describes the purpose of this personal story. All of the other choices are too abstract or outside the scope.

34. A

In the cited lines, Blue-Star Woman is compared to the ground squirrel, a creature living in nature. The author has probably chosen this simile in order to reinforce the connection between her character and the natural world, (A).

35. C

Since the landowner's attitude toward Blue-Star Woman's occupation of his land is described as *easy*, we can assume that she is allowed to stay there. *Permission* (C) conveys this idea. Choices (A) and (E) are negative words, and (B) and (D) don't work in this context.

36. A

In the second paragraph, the formal nature of the white man's law is contrasted with Blue-Star Woman's more emotional view of what is right. While the law of the land requires proof of tribal membership, the *law of heart* allows a person a piece of earth by virtue of her existence, as a *birthrights*. This is paraphrased in (A).

37. C

You may need to carefully reread the third paragraph to get this one right. In lines 33–43, the official requires Blue-Star Woman to name her parents, which goes against her belief that the names of the dead shouldn't be spoken. This point, (C), is the key juxtaposition. Choice (A) might have been tempting, but earlier in the paragraph the author explains that pronouncing one's own name is no longer forbidden.

38. C

As we see throughout the passage, Blue-Star Woman's name is a symbol of her identity and culture. By stating that her name seems meaningless, she implies that her culture and customs are also losing their meaning.

Rowan Passage

This short passage is most likely an excerpt from a fictional work. Rowan proposed to Miss Ashley, and she accepted. The relationship seems to be one-sided: he talks and she listens.

39. D

This is an old-fashioned expression that means dating (D). If you weren't sure of the meaning, the context is a help, and you can always eliminate clearly wrong answers. For example, the author doesn't tell you how Rowan and Miss Ashley spent all their time (A). Be wary of extreme language in answer choices like *all*. This is a trap for those test takers who read *stepping out* too literally. Also, although you know they have been dating for a year, you don't know whether the author thinks that's too long (E).

40. A

Prior to this sentence, you read about how quiet Miss Ashley was and how Rowan did most of the talking. You can infer that he likes quiet women who let him talk (A). Choice (D) might be tempting, since Rowan did discuss business, but this is not in keeping with the rest of the passage. (Rowan doesn't seem to have such progressive views.) Although (E) might also seem tempting at first, since Rowan spun dreams about the future, the author doesn't tell you if Miss Ashley shared these dreams.

The Black Leaders Passages

You're presented with a pair of passages, both excerpted from the writings of American black leaders. You should begin by reading through the first passage and answering the questions that pertain to it, questions 41–43. You can then read the second passage and attack the rest of the questions. Passage 1 is from the writings of Booker T. Washington. It outlines Washington's views on the means by which black Americans could win individual and political rights, focusing on his belief that *slow but sure influences* and *natural, slow growth* are most likely to be successful.

41. C

Washington first refers to Southern whites in the first paragraph, in which he declares his belief that political rights will eventually be granted to blacks, once whites no longer feel forced to do so. This sentiment is echoed in (C). None of the other choices can be substantiated.

42. E

Washington states his beliefs about the reasons that the Atlanta officials invited him to speak at the exposition. He viewed his selection as a reward for *merit in the Negro race* and not solely a reflection of his own talent or status, (E).

43. A

Reread the whole sentence surrounding the cited words. The *slow but sure influences* proceed from accomplishments such as the possession of property and good character, which is a paraphrase of (A).

44. C

Passage 2 contrasts sharply with the first passage, as Du Bois accuses Washington of representing *the old attitude of adjustment and submission*. Du Bois advocates a more proactive approach and condemns Washington's methods, claiming that they have caused more harm than good.

Reread lines 10–17 in Passage 2. In the latter part of the sentence, Du Bois explains that, historically, races that have allowed themselves to surrender respect have been seen by their oppressors as unworthy of civilization. Du Bois cites this historical context to highlight the status of black people, showing that submission is not the way to win respect. Choice (C) is a good paraphrase of this idea.

45. C

This question might seem a little tricky, but if you reread the surrounding lines, it should become clearer. In lines 20–27, Du Bois describes the *palm-branch*, Washington's policy of asking black people to give up certain rights. In lines 31–37, Du Bois outlines the negative consequences of this policy, a policy with which he clearly does not agree. Thus, we can see that his reference to the palm-branch, usually a metaphor for a gesture of peace, is ironic, and his tone critical, as described in (C). Other negative-sounding choices may have been tempting, but he is certainly not *distanced* (A), *mournful* (B), *surprised* (D), or *apathetic* (E).

46. A

As you may remember from question 43, Washington believed that whites would eventually grant blacks rights without any undue pressure, due to the essential goodness of human nature. Du Bois has a much more cynical attitude (which he justifies in his passage), and he would surely view Washington's view of human nature as excessively *naive*, (A). None of the other choices can be inferred from what we know of Du Bois's views.

47. C

It's hard to imagine that these two authors would agree on anything! Choice (C), however, seems to be the most reasonable assumption, because Washington speaks about the need for patience and Du Bois about the need for meaningful action. Choice (A), the use of force, is not discussed by either writer. Choice (B) vaguely contradicts Washington's feelings about the inclination of whites to reward the accomplishments of blacks. Choices (D) and (E) aren't supported by either passage.

48. E

None of the other choices is specific enough to reflect the content of these two passages.

SECTION 4

 Picking Numbers

 Backsolving

 Eyeballing

21. E

Don't be intimidated by the number of variables in this question. Take one step at a time, keeping in mind that sometimes the data that are most helpful to use first are provided last—in this case, the first useful piece of information is the fact that $z = 4$:

Use $z = 4$ to determine y:

$$y = 5z$$
$$y = 5(4)$$
$$y = 20$$

Now use $y = 20$ to solve for x:

$$x - y = 6$$
$$x - 20 = 6$$
$$x = 26$$

22. B

Translate bit by bit:

"The sum of $9a$ and the square root of $2b$" means $9a + \sqrt{2b}$; "is equal to" means $=$; and "the square of the sum of $3a$ and $3b$" means $(3a + 3b)^2$.

23. D

If 1 pound serves 9 children and there are 15 children, then we need $\frac{15}{9}$ or 1.67 pounds to feed the children. If one pound serves 7 adults, and we have 60 adults, then we need $\frac{60}{7}$ or 8.57 pounds to feed the adults. So in total we need $1.67 + 8.57$ or 10.24 pounds to feed all 75 people, which rounds up to 11 pounds.

24. C

Replace every x in the expression with $\frac{1}{2}$ and then evaluate:

$$\frac{2}{x} + \frac{2}{(x-1)} = \frac{2}{\left(\frac{1}{2}\right)} + \frac{2}{\left(\left(\frac{1}{2}\right)-1\right)} = 4 + \left(\frac{2}{-\frac{1}{2}}\right) =$$
$$4 + (-4) = 0$$

25. A

If $0.2J = 1{,}500$, then $J = \frac{1{,}500}{0.2} = 7{,}500$, and $0.15J = 0.15(7{,}500) = 1{,}125$. Another road to the answer is to realize that because 15 is $\frac{3}{4}$ of 20, 15% of J must be $\frac{3}{4}$ of 20% of J, and $\frac{3}{4}(1{,}500) = 1{,}125$.

26. A

All of the answer choices are perfect squares, but all the ones other than (A) have other factors besides themselves, their square roots, and 1. To consider just some examples: (B) has 27 as a factor; (C) has 25 and 50; (D) has 72; (E) has 25. Choice (A) is the only one that fits the criteria of the question, its only factors being 49, 7, and 1. Why? Only (A) is the square of a prime number.

27. B

Pick numbers. All of the choices, except (B), can be ruled out by squaring the first few integers: $1^2 = 1$; $5^2 = 25$; $6^2 = 36$; $7^2 = 49$. Nothing squared ends in 3.

28. E

Raise each of the three terms in the expression to the fourth power:

$$(-3x^5y^4)^4 = (-3)^4[(x^5)^4][(y^4)^4] = 81x^{20}y^{16}$$

29. 5

The intersection of sets is their overlap. $A = \{1, 2, 3, 4, 5, 6, 7, 8, 9, 0\}$ and $B = \{$even numbers$\}$. The overlap of these sets is $\{2, 4, 6, 8, 0\}$, which contains five elements.

30. 1

Radical equations follow the same rules as other equations; just remember that the solution to radical equations often entails squaring both sides:

$$\sqrt{2-x} - 1 = 0$$
$$\sqrt{2-x} = 1$$
$$\left(\sqrt{2-x}\right)^2 = (1)^2$$
$$2 - x = 1$$
$$1 = x$$

31. 1,296

You just need to do some quick calculations. $8 \times 9 = 72$. Half of 72 is 36, and 36 squared is 1,296, your answer.

32. $\frac{5}{24}$ or 0.208

Use the average formula.

$\text{Average} = \dfrac{\text{Sum}}{\text{Number of elements}}$. The sum equals $\dfrac{1}{4} + \dfrac{1}{6} = \dfrac{6}{24} + \dfrac{4}{24} = \dfrac{10}{24}$, so the average is half that, or $\dfrac{5}{24}$.

33. 9

Begin by picking a number for A. A can only be 4 or 9, because the unit digit of $A + A$ equals 8. Start with 4: you get $4 + 4 = 8$ in the ones' column. In the

tens column, plug in 4 for A. What number could you plug in for B so that you have the same number for both Bs? Let's try 9; $9 + 9 = 18$, so you carry a 1. In the tens column, 9, plus the 1 you carried, plus what would give you the same number for both Bs? In fact, any digit except for 0 and 9 could be B. So 9 is the correct answer.

34. 36

Start by finding the measure of $\angle BAC$. Because $\angle CAE$ is 73 degrees, and BAE is 90 degrees, you can subtract $90 - 73 = 17$ to get the degree measure of $\angle BAC$. $\angle BAD$ is 53 degrees, so subtract again: $53 - 17 = 36$, your answer.

35. 45

We know that the circumference is 9π, and because the circumference formula is $2\pi r$, the radius is 4.5. Each short side of the rectangle is $4.5 \times 2 = 9$. Each long side is $4.5 \times 3 = 13.5$. Add the sides:

$$13.5 + 13.5 + 9 + 9 = 45$$

36. 5

Start by figuring out how many cookies were eaten. Nuala started with 64, and 9 were left: $64 - 9 = 55$. You need to pick a number of guests, a number greater than 9. Pick 11, because it's a factor of 55. If 11 guests ate 5 cookies each, you would be left with 9 cookies, which makes 5 the correct answer.

37. 48

We want to translate this problem into two equations and solve for the variables. If X is the number of \$2 boxes and Y is the number of \$5 boxes, we can say $X + Y = 150$ because we have 150 total boxes, and $2X + 5Y = 444$ because $2X$ is the number of dollars made from X boxes and $5Y$ is the number of dollars made from Y boxes. Using elimination, we see:

$$2X + 5Y = 444$$
$$- (2X + 2Y = 300)$$
$$3Y = 144$$
$$Y = 48$$

38. $\frac{49}{4}$ or 12.25

Begin by picking numbers for the sides of the rectangle. You could have 1 for the short sides and 6 for the long sides, giving you an area of 6. Picking 2 for the short sides and 5 for the long gives you an area of 10. Picking 3 for the short sides and 4 for the long sides gives you area 12. Did you notice that the closer the numbers get, the larger the resulting area? Therefore, two numbers that are the same, 3.5 and 3.5, will give you the largest possible area, 12.25. Remember that squares fall under the category of rectangles, so it's okay to have a rectangle with equal sides. And it's handy to know that squares have the highest area-to-perimeter ratios of all rectangles.

SECTION 5

1. C

The problem here is subject-verb agreement. The gerund *bleeding*, which is singular, is the subject of the verb *to be considered*—not the leeches. Therefore, the verb shouldn't be the plural form *were*, but the singular *was*.

2. C

The verb *improved* needs to be modified by an adverb. The adjective *dramatic* should be the adverb *dramatically*.

3. D

This sentence has a word choice problem. *Respectively* is used when you consider one or more members of a group separately. In this case,

the author is probably looking for the word *respectfully*, since the counselors are standing below the king's throne, showing their respect.

4. B

The phrase *have agreement* is ungrammatical. *Agreement*, a noun, either needs to be used with the article *an* (*have an agreement*) or changed to the verb form *have agreed*. The latter makes the most sense in the context of this sentence, but of course because this is an Identifying Sentence Errors question, you only have to spot the mistake, not fix it.

5. A

Have you ever heard "people aren't whiches" in your English class? That old grammar saying applies here: The delegates are people, so the sentence requires *who* instead of *which*.

6. E

This sentence contains no error. Choices (C) and (D) are perfectly parallel.

7. B

The effort is the subject of the verb *to result*, and because *effort* is singular, the verb should be changed to *results*.

8. A

Every one is the subject of the verb *to be closed*. *Every one* takes the singular form of the verb, so it should read *was closed*.

9. D

Should not hardly just sounds wrong. It's a double negative. There's no need for the word *hardly*.

10. A

This question focuses on word choice. *Imaginary* refers to something that is not real, and the paper in question is surely real. *Imaginative* is a better choice here.

11. C

The *memoirs* are the subject of the verb *to promise*. Because *memoirs* is plural, you need the singular form, *promise*.

12. A

This question tests the idiomatic use of a preposition. The correct idiom is *point at issue*.

13. A

Raising is a form of the active verb *to raise*. Because no one is performing an action, the passive verb *to rise* works better here: *rising living costs*.

14. E

This sentence contains no error.

15. A

The original sentence is best.

16. E

Choices (A), (B), and (D) contain *that* or *who*. These words seem to introduce an additional clause that never appears. Choice (E) uses the correct verb form *believe* and is correct.

17. C

The problem here is a misplaced modifier. Ask yourself: What was developed? As it stands, the sentence tells us that the president himself was developed by a scientific team (a scary thought!). Choice (C) corrects the problem by providing a phrase that logically modifies *the president*. Choice (D) also could modify *the president*, but it changes the meaning of the sentence.

18. D

The second part of the sentence describes regions that have certain characteristics. *Only* is the correct linking word to set those regions apart. Choice (C) doesn't make sense, so (D) is correct.

19. B

The sentence as given is a run-on, but there is a contrasting relationship between the *political death* in the first clause and the attempts *to prevent its demise* in the second. Choice (B) clarifies this contrast and makes the second clause dependent by using the conjunction *although*. Choice (D) does something similar with *despite*, but it is wordy and shows poor diction.

20. A

This is a complex sentence, but the original sentence is best. None of the other options manage to present all of the information in a clear and concise way.

21. E

Choice (E) is the most clear and concise, omitting the unnecessary *when you are* from the original sentence.

22. B

Choices (A) and (C) use the passive voice, which is awkward. Choices (D) and (E) use incorrect forms of the conditional. Choice (B) is the clearest choice.

23. E

The company is singular, so the use of the pronoun *they* in (A) and (C) is incorrect. Choices (B) and (D) awkwardly use the passive voice. Choice (E) is the most clear and concise choice.

24. E

When comparing two people, *better* should be used instead of *best*. Only (E) does this correctly.

25. A

The original sentence is best. It is the only one of the options to correctly use the past perfect verb tense.

26. B

The original sentence compares *the variety...of services* with *low-cost programs*, which doesn't make much sense. Choices (B) and (D) clarify the sentence by inserting *the number of*, and making a more appropriate comparison. However, (D) uses the wrong verb form, making (B) the best choice.

27. C

Choices (B), (C), and (E) all correctly use a semicolon to join the two independent clauses. Only (C), however, makes sense of the sentence by using *he* to refer to the politician.

28. C

Choice (C) is the only choice that corrects this run-on sentence in a logical way: *Known for his aphoristic wit and brilliant conversation* introduces Oscar Wilde; the rest of the sentence provides additional information about him. Choice (B) contains a fragment, (D) is a run-on which presents an illogical contrast between Wilde's wit and his writing, and (E) is extremely garbled.

29. A

The sentence is correct: *Maintaining* and *securing* are in the proper parallel form (both gerunds). Choice (B) is convoluted and slightly alters the meaning of the sentence. Choice (C) is a fragment. Choice (D) is verbose and tangled. Choice (E) has sacrificed correct parallel structure for the sake of brevity, comparing the *appearance* (a noun) to *securing* (a gerund).

30. B

The sentence contains a misplaced modifier: *Once an enclave of privileged white males* refers to the Wodehouse Club, not to its directors. Choice (B) correctly places the modifying phrase right next to the thing it's describing. Choices (C) and (D) do not correct the misplaced modifier, and (D) is a fragment. Choice (E) is poorly worded, and the verb *has* does not agree with the subject, *directors*.

31. B

What actually occurred when alcohol was banned turned out to be the opposite of what the prohibitionists had envisioned. Drinking continued (illegally), and crime actually increased. Therefore, you're looking for words that will express this ironic contrast between the idea and the reality. *In fact* is the best choice. Choice (D) is wrong because although *but* expresses a contrast, it also creates a fragment (*but* must follow a comma, not a semicolon). Choices (A), (C), and (E) fail to express the logical contrast between the two halves of the sentence.

32. C

What is being compared here? You can't compare an action (watching a video) to an object (a book)—it's not logical, and it violates the rules of parallelism. Choice (C) corrects the sentence by putting the two activities in parallel form. Choice (B) fails to fix the parallelism problem, and it introduces strange and unnecessary changes in verb tense. Choice (D) is awkwardly phrased (would you say *book-reading*?), and (E) also fails to fix the parallelism problem, creating a somewhat confusing comparison.

33. E

To correct this sentence fragment, all you need to do is insert the helping verb *is* before the participle *based. Based, being based*, and *basing* are all verb forms that cannot stand on their own as a sentence's main verb.

34. D

The underlined portion of the sentence is wordy and awkward. Choice (D) expresses the same thought in a clearer, more concise way. Choices (B) and (E) are just as convoluted as the original sentence, and (C) is a fragment.

35. C

They, the subject of the sentence, refers to the supervisors, while *them* refers to the workers. You need to change the sentence to clarify the fact that the supervisors only allowed the workers to go to the bathroom twice a day. Choice (C) clears things up: *They* (the supervisors) *allowed them* (the workers) *to go to the bathroom only twice a day.*

36. D

This question asks you to clear up the excessive use of pronouns in the paragraph. Choice (D), *the company's*, makes the most sense, because the factories belong to the company. Choice (B), *its*, corrects the use of *their* in the original sentence, but isn't as good a choice because it doesn't solve the problem of overuse of pronouns.

37. B

As it stands, the verb tenses in this sentence are confusing. Choice (B) makes the sentence clearer by eliminating the use of *would*. All of the other choices are unnecessarily wordy.

38. A

When you reread the surrounding lines, you will see that sentence 9 provides additional information but does not set up a contrast to earlier information. Only *moreover* (A) conveys this, because the linking words in all the other choices set up a contrast.

39. C

The original sentence misuses the passive voice and incorrectly joins independent clauses with a comma. Choice (C) clarifies the sentence by creating a dependent clause and using the correct active form of the verb *to urge*.

CHAPTER 9: PRACTICE TEST TWO

HOW TO TAKE THIS PRACTICE TEST

Before taking this Practice Test, find a quiet room where you can work uninterrupted for two and a half hours. Make sure you have a comfortable desk, your calculator, and several No. 2 pencils. Use the answer sheet to record your answers. Once you start, don't stop until you've finished. Take a five-minute rest break after section two and a one-minute stretch break after section four. Remember—you may review any questions within a section, but you may not jump from one section to another.

PSAT PRACTICE TEST TWO ANSWER SHEET

Remove (or photocopy) this answer sheet and use it to complete the test. See the answer key following the test when finished. Chapter 11 will show you how to find your score.

Start with number 1 for each section. If a section has fewer questions than answer spaces, leave the extra spaces blank.

SECTION 1

1. Ⓐ Ⓑ Ⓒ Ⓓ Ⓔ 7. Ⓐ Ⓑ Ⓒ Ⓓ Ⓔ 13. Ⓐ Ⓑ Ⓒ Ⓓ Ⓔ 19. Ⓐ Ⓑ Ⓒ Ⓓ Ⓔ
2. Ⓐ Ⓑ Ⓒ Ⓓ Ⓔ 8. Ⓐ Ⓑ Ⓒ Ⓓ Ⓔ 14. Ⓐ Ⓑ Ⓒ Ⓓ Ⓔ 20. Ⓐ Ⓑ Ⓒ Ⓓ Ⓔ
3. Ⓐ Ⓑ Ⓒ Ⓓ Ⓔ 9. Ⓐ Ⓑ Ⓒ Ⓓ Ⓔ 15. Ⓐ Ⓑ Ⓒ Ⓓ Ⓔ 21. Ⓐ Ⓑ Ⓒ Ⓓ Ⓔ
4. Ⓐ Ⓑ Ⓒ Ⓓ Ⓔ 10. Ⓐ Ⓑ Ⓒ Ⓓ Ⓔ 16. Ⓐ Ⓑ Ⓒ Ⓓ Ⓔ 22. Ⓐ Ⓑ Ⓒ Ⓓ Ⓔ
5. Ⓐ Ⓑ Ⓒ Ⓓ Ⓔ 11. Ⓐ Ⓑ Ⓒ Ⓓ Ⓔ 17. Ⓐ Ⓑ Ⓒ Ⓓ Ⓔ 23. Ⓐ Ⓑ Ⓒ Ⓓ Ⓔ
6. Ⓐ Ⓑ Ⓒ Ⓓ Ⓔ 12. Ⓐ Ⓑ Ⓒ Ⓓ Ⓔ 18. Ⓐ Ⓑ Ⓒ Ⓓ Ⓔ 24. Ⓐ Ⓑ Ⓒ Ⓓ Ⓔ

☐ # right in Section 1

☐ # wrong in Section 1

SECTION 2

1. Ⓐ Ⓑ Ⓒ Ⓓ Ⓔ 6. Ⓐ Ⓑ Ⓒ Ⓓ Ⓔ 11. Ⓐ Ⓑ Ⓒ Ⓓ Ⓔ 16. Ⓐ Ⓑ Ⓒ Ⓓ Ⓔ
2. Ⓐ Ⓑ Ⓒ Ⓓ Ⓔ 7. Ⓐ Ⓑ Ⓒ Ⓓ Ⓔ 12. Ⓐ Ⓑ Ⓒ Ⓓ Ⓔ 17. Ⓐ Ⓑ Ⓒ Ⓓ Ⓔ
3. Ⓐ Ⓑ Ⓒ Ⓓ Ⓔ 8. Ⓐ Ⓑ Ⓒ Ⓓ Ⓔ 13. Ⓐ Ⓑ Ⓒ Ⓓ Ⓔ 18. Ⓐ Ⓑ Ⓒ Ⓓ Ⓔ
4. Ⓐ Ⓑ Ⓒ Ⓓ Ⓔ 9. Ⓐ Ⓑ Ⓒ Ⓓ Ⓔ 14. Ⓐ Ⓑ Ⓒ Ⓓ Ⓔ
5. Ⓐ Ⓑ Ⓒ Ⓓ Ⓔ 10. Ⓐ Ⓑ Ⓒ Ⓓ Ⓔ 15. Ⓐ Ⓑ Ⓒ Ⓓ Ⓔ

☐ # right in Section 2

☐ # wrong in Section 2

SECTION 3

25. Ⓐ Ⓑ Ⓒ Ⓓ Ⓔ 31. Ⓐ Ⓑ Ⓒ Ⓓ Ⓔ 37. Ⓐ Ⓑ Ⓒ Ⓓ Ⓔ 43. Ⓐ Ⓑ Ⓒ Ⓓ Ⓔ
26. Ⓐ Ⓑ Ⓒ Ⓓ Ⓔ 32. Ⓐ Ⓑ Ⓒ Ⓓ Ⓔ 38. Ⓐ Ⓑ Ⓒ Ⓓ Ⓔ 44. Ⓐ Ⓑ Ⓒ Ⓓ Ⓔ
27. Ⓐ Ⓑ Ⓒ Ⓓ Ⓔ 33. Ⓐ Ⓑ Ⓒ Ⓓ Ⓔ 39. Ⓐ Ⓑ Ⓒ Ⓓ Ⓔ 45. Ⓐ Ⓑ Ⓒ Ⓓ Ⓔ
28. Ⓐ Ⓑ Ⓒ Ⓓ Ⓔ 34. Ⓐ Ⓑ Ⓒ Ⓓ Ⓔ 40. Ⓐ Ⓑ Ⓒ Ⓓ Ⓔ 46. Ⓐ Ⓑ Ⓒ Ⓓ Ⓔ
29. Ⓐ Ⓑ Ⓒ Ⓓ Ⓔ 35. Ⓐ Ⓑ Ⓒ Ⓓ Ⓔ 41. Ⓐ Ⓑ Ⓒ Ⓓ Ⓔ 47. Ⓐ Ⓑ Ⓒ Ⓓ Ⓔ
30. Ⓐ Ⓑ Ⓒ Ⓓ Ⓔ 36. Ⓐ Ⓑ Ⓒ Ⓓ Ⓔ 42. Ⓐ Ⓑ Ⓒ Ⓓ Ⓔ 48. Ⓐ Ⓑ Ⓒ Ⓓ Ⓔ

☐ # right in Section 3

☐ # wrong in Section 3

SECTION

4

19. Ⓐ Ⓑ Ⓒ Ⓓ Ⓔ	24. Ⓐ Ⓑ Ⓒ Ⓓ Ⓔ	29. Ⓐ Ⓑ Ⓒ Ⓓ Ⓔ	34. Ⓐ Ⓑ Ⓒ Ⓓ Ⓔ
20. Ⓐ Ⓑ Ⓒ Ⓓ Ⓔ	25. Ⓐ Ⓑ Ⓒ Ⓓ Ⓔ	30. Ⓐ Ⓑ Ⓒ Ⓓ Ⓔ	35. Ⓐ Ⓑ Ⓒ Ⓓ Ⓔ
21. Ⓐ Ⓑ Ⓒ Ⓓ Ⓔ	26. Ⓐ Ⓑ Ⓒ Ⓓ Ⓔ	31. Ⓐ Ⓑ Ⓒ Ⓓ Ⓔ	36. Ⓐ Ⓑ Ⓒ Ⓓ Ⓔ
22. Ⓐ Ⓑ Ⓒ Ⓓ Ⓔ	27. Ⓐ Ⓑ Ⓒ Ⓓ Ⓔ	32. Ⓐ Ⓑ Ⓒ Ⓓ Ⓔ	37. Ⓐ Ⓑ Ⓒ Ⓓ Ⓔ
23. Ⓐ Ⓑ Ⓒ Ⓓ Ⓔ	28. Ⓐ Ⓑ Ⓒ Ⓓ Ⓔ	33. Ⓐ Ⓑ Ⓒ Ⓓ Ⓔ	38. Ⓐ Ⓑ Ⓒ Ⓓ Ⓔ

right in Section 4

wrong in Section 4

If Section 4 of your test book contains math questions that are not multiple-choice, continue to item 29 below. Otherwise, continue to item 29 above.

29. 30. 31. 32. 33.
34. 35. 36. 37. 38.

SECTION

5

1. Ⓐ Ⓑ Ⓒ Ⓓ Ⓔ	11. Ⓐ Ⓑ Ⓒ Ⓓ Ⓔ	21. Ⓐ Ⓑ Ⓒ Ⓓ Ⓔ	31. Ⓐ Ⓑ Ⓒ Ⓓ Ⓔ
2. Ⓐ Ⓑ Ⓒ Ⓓ Ⓔ	12. Ⓐ Ⓑ Ⓒ Ⓓ Ⓔ	22. Ⓐ Ⓑ Ⓒ Ⓓ Ⓔ	32. Ⓐ Ⓑ Ⓒ Ⓓ Ⓔ
3. Ⓐ Ⓑ Ⓒ Ⓓ Ⓔ	13. Ⓐ Ⓑ Ⓒ Ⓓ Ⓔ	23. Ⓐ Ⓑ Ⓒ Ⓓ Ⓔ	33. Ⓐ Ⓑ Ⓒ Ⓓ Ⓔ
4. Ⓐ Ⓑ Ⓒ Ⓓ Ⓔ	14. Ⓐ Ⓑ Ⓒ Ⓓ Ⓔ	24. Ⓐ Ⓑ Ⓒ Ⓓ Ⓔ	34. Ⓐ Ⓑ Ⓒ Ⓓ Ⓔ
5. Ⓐ Ⓑ Ⓒ Ⓓ Ⓔ	15. Ⓐ Ⓑ Ⓒ Ⓓ Ⓔ	25. Ⓐ Ⓑ Ⓒ Ⓓ Ⓔ	35. Ⓐ Ⓑ Ⓒ Ⓓ Ⓔ
6. Ⓐ Ⓑ Ⓒ Ⓓ Ⓔ	16. Ⓐ Ⓑ Ⓒ Ⓓ Ⓔ	26. Ⓐ Ⓑ Ⓒ Ⓓ Ⓔ	36. Ⓐ Ⓑ Ⓒ Ⓓ Ⓔ
7. Ⓐ Ⓑ Ⓒ Ⓓ Ⓔ	17. Ⓐ Ⓑ Ⓒ Ⓓ Ⓔ	27. Ⓐ Ⓑ Ⓒ Ⓓ Ⓔ	37. Ⓐ Ⓑ Ⓒ Ⓓ Ⓔ
8. Ⓐ Ⓑ Ⓒ Ⓓ Ⓔ	18. Ⓐ Ⓑ Ⓒ Ⓓ Ⓔ	28. Ⓐ Ⓑ Ⓒ Ⓓ Ⓔ	38. Ⓐ Ⓑ Ⓒ Ⓓ Ⓔ
9. Ⓐ Ⓑ Ⓒ Ⓓ Ⓔ	19. Ⓐ Ⓑ Ⓒ Ⓓ Ⓔ	29. Ⓐ Ⓑ Ⓒ Ⓓ Ⓔ	39. Ⓐ Ⓑ Ⓒ Ⓓ Ⓔ
10. Ⓐ Ⓑ Ⓒ Ⓓ Ⓔ	20. Ⓐ Ⓑ Ⓒ Ⓓ Ⓔ	30. Ⓐ Ⓑ Ⓒ Ⓓ Ⓔ	40. Ⓐ Ⓑ Ⓒ Ⓓ Ⓔ

right in Section 5

wrong in Section 5

PRACTICE TEST TWO

SECTION 1

Time—25 Minutes   For each of the following questions, choose the best answer and darken the
  24 Questions   corresponding oval on the answer sheet.

Select the lettered word or set of words that best completes the sentence.

Example:

Today's small, portable computers contrast markedly with the earliest electronic computers, which were ----.

(A) effective

(B) invented

(C) useful

(D) destructive

(E) enormous

---

1. A drill sergeant ---- new recruits to be tractable and to ---- his orders.

    (A) presumes . . . conform to

    (B) encourages . . . look at

    (C) expects . . . comply with

    (D) trains . . . apply for

    (E) compels . . . retreat from

2. In spite of its ---- climate, the Sonoran Desert ---- many forms of plant and animal life.

    (A) arid . . . supports

    (B) extreme . . . uproots

    (C) harsh . . . destroys

    (D) temperate . . . rejects

    (E) changing . . . retains

3. During the Han Dynasty in China, manual work was respected by all; even noblemen felt that they could engage in it without ----.

    (A) difficulty

    (B) training

    (C) remuneration

    (D) discomfort

    (E) dishonor

GO ON TO THE NEXT PAGE

4. Until recently, modern historians have tended to attribute great influence to individual heroes, whereas now, many historians recognize the importance of social climate and ---- action.

   (A) collaborative

   (B) geographic

   (C) deliberate

   (D) subjective

   (E) ulterior

5. Although critics consider the author's first novel both original and ----, her publishers are apprehensive about its ---- appeal.

   (A) moving . . . emotional

   (B) suspenseful . . . vital

   (C) obscure . . . lasting

   (D) sophisticated . . . popular

   (E) entertaining . . . obsolete

GO ON TO THE NEXT PAGE

Answer the questions below based on the information in the accompanying passages.

Questions 6–9 are based on the following passages.

Passage 1

Music is the perfect medium for the expression of political points of view. In fact, the motivational songs of repressed peoples have been sung in streets, at music halls, and around
(5) campfires for centuries. In America in particular, there is an honored history of musicians speaking for the people and bringing to light political problems largely disregarded by the rest of the mass media. Woody Guthrie, a stel-
(10) lar creator of socially conscious music, serves as an excellent example. Some musicians, those of little heart, fear that taking a strong stand will cost them precious listeners. In fact, outspoken assertive musical artists like Guthrie
(15) tend to have the most loyal fans.

Passage 2

I listen to music to escape the troubles of my daily life. If I'm in the mood for social crises and political opinion, I'll go to the editorial section of the daily paper. Musicians
(5) should play music, not dabble in politics as a hobby. After all, what insights can a musician offer that cannot be more fully explored by professional journalists and reporters? No one expects a novice to sit down at a piano
(10) and produce beautiful music. Likewise, I don't expect someone who has spent his life on stage and in practice rooms to produce a political analysis of any great depth.

6. In Passage 1, "medium" (line 1) most nearly means

(A) middle
(B) fair
(C) average
(D) instrument
(E) clairvoyant

7. The phrase "those of little heart" (lines 11–12) in Passage 1 serves to emphasize

(A) the author's disdain for musicians who suppress their political beliefs
(B) a political musician's loss of loyal listeners
(C) the author's negative opinion of many music listeners
(D) the difficulty of writing effective political-protest music
(E) Woody Guthrie's importance in American musical history

8. For the author of Passage 2, musicians who express political views are

(A) artists who use their music in the best way possible
(B) people who should run for political office
(C) artists who bore all of their listeners
(D) not interested in music as an escape
(E) people who toy with serious topics outside of their specialty

GO ON TO THE NEXT PAGE

9. The authors of the passages disagree about the

(A) legal right of musicians to compose music with a political message

(B) talent of Woody Guthrie

(C) importance of political analysis

(D) validity of political commentary in music

(E) loyalty of Guthrie's fans

Questions 10–14 are based on the following passage.

The following passage presents a scientific discussion of the human ability to use language.

It is the use of language that sets apart humans from the animals. Language is what enables us to reveal our conscious selves, to transmit knowledge to each other and to suc-
(5) ceeding generations, to discuss and debate ideas, and to build and maintain the framework of civilization. Though research has been done and claims have been made that intelligent animals such as chimpanzees can
(10) learn to understand human language in a limited way, the evidence seems to indicate that true language is exclusively the province of humans.

Is a human born with the innate capac-
(15) ity for language, or is language a complex form of behavior that one learns as a child? The linguist Noam Chomsky has argued that humans possess innate structures in the brain that govern language acquisition; in other
(20) words, our brains are not unlike computers preprogrammed with the ability to learn how to use language creatively. Behavioral psychologists, on the other hand, see language as nothing more than "verbal behavior" that
(25) a child learns through experience.

Although this question is still unanswered, it is clear from the work of neuroscientists that once a human possesses language, certain structures and areas of the brain do control
(30) its use. Language tends to reside in only one hemisphere of the brain. Which hemisphere this is, the right or the left, is related to the "handedness" of a person: right-handers, for example, usually process language on the left-
(35) hand side of the brain. Neuroscientists have further determined that language is not localized to one specific area within the hemisphere. Rather, activities such as speaking and understanding written words seem to be handled
(40) by different areas.

Much of this information comes from studies of people who have suffered injuries to specific parts of the brain. Nineteenth-century scientist Pierre Paul Broca, for exam-
(45) ple, discovered the specific region of the brain that controls the flow of words from brain to mouth: he did the autopsy of a brain-damaged patient who had been incapable of speaking for over twenty years and found the
(50) lesion in the brain tissue that had caused the problem. The area of the brain that enables us to comprehend speech was located by Broca's contemporary Carl Wernicke in a similar way.

A modern technique known as PET (posi-
(55) tron emission tomography) scanning has made the study of language processing possible in normal subjects. Using PET, scientists are able to "see" how normal people think by monitoring the brain's use of oxygen during
(60) mental activity. The part of the brain that lights up in a PET scan of a person hearing words has been shown to be completely different from the spot that lights up when the person speaks. In addition, it seems that even
(65) verbs and nouns are handled by different areas. Exactly why the various components of language should be distributed across the brain in this way remains, however, the subject of speculation.

GO ON TO THE NEXT PAGE

10. The author's statement about what "language" entails (lines 2–7) is made primarily by using

    (A) quotations

    (B) scientific data

    (C) generalizations

    (D) analogies

    (E) inferences

11. The question that begins the second paragraph chiefly serves to

    (A) present a scientific dilemma that has been resolved

    (B) suggest that there are some questions not being addressed by scientists

    (C) summarize an issue that is the subject of continued debate

    (D) outline the position of the author

    (E) introduce a topic that will be discussed for the rest of the passage

12. The author mentions computers in the second paragraph primarily to illustrate the

    (A) way humans learn language through experience

    (B) importance of computer use to a child's language acquisition

    (C) progress in understanding language made using computer models

    (D) inability of computers to use language creatively

    (E) possibility that humans are born knowing how to use language

13. The best evidence that the brain processes speaking and hearing words in different areas is provided by the

    (A) studies of Pierre Paul Broca

    (B) experiments on chimpanzees

    (C) results of PET scans

    (D) observations of children learning language

    (E) studies of Carl Wernicke

14. The author discusses the work of Broca and Wernicke in the fourth paragraph to illustrate the

    (A) method by which early discoveries were made about the brain and language

    (B) imprecision of the techniques of 19th-century scientists

    (C) extent to which the localization of speech in the brain is understood

    (D) study of language processing in the brains of normal patients

    (E) range of early neuroscientific ideas about where language is processed in the brain

GO ON TO THE NEXT PAGE

Questions 15–24 are based on the following passage.

In this passage, an essayist and author of children's stories recalls being captivated by the sight of a young circus rider rehearsing.

After the lions had returned to their cages, creeping angrily through the chutes, a little bunch of us drifted away and into an open doorway nearby, where we stood for a while
(5) in semidarkness, watching a big brown circus horse go harumphing around the practice ring. The long rein, or tape, by which his trainer guided her charge counterclockwise in his dull career formed the radius of their
(10) private circle, of which she was the revolving center. The great size and meekness of the horse, the repetitious exercise, the heat of the afternoon, all exerted a hypnotic charm.
Behind me I heard someone say, "Excuse
(15) me, please," in a low voice. She was halfway into the building when I turned and saw her—a girl of sixteen or seventeen. In most respects she was like any of two or three dozen showgirls you encounter if you wander
(20) about the winter quarters of Mr. John Ringling North's circus, in Sarasota. But her grave face and the naturalness of her manner gave her a sort of quick distinction and brought a new note into the gloomy octago-
(25) nal building. As soon as she had squeezed through the crowd, she spoke a word or two to the older woman, whom I took to be her mother, stepped to the ring, and waited while the horse coasted to a stop in front of her.
(30) She gave the animal a couple of affectionate swipes on his enormous neck and then swung herself aboard. The horse immediately resumed his rocking canter, the woman goading him on, chanting something that sounded
(35) like "Hop! Hop!"

In attempting to recapture this mild spectacle, I am merely acting as recording secretary for one of the oldest of societies—the society of those who, at one time or another, have
(40) surrendered, without even a show of resistance, to the bedazzlement of a circus rider. It is not easy to communicate anything of this nature. The circus comes as close to being the world in microcosm as anything I know; in
(45) a way, it puts all the rest of show business in the shade. Its magic is universal and complex. Out of its wild disorder comes order; from its rank smell rises the good aroma of courage and daring; out of its preliminary shabbi-
(50) ness comes the final splendor. And buried in the familiar boasts of its advance agents lies the modesty of most of its people. For me the circus is at its best before it has been put together. In short, a man has to catch the cir-
(55) cus unawares to experience its full impact and share its gaudy dream.
The ten-minute ride the girl took achieved—as far as I was concerned, who wasn't looking for it, and quite unbeknownst
(60) to her, who wasn't even striving for it—the thing that is sought by performers everywhere: a means of improving a shining ten minutes in the diligent way all serious artists seize free moments to hone the blade
(65) of their talent. Her brief tour included only elementary postures and tricks, perhaps because they were all she was capable of, perhaps because her warmup at this hour was unscheduled and the ring was not rigged
(70) for a real practice session. She swung herself off and on the horse several times, gripping his mane. She did a few knee-stands—or whatever they are called—dropping to her knees and quickly bouncing back up on her
(75) feet again. Most of the time she simply rode in a standing position, well aft on the beast, her hands hanging easily at her sides, her

GO ON TO THE NEXT PAGE

head erect, her straw-colored ponytail lightly
brushing her shoulders, the blood of exer-
(80) tion showing faintly through the tan of her
skin. Twice she managed a one-foot stance—
a sort of ballet pose, with arms outstretched.

The richness of the scene was in its plainness, its natural condition—of horse, of ring,
(85) of girl, even to the girl's bare feet that gripped
the bare back of her proud and ridiculous
mount. The enchantment grew not out of
anything that happened or was performed but
out of something that seemed to go round and
(90) around and around with the girl, attending
her, a steady gleam in the shape of a circle—
a ring of ambition, of happiness, of youth.
(And the positive pleasures of equilibrium
under difficulties.) In a week or two, all
(95) would be changed, all (or almost all) lost:
the girl would wear makeup, the horse would
wear gold, the ring would be painted, the
bark would be clean for the feet of the horse,
the girl's feet would be clean for the slippers
(100) that she'd wear. All, all would be lost.

15. In the first paragraph, the author describes the
horse as

(A) spirited and energetic
(B) fierce and threatening
(C) good-natured but unpredictable
(D) old and frightened
(E) huge but submissive

16. The word "charge" in line 8 most nearly
means

(A) a definite quantity of electricity
(B) an accusation of blame
(C) something under supervision
(D) a formal requirement
(E) a round of ammunition

17. In lines 15–25, the author's first description of
the circus showgirl is intended to convey the
idea that she

(A) was bothered by the heat of the day
(B) tried hard to fit in with the other
showgirls
(C) was obviously more talented than her
peers
(D) wished to entertain the spectators
(E) resembled her peers yet stood apart
from them

18. In lines 41–43, the author comments that
"It is not easy to communicate anything of
this nature" in order to

(A) emphasize that he is describing an
uncommon experience
(B) admit the inadequacy of his powers as
a writer
(C) stress that the emotional reaction he is
describing is complex and elusive
(D) point out that people don't like to admit
how attractive the circus is
(E) confess that he envied the circus rider's
prowess

19. The author mentions the boasts of circus
advance agents (lines 51–52) to provide
evidence of the

(A) problems that beset those who spend
their lives in the circus
(B) pressures driving the girl rider to succeed
(C) ways in which circus employees regularly
deceive the public
(D) contrasts and paradoxes that make the
circus a world in miniature
(E) author's disillusionment with show
business in general

GO ON TO THE NEXT PAGE

20. The author indicates that, as she rode around the ring, the girl was

   (A) concentrating on simple tricks
   (B) receiving instructions from her mother
   (C) distracted by the crowd of onlookers
   (D) irritated by the horse's behavior
   (E) rehearsing for the evening's performance

21. In paragraph 4, the author suggests that the girl can be called a "serious artist" because of her

   (A) physical grace and acrobatic talent
   (B) devotion to improving her skills
   (C) unusual rapport with the horse
   (D) ability to do a lot of tricks in a short time
   (E) meticulous attention to detail

22. In lines 72–73, the author adds the phrase "or whatever they are called" primarily to emphasize

   (A) his inability to remember what he knew as a child
   (B) his interest in the girl's attitude toward her work rather than her technical skill
   (C) the unimportance of the practice session in comparison to an actual circus performance
   (D) his ignorance of even the simplest acrobatic maneuvers
   (E) the girl's inability to perform correctly a particular maneuver

23. By mentioning the "plainness" of the scene in lines 83–87, the author underscores the point that

   (A) the life of a circus performer is often dangerous and difficult
   (B) circus audiences fail to appreciate the hard work that show riders must do
   (C) the girl riding the horse was unaware of the onlookers
   (D) horse and rider would appear more glamorous during an actual performance
   (E) something other than the physical setting made the experience special

24. In the last paragraph of the passage, the author uses the phrase, "a ring of ambition, of happiness, of youth" to reflect

   (A) the gold rings on the girl's fingers
   (B) the ring of the circus stage
   (C) the ringing sound of the circus music
   (D) his desire to get married
   (E) the shape of the horse's stirrups

IF YOU FINISH BEFORE TIME IS CALLED, YOU MAY CHECK YOUR WORK ON THIS SECTION ONLY. DO NOT TURN TO ANY OTHER SECTION IN THE TEST.   STOP

SECTION 2

Time—25 Minutes
18 Questions

Solve each of the following problems, decide which is the best answer choice, and darken the corresponding oval on the answer sheet.

Notes:

(1) Calculator use is permitted.

(2) All numbers used are real numbers.

(3) Figures are provided for some problems. All figures are drawn to scale and lie in a plane UNLESS otherwise indicated.

(4) Unless otherwise specified, the domain of any function f is assumed to be the set of all real numbers x for which $f(x)$ is a real number.

Reference Information

$A = \frac{1}{2}bh$ $c^2 = a^2 + b^2$ Special right triangles $A = \pi r^2$ $C = 2\pi r$ $V = \ell wh$ $V = \pi r^2 h$ $A = \ell w$

The sum of the degree measures of the angles in a triangle is 180.
The number of degrees of arc in a circle is 360.
A straight angle has a degree measure of 180.

---

1. If $r = 8$, then $(r + 4)^2 =$

   (A)   24
   (B)   64
   (C)   68
   (D)   80
   (E)   144

2. A stationery store ordered a shipment of 800 erasers and sold 360 of them. What percent of the shipment did it sell?

   (A) 3.6%
   (B) 4.5%
   (C) 18%
   (D) 36%
   (E) 45%

GO ON TO THE NEXT PAGE

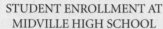

STUDENT ENROLLMENT AT
MIDVILLE HIGH SCHOOL

3. According to the bar graph above, the total number of students enrolled at Midville High School is approximately

(A) 1,325

(B) 1,375

(C) 1,400

(D) 1,425

(E) 1,500

4. In the figure above, what is the value of $a + b$?

(A) 90

(B) 120

(C) 150

(D) 180

(E) 240

5. Josephine types 12 words every 20 seconds. At this rate, how many words does she type every two minutes?

(A) 18

(B) 20

(C) 36

(D) 42

(E) 72

6. Which of the following is an expression for "12 greater than the square root of the product of 10 and a"?

(A) $12 + \sqrt{10a}$

(B) $12 + \sqrt{10+a}$

(C) $12\sqrt{10a}$

(D) $12 + \sqrt{a}$

(E) $\sqrt{10a+12}$

7. The sum of the odd integers between 8 and 26 is how much greater than the sum of the even integers between 5 and 23?

(A) 18

(B) 19

(C) 21

(D) 27

(E) 33

8. If $\dfrac{\frac{1}{a}}{\frac{1}{9}} = 3$, what is the value of a?

(A) 1

(B) 3

(C) 9

(D) 18

(E) 27

GO ON TO THE NEXT PAGE

9. The total cost of five books is $70. If the average (arithmetic mean) cost of two of the books is $15, what is the total cost of the remaining three books?

(A) $40
(B) $45
(C) $50
(D) $55
(E) $60

Note: Figure not drawn to scale.

10. In the figure above, if $AC = 2CD$, $AC = 10$, and $BD = 9$, what is the length of BC?

(A) 1
(B) 3
(C) 4
(D) 6
(E) 8

Note: Figure not drawn to scale.

11. In the triangle above, the sides have been extended as shown. What is the value of r?

(A) 34
(B) 42
(C) 74
(D) 84
(E) 96

12. If $0 \leq x \leq 6$ and $-2 \leq y \leq 5$, which of the following gives the set of all possible values for xy?

(A) $xy = 2$
(B) $0 \leq xy \leq 30$
(C) $-2 \leq xy \leq 11$
(D) $-2 \leq xy \leq 30$
(E) $-12 \leq xy \leq 30$

13. If a number is divisible by the first six positive even integers, the number must be divisible by all of the following EXCEPT

(A) 18
(B) 20
(C) 24
(D) 30
(E) 40

14. If two points on a certain line in a coordinate plane have coordinates $(2, 6)$ and $(4, 9)$, what is the slope of the line?

(A) $\dfrac{3}{4}$
(B) $\dfrac{5}{4}$
(C) $\dfrac{3}{2}$
(D) 2
(E) 3

15. If $rs < 0$, which of the following statements CANNOT be true?

(A) $r < 0$
(B) $r > 0$
(C) $r - s = 0$
(D) $r + s = 0$
(E) $r + s = 1$

GO ON TO THE NEXT PAGE

Note: Figure not drawn to scale.

16. The figure above is composed of a rectangle and a semicircle. If the area of the rectangle is 48, what is the area of the semicircle?

    (A) π

    (B) 2π

    (C) 4π

    (D) 8π

    (E) 12π

17. If $x^2 + 4x - 12 = 0$, which of the following is a possible value for x?

    (A) -6

    (B) -4

    (C) -2

    (D) 4

    (E) 6

18. If $a \otimes b$ is defined for all positive integers a and b by the equation $a \otimes b = a(b - a)$, then $4 \otimes (3 \otimes 5) =$

    (A) 2

    (B) 6

    (C) 8

    (D) 22

    (E) 28

19. In a crate of 56 oranges and apples, the ratio of the number of oranges to the number of apples is 4:3. After n apples and n oranges are removed, the ratio of the number of oranges to the number of apples is 3:2. What is the value of n?

    (A) 2

    (B) 5

    (C) 7

    (D) 8

    (E) 12

20. When the sum of a set of numbers is divided by the average (arithmetic mean) of these numbers, the result is j. What does j represent?

    (A) half of the sum of the numbers in the set

    (B) the average of the numbers in the set

    (C) the sum of the numbers in the set

    (D) half of the average of the numbers in the set

    (E) the quantity of numbers in the set

SECTION 3

Time—25 Minutes
24 Questions

For each of the following questions, choose the best answer and darken the corresponding oval on the answer sheet.

Select the lettered word or set of words that best completes the sentence.

Example:

Today's small, portable computers contrast markedly with the earliest electronic computers, which were ----.

(A) effective

(B) invented

(C) useful

(D) destructive

(E) enormous

---

25. Highly influenced by Frank Lloyd Wright's principles of design, the architect E. Fay Jones has built homes reputed to equal and even ---- Wright's successes at building in harmony with natural surroundings.

    (A) echo

    (B) question

    (C) reconstruct

    (D) surpass

    (E) revise

26. Trumpets, including Pacific conch-shell trumpets, African ivory trumpets, orchestral valve trumpets, and tubas, comprise one of the most ---- categories of wind instruments.

    (A) excessive

    (B) discordant

    (C) coherent

    (D) absolute

    (E) diverse

27. Weighing over 70 tons, *Brachiosaurus* was ---- creature, yet its brain was quite ----.

    (A) an intelligent . . . enormous

    (B) a gargantuan . . . small

    (C) a minute . . . tiny

    (D) a prodigious . . . fossilized

    (E) an extinct . . . extant

28. The ---- nature of the platypus makes it difficult to sight, even in the ---- space of a zoological exhibit.

    (A) elusive . . . confined

    (B) crafty . . . massive

    (C) amiable . . . inhabited

    (D) playful . . . structured

    (E) slothful . . . open

29. The original American colonies were ---- entities, each having its own government, maintaining its own militia, and functioning ----.

    (A) dependent . . . competitively

    (B) distinct . . . autonomously

    (C) independent . . . devotedly

    (D) prosperous . . . austerely

    (E) united . . . expressively

GO ON TO THE NEXT PAGE

30. Kudzu, a vine ---- to Japan, was introduced in
the United States in 1876 and is now widely
grown in the South.

    (A) segregated
    (B) unaccustomed
    (C) relative
    (D) contiguous
    (E) indigenous

31. By most contemporary European accounts,
Tsar Peter the Great of Russia was ----,
towering over others of his generation both
physically and intellectually.

    (A) an egotist
    (B) an archetype
    (C) a celebrity
    (D) a titan
    (E) a sage

32. During the late 1860s, Emily Dickinson
became increasingly ----, generally shunning
personal contact with those outside her family
circle.

    (A) conciliatory
    (B) reclusive
    (C) intemperate
    (D) meticulous
    (E) garrulous

GO ON TO THE NEXT PAGE

Answer the following questions based on the information in the accompanying passages.

Questions 33–34 are based on the following passage.

Recent research indicates that the Malagasy people of Madagascar likely originated in Indonesia, some 3,700 miles to the east of Madagascar in the Indian
(5) Ocean. Although there have never been any archaeological finds on the island that point unequivocally to Indonesia, linguistic and cultural evidence strongly supports this theory. Malagasy, for example, is a
(10) Malayo-Polynesian language that strikingly overlaps with Ma'anyan, a tongue spoken in Kalimantan in southeastern Indonesia. This linguistic lineage has cultural parallels such as rice cultivation, the cult of ancestors, and
(15) the widespread use of outrigger canoes which have a strong Indonesian resonance.

33. According to the passage, some of the strongest evidence for the claim that the settlers of Madagascar originated in Indonesia is to be found in

(A) the location of Indonesia 3,700 miles to the east in the Indian Ocean

(B) archaeological finds of outrigger canoes in Madagascar

(C) the linguistic overlap between Malagasy and a language spoken in Kalimantan

(D) the cultural overlap reflected in housing styles of the two regions

(E) references to Indonesian islands in the poetry of Madagascar

34. As used in the passage, "resonance" (line 16) most nearly means

(A) reverberation

(B) evidence

(C) consequence

(D) timbre

(E) character

GO ON TO THE NEXT PAGE

Questions 35–36 refer to the following passage.

Mammalian predator territories are dynamic rather than static spaces, constantly shifting over time in accordance with several factors, such as the population size of prey
(5) species and the dynamics between different predatory species. This complex interplay was dramatically illustrated at Yellowstone National Park, where the reintroduction of wolves (Canis lupus) in 1995 after half a
(10) century's absence reshaped the ecosystem within two years. The new arrivals had a major impact on the Yellowstone coyotes (Canis latrans), who were suddenly demoted to the position of second-ranking predator.
(15) The coyote population was cut in half, with a corresponding increase in rodents, while elk were forced to become far more vigilant.

35. The author cites the introduction of wolves at Yellowstone primarily to

(A) stress that the territories of predators are continually changing in response to various factors

(B) emphasize that wolves are a more dominant predator than coyotes

(C) reinforce the claim that, once a predator has marked out a territory, it will maintain that area at any cost

(D) illustrate the influence of the population size of prey species on predator territories

(E) argue that human intervention in ecosystems can have unforeseen consequences

36. Which of the following statements, taken with the information in the paragraph, would best explain the cited increase in the rodent population of Yellowstone?

(A) Rodents were introduced into the park well before 1995.

(B) The rodent population has not increased in other national parks.

(C) Rodents are common prey for coyotes, but not for wolves.

(D) The population of elk has decreased substantially.

(E) Other species have increased even more dramatically.

GO ON TO THE NEXT PAGE

Questions 37–48 are based on the following passages.

The passages below are drawn from two articles that discuss the recent restoration of the ceiling of the Sistine Chapel.

Passage 1

One shudders to contemplate Michelangelo's reaction if he were to gaze up today at the famous frescoes* he painted on the ceiling of the Sistine Chapel over four centu-
(5) ries ago. A practical man, he would no doubt be unsurprised by the effects of time and environment on his masterpiece. He would be philosophical about the damage wrought by mineral salts left behind when rainwater
(10) leaked through the roof. The layers of dirt and soot from coal braziers that heated the chapel and from candles and incense burned during religious functions would—prior to their removal during restoration—likely have
(15) been taken in stride as well. But he would be appalled at the ravages inflicted on his work by the recent restorers.

The Vatican restoration team reveled in inducing a jarringly colorful transformation
(20) in the frescoes with their special cleaning solvents and computerized analysis equipment. But this effect was not, as they claim, achieved merely by removing the dirt and animal glue (employed by earlier restorers to
(25) revive muted colors) from the frescoes; they removed Michelangelo's final touches as well. Gone from the ceiling is the quality of suppressed anger and thunderous pessimism so often commented on by admiring scholars.
(30) That quality was not an artifact of grime, not a misleading monochrome imposed on the ceiling by time, for Michelangelo himself applied a veil of glaze to the frescoes to darken them after he had deemed his work too
(35) bright. The master would have felt compelled to add a few more layers of glaze had the ceiling radiated forth as it does now. The solvents of the restorers, in addition to stripping away the shadows, reacted chemically with
(40) Michelangelo's pigments to produce hues the painter never beheld.

Of course, the restorers left open an avenue for the reversal of their own progress towards color and brightness. Since the layers of
(45) animal glue are no longer there to serve as protection, the atmospheric pollutants from the city of Rome gained direct access to the frescoes. Significant darkening was already noticed in some of the restored work a mere
(50) four years after it was completed. It remains to be seen whether the measure introduced to arrest this process—an extensive climate-control system—will itself have any long-term effect on the chapel's ceiling.

fresco: a style of painting on plaster using water-based pigments.

Passage 2

The question lingers long after one contrasts the areas of the Sistine Chapel's ceiling still shackled by grime with the colorful splendor of the frescoes that have
(5) been cleaned: how could Michelangelo's masterpiece have been allowed to fall into such ruin? The amount of responsibility shouldered in restoring such a work is daunting to even the most ambitious of experts, naturally,
(10) but this does not explain the inaction. Rather, we had come to believe from centuries of habituation to the darkness of the ceiling that Michelangelo had actually desired it to be part of the effect. The courageous work
(15) of the restorers has wiped away not only the dirt but also—painfully for those in certain circles—cherished myths as well.

GO ON TO THE NEXT PAGE

The armament of the restorer has expanded in recent decades beyond artistic sensibil-
(20) ity and historical knowledge. A chemist on
the Vatican restoration team identified the
composition of the layers covering Michelangelo's original colors. Since there was a
stratum of dirt between the painting and the
(25) first layer of glaze, it was clear that several
decades had elapsed between the comple-
tion of the ceiling and the application of
the glaze. This justified the use of cleaning
solvents that would lift off all but that final
(30) layer of dirt, which was kept for the sake
of protection of the frescoes. The particular solvent employed, AB 57, was chosen
because of the overall neutral action of its
two chemicals on pigments: one temporarily
(35) tones them down, but the other livens them
up to the same degree. Thus the colors that
emerged from the shadows are truly what
Michelangelo intended to be seen.
    One member of the team asserted that the
(40) cleaning brought to light a painting that can
be considered "the equivalent of a treatise,
not written but painted, on the art of fresco
painting." The luminous figures are without
doubt the work of a master craftsman who
(45) executed typical Renaissance painting techniques to perfection. This is the source of the
difficulty critics have with the restoration:
the ceiling of the Sistine Chapel no longer
seems to be the fruit of the wayward genius,
(50) defiant of Renaissance fresco-painting protocol, that Michelangelo was thought to be.
They balk at the fact that the painter seems,
like a vagabond given a good scrubbing, to
be a complete stranger, rational and tradi-
(55) tional and devoid of fearfulness and anger.
But the veil that led to the misperceptions of
Michelangelo has now been lifted, and we
may better acquaint ourselves with him.

37. The word "philosophical" in Passage 1, line 8,
    is best interpreted to mean

    (A) overwhelmed

    (B) knowledgeable

    (C) abstract

    (D) unruffled

    (E) pensive

38. The author of Passage 1 implies in the
    first paragraph that the deterioration of
    Michelangelo's frescoes

    (A) has not resulted in an appreciable
         difference in their visual impact

    (B) could have been prevented if the chapel
         were not kept in use

    (C) was not abated by the misguided efforts
         of the restorers

    (D) should have been accepted as an
         unfortunate but natural process

    (E) was considered inevitable and irrevers-
         ible at the time they were painted

GO ON TO THE NEXT PAGE

39. In the second paragraph of Passage 1, the author creates a sense of irony by juxtaposing which two of the following elements?

    (A) appreciation of the removal of grime from the ceiling versus sadness over the change of color

    (B) description of the restorers' technical equipment versus description of Michelangelo's antiquated painting technique

    (C) the claim that the color came from removing the dirt and glue versus the claim that glue had never been used

    (D) the assertion that Michelangelo's glaze had been removed versus the assertion that the colors had been chemically enhanced

    (E) the restorers' attitude toward brightly colored frescoes versus Michelangelo's attitude toward brightly colored frescoes

40. In Passage 1, line 52, the word "arrest" most nearly means

    (A) attract
    (B) detain
    (C) capture
    (D) retard
    (E) contain

41. The author of Passage 2 apparently thinks that the "amount of responsibility" (line 7) involved in restoring the ceiling of the Sistine Chapel

    (A) was the reason that restorers allowed the masterpiece to deteriorate

    (B) reflects the fact that the frescoes are the greatest work of the Renaissance period

    (C) was not by itself a strong enough deterrent to have stopped restorers

    (D) protected the ceiling from premature efforts at restoration in the past

    (E) kept all but the finest restorers from attempting to work on the ceiling

42. The author of Passage 2 uses the evidence of the "stratum of dirt between the painting and the first layer of glaze" (lines 24–25) to establish that

    (A) good care had not been taken of the frescoes from the beginning

    (B) science has replaced art history as the driving force behind art restoration

    (C) the first layer of glaze was not part of the original masterpiece

    (D) it took an extremely long period of time to complete the whole work

    (E) the work of the Vatican chemist was extremely accurate

GO ON TO THE NEXT PAGE

43. The quotation from a member of the restoration team (Passage 2, lines 41–43) suggests that he viewed the chapel ceiling as

(A) a more educational experience than reading a book

(B) a valuable source of information about fresco-painting techniques

(C) a work that could have served as a model for other fresco painters

(D) a repository of lost literature as well as an artistic masterpiece

(E) the only good surviving example of a Renaissance fresco

44. It can be inferred from Michelangelo's reputation for being "defiant of Renaissance fresco-painting protocol" (Passage 2, lines 50–51) that

(A) his work was considered inferior by other Renaissance artists

(B) he was a fiercely independent and individualistic thinker

(C) historical conceptions of the artist have overestimated his negative traits

(D) darkening of colors to produce a gloomy effect was not common practice

(E) the restoration has jeopardized his position in history as a great artist

45. The reference to "a vagabond given a good scrubbing" (Passage 2, line 53) serves to

(A) give an idea of the simplicity of the cleaning operation

(B) explain the disconcerting effect of the colorful frescoes on some critics

(C) provide some biographical information about the painter

(D) indicate that the cleaning of the chapel ceiling should not alter the artist's image

(E) show that no art historian has ever really understood Michelangelo

46. The authors of Passages 1 and 2 disagree primarily on which aspect of the painting on the ceiling of the Sistine Chapel?

(A) Whether the former darkened quality was to any degree intentional

(B) The reason that the restoration of the painting was so long delayed

(C) The specific techniques the restorers should have used

(D) Whether or not the frescoes were originally done in color

(E) The extent of the damage that was caused by the grime

GO ON TO THE NEXT PAGE →

47. Which statement best expresses the objection that the author of Passage 2 would make about Passage 1's argument regarding the painting's "suppressed anger and thunderous pessimism" (lines 27–28)?

   (A) It makes little sense because the essential elements of the painting were not changed during the restoration.

   (B) It is weak because the painting has been the subject of many different and often contradictory interpretations.

   (C) It summarizes the long-held ideas that the restoration has proved to be erroneous.

   (D) It is unfounded because the restored painting does not exhibit the quality discussed.

   (E) It distorts the actual views of past art historical experts.

48. How would the author of Passage 1 respond to the fact mentioned in Passage 2 that a layer of dirt was kept "for the sake of protection of the frescoes" (lines 30–31)?

   (A) The protection clearly was not as effective as the restorers had hoped.

   (B) Nothing will be able to protect the frescoes now that the animal glue has been removed.

   (C) Chemical agents left in the dirt are continuing to cause damage to the ceiling.

   (D) The dirt layer will allow the painting to retain its dark and angry quality.

   (E) The restorers really kept the final layer of dirt in a futile attempt to pacify their critics.

IF YOU FINISH BEFORE TIME IS CALLED, YOU MAY CHECK YOUR WORK ON THIS SECTION ONLY. DO NOT TURN TO ANY OTHER SECTION IN THE TEST. STOP

SECTION 4

Time—25 Minutes
20 Questions

Solve each of the following problems, decide which is the best answer choice, and darken the corresponding oval on the answer sheet.

Notes:

(1) Calculator use is permitted.

(2) All numbers used are real numbers.

(3) Figures are provided for some problems. All figures are drawn to scale and lie in a plane UNLESS otherwise indicated.

(4) Unless otherwise specified, the domain of any function f is assumed to be the set of all real numbers x for which $f(x)$ is a real number.

$A = \frac{1}{2}bh$ $c^2 = a^2 + b^2$ Special right triangles $A = \pi r^2$ $V = \ell wh$ $V = \pi r^2 h$ $A = \ell w$
$C = 2\pi r$

The sum of the degree measures of the angles in a triangle is 180.
The number of degrees of arc in a circle is 360.
A straight angle has a degree measure of 180.

21. When Mr. Schafer arrived at the grocery store, there were 8 cases of soda left on the shelf. One case contained 11 cans of soda, and each of the others contained 6. If Mr. Schafer bought all 8 cases, how many cans of soda did he purchase at this store?

(A) 53

(B) 54

(C) 57

(D) 59

(E) 65

22. A, B, and C are consecutive points on a line. The length of $\overline{AB}$ is 10, and the length of $\overline{BC}$ is 16 more than the length of $\overline{AB}$. What is the length of $\overline{AC}$?

(A) 26

(B) 36

(C) 46

(D) 56

(E) 66

23. If $x + 5 = a$, then $3x + 15 =$

    (A) $a + 5$
    (B) $a + 15$
    (C) $3a$
    (D) $3a + 5$
    (E) $3a + 15$

24. If the sum of the areas of two regions is 7, what is the average (arithmetic mean) of the areas of the regions?

    (A) 0
    (B) $\dfrac{7}{2}$
    (C) $\dfrac{7}{4}$
    (D) 7
    (E) 14

25. Which of the following is equal to $(3 \times 10^3) + (3 \times 10^4)$?

    (A) 33×10
    (B) 33×10^3
    (C) 33×10^4
    (D) 3×10^7
    (E) 6×10^7

26. If the area of the square in the figure above is 25 and the perimeter of each of the two triangles is 21, what is the perimeter of the entire figure?

    (A) 30
    (B) 38
    (C) 42
    (D) 48
    (E) 80

GO ON TO THE NEXT PAGE

Note: Figure not drawn to scale.

27. In the figure above, $AB = BC$ and $DE = EF = DF$. If the measure of $\angle ABC$ is 50 degrees and the measure of $\angle BDE$ is 70 degrees, what is the degree measure of $\angle DFA$?

(A) 50

(B) 55

(C) 60

(D) 65

(E) 70

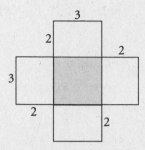

28. In the figure above, the shaded region and each of the four unshaded regions are rectangles. If a point on the figure is chosen at random, what is the probability that point is in the shaded region?

(A) $\dfrac{1}{9}$

(B) $\dfrac{3}{14}$

(C) $\dfrac{3}{11}$

(D) $\dfrac{3}{8}$

(E) $\dfrac{3}{7}$

GO ON TO THE NEXT PAGE

DIRECTIONS FOR STUDENT-PRODUCED RESPONSE QUESTIONS

For each of the questions below (29–38), solve the problem and indicate your answer by darkening the ovals in the special grid. For example:

Answer: 1.25 or $\frac{5}{4}$ or 5/4

Write answer in boxes. → Grid-in result. →

→ Fraction line
→ Decimal point

Either position is correct.

You may start your answers in any column, space permitting. Columns not needed should be left blank.

- It is recommended, though not required, that you write your answer in the boxes at the top of the columns. However, you will receive credit only for darkening the ovals correctly.

- Grid only one answer to a question, even though some problems have more than one correct answer.

- Darken no more than one oval in a column.

- No answers are negative.

- Mixed numbers cannot be gridded. For example: the number $1\frac{1}{4}$ must be gridded as 1.25 or 5/4.

  (If $1\,1\,/\,4$ is gridded, it will be interpreted as $\frac{11}{4}$, not $1\frac{1}{4}$.)

- <u>Decimal Accuracy:</u> Decimal answers must be entered as accurately as possible. For example, if you obtain an answer such as 0.1666..., you should record the result as .166 or .167. **Less accurate values such as .16 or .17 are not acceptable.**

Acceptable ways to grid $\frac{1}{6}$ = .1666...

29. The height of a particular species of tree is directly proportional to the average yearly rainfall where it grows. If a tree that lives in an area with an average yearly rainfall of 200 centimeters is 30 meters tall, how tall, in meters, is a tree that lives in an area with an average yearly rainfall of 10 centimeters?

30. A scientist begins an experiment with 50 bacteria in a petri dish. If the population doubles every two days, the number of bacteria in the dish can be expressed as $(50)2^{\frac{t}{2}}$, where t is the number of days that have passed since the start of the experiment. How many bacteria will be in the petri dish at the end of the sixth day of the experiment?

GO ON TO THE NEXT PAGE →

31. If $6y = 12$ and $x - 2y = 3$, what is the value of x?

33. A rectangular floor 56 inches by 60 inches is to be completely covered with non-overlapping rectangular tiles, each 6 inches by 8 inches. How many tiles are needed to cover the floor?

32. Bill bought three books at $14.50 each. If the tax was already included in the cost, how much change did he receive from a $50 bill? (Disregard the $ sign when gridding your answer.)

34. If $4^{n+1} = 64$, then $n^3 = ?$

GO ON TO THE NEXT PAGE

35. If the ratio of *a* to *b* is 3 to 4 and the ratio of *a* to *c* is 2 to 5, what is the ratio of *b* to *c*?

36. If three coins are tossed simultaneously, what is the probability of getting exactly two tails?

37. What is the least positive integer *j* such that 28*j* is a perfect square?

Note: Figure not drawn to scale.

38. In the figure above, *AC* has length 6 and is perpendicular to *OB*. If the circle has center *O* and radius 5, what is the length of *BD*?

SECTION 5

Time—30 Minutes
39 Questions

For each of the following questions, choose the best answer and darken the corresponding oval on the answer sheet.

Directions: The following sentences test your knowledge of grammar, usage, diction (choice of words), and idioms.

Some sentences are correct.

No sentence contains more than one error.

You will find that the error, if there is one, is underlined and lettered. Elements of the sentence that are not underlined will not be changed. In choosing answers, follow the requirements of standard written English.

If there is an error, select the <u>one underlined part</u> that must be changed to make the sentence correct, and fill in the corresponding oval on your answer sheet.

If there is no error, fill in answer oval (E).

1. The first female aviator <u>to cross</u> the English
                            A
   Channel, Harriet Quimby <u>flown</u> <u>by monoplane</u>
                            B   C
   from Dover, England, to Hardelot, France, <u>in</u>
                                              D
   1912. <u>No error</u>
         E

2. The reproductive behavior of sea horses <u>is</u>
                                            A
   <u>notable</u> <u>in respect of</u> the male, <u>who,</u> <u>instead of</u>
   A   B   C   D
   the female, carries the fertilized eggs. <u>No error</u>
                                            E

3. Early <u>experience</u> of racial discrimination
         A
   <u>made</u> an <u>indelible</u> <u>impression for</u> the late
   B   C   D
   Supreme Court Justice Thurgood Marshall.
   <u>No error</u>
   E

4. More journalists <u>as</u> you would suspect are
                     A
   <u>secretly</u> writing plays or novels, <u>which</u> they
   B   C
   hope someday <u>to have published</u>. <u>No error</u>
                D   E

GO ON TO THE NEXT PAGE

5. <u>As long ago as</u> the 12th century, French
    A

    alchemists <u>have</u> perfected techniques
            B

    <u>for refining</u> precious metals <u>from</u> other ores.
       C   D

    <u>No error</u>
      E

6. Galileo begged Rome's indulgence for his

    <u>support of</u> a Copernican system <u>in which</u> the
      A   B

    Earth circled the sun <u>instead of</u> <u>occupied</u> a
                      C   D

    central position in the universe. <u>No error</u>
                                E

7. <u>Squandering</u> his inheritance, the prodigal son
    A

    <u>felt no compunction</u> in <u>wasting</u> his <u>father's</u>
          B   C   D

    hard-earned fortune. <u>No error</u>
                  E

8. Although the piano <u>as we know it today</u> did
                   A

    not exist in his time, Bach <u>was writing</u>
                      B

    many pieces <u>that are</u> now frequently played
              C

    <u>on that instrument.</u> <u>No error</u>
         D   E

9. The chemist Sir Humphrey Davy was a friend

    <u>of the poet</u> William Wordsworth; <u>he</u> <u>would</u>
      A   B   C

    <u>visit</u> with several other guests <u>at</u> a tiny cottage
      C   D

    in the English Lake District. <u>No error</u>
                       E

10. <u>Grading</u> research papers <u>over the years</u>, the
    A   B

    professor became expert <u>at recognizing</u>
                       C

    submissions that <u>have been plagiarized</u> or
                    D

    inadequately documented. <u>No error</u>
                    E

11. <u>During</u> the military coup, the deposed prime
    A

    minister's property was <u>put up</u> for sale without
                    B

    <u>him</u> <u>having</u> any opportunity to object.
      C   D

    <u>No error</u>
      E

12. The primary difference <u>between</u> the two
                 A

    positions advertised <u>is</u> <u>that</u> one is exciting;
                 B C

    <u>the other is boring.</u> <u>No error</u>
         D   E

13. <u>To conserve calories</u>, to promote digestion,
    A

    <u>or so that they are</u> less vulnerable to predators,
              B

    wild animals <u>rest</u> during <u>many of</u> their
             C   D

    waking hours. <u>No error</u>
             E

14. <u>It</u> did not occur to the interviewer <u>to ask</u>
    A   B

    either the job applicant <u>nor</u> his reference
                  C

    <u>whether</u> the applicant had completed the
      D

    project he initiated. <u>No error</u>
                 E

GO ON TO THE NEXT PAGE →

Directions: The following sentences test correctness and effectiveness of expression. In choosing answers, follow the requirements of standard written English; that is, pay attention to grammar, choice of words, sentence construction, and punctuation.

In each of the following sentences, part of the sentence or the entire sentence is underlined. Beneath each sentence, you will find five ways of phrasing the underlined part. Choice (A) repeats the original; the other four are different.

Choose the answer that best expresses the meaning of the original sentence. If you think the original is better than any of the alternatives, choose it; otherwise, choose one of the others. Your choice should produce the most effective sentence—clear and precise, without awkwardness or ambiguity.

15. James's ambition was <u>not only to study but also mastering</u> the craft of journalism.

    (A) not only to study but also mastering
    (B) not only studying but to try and master
    (C) not studying only, but also mastering
    (D) not only to study but also to master
    (E) to study and as well to master

16. The Islandian government, under pressure to satisfy the needs of consumers, <u>and loosening its</u> control of the economy.

    (A) and loosening its
    (B) by loosening its
    (C) is loosening their
    (D) but loosening their
    (E) is loosening its

17. To the surprise of the school's staff, the new freshman class at Ridgewood High <u>being larger than last year's</u>.

    (A) being larger than last year's
    (B) is large, more so than last year
    (C) which is larger than the one last year
    (D) is larger than last year's
    (E) by far larger than the last

18. Night shift workers lead a strange life, working while the rest of us are sleeping, <u>then sleeping</u> while the rest of us are working.

    (A) then sleeping
    (B) after which they sleep
    (C) then they sleep
    (D) until they go to sleep
    (E) but soon they are sleeping

19. <u>The young couple eventually returned to the grassy spot where they had left their sandwiches, strolling hand in hand.</u>

    (A) The young couple eventually returned to the grassy spot where they had left their sandwiches, strolling hand in hand.
    (B) Eventually, the young couple returned to the grassy spot where they had left their sandwiches, strolling hand in hand.
    (C) Strolling hand in hand, the grassy spot where they had left their sandwiches was returned to by the young couple.
    (D) The young couple, returning to the grassy spot where they had left their sandwiches, while strolling hand in hand.
    (E) Strolling hand in hand, the young couple eventually returned to the grassy spot where they had left their sandwiches.

GO ON TO THE NEXT PAGE

20. <u>Amelia Earhart was born in Kansas the first person to fly from Hawaii to California.</u>

    (A) Amelia Earhart was born in Kansas the first person to fly from Hawaii to California.

    (B) Amelia Earhart being the first person to fly from Hawaii to California and was born in Kansas.

    (C) Being the first person to fly from Hawaii to California, Amelia Earhart was born in Kansas.

    (D) Amelia Earhart was the first person to fly from Hawaii to California and was born in Kansas.

    (E) Amelia Earhart, who was born in Kansas, was the first person to fly from Hawaii to California.

21. Samuel Johnson's Dictionary, published in 1755, <u>was neither the first in English nor the largest</u>, but its quotations illustrating definitions made it the best for many decades.

    (A) was neither the first in English nor the largest

    (B) neither was it the first in English nor the largest

    (C) neither was the first in English nor the largest

    (D) neither was the first in English, and it was not the largest either

    (E) was neither the first in English, nor was it the largest

22: In the Middle Ages, when astronomical phenomena were poorly understood, <u>the comets that seemed to portend</u> military conflicts or other social crises.

    (A) the comets that seemed to portend

    (B) the comets seeming to portend

    (C) the comets seemed to portend

    (D) the comets apparently portending

    (E) and when the comets seemed to portend

23. Unusual numbers of playwrights and artists <u>flourishing in the England of Shakespeare's time</u> and the Italy of Michelangelo's day, when cultural conditions were particularly conducive to creativity.

    (A) flourishing in the England of Shakespeare's time

    (B) by flourishing in the England of Shakespeare's time

    (C) while flourishing in Shakespeare's England

    (D) flourished in the England of Shakespeare's time

    (E) having flourished in Shakespeare's England

24. During World War I, United States Army psychologists administered a forerunner of today's IQ tests, <u>where it had directions that</u> were given orally in acoustically poor and crowded rooms.

    (A) where it had directions that

    (B) whereby there were directions that

    (C) whose directions

    (D) and for it they had directions which

    (E) and it had directions which

GO ON TO THE NEXT PAGE

25. A dispute arose between Rimland and Heartland over the eastern provinces from which 20 years before a great many people <u>had emigrated</u>.

    (A) had emigrated
    (B) emigrated
    (C) had immigrated
    (D) immigrated
    (E) migrated

26. In an effort to sound like an expert, <u>the director's speech which was riddled with esoteric references</u> and specialized terms.

    (A) the director's speech which was riddled with esoteric references
    (B) the director's speech was riddled with esoteric references
    (C) the director delivered a speech riddled with esoteric references
    (D) his speech which was riddled with esoteric references
    (E) the speech of the director was riddled with esoteric references

27. <u>If the construction strike has not occurred,</u> the contractor would have had no difficulty in finishing the renovation of the restaurant on time.

    (A) If the construction strike has not occurred
    (B) If the construction strike would not have occurred
    (C) Had the construction strike not of occurred
    (D) Had it not been that the construction strike had occurred
    (E) Had it not been for the construction strike

28. In retrospect, one can see the folly of trying to unite a region containing some four hundred distinct ethnic groups, <u>each with its own language, laws, and traditions</u>.

    (A) each with its own language, laws, and traditions
    (B) each of them has its own language, laws, and traditions
    (C) each with their own language, laws, and traditions
    (D) and each of them having its own language, laws, and traditions
    (E) when they each have their own language, laws, and traditions

29. Proponents of campaign finance reform point out that people who make large donations to politicians expect to be rewarded with special favors <u>and gaining easy access</u> to the corridors of power.

    (A) and gaining easy access
    (B) and they gain easy access
    (C) and easy access
    (D) as well as gaining easy access
    (E) and to be rewarded with easy access

30. <u>Had Churchill sent planes to defend Coventry</u> from the German air raid, the Nazis would have realized that their secret code had been broken by the Allies.

    (A) Had Churchill sent planes to defend Coventry
    (B) If Churchill would have sent planes to defend Coventry
    (C) Churchill having sent planes to defend Coventry
    (D) If Churchill sent planes to defend Coventry
    (E) Churchill, by sending planes to Coventry to defend it

GO ON TO THE NEXT PAGE

31. <u>Television shows such as *M*A*S*H* and *All in the Family* took</u> months or even years to build a large audience, most new series today never get that chance.

   (A) Television shows such as *M*A*S*H* and *All in the Family* took

   (B) Although television shows such as *M*A*S*H* and *All in the Family* took

   (C) With television shows such as *M*A*S*H* and *All in the Family* taking

   (D) Such television shows as *M*A*S*H* and *All in the Family* took

   (E) When television shows such as *M*A*S*H* and *All in the Family* took

32. Returning to her home town after a 20-year absence, <u>the desperate poverty Savka saw there shocked and saddened her</u>.

   (A) the desperate poverty Savka saw there shocked and saddened her

   (B) the desperate poverty Savka saw there was shocking and also sad to her

   (C) Savka, shocked and saddened by the desperate poverty she saw there

   (D) Savka was shocked and saddened by the desperate poverty she saw there

   (E) was a desperate poverty that shocked and saddened Savka

33. The brochure for the writing camp promises that by the time you leave the camp, you <u>complete an entire manuscript</u>.

   (A) complete an entire manuscript

   (B) would complete an entire manuscript

   (C) will have completed an entire manuscript

   (D) have complete an entire manuscript

   (E) had completed an entire manuscript

34. When the electrochemists Stanley Pons and Martin Fleischmann declared in 1989 that they had achieved <u>cold fusion; scientists around the world tried to duplicate the process, they were not successful</u>.

   (A) cold fusion; scientists around the world tried to duplicate the process, they were not successful

   (B) cold fusion then scientists around the world tried to duplicate the process only without succeeding

   (C) cold fusion, consequently scientists around the world, without success, tried to duplicate the process

   (D) cold fusion, scientists around the world tried without success to duplicate the process

   (E) cold fusion; however, scientists around the world tried to duplicate the process, without success

GO ON TO THE NEXT PAGE

Directions: The passage below is an early draft of an essay. Parts of the passage need to be rewritten.

Read the passage, and answer the questions that follow. Some questions are about individual sentences or parts of sentences; in these questions, you are asked to select the choice which will improve sentence structure and word choice. Other questions refer to parts of the essay or the entire essay and ask you to consider the organization and development. You should follow the conventions of standard written English in answering the questions. After you have chosen your answer, fill in the corresponding oval on your answer sheet.

Questions 35–39 are based on the following passage.

(1) *Last summer I was fortunate enough to be able to spend a month in France. (2) It was the most exciting time of my life. (3) I stayed with a family in Montpellier, who were in the south of France. (4) It was very different from my life back in the United States. (5) Every morning we bought fresh bread from the bakery and had coffee in a bowl instead of a cup. (6) The milk came in bottles fresh from the dairy.*

(7) *Back home in Winnetka, Illinois, I wouldn't think anything of taking a ten-minute shower every day, or even twice a day in the summer. (8) In Montpellier, we showered only once every two days and were using far less water. (9) First you turn the water on to get wet, then turn it off and soap yourself up, then you turned it on again to rinse off, so the water is only on for about maybe two minutes. (10) And it was pretty hot there in the summer, I'd never taken showers in cold water before! (11) I couldn't imagine what it was like in the winter. (12) I also noticed that although the family had a car, they hardly ever used it. (13) The father took the bus to work in the morning and the mother rode her bicycle when doing errands. (14) Since the family wasn't poor, they were well-off, I realized that gas is much more expensive in France than in the United States (15) I realized that as Americans, we can afford to take long showers and drive everywhere because we pay much less for energy. (16) Living in Montpellier and seeing how frugally people lived there, I get angry thinking of the resources wasted in the United States (17) When I came home, I was much more energy conscious. (18) I didn't drink coffee out of a bowl anymore, but I started riding my bike to school and turning the thermostat down at night.*

35. In context, which of the following is the best way to revise sentence 3 (reproduced below)?

    I stayed with a family in Montpellier, who were in the south of France.

    (A) I stayed with a family in Montpellier, who were living in the south of France.

    (B) I stayed with a family in Montpellier, which is in the south of France.

    (C) In the south of France in Montpellier were living the family that I stayed with.

    (D) The south of France in Montpellier is where I stayed with a family.

    (E) I stayed in the south of France in Montpellier where lived a family.

GO ON TO THE NEXT PAGE

36. Which of the following sentences, if added after sentence 6, would best link the first paragraph with the rest of the essay?

    (A) These differences were superficial, however; I was soon to discover other, more important ones.

    (B) How I longed for my familiar existence back in the United States!

    (C) I was not prepared for the culture shock I experienced.

    (D) But I didn't let such minor inconveniences ruin my overseas experience.

    (E) Although it took a while, eventually I got used to the new way of doing things.

37. In context, which of the following versions of sentence 8 (reproduced below) is best?

    In Montpellier, we only showered once every two days and were using far less water.

    (A) Showering only once every two days, Montpellier was where I used far less water.

    (B) Showering only once every two days and using far less water were things we did in Montpellier.

    (C) In Montpellier, we showered only once every two days and used far less water.

    (D) In Montpellier, where once every two days was when we showered, a lot less water was used.

    (E) In Montpellier, we were only showering once every two days and using far less water.

38. Which of the following best replaces the word "And" at the beginning of sentence 10 (reproduced below)?

    And it was pretty hot there in the summer, I'd never taken showers in cold water before!

    (A) But
    (B) Although
    (C) Yet
    (D) When
    (E) Which

39. In context, which is the best version of the underlined portion of sentence 14 (reproduced below)?

    Since the family wasn't poor, they were well-off, I realized that gas is much more expensive in France than in the United States.

    (A) The family not being poor, they were well-off

    (B) Well-off, not poor, being the family

    (C) Since the family was well-off, they were not poor

    (D) The family wasn't poor but well-off

    (E) Since the family was well-off rather than poor

IF YOU FINISH BEFORE TIME IS CALLED, YOU MAY CHECK YOUR WORK ON THIS SECTION ONLY. DO NOT TURN TO ANY OTHER SECTION IN THE TEST. **STOP**

PRACTICE TEST TWO: **ANSWER KEY**

SECTION 1

1. C	9. D	17. E
2. A	10. C	18. C
3. E	11. C	19. D
4. A	12. E	20. A
5. D	13. C	21. B
6. D	14. A	22. B
7. A	15. E	23. E
8. E	16. C	24. B

SECTION 2

1. E	8. B	15. C
2. E	9. A	16. B
3. D	10. C	17. A
4. B	11. E	18. C
5. E	12. E	19. D
6. A	13. A	20. E
7. D	14. C	

SECTION 3

25. D	33. C	41. C
26. E	34. E	42. C
27. B	35. A	43. B
28. A	36. C	44. D
29. B	37. D	45. B
30. E	38. D	46. A
31. D	39. E	47. C
32. B	40. D	48. A

SECTION 4

21. A	29. 1.5 or $\dfrac{3}{2}$
22. B	30. 400
23. C	31. 7
24. B	32. 6.5 or $\dfrac{13}{2}$
25. B	33. 70
26. C	34. 8
27. D	35. $\dfrac{8}{15}$ or 0.533
28. C	36. $\dfrac{3}{8}$ or 0.375
	37. 7
	38. 1

SECTION 5

1. B	14. C	27. E
2. B	15. D	28. A
3. D	16. E	29. C
4. A	17. D	30. A
5. B	18. A	31. B
6. D	19. E	32. D
7. E	20. E	33. C
8. B	21. A	34. D
9. B	22. C	35. B
10. D	23. D	36. A
11. C	24. C	37. C
12. E	25. A	38. B
13. B	26. C	39. E

PRACTICE TEST TWO: ASSESS YOUR STRENGTHS

Use the following tables to determine which question types you need to review most.

Question Type	Section and Question
Sentence Completion	Section 1, 1–5
	Section 3, 25–32
Reading Comprehension	Section 1, 6–24
	Section 3, 33–48
Regular Math	Section 2, 1–18
	Section 4, 19–28
Grid-in Math	Section 4, 29–38
Identifying Sentence Errors	Section 5, 1–14
Improving Sentences	Section 5, 15–34
Improving Paragraphs	Section 5, 35–39

Question Type	Number of Questions on Test	Number Correct
Sentence Completion	13	
Reading Comprehension	35	
Regular Math	28	
Grid-in Math	10	
Identifying Sentence Errors	14	
Improving Sentences	20	
Improving Paragraphs	5	

ANSWERS AND EXPLANATIONS

SECTION 1

1. C

Take this straight-ahead sentence one blank at a time. The second blank may be the easier of the two to predict. A drill sergeant naturally would want new recruits to follow his orders. The only answer choice that matches this prediction is (C), *comply with*. Checking out the first words confirms that this answer choice works.

2. A

The first blank describes the climate of the Sonoran Desert, therefore you can eliminate (D) and (E). You might expect a desert to have relatively little plant and animal life, but this is a contrasting sentence; the second blank will tell us what the desert does *in spite of* the climate, so you can expect a positive action, such as *sustain*. Only (A) matches this prediction.

3. E

In sentences with a semicolon, you should refer to the other part of the sentence (the part that doesn't have a blank space) to find the clue. Here you're told in the first part of the sentence that manual work is *respected by all*; thus, you could predict that even noblemen could engage in it without *dishonor*.

4. A

In this contrasting sentence, you can expect the missing word to counter the concept of *individual* heroes discussed in the first part of the sentence. *Collaborative* (A) matches this prediction.

5. D

In this two-blank contrasting sentence, it's probably easier to begin with the second blank. Although critics clearly like the book, the publishers are likely to be worried about its popular appeal, which is exactly what (D) gives you. And the first word, *sophisticated*, is a positive adjective, which is what we expect as well.

MUSIC PASSAGES

These two short passages are both about music. The writer of Passage 1 believes that music and politics go hand in hand, citing Woody Guthrie as an example of a musician who takes a strong stand on political problems. Passage 2 takes a more personal tone. The author writes that musicians and politics do not go together because musicians are not experts at political analysis.

6. D

The sentence reads, *Music is the perfect medium for the expression of political points of view.* Music is a *way* for people to express political opinions—*way* and *method* are good predictions, which fit well with (D), *instrument*. Note that *instrument* here has nothing to do with musical instruments; it means something more like *tool*. All the other choices are common meanings of *medium* that don't fit here.

7. A

This author supports musicians who express political views. The sentence in question is about musicians who are afraid to be political: *Some musicians, those of little heart, fear that taking a strong stand will cost them precious listeners.* So *those of little heart* is an insult; the writer is saying they lack courage (A). Choice (B) is out, because the author says that listeners are actually more loyal to political musicians. The quote in question refers to musicians, not fans (C). The author never addresses the difficulty of writing political music (D). Choice (E) is off base, because the phrase in question refers to non-political musicians, and Guthrie is described as just the opposite.

8. E

The author of Passage 2 does not like to see politics mixed with music: *Musicians should play music, not dabble in politics as a hobby.* So, musicians who deal in political issues are dabblers, (E). Choice (A) is the viewpoint of Author 1, not Author 2. Choice (B) is out of scope, since the idea of musicians running for office does not come up in either paragraph. Choice (C) might be tempting but is too extreme. The author might find political music boring, but he never says that all listeners find it boring. Choice (D) is also too extreme. The author says that he listens to music to escape, but doesn't imply that political musicians *never* write music that helps listeners escape their troubles.

9. D

Author 1 thinks that political music is great, while Author 2 thinks that musicians should stick to music, and not dabble in politics. This point of disagreement is summed up by (D). Author 2 thinks that it's not a good idea for musicians to mess around with politics, but never implies that it's illegal (A). Choices (B) and (E) are out of scope, since Author 2 never mentions Guthrie or his fans—remember that Author 2 doesn't like political music, but that doesn't mean that those musicians are untalented. Choice (C) is a distortion; Author 2 enjoys political analysis—he just thinks it should be left to professionals.

LANGUAGE ABILITY PASSAGE

This science passage shouldn't present too many difficulties for the reader who knows better than to get bogged down in the wealth of information presented in a typical science passage. When you first read the passage, instead of trying to take it all in, you should work on just getting a general sense of the structure of the passage and the broad themes under discussion.

The first paragraph introduces the main idea of the passage, which is that language separates humans from animals. The second paragraph mentions Chomsky's theory that humans are hardwired to acquire language. The third paragraph discusses the areas in the brain where language is processed. Paragraph 4 looks at how scientists originally came to know what they do about the way the brain processes language, and the final paragraph mentions a promising new investigative tool for brain-language research. If you can glean that from reading the passage, you're more than ready to attack the questions.

10. C

This is a line reference question, so reread the sentence in question. It's easy to see that the author here is not using *quotations,* (A), or *scientific data,* (B). Nor is she using *analogies,* (D), or *inferences,* (E). Phrases such as *to discuss and debate ideas* are *generalizations,* (C).

11. C

The question that begins paragraph 2 serves to introduce and summarize the debate that is discussed in the rest of the paragraph. Choices (A), (B), and (D) are wrong, and (E) is wrong because the topic shifts in the middle of the next paragraph.

12. E

The author mentions computers in his discussion of Chomsky's theory that our brains, like computers, are hardwired to acquire language. Choice (E) paraphrases Chomsky's theory.

13. C

You should have suspected that this information is found in the latter part of the passage, and if you scan there for the words *speak* and *hear*, you'll find them in the sentence that begins on line 60, which discusses PET scans (C).

14. A

Scan for the reference to Broca and Wernicke in the fourth paragraph and reread this portion to figure out its relevance to the passage. As the passage notes, much of the information about the brain's acquisition of language comes from their studies. In other words, the author discusses the work of Broca and Wernicke to illustrate the method by which early discoveries were made about the brain and language (A).

CIRCUS RIDER PASSAGE

This passage can be tough slogging through because the prose is very florid and rich in descriptive detail. Because this is a narrative passage, you should just try to concentrate on the author's attitude toward the subject of his reminiscence, in this case a young circus performer practicing her equestrian act. Clearly, the author was extremely moved by the young showgirl's performance, particularly by her seriousness and dedication to her craft. Once you figure that out, you are ready to proceed to the questions.

15. E

In this specific question, you'll have to scan the first paragraph for the author's description of the horse. There you'll read of its *great size and meekness*. The

correct answer, *huge but submissive*, (E), is a direct paraphrase of this.

16. C

This is a Vocabulary-in-Context question, so reread the sentence and predict the meaning of *charge* here, much as you would in a Sentence Completion. "The trainer guided her *charge*"—clearly here the charge refers to the horse and is a secondary definition of *charge*, which can mean "something under supervision."

17. E

Reread the lines before you try to answer the question. There you'll find that the showgirl is in *most respects* like the others, but that *her manner* distinguished her from them; in other words, she resembled her peers but stood apart from them (E). Avoid answer choices that are too strongly worded, such as (C).

18. C

Read before and after this line to get a sense of the context. You should get a sense that the sentence exists to stress that the author is trying to convey a feeling that is difficult to describe, which is what (C) says.

19. D

The sentence in question contrasts the boasts of the advance agents with the modesty of most circus workers. Choices (A), (B), (C), and (E) simply don't make sense in reference to this sentence. Choice (D), with its mention of *contrasts*, fits the theme and tone of the paragraph.

20. A

Reread the description of the showgirl's performance in the ring, located in the fourth paragraph. There it notes that *her brief tour included only elementary postures and tricks*; in other words, she was concentrating on simple tricks (A).

21. B

Scan for a reference to *serious artist*, where the girl reminds the author of the *way all serious artists seize free minutes to hone the blade of their talent*. In other words, the girl is a serious artist because of her devotion to improving her skills (B).

22. B

Stay close to the broad theme of the passage. Here, the author is not so much interested in giving a play-by-play of the girl's technical skills as in describing her dedication to her craft. For this question, it may have been easier to find evidence to eliminate all the wrong answer choices. Any time you can find four wrong answers, you've found the right answer.

23. E

Again, reread the lines in question and stay close to the broad theme of the passage. The physical setting was plain, but the scene was elevated by the girl's performance and her obvious devotion to her craft. The other choices may be true statements, but they aren't related to the use of *plainness* or the author's main point.

24. B

Reread the last paragraph if you are unsure of the answer. The author is talking about the ring, or stage, where the girl is performing. The *ring of ambition* is reflected by the ring of the circus stage.

SECTION 2

 Picking Numbers

 Backsolving

 Eyeballing

1. E

Just substitute 8 for r in the equation. $(8 + 4)^2 = (12)^2 = 144$.

2. E

$\text{Percent} = \dfrac{\text{Part}}{\text{Whole}} \times 100\%$. Here, the percent is $\dfrac{360}{800} \times 100\% = 45\%$.

3. D

Refer to the scale and translate the bars into numbers; 9th grade is 200, 10th grade is 400, 11th is 450, and 12th is about 380, so together they add up to $200 + 400 + 450 + 380 = 1{,}430$, which is closest to (D).

4. B

Because all the angles together add up to $360°$, you know that $3a + 3b = 360$. Divide both sides of the equation by 3 and you get $a + b = 120$.

5. E

Take this rate problem one step at a time. If Josephine types 12 words in 20 seconds, then she types 36 words in 60 seconds or one minute; thus, she types twice that, or 72 words, in two minutes.

6. A

Translate the English into math. For instance, "12 greater than" means you add 12 to the expression, and "the square root of the product of 10 and a" would translate as $\sqrt{10a}$, so the entire expression would translate to $12 + \sqrt{10a}$.

7. D

The odd integers between 8 and 26 start at 9 and go to 25, and there are 9 integers in all. The even integers between 5 and 23 start at 6 and go to 22, and once again there are 9 integers in all. Note that each integer in the first set is 3 more than the corresponding integer in the second set. Thus, the difference between the sums should be $3 \times 9 = 27$.

8. B ⤺

Begin by simplifying the fraction:

$\dfrac{\frac{1}{a}}{\frac{1}{9}} = \dfrac{1}{a} \div \dfrac{1}{9} = \dfrac{1}{a} \times \dfrac{9}{1} = \dfrac{9}{a}$. Thus, $\dfrac{9}{a} = \dfrac{3}{1}$.

Cross-multiply and you get $3a = 9$, so $a = 3$.

9. A

If the average cost of two of the books is $15, the total cost of the two books is $30, which means that the total cost of the three remaining books is $70 − $30 = $40.

10. C

Note that the figure is not drawn to scale, so even though the points look evenly spaced, they're not. Label the lengths you're given and see what comes of it. For instance, you're told that $AC = 10$ and that it's twice the length of CD, so $CD = 5$. $BD = 9$, and since BD is composed of BC and CD, $BC = 9 - 5 = 4$.

11. E

To figure out the value of r, begin by filling in the angle measures for the triangle. For instance, the angle vertical to the 54° angle is also 54°, and the angle supplementary to the 138° angle has a degree measure of $180° - 138° = 42°$. Now that you know two of the angles in the triangle, you can calculate the angle measure of the third angle (which we'll call x): $x + 54 + 42 = 180$, so $x = 84$. The angle

measure we're looking for is supplementary to this angle, so $84 + r = 180$. Thus, $r = 96$.

12. E

Find the range of values for the product xy by multiplying the maximum and minimum values of each variable, in every combination:

xy could equal $(0)(-2) = 0$
xy could equal $(0)(5) = 0$
xy could equal $(6)(-2) = -12$
xy could equal $(6)(5) = 30$

So the smallest value of xy is −12 and the largest is 30.

13. A ₁②₃

First, list out the first six positive integers: 2, 4, 6, 8, 10, and 12. It would be helpful to figure out the least common multiple of these integers, which is most easily accomplished by figuring out the prime factorization of each; 2 is prime; $4 = 2 \times 2$; $6 = 2 \times 3$; $8 = 2 \times 2 \times 2$; $10 = 2 \times 5$; $12 = 2 \times 2 \times 3$. So the smallest integer that would incorporate all of the necessary prime factors (i.e., the least common multiple) would be $2 \times 2 \times 2 \times 3 \times 5 = 120$. All of the answer choices can be divided into 120 except for 18, which contains an extra 3 among its prime factors.

14. C

Here you just have to know that slope is equal to $\dfrac{\text{rise}}{\text{run}}$, or in mathematical terms, $\dfrac{y_2 - y_1}{x_2 - x_1}$. So here the slope equals $\dfrac{9 - 6}{4 - 2} = \dfrac{3}{2}$.

15. C ₁②₃

If $rs < 0$, then either r is negative and s is positive, or s is negative and r is positive. So clearly, (A) and (B) can be eliminated. You could try to pick numbers to eliminate other answer choices. For instance, if $r = -1$ and $s = 1$, then (D) is true, and if $r = -1$ and $s = 2$, then (E) is true. Moreover, (C) *cannot* be true, because if $r - s = 0$, then $r = s$, which we know cannot be the case.

16. B

If the area of the rectangle is 48, then BC, which is the diameter of the semicircle, must be 4, because the area of a rectangle equals *length* × *width*. So the radius of the semicircle is half the diameter, or 2, and the area of the semicircle is $\frac{1}{2}(\pi r^2) = \frac{1}{2}[\pi(2)^2] = \frac{1}{2}(4\pi) = 2\pi$.

17. A

Use reverse FOIL to factor the quadratic equation. $x^2 + 4x - 12 = (x + 6)(x - 2)$, so $(x + 6)(x - 2) = 0$. Now set the terms in the parentheses to equal 0 in order to find the possible values for x; $(x + 6) = 0$ or $(x - 2) = 0$, so x is either -6 or 2.

18. C

Don't be freaked out by symbol questions. Just plug the numbers into the right-hand side of the symbol equation. Here, you have a two-step symbol problem, so as with any equation you should begin inside the parentheses: $3 \, ❂ \, 5 = 3(5 - 3) = 3 \times 2 = 6$. So now you are looking for $4 \, ❂ \, 6$, which is $4(6 - 4) = 4 \times 2 = 8$.

19. D

Begin by applying your knowledge of ratios to the numbers you are given. Here, you are told that the *before* ratio is 4:3, so the *before* ratio total is $4 + 3 = 7$. That means to start with, $\frac{4}{7}$ of the fruits are oranges and $\frac{3}{7}$ are apples. So we have $\frac{4}{7} \times 56 = 32$ oranges and $\frac{3}{7} \times 56 = 24$ apples. Now you can backsolve to get the correct answer. We'll start with (C): If 7 apples and 7 oranges are removed, you'd be left with 25 oranges and 17 apples. $\frac{25}{17} \neq \frac{3}{2}$, but it's close, so let's try the next closest number, $n = 8$ (D). If 8 apples and 8 oranges are removed, you'd

be left with 24 oranges and 16 apples. $\frac{24}{16} = \frac{3}{2}$, so (D) is the correct answer.

20. E

Translating word problems into written equations can help you figure out where to get started on complicated questions. Solve for j using the average formula:

$$\text{Average} = \frac{\text{Sum of terms}}{\text{Number of terms}}$$

Now, express this as:

$$\frac{\text{Sum of terms}}{\text{Average of terms}} = \text{Number of terms} = j$$

SECTION 3

25. D

The key phrase here is *to equal and even----Wright's successes.* So we are looking for a word that means *more than equal.* Choice (D), *surpass*, works nicely.

26. E

We are looking for a word that covers the wide variety of trumpets described in this sentence. Look for a word that means "varied" among the answer choices. Choice (E), *diverse*, works best here.

27. B

Weighing over 70 tons leads us to predict a word like *large* or *gigantic* for the first blank. The word *yet* sets up a contrast for the second blank. We want a word like *small* or *tiny* for the second blank. Only (B), *gargantuan*, and (D), *prodigious*, work for the first blank. Of these two options, only (B), *small*, works for the second blank. So (B) is correct.

28. A

Take this two-blank sentence one word at a time. Here, it might be easier to begin with the first blank.

You're looking for a word that works with *difficult to sight* in the first blank. *Elusive* (A) and *crafty* (B) are the only choices that work. Now predict a word for the second blank to choose between (A) and (B). We're looking for a word that sets up a contrast with *difficult to sight*. Choice (A), *confined*, works here.

29. B

The key phrase here is *each having its own government, maintaining its own militia…* So we want to choose words that describe the colonies as independent and autonomous. Both *distinct* (B) and *independent* (C) work for the first blank. There isn't a contrast in this sentence, so you would expect the second blank to express a similar idea to the first. That makes (B), *distinct. . . autonomously*, the correct choice.

30. E

Because kudzu was introduced to the United States in 1876, it must have flourished in Japan prior to then. So we are looking for a choice that is consistent with this idea. *Indigenous* means "native to a specific area or region," so (E) is correct.

31. D

We are looking for an answer choice that is consistent with the phrase *towering over others of his generation both physically and intellectually*. A choice that connotes largeness is what we're looking for here. So (D), *a titan*, is right on the money.

32. B

Look for an answer that is consistent with *shunning personal contact with those outside her family circle*. Choice (B), *reclusive*, is just what we're looking for.

MALAGASY PEOPLE PASSAGES

This short passage explains that research has found that the Malagasy people in Madagascar are probably originally from Indonesia. That theory is based not on physical findings, but on linguistic and cultural findings.

33. C

The passage states that there is *linguistic and cultural evidence* to support the theory. Choice (C) cites the linguistic evidence that the Malagasy language is similar to a language spoke in Indonesia. The author mentions the geographical relationship of Indonesia to Madagascar, but the passage does not use this relationship as evidence for the claim that Indonesians settled Madagascar (A). Choice (B) is directly contradicted by the passage, which explicitly states that there have been no archaeological finds that point unequivocally to Indonesia. Choices (D) and (E) are out of scope, since the passage never refers to housing styles or poetry.

34. E

The author argues that rice cultivation, ancestor worship, and outrigger canoes are cultural evidence of a connection with Indonesia. So a good prediction for the word *resonance* would be *origin*, or *style*. Choice (E) fits well with these predictions. Choices (A) and (D) are related to common meanings of resonance but are too literal to work here, since there is no reference to sounds. The resonance is *used* as *evidence*, but the word resonance doesn't *mean* evidence (B). Choice (C) doesn't fit at all in the sentence.

PREDATOR TERRITORIES PASSAGE

This short passage discusses how territories controlled by predators are always changing, using the wolf and coyote populations in Yellowstone National Park as examples. After wolves were reintroduced in the park, the population of coyotes dropped because wolves were more dominant. That caused the population of rodents to increase and probably the population of elk to decrease.

35. A

The author writes *this complex interplay was dramatically illustrated…* So, what is the interplay? The first sentence says *mammalian predator territories…constantly [shift] over time.* This is nicely summed up by (A). Although the wolves did push the coyotes down the food chain, (B) doesn't show the primary purpose of the Yellowstone example. Choice (C) is the opposite of the main idea of the passage. Although the passage states in the first sentence that predator territories are affected by the size of prey populations (D), the Yellowstone example instead shows that one predator can affect the territory of another. Choice (E) is out of the scope of the passage, since you don't know whether the consequence was unforeseen.

36. C

The author notes that *the coyote population was cut in half, with a corresponding increase in rodents…* Why would a decrease in coyotes lead to an increase in rodents? Choice (C) provides an explanation; if the coyotes ate the rodents (but the wolves didn't), then a decrease in coyotes would likely lead to an increase in rodents. Choices (A), (B), (D), and (E) all mention factors that cannot directly explain an increase in rodents.

THE SISTINE CHAPEL PASSAGES

Here we have a pair of passages written by authors who have diametrically opposed points of view about the recent restoration of the Sistine Chapel. The author of Passage 1 goes after the restoration team with all the ammunition he's got. After spending a paragraph making the point that Michelangelo himself would have been appalled at the effects of the cleaning, the author goes on to assert that the cleaning process removed an essential artistic element of the frescoes. This element—of anger and pessimism—was, according to the author, not the result of centuries of dirt but was rather put there by the master himself. To add insult to injury, the restorers removed protective layers of glue in the process. After reading the first passage, you're ready answer questions 37–40.

Now it's time to focus on Passage 2, which counters the attack of Passage 1 by claiming that the dark, forbidding quality of the frescoes was not, as the author of Passage 1 argues, an effect intended by Michelangelo, but just dirt. The problem, according to Passage 2, is that people had gotten so used to how the frescoes looked before they were cleaned that the cleaning has wiped away *cherished myths* about Michelangelo as well as grime. According to the author, the process has revealed Michelangelo to be a master Renaissance craftsman. This, he states, is why people such as the author of Passage 1 don't like what was done; they are used to seeing Michelangelo as a *wayward genius* rather than a great but conventional artist.

37. D

The point of this paragraph is that Michelangelo would not be bothered by the damage done by time and nature to the Sistine Chapel, but he would be upset by what the restorers did. In this vein, being *philosophical about the damage* wrought by rain means being "unruffled" by it, so (D) is correct.

38. D

The author of Passage 1 is not unhappy with the deterioration of the frescoes over time; he's unhappy with the restoration. The inference he wants the reader to make in the first paragraph is that if Michelangelo would have accepted the deterioration as unfortunate but natural, we should have accepted it also (D). Choice (A) is wrong because the author of Passage 1 says that Michelangelo would be able to perceive the effect of time and the environment on the frescoes. Choice (B) is wrong because there still would have been water damage, even if the chapel were not kept in use. Choice (C) is tricky: It's something the author implies, but not in the first paragraph. Choice (E) is another close choice; it's wrong because we don't know for sure what Michelangelo thought about the deterioration of his frescoes when he was painting them. All we know is that the author thinks Michelangelo wouldn't be bothered by the damage if he saw it now.

39. E

The choices for this question are rather long, but if even just one of the two *elements* in a choice didn't make sense, you could have eliminated it. For example, (A) is wrong because Author 1 does not appreciate the removal of grime at all. Choice (B) is out because Michelangelo's painting techniques—other than the final application of glaze—are not described, nor is the claim made or mentioned that glue was never used on the painting (C). The *elements* in (D) and (E) can all be found in the second paragraph. Choice (D) is wrong, and (E) is correct because it points out the author's use of irony in emphasizing that Michelangelo disliked what the restorers revel in: bright colors.

40. D

For this Vocabulary-in-Context question, refer to the line in question. The climate control system will *arrest*—that is, retard—the process of darkening by pollution (D). The other words are synonyms of *arrest* as it is used in other contexts.

41. C

In the second sentence of Passage 2, the author says that the responsibility of restoring the Sistine Chapel is great but *does not explain* why the chapel had been allowed to fall into disrepair. In other words, the responsibility was not a strong enough deterrent by itself (C) to have stopped restorers. This makes (A), (D), and (E) wrong and (C) correct. Neither author claims that the frescoes are *the greatest work of the Renaissance period,* (B)—this is an extreme choice.

42. C

The author of Passage 2 says that the layer of dirt between the painting and the first layer of glaze shows that the first layer of glaze was put on the painting a long time after Michelangelo finished it (if the glaze had been put on right after he finished it, dirt would have had no time to accumulate). The author is establishing that the first layer of glaze was not put on by Michelangelo (C) and therefore was acceptable to remove. Choices (A), (D), and (E) miss the author's purpose here, which is to justify the removal of that first layer of glaze. Choice (B) is too broad in scope.

43. B

The point of the quotation from the member of the restoration team is that the Sistine Chapel is such a good example of fresco painting that it can be regarded as a *valuable source of information about fresco-painting techniques*, (B). Choices (A) and (D) both distort the author's comparison of the painting to a treatise on fresco art. There is no evidence in the passage that either (C) or (E) is true.

44. D

The author of Passage 2 says that as a result of the restoration's brightening of the fresco colors, Michelangelo no longer seems to have been a *wayward genius, defiant of Renaissance fresco-painting protocol.* The inference you are required to make is that since the brightening of colors made Michelangelo seem to be more conventional as a Renaissance artist, it must have been standard at the time to paint frescoes in bright colors. In other words, darkening colors intentionally was not common practice (D). Choices (A) and (B) may be true, but there is no direct evidence in the passage to support them. (Michelangelo could have painted differently from others and still have been considered superior at the time; he also didn't necessarily need to be a *fiercely independent and individualistic thinker* to be defiant of fresco-painting protocol.) Being defiant of Renaissance fresco-painting protocol is not a negative trait, so (C) is out. As for (E), the author of Passage 2 still considers Michelangelo a great artist even though he may not be a *wayward genius.*

45. B

The author of Passage 2 uses the image of the cleaned-up vagabond to explain the reason critics don't like the effects of the restoration: they no longer recognize their beloved artist without the dark anger and fearfulness. Choice (B) is correct. Choices (A) and (C) can be ruled out as completely irrelevant. Choice (D) contradicts the author of Passage 2's belief that the artist's image has been altered—it is now more accurate. This does not mean, though,

that every single art historian has been wrong about Michelangelo; we have no way of knowing whether this extreme statement is true or not, so (E) is out.

46. A

The heart of the controversy over the Sistine Chapel is the question of color brightness: Was the darkening of the ceiling intentional or not? Author 1 says yes, while Author 2 says no. Choice (A) is correct. Choice (D) may have stopped you for a second, but both authors acknowledge that the frescoes were originally done in color. The delay of restoration (B) is something only Author 2 discusses. Choice (C) is wrong because Author 1 doesn't think the restorers should have used anything. Choice (E) is out because the amount of damage done by the dirt is not a point of contention between the authors.

47. C

As we've established, Author 1 thinks that the quality of suppressed anger and thunderous pessimism was intentional. Author 2 considers Author 1's view to be nothing but a *cherished myth* that the restoration has proved to be false (C). Choice (A) is wrong because Author 2 delights in the fact that the essential element of brightness was changed during the restoration. Choice (B) is out because we know nothing about *many different and contradictory interpretations* of the painting. Choice (D) makes no sense as a rebuttal to Passage 1 because the heart of Author 1's argument is that the restoration destroyed the painting's quality of anger and pessimism. Finally, (E) is wrong because the views of Author 1 are representative of the views of past historical experts.

48. A

Author 1's opinion of the restorers' protection of the frescoes can be found in the final paragraph of Passage 1: The paintings are now being directly affected by pollution, he says. No doubt Author 1 would say sarcastically that the protection of one layer of dirt was *not as effective as the restorers had hoped* (A). Choice (B) is too extreme; Author 1 may be skeptical about protection of the frescoes, but it's always possible that something can do the job. Evidence that Author 1 would respond as in (C) or (E) cannot be found in Passage 1, and (D) contradicts Author 1's argument.

SECTION 4

 Picking Numbers

 Backsolving

 Eyeballing

21. A

Mr. Schafer bought 1 case with 11 cans of soda and 7 cases with 6 cans of soda each, so he bought $1(11) + 7(6)$ or $11 + 42 = 53$ cans of soda.

22. B

Use $AB = 10$ to solve for BC:

$$BC = 16 + AB$$
$$BC = 16 + 10$$
$$BC = 26$$

Now use $AB = 10$ and $BC = 26$ to solve for AC:

$$AC = AB + BC$$
$$AC = 10 + 26$$
$$AC = 36$$

23. C

Notice that $3x + 15$ is equivalent to $3(x + 5)$. Since $x + 5$ is a, $3x + 15 = 3(x + 5) = 3a$.

24. B

If you are uncertain of how to solve a problem, think logically and eliminate unrealistic answer choices. This will increase your odds of guessing the correct answer. Use *sum of terms* = 7 to solve for average:

$$\text{Average} = \frac{\text{Sum of terms}}{\text{Number of terms}}$$
$$\text{Average} = \frac{7}{2}$$

25. B

$(3 \times 10^3) + (3 \times 10^4) = 3{,}000 + 30{,}000 = 33{,}000 = 33 \times 1{,}000 = 33 \times 10^3$

26. C

If the area of the square is 25, each side is 5. Use this fact to identify the sum of the lengths of the other two sides of each triangles. If each triangle has a perimeter of 21, the other two sides must add up to $21 - 5 = 16$. What's more, each of the two vertical sides of the square is 5. So the perimeter of the entire figure is $2(16) + 2(5) = 42$.

27. D

Since $AB = BC$, the angles across from them must be equal, too. If $\angle ABC$ is 50 degrees, $\angle BAC$ and $\angle BCA = \frac{(180 - 50)}{2} = 65$ degrees. Since $DE = EF = DF$, triangle DEF is equilateral, with all angles measuring 60 degrees. You are given that $\angle BDE = 70$, so you can solve: $\angle ADF = 180 - (\angle BDE + \angle EDF) = 180 - (70 + 60) = 50$. Finally, $\angle DFA = 180 - (\angle ADF + \angle DAF) = 180 - (50 + 65) = 65$.

28. C

As with all probability questions, the trick is to compare a part with a whole. As soon as you can pinpoint the part—the shaded region—in relation to the whole—the entire figure—you can solve the problem.

Area of unshaded region $= 4 \times (2 \times 3) = 24$
Area of shaded region $= (3 \times 3) = 9$
Total area of figure $= 24 + 9 = 33$

$$\text{Probability} = \frac{\text{Desired outcome}}{\text{Possible outcomes}} = \frac{9}{33} = \frac{3}{11}$$

29. 1.5 or $\frac{3}{2}$

Find an equation to relate the height of the tree to the yearly rainfall. Because height is directly proportional to rainfall, you can represent their relationship as $h = kr$, where h is height, r is rainfall, and k is a constant. Use the given values to find k; then, use the equation to find the height of the tree in the low-rainfall area:

$$30 = k(200)$$
$$0.15 = k$$
$$h = 0.15(10) = 1.5 \text{ meters}$$

30. 400

This problem conveniently provides an equation you can use to find the answer:

$$(50)2^{\frac{6}{2}} = (50)2^3 = 50(8) = 400$$

(You could also calculate the number of bacteria two, four, and six days after the start of the experiment by doubling the number each time, beginning with the initial population of 50.)

31. 7

If $6y = 12$, then $y = 2$. So $x - 2y = 3$ can be rewritten as $x - 2(2) = 3$; $x - 4 = 3$, so x must equal 7.

32. 6.5 or $\frac{13}{2}$

Three books at $14.50 = 3(\$14.50) = \$43.50$.
If Bill paid with a $50 bill, he would receive $50 - \$43.50 = \$6.50$ in change.

33. 70

To determine the total number of tiles necessary to cover the floor, figure out the total area of the floor and divide that value by the total area of a single tile.

So $\dfrac{\text{Total area}}{\text{Tile area}} = \dfrac{56 \times 60}{6 \times 8} = \dfrac{56 \times 60}{8 \times 6} =$
$7 \times 10 = 70$ tiles.

34. 8

Begin by solving for n. We know that $4^{n+1} = 64$; $64 = 4^3$. So $n + 1 = 3$, and $n = 2$. Thus, $n^3 = 2^3 = 8$.

35. $\frac{8}{15}$ or 0.533

If you are given two ratios with one term in common, in this case a, you can compare ratios if you have the same number for as in each ratio. We're told that $a{:}b$ is 3:4, and $a{:}c$ is 2:5. The least common multiple of 2 and 3 is 6, so we need to double the first ratio and triple the second ratio. So $a{:}b$ can be rewritten as 6:8, and $a{:}c$ can be rewritten as 6:15. Now because we have the same number of as in each ratio, we can compare bs to cs. The ratio of b to c is $\dfrac{8}{15}$ or 0.533.

36. $\frac{3}{8}$ or 0.375

We must determine how many different ways the three coins could land, and then count the number of possibilities that have exactly two coins tails up. It's easiest to do this systematically on paper, using "H" for Heads and "T" for Tails.

H-H-H	T-H-H
H-H-T	T-H-T
H-T-H	T-T-H
H-T-T	T-T-T

Be sure to find every combination. There are eight possible outcomes, but only three of them have exactly two tails showing. (Remember: the combination with three tails up doesn't fit the description.) So the probability of getting exactly two tails is 3 out of 8, or $\frac{3}{8}$.

37. 7

Begin by finding the prime factorization of 28: $28 = 7 \times 4 = 7 \times 2 \times 2$. Notice that 2×2 gives us a perfect square. In this case, the smallest perfect square will consist of two pairs of prime factors. So we need to multiply 28 by 7 to get the smallest perfect square. So $j = 7$.

38. 1

To find the length of BD, first find the length of OD and subtract that from the length of BO. To find the length of OD, look at the right triangle of ADO. Since the radius is 5, you know the hypotenuse, AO, is 5. Because BO is perpendicular to chord AC, BO bisects it. Because AC has a length of 6, AD has a length of 3. So ADO is a 3-4-5 right triangle, and the missing side OD must be of length 4. BO is a radius with a length of 5. So the length of $BO - OD = 5 - 4 = 1$.

SECTION 5

1. B

The use of the word *flown* isn't right. *Flown*, the past participle form of *fly*, can't be used as a main verb by itself. What's needed here is the simple past form of *fly*, which is *flew*.

2. B

In respect of is incorrect. The prepositional phrase is *with respect to*.

3. D

Does something make an *impression for* someone? No, it makes an *impression on* someone.

4. A

The correct comparative form is *more...than*, not *more...as*.

5. B

This sentence describes events prior to a time in the past, so instead of the present perfect *have perfected*, it should use the past perfect *had perfected*.

6. D

Instead of takes a participle: *occupied* should be corrected to *occupying*.

7. E

This sentence contains no error. The verb forms are correct, and the preposition *in* is used idiomatically with *compunction*.

8. B

The past participle—*was writing*—is used to describe an ongoing action contemporary with another action. In this case, the simple past tense, *wrote*, should be used.

9. B

He could refer to either *Davy* or *Wordsworth*; this pronoun has no clear antecedent.

10. D

To indicate that plagiarism or documentation came before both the recognition and the becoming expert, this sentence needs the past perfect tense: *had been plagiarized or inadequately documented*.

11. C

The gerund, not the pronoun, should be the object of the preposition *without*, so the objective pronoun *him* should be changed to the possessive *his*.

12. E

A semicolon is used to separate two independent clauses. The second half of the sentence, *the other is boring*, is an independent clause.

13. B

Items in a list need to be parallel. The underlined portion should read something like *or to be less vulnerable to predators*.

14. C

Either should be paired with *or*, not *nor*.

15. D

This sentence contains a parallelism problem. The idea in this sentence is best expressed with the *not only ... but also* formula. When this formula is used, the two items connected by it have to be in the same grammatical form. Because what are described are *ambitions*, it's idiomatic to use infinitives.

16. E

The original sentence doesn't have a verb, because an *-ing* word without a helping verb isn't a verb. Choices (C) and (E) supply verbs, but (C) introduces an incorrect pronoun. The pronoun must refer to *government*, which is singular. So the pronoun must be *its*.

17. D

Again, the original sentence doesn't have a verb. Choices (B) and (D) supply the missing verb, but (B) makes other changes that introduce new mistakes.

18. A

The original sentence is best. This sentence describes a two-step process. It's a bit like a very short list. Therefore, both steps must be given in parallel forms. The first step is *working* (with no pronoun), so the second step should be simply *sleeping* (with no pronoun).

19. E

Strolling hand-in-hand is a modifying phrase that modifies the noun *couple*. Only (E) places the modifying phrase next to *couple*. The other options misplace the modifier, making it sound as if the sandwiches or the grassy spot are strolling.

20. E

The original sentence is a run-on. Choice (E) provides the best fix, by introducing a subordinate clause.

21. A

The original sentence is the most clear and concise.

22. C

The original sentence has no independent clause. This problem is corrected by getting rid of *that*. All of the other choices simply supply different dependent clauses, and thus fail to address the problem.

23. D

Only (D) corrects the problem with the sentence by turning *flourishing* into *flourished*—a main verb in the past tense.

24. C

Choice (C) most clearly shows the connection between the first clause of the sentence, which identifies a kind of test, and the second clause of the sentence, which asserts something about the directions of the test. *Whose directions* compactly states the relation between these clauses.

25. A

The original sentence is best. The past perfect tense is correct because it describes an action that occurred prior to the main action of the sentence, which is in the past tense (*arose*). Note that *emigrated*, not *immigrated*, is the correct word here: You *emigrate* from a place and *immigrate* to a place.

26. C

Logically, the introductory phrase should refer to the director himself, not to his speech. Therefore, the correct answer has to begin with *the director*.

27. E

This is the first clause of a past conditional statement. Only (E) formulates the conditional mood correctly.

28. A

The sentence is fine as it is. Choice (B) is a run-on. Choices (C) and (E) contain plural pronouns that don't agree with their singular antecedents, and (D) creates a fragment.

29. C

The donors expect to be rewarded with two things: *special favors* and *easy access*. For the sake of parallelism, both these things should be expressed in the same grammatical form: adjective + noun. The other choices are wordy and lack parallel structure; (E) is also redundant.

30. A

The first clause of the sentence correctly sets up a condition which was not fulfilled: Churchill did not send planes to defend Coventry, and hence the Nazis did not realize the Allies had broken their code. Choice (A) is another way of saying *If Churchill had sent planes to defend Coventry*. Choice (B) is gramatically unsound: *if he would have* is a very common error. Watch out for it! Choices (C) and (E) are fragments, and (D) uses the wrong verb tense (*sent* for the past perfect *had sent*).

31. B

The conjunction *although* correctly expresses the contrast that is implied here: television shows were formerly given time to build up an audience, but now they are not. Choices (A) and (D) are run-on sentences, and (C) and (E) are illogical.

32. D

The opening phrase describes Savka, but the way the sentence is phrased, it sounds as though *the desperate poverty* is returning home after a 20-year absence. You know the correct answer will begin with *Savka* to correct the misplaced modifier. Choice (C) creates a sentence fragment, so (D) is the correct answer.

33. C

The phrase *by the time you leave* is the clue to the sentence's meaning. Some time in the future you will leave the camp, but before that happens, you will complete a manuscript. To express this sequence of events clearly, you need to use the future perfect tense: *you will have completed*.

34. D

The sentence as it stands contains a fragment before the semicolon and a run-on after it. Choices (B), (C), and (E) are all awkward and ungrammatical.

35. B

The word *who* modifies a person not a place. Since the first clause in this sentence ends with a place,

Montpellier, you need to modify this with the word *which*.

36. A

The second paragraph explores differences between French and American lifestyles that are more substantial than those outlined in the first paragraph. (Sentence 18 nicely encapsulates the difference between the two paragraphs with its reference to fleeting versus long-lasting changes.) Thus, (A), which hints at the *more important* distinctions described in the second paragraph, is the best connection. Choices (B) and (C) come out of nowhere: the writer is merely noting, not lamenting, certain cultural differences. Choice (D) is illogical because the writer describes her time in France as *exciting*. Choice (E) isn't bad as a conclusion to the first paragraph, but it doesn't work as a tie-in to the second paragraph.

37. C

Choice (C) fixes sentence 8's inconsistency in tense by employing the simple past of both verbs, which is correct in context. Choice (A) contains a misplaced modifier: Montpellier cannot be modified by a clause beginning with *showering*. Choice (B) contains an awkward and unnecessary shift to the passive voice. Choice (D) is awkwardly worded and changes the meaning of the original sentence. Choice (E) is consistent in tense, but its use of the past continuous (*were...showering*) instead of the simple past doesn't work in context.

38. B

From context, we know that the writer is trying to say that despite the summer heat, cold-water showers were a new and different experience. Choice (B) makes this clear. Choices (A) and (C), although they seem to provide the requisite sense of contrast, produce ungrammatical sentences. Choices (D) and (E) make no sense and do not form grammatical sentences either.

39. E

Choice (E) successfully combines the first two clauses of the sentence into a single dependent clause, relieving the awkwardness in the original version. Choice (B) is completely nonsensical. Choice (C) merely reorders the first two clauses without solving the problem, and (D) creates a run-on.

CHAPTER 10: PRACTICE TEST THREE

HOW TO TAKE THIS PRACTICE TEST

Before taking this Practice Test, find a quiet room where you can work uninterrupted for two and a half hours. Make sure you have a comfortable desk, your calculator, and several No. 2 pencils. Use the answer sheet to record your answers. Once you start, don't stop until you've finished. Take a five-minute rest break after section two and a one-minute stretch break after section four. Remember—you may review any questions within a section, but you may not jump from one section to another.

PSAT PRACTICE TEST THREE ANSWER SHEET

Remove (or photocopy) this answer sheet and use it to complete the test. See the answer key following the test when finished. Chapter 11 will show you how to find your score.

Start with number 1 for each section. If a section has fewer questions than answer spaces, leave the extra spaces blank.

SECTION 1

1. Ⓐ Ⓑ Ⓒ Ⓓ Ⓔ
2. Ⓐ Ⓑ Ⓒ Ⓓ Ⓔ
3. Ⓐ Ⓑ Ⓒ Ⓓ Ⓔ
4. Ⓐ Ⓑ Ⓒ Ⓓ Ⓔ
5. Ⓐ Ⓑ Ⓒ Ⓓ Ⓔ
6. Ⓐ Ⓑ Ⓒ Ⓓ Ⓔ

7. Ⓐ Ⓑ Ⓒ Ⓓ Ⓔ
8. Ⓐ Ⓑ Ⓒ Ⓓ Ⓔ
9. Ⓐ Ⓑ Ⓒ Ⓓ Ⓔ
10. Ⓐ Ⓑ Ⓒ Ⓓ Ⓔ
11. Ⓐ Ⓑ Ⓒ Ⓓ Ⓔ
12. Ⓐ Ⓑ Ⓒ Ⓓ Ⓔ

13. Ⓐ Ⓑ Ⓒ Ⓓ Ⓔ
14. Ⓐ Ⓑ Ⓒ Ⓓ Ⓔ
15. Ⓐ Ⓑ Ⓒ Ⓓ Ⓔ
16. Ⓐ Ⓑ Ⓒ Ⓓ Ⓔ
17. Ⓐ Ⓑ Ⓒ Ⓓ Ⓔ
18. Ⓐ Ⓑ Ⓒ Ⓓ Ⓔ

19. Ⓐ Ⓑ Ⓒ Ⓓ Ⓔ
20. Ⓐ Ⓑ Ⓒ Ⓓ Ⓔ
21. Ⓐ Ⓑ Ⓒ Ⓓ Ⓔ
22. Ⓐ Ⓑ Ⓒ Ⓓ Ⓔ
23. Ⓐ Ⓑ Ⓒ Ⓓ Ⓔ
24. Ⓐ Ⓑ Ⓒ Ⓓ Ⓔ

☐ # right in Section 1

☐ # wrong in Section 1

SECTION 2

1. Ⓐ Ⓑ Ⓒ Ⓓ Ⓔ
2. Ⓐ Ⓑ Ⓒ Ⓓ Ⓔ
3. Ⓐ Ⓑ Ⓒ Ⓓ Ⓔ
4. Ⓐ Ⓑ Ⓒ Ⓓ Ⓔ
5. Ⓐ Ⓑ Ⓒ Ⓓ Ⓔ

6. Ⓐ Ⓑ Ⓒ Ⓓ Ⓔ
7. Ⓐ Ⓑ Ⓒ Ⓓ Ⓔ
8. Ⓐ Ⓑ Ⓒ Ⓓ Ⓔ
9. Ⓐ Ⓑ Ⓒ Ⓓ Ⓔ
10. Ⓐ Ⓑ Ⓒ Ⓓ Ⓔ

11. Ⓐ Ⓑ Ⓒ Ⓓ Ⓔ
12. Ⓐ Ⓑ Ⓒ Ⓓ Ⓔ
13. Ⓐ Ⓑ Ⓒ Ⓓ Ⓔ
14. Ⓐ Ⓑ Ⓒ Ⓓ Ⓔ
15. Ⓐ Ⓑ Ⓒ Ⓓ Ⓔ

16. Ⓐ Ⓑ Ⓒ Ⓓ Ⓔ
17. Ⓐ Ⓑ Ⓒ Ⓓ Ⓔ
18. Ⓐ Ⓑ Ⓒ Ⓓ Ⓔ

☐ # right in Section 2

☐ # wrong in Section 2

SECTION 3

25. Ⓐ Ⓑ Ⓒ Ⓓ Ⓔ
26. Ⓐ Ⓑ Ⓒ Ⓓ Ⓔ
27. Ⓐ Ⓑ Ⓒ Ⓓ Ⓔ
28. Ⓐ Ⓑ Ⓒ Ⓓ Ⓔ
29. Ⓐ Ⓑ Ⓒ Ⓓ Ⓔ
30. Ⓐ Ⓑ Ⓒ Ⓓ Ⓔ

31. Ⓐ Ⓑ Ⓒ Ⓓ Ⓔ
32. Ⓐ Ⓑ Ⓒ Ⓓ Ⓔ
33. Ⓐ Ⓑ Ⓒ Ⓓ Ⓔ
34. Ⓐ Ⓑ Ⓒ Ⓓ Ⓔ
35. Ⓐ Ⓑ Ⓒ Ⓓ Ⓔ
36. Ⓐ Ⓑ Ⓒ Ⓓ Ⓔ

37. Ⓐ Ⓑ Ⓒ Ⓓ Ⓔ
38. Ⓐ Ⓑ Ⓒ Ⓓ Ⓔ
39. Ⓐ Ⓑ Ⓒ Ⓓ Ⓔ
40. Ⓐ Ⓑ Ⓒ Ⓓ Ⓔ
41. Ⓐ Ⓑ Ⓒ Ⓓ Ⓔ
42. Ⓐ Ⓑ Ⓒ Ⓓ Ⓔ

43. Ⓐ Ⓑ Ⓒ Ⓓ Ⓔ
44. Ⓐ Ⓑ Ⓒ Ⓓ Ⓔ
45. Ⓐ Ⓑ Ⓒ Ⓓ Ⓔ
46. Ⓐ Ⓑ Ⓒ Ⓓ Ⓔ
47. Ⓐ Ⓑ Ⓒ Ⓓ Ⓔ
48. Ⓐ Ⓑ Ⓒ Ⓓ Ⓔ

☐ # right in Section 3

☐ # wrong in Section 3

SECTION 4

19. Ⓐ Ⓑ Ⓒ Ⓓ Ⓔ	24. Ⓐ Ⓑ Ⓒ Ⓓ Ⓔ	29. Ⓐ Ⓑ Ⓒ Ⓓ Ⓔ	34. Ⓐ Ⓑ Ⓒ Ⓓ Ⓔ	
20. Ⓐ Ⓑ Ⓒ Ⓓ Ⓔ	25. Ⓐ Ⓑ Ⓒ Ⓓ Ⓔ	30. Ⓐ Ⓑ Ⓒ Ⓓ Ⓔ	35. Ⓐ Ⓑ Ⓒ Ⓓ Ⓔ	# right in Section 4
21. Ⓐ Ⓑ Ⓒ Ⓓ Ⓔ	26. Ⓐ Ⓑ Ⓒ Ⓓ Ⓔ	31. Ⓐ Ⓑ Ⓒ Ⓓ Ⓔ	36. Ⓐ Ⓑ Ⓒ Ⓓ Ⓔ	
22. Ⓐ Ⓑ Ⓒ Ⓓ Ⓔ	27. Ⓐ Ⓑ Ⓒ Ⓓ Ⓔ	32. Ⓐ Ⓑ Ⓒ Ⓓ Ⓔ	37. Ⓐ Ⓑ Ⓒ Ⓓ Ⓔ	# wrong in Section 4
23. Ⓐ Ⓑ Ⓒ Ⓓ Ⓔ	28. Ⓐ Ⓑ Ⓒ Ⓓ Ⓔ	33. Ⓐ Ⓑ Ⓒ Ⓓ Ⓔ	38. Ⓐ Ⓑ Ⓒ Ⓓ Ⓔ	

If Section 4 of your test book contains math questions that are not multiple-choice, continue to item 29 below. Otherwise, continue to item 29 above.

29. 30. 31. 32. 33.

34. 35. 36. 37. 38.

SECTION 5

1. Ⓐ Ⓑ Ⓒ Ⓓ Ⓔ	11. Ⓐ Ⓑ Ⓒ Ⓓ Ⓔ	21. Ⓐ Ⓑ Ⓒ Ⓓ Ⓔ	31. Ⓐ Ⓑ Ⓒ Ⓓ Ⓔ	
2. Ⓐ Ⓑ Ⓒ Ⓓ Ⓔ	12. Ⓐ Ⓑ Ⓒ Ⓓ Ⓔ	22. Ⓐ Ⓑ Ⓒ Ⓓ Ⓔ	32. Ⓐ Ⓑ Ⓒ Ⓓ Ⓔ	
3. Ⓐ Ⓑ Ⓒ Ⓓ Ⓔ	13. Ⓐ Ⓑ Ⓒ Ⓓ Ⓔ	23. Ⓐ Ⓑ Ⓒ Ⓓ Ⓔ	33. Ⓐ Ⓑ Ⓒ Ⓓ Ⓔ	
4. Ⓐ Ⓑ Ⓒ Ⓓ Ⓔ	14. Ⓐ Ⓑ Ⓒ Ⓓ Ⓔ	24. Ⓐ Ⓑ Ⓒ Ⓓ Ⓔ	34. Ⓐ Ⓑ Ⓒ Ⓓ Ⓔ	# right in Section 5
5. Ⓐ Ⓑ Ⓒ Ⓓ Ⓔ	15. Ⓐ Ⓑ Ⓒ Ⓓ Ⓔ	25. Ⓐ Ⓑ Ⓒ Ⓓ Ⓔ	35. Ⓐ Ⓑ Ⓒ Ⓓ Ⓔ	
6. Ⓐ Ⓑ Ⓒ Ⓓ Ⓔ	16. Ⓐ Ⓑ Ⓒ Ⓓ Ⓔ	26. Ⓐ Ⓑ Ⓒ Ⓓ Ⓔ	36. Ⓐ Ⓑ Ⓒ Ⓓ Ⓔ	
7. Ⓐ Ⓑ Ⓒ Ⓓ Ⓔ	17. Ⓐ Ⓑ Ⓒ Ⓓ Ⓔ	27. Ⓐ Ⓑ Ⓒ Ⓓ Ⓔ	37. Ⓐ Ⓑ Ⓒ Ⓓ Ⓔ	
8. Ⓐ Ⓑ Ⓒ Ⓓ Ⓔ	18. Ⓐ Ⓑ Ⓒ Ⓓ Ⓔ	28. Ⓐ Ⓑ Ⓒ Ⓓ Ⓔ	38. Ⓐ Ⓑ Ⓒ Ⓓ Ⓔ	
9. Ⓐ Ⓑ Ⓒ Ⓓ Ⓔ	19. Ⓐ Ⓑ Ⓒ Ⓓ Ⓔ	29. Ⓐ Ⓑ Ⓒ Ⓓ Ⓔ	39. Ⓐ Ⓑ Ⓒ Ⓓ Ⓔ	# wrong in Section 5
10. Ⓐ Ⓑ Ⓒ Ⓓ Ⓔ	20. Ⓐ Ⓑ Ⓒ Ⓓ Ⓔ	30. Ⓐ Ⓑ Ⓒ Ⓓ Ⓔ	40. Ⓐ Ⓑ Ⓒ Ⓓ Ⓔ	

PRACTICE TEST THREE

SECTION 1

Time—25 Minutes
24 Questions

For each of the following questions, choose the best answer and darken the corresponding oval on the answer sheet.

Select the lettered word or set of words that best completes the sentence.

Example:

Today's small, portable computers contrast markedly with the earliest electronic computers, which were ----.

(A) effective
(B) invented
(C) useful
(D) destructive
(E) enormous

1. The artist's students admired his work so much that they often sacrificed their own sense of originality and simply ---- the work of their teacher.

   (A) censured
   (B) praised
   (C) discussed
   (D) emulated
   (E) demeaned

2. After swimming in the ---- English Channel for several hours, the athlete's body temperature dropped dramatically, causing her to shiver uncontrollably.

   (A) calm
   (B) frigid
   (C) turbulent
   (D) balmy
   (E) polluted

3. Only ---- dogs can be trained to assist the blind, since the dogs' unwavering ---- is essential to the personal safety of the blind person.

   (A) tractable . . . obedience
   (B) docile . . . negligence
   (C) clever . . . dexterity
   (D) unseasoned . . . restraint
   (E) smart . . . domestication

GO ON TO THE NEXT PAGE

4. In order to relieve the drought in the ----
valley region of the state, the governor ----
water-saving measures throughout the area.

   (A) populous ... recalled
   (B) sodden ... encouraged
   (C) depleted ... decried
   (D) parched ... rescinded
   (E) arid ... instituted

5. The majority of the models at the car
show were boxy and awkward in design,
making the new Phantom model appear
particularly ----.

   (A) modern
   (B) swift
   (C) ungainly
   (D) sleek
   (E) burnished

6. Despite the ---- of a thunderstorm quickly
approaching from the horizon, the farm
workers were ---- in completing their work
before seeking shelter indoors.

   (A) expectation ... negligent
   (B) menace ... dilatory
   (C) threat ... diligent
   (D) absence ... languid
   (E) forecast ... unfortunate

7. In *The Prince*, Machiavelli argues that a prince
can scheme and plot to maintain his power as
long as these ---- are hidden from the public.

   (A) digressions
   (B) condemnations
   (C) antagonisms
   (D) machinations
   (E) pronouncements

GO ON TO THE NEXT PAGE

Answer the questions below based on the information in the accompanying passages.

Questions 8–12 refer to the following passage.

The following article, adapted from a popular science magazine, explains a natural phenomenon known as the lunar eclipse.

Many people are aware of the beauty of a solar eclipse, but are surprised to learn that lunar eclipses are often just as spectacular, and are both more common and easier to
(5) observe. The filtering and refraction of light from the Earth's atmosphere during a lunar eclipse creates stunning color effects that range from dark brown to red, orange, and yellow. Each of these light shows is unique
(10) since they are the result of the amount of dust and cloud cover in the Earth's atmosphere at the time of the eclipse. While total solar eclipses last only for a few minutes and can be seen only in a small area of a few kilometers,
(15) total lunar eclipses can last for several hours and can be seen over much of the planet. In fact, the beauty and stability of lunar eclipses make them a favorite of both amateur and professional photographers.
(20) Lunar eclipses generally occur two to three times a year, and are possible only when the Moon is in its full phase. When we see the Moon, we are actually seeing sunlight reflected off the surface of the Moon. When
(25) the Earth is positioned in between the Moon and the Sun, however, the Earth's shadow falls on the Moon, and a lunar eclipse occurs. To better understand this process, it's helpful to imagine the Earth's shadow on the Moon as
(30) a pair of nested cones, with the Earth at the apex of the cones, and the Moon at their bases. The outer, more diffuse cone of shadow is called the penumbral shadow, while the inner, darker cone is the umbral shadow.

(35) The type of lunar eclipse—total, partial, or penumbral—that occurs depends both on how much of the Moon passes through the Earth's shadow and through which part of the shadows it passes. A penumbral eclipse occurs
(40) when the Moon passes through the Earth's outer shadow. This type of eclipse is both brief and subtle, and frequently goes unobserved by all but astronomers and the most avid devotees. By contrast, total and partial
(45) eclipses occur when all or part, respectively, of the Moon passes through of the umbral shadow of the Earth. These eclipses are quite easy to see and are widely observed.
Unlike solar eclipses lunar eclipses are safe
(50) to watch. Solar radiation at the intensity that occurs during an eclipse of the Sun can cause a form of retinal burns known as eclipse blindness. In fact, the only way to safely view a solar eclipse is by using specially designed
(55) filters. However, since the Moon's light is dissipated, reflected sunlight, it is completely safe to watch a lunar eclipse without any special equipment, although a pair of binoculars can certainly help the viewer appreciate the splen-
(60) dor of this beautiful phenomenon.

8. The main purpose of the passage is to

   (A) contrast lunar and solar eclipses

   (B) discuss lunar eclipses

   (C) explain why solar and lunar eclipses occur

   (D) demonstrate the equipment needed to safely view a solar eclipse

   (E) argue that lunar eclipses are more beautiful than solar eclipses

GO ON TO THE NEXT PAGE

9. In line 17 "stability" most nearly means

   (A) visibility

   (B) equilibrium

   (C) strength

   (D) duration

   (E) poise

10. According to the author, a partial lunar eclipse occurs

    (A) when all of the Moon passes through the Earth's umbral shadow

    (B) two to three times a year

    (C) when only a part of the Moon passes through the Earth's umbral shadow

    (D) when a part of the Moon passes through only the Earth's penumbral shadow

    (E) when the Moon passes between the Sun and the Earth

11. The author implies that penumbral eclipses are

    (A) more common than partial or full lunar eclipses

    (B) the result of a "cone" of shadow cast by the Moon onto the Earth

    (C) longer-lasting than most solar eclipses

    (D) more difficult to observe than other types of lunar eclipses

    (E) visible within only a small area

12. According to the passage, it is safe to watch a lunar eclipse, unlike a solar eclipse, because

    (A) a lunar eclipse is more subtle and brief than a solar eclipse

    (B) a lunar eclipse lasts much longer than a solar eclipse

    (C) moonlight is less intense than sunlight

    (D) special filters can be employed to view a lunar eclipse

    (E) a lunar eclipse results from the Moon passing through the Earth's shadow

GO ON TO THE NEXT PAGE

Questions 13–14 refer to the following passage.

Many people are surprised to learn that the idea of a flying machine stretches all the way back to ancient Greece. Archimedes, who identified the principle of buoyancy
(5) more than 2,000 years ago, may also have conceived of a flying machine using this principle. Throughout the years, other scientists and philosophers, Roger Bacon and Albertus Magnus among them, advanced designs for
(10) flying machines based on buoyancy. It wasn't until 1783, however, that the principle was tested. In the late summer of that year, Joseph and Etienne Montgolfier built a hot air balloon propelled by a manure-and-straw fire
(15) that safely held aloft a trio of farm animals for eight minutes.

13. The passage implies that the principle of buoyancy

(A) is Archimedes's main contribution to science

(B) was invented by the Montgolfier brothers

(C) is important for the functioning of hot air balloons

(D) confounded both Roger Bacon and Albertus Magnus

(E) was first fully understood in 1783

14. In line 9, the word "advanced" most nearly means

(A) proposed

(B) contemplated

(C) proceeded

(D) moved

(E) progressed

Questions 15–18 refer to the following passages.

Passage 1

Although movies depend on a host of contributors, every worthwhile film ultimately reflects the vision of only one individual—the director, or *auteur*. Without an *auteur*, a film
(5) would be a hodgepodge of disjointed camera angles, erratic performances, and inappropriate dialogue—a confused muddle of dozens of opinions about what should and should not be occurring on the screen. Instead, the
(10) *auteur* takes this raw material and gives it shape, texture, and meaning. Just as an author creates a book or an artist creates a painting, it is the *auteur* who creates the film to which we respond.

Passage 2

Unlike a book or a painting, a film is a collaborative work. We might be drawn to the cinema because we want to see our favorite star, but we can also appreciate a wonderful
(5) score, a great screenplay, or beautiful camerawork. How often have we heard someone say, "I loved the story but I hated the acting," or "The costumes were interesting but the special effects were boring"? Any sensitive viewer
(10) responds not to a single artistic vision in a film, but to dozens of such visions. In fact, it may well be this rich synthesis of creativity that makes the art form so exciting.

GO ON TO THE NEXT PAGE

15. With which of the following statements would
the writer of Passage 1 most strongly disagree?

(A) The director is the most important person in filmmaking.

(B) Many kinds of artists contribute to the
making of a movie.

(C) A worthwhile work of art reflects the
vision of a single person.

(D) The main purpose of movies is to
entertain.

(E) Movies do not have authors in the same
way that books do.

16. Which statement best expresses the main idea
of Passage 2?

(A) Moviegoers are primarily drawn to films
by the performances of actors.

(B) Many contributors influence the viewer's
experience of a film.

(C) Viewers must be sensitive to identify the
many contributions to a movie.

(D) A person may enjoy one aspect of a
movie, but find another aspect disappointing.

(E) Books and films are fundamentally different art forms.

17. The author of Passage 2 would most likely
regard the statement that "it is the *auteur*
who creates the film to which we respond"
(Passage 1, lines 13–14) as

(A) a shameful omission

(B) a sound argument

(C) an unfortunate simplification

(D) an unresolved hypothesis

(E) a regrettable necessity

18. Both passages refer to "a painting," but they
differ in that

(A) Passage 1 distinguishes between a painting and a movie, but Passage 2 concentrates on the similarities between the two
art forms

(B) Passage 1 attributes equal value to a
painting and a movie, but Passage 2
states that a movie is usually more interesting

(C) Passage 1 asserts that a painting has
an individual creator, but Passage 2
declares that a painting is a collaborative
work

(D) Passage 1 compares the creation of a
film to the creation of a painting, but
Passage 2 draws a contrast between them

(E) Passage 1 says that viewers respond to
a painting as a whole, but Passage 2
points out that a painting is made of
individual components

GO ON TO THE NEXT PAGE

Questions 19–24 refer to the following passage.

The following is adapted from two excerpts from a 1926 diary of a resident of Moscow, Russia. At that time, Russia, as part of the Soviet Union, was ruled by a dictatorial government and was experiencing a severe economic depression.

Late afternoon, blustery and gray.

It has been many years since I have attended a performance of a play. My black fox fur is quite tattered, but I have spent the last two
(5) evenings before the fire mending it. Before the children were born, we went to the theater at least once a week. I wished later, during the upheaval, that we had not given it up. Once it was gone, truly gone, I missed it so.
(10) I did not expect to be this nervous. It's as if I've never been to a proper theater, and I can scarcely remember a time when I've so fussed over the state of my hair. I'm wondering if I will remember how to behave. In truth, the
(15) cause of my nervous condition is this feeling that the whole of Moscow has contrived to engage in a rebellious act. Will we be putting ourselves in danger tonight? It's hard to believe we will not. Perhaps only a handful
(20) of people will attend.

Later the same night, very cold.

I certainly had no need to fret over the condition of my fox fur. Others even attended the performance with tattered bits of sweat-
(25) ers wrapped around their necks, but people were not judged for the state of their clothing. Triumph Square was abuzz with energy and anticipation. Once among the throng, all of my fears of punishment evaporated. Moscow
(30) was united tonight in support of its theater. The play was by Gogol and of course I've seen it many times, but never like this. The director was a man whose name I had almost forgotten, Vsevolod Meyerhold. The pace of
(35) the show was breathtaking. I found that I could scarcely keep up—it's very lucky I'm familiar with the script. The audience was quite bowled over. At the curtain call, much of the audience rose to their feet. The roar of
(40) the crowd was a mix of jeering and applause. I was so overwhelmed with emotion, I found myself on my feet clapping loudly—until I realized that the figures on stage for the curtain call were only papier-mâché* dummies,
(45) rather than the actors from the performance. I even felt momentarily foolish for being taken in by the ruse. I wonder if this was why others in the crowd were scoffing, or if they were indeed unhappy with the entire produc-
(50) tion. I did not stop to ask anyone—the paper tomorrow morning will tell me. I rushed home, not bothered by the cold.
a material made of paper pulp and glue

19. As used in the passage, "proper" (line 11) most nearly means

(A) polite

(B) correct

(C) legitimate

(D) adequate

(E) moral

20. The author speculates that "Perhaps only a handful of people will attend" (lines 19–20) because she believes that

(A) the citizens of Moscow have little interest in the theater

(B) many people would be too afraid of punishment to attend

(C) the audience will likely be unhappy with the entire production

(D) people will be embarrassed to attend the theater in tattered clothes

(E) the cold weather will deter many people from coming

GO ON TO THE NEXT PAGE

21. In lines 22–23, the author notes that "I certainly had no need to fret over the condition of my fox fur" because

    (A) the author was among the most elegant of the attendees

    (B) the physical appearance of the play's attendees was immaterial

    (C) the author had successfully repaired the fur

    (D) the fur was less important than other aspects of her appearance

    (E) she would not be identified in such a large crowd

22. The pace of the play could be best described as

    (A) brisk

    (B) deliberate

    (C) unintelligible

    (D) typical

    (E) tedious

23. Based on the passage, which of the following best expresses the author's experience of the play?

    (A) She was scandalized by the appearance of the crowd.

    (B) She was angered by the papier-mâché dummies.

    (C) She was torn between appreciation and embarrassment.

    (D) She was confused by the pace of the scenes.

    (E) She was elated to be in the theater again.

24. The change in the author's mood from afternoon to evening can best be described as a transition from

    (A) agitated to lethargic

    (B) jealous to confident

    (C) sorrowful to joyful

    (D) anxious to exhilarated

    (E) explosive to tranquil

IF YOU FINISH BEFORE TIME IS CALLED, YOU MAY CHECK YOUR WORK ON THIS SECTION ONLY. DO NOT TURN TO ANY OTHER SECTION IN THE TEST. **STOP**

SECTION 2

Time—25 Minutes
18 Questions

Solve each of the following problems, decide which is the best answer choice, and darken the corresponding oval on the answer sheet.

Notes:

(1) Calculator use is permitted.

(2) All numbers used are real numbers.

(3) Figures are provided for some problems. All figures are drawn to scale and lie in a plane UNLESS otherwise indicated.

(4) Unless otherwise specified, the domain of any function f is assumed to be the set of all real numbers x for which $f(x)$ is a real number.

Reference Information

$A = \frac{1}{2}bh$ $c^2 = a^2 + b^2$ Special right triangles $A = \pi r^2$ $C = 2\pi r$ $V = \ell w h$ $V = \pi r^2 h$ $A = \ell w$

The sum of the degree measures of the angles in a triangle is 180.
The number of degrees of arc in a circle is 360.
A straight angle has a degree measure of 180.

1. If $7x - 2 = 12x + 13$, then $6x =$

   (A) −18
   (B) −5
   (C) −3
   (D) 5
   (E) 18

2. Two lines intersect as shown in the figure above. Which of the following could be false?

   (A) $2c = 2d$
   (B) $a + d = b + d$
   (C) $a - b = d - c$
   (D) $a + b = c + d$
   (E) $2(a + c) = 2(b + d)$

GO ON TO THE NEXT PAGE

3. In a certain bag, the only coins are two pennies, one nickel, three dimes, and two quarters. If one coin is drawn at random from the bag, what is the probability that the coin drawn is a dime?

(A) $\dfrac{1}{8}$

(B) $\dfrac{3}{8}$

(C) $\dfrac{1}{2}$

(D) $\dfrac{5}{8}$

(E) 1

4. The cost of a dozen pencils and six pens is $3.34. If three pencils cost $0.10, what is the cost of one pen, in cents?

(A) 36

(B) 42

(C) 49

(D) 53

(E) 59

5. If $\overline{BD}$ bisects $\angle ABC$ in the figure above, what is the value of x?

(A) 40

(B) 50

(C) 60

(D) 70

(E) 80

6. If a is an odd integer and b is an even integer, which of the following must be odd?

(A) $2a + b$

(B) $3a + b$

(C) $2(a + b)$

(D) $\dfrac{b}{a}$

(E) $a + \dfrac{b}{2}$

7. If $x > 0$ and $x^{-3} = 8$, what is the value of x^2?

(A) $\dfrac{1}{4}$

(B) $\dfrac{1}{2}$

(C) 4

(D) 8

(E) 64

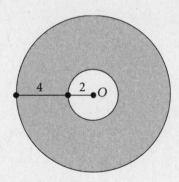

8. In the figure above, O is the center of both circles. What is the ratio of the shaded area to the unshaded area?

(A) 2:1

(B) 4:1

(C) 6:1

(D) 8:1

(E) 9:1

GO ON TO THE NEXT PAGE

Composition of Football
Team by Grade Level

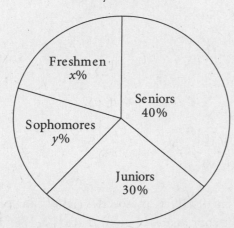

9. The graph above shows the composition by
   grade level of a high school football team. If
   the team has 60 players and there are exactly
   half as many freshmen as there are seniors,
   how many sophomores are on the team?

   (A)   6
   (B) 10
   (C) 12
   (D) 18
   (E) 20

Note: Figure not drawn to scale.

10. In the previous figure, if $a > 50°$, which of the
    following describes *all* possible values of b?

    (A) $b < 70$
    (B) $b > 70$
    (C) $b = 70$
    (D) $b \leq 70$
    (E) $b \geq 70$

11. If $0.005 \leq x \leq 0.5$ and $0.25 \leq y \leq 25$, what is the
    maximum value of $\dfrac{x}{y}$?

    (A) 0.0002
    (B) 0.002
    (C) 0.02
    (D) 0.2
    (E) 2

M

12. N and P are two points to the right of M on
    the number line above. If $2\overline{MN} = 5\overline{MP}$ what
    is the ratio of PN to MP?

    (A) 2:5
    (B) 2:3
    (C) 3:2
    (D) 5:2
    (E) 5:7

13. Which of the following is the best estimate for
    the slope of the line that best fits the data shown
    in the scatterplot above? (Assume that the black
    bordered area is a square and that the scale of
    measurement is the same on every side.)

    (A) -3
    (B) $-\dfrac{1}{3}$
    (C) $\dfrac{1}{3}$
    (D) $\dfrac{2}{3}$
    (E) 3

GO ON TO THE NEXT PAGE

14. If $x = a - 5$ and $y = a + 1$, then $x - y =$

(A) -6

(B) -4

(C) 2

(D) 4

(E) 6

15. In the figure above, square $ABCD$ is divided into 16 small squares of equal size. The perimeter of $ABCD$ is 8. The perimeter of each of the small squares is

(A) $\dfrac{1}{4}$

(B) $\dfrac{1}{2}$

(C) 1

(D) 2

(E) 4

16. If $5x + 5y = 20$, what is the average (arithmetic mean) of x and y?

(A) 1

(B) 2

(C) 4

(D) 5

(E) 10

17. If a, b, and c are positive integers and

$$a\!\!\triangle\!\!\begin{smallmatrix}b\end{smallmatrix}\!\!c = \frac{b+c}{a} - \frac{a+c}{b} - \frac{a+b}{c},$$

then $2\!\!\triangle\!\!\begin{smallmatrix}4\end{smallmatrix}\!\!6 =$

(A) 2

(B) 4

(C) 8

(D) 12

(E) 18

18. Triangle DEF is an isosceles right triangle. The coordinates of point D are $(-2, 1)$ and the coordinates of point E are $(-2, 7)$. Which of the following could be the coordinates of point F?

I. $(-8, 1)$

II. $(4, 1)$

III. $(4, 7)$

(A) I only

(B) II only

(C) III only

(D) II and III

(E) I, II, and III

IF YOU FINISH BEFORE TIME IS CALLED, YOU MAY CHECK YOUR WORK ON THIS SECTION ONLY. DO NOT TURN TO ANY OTHER SECTION IN THE TEST.

STOP

SECTION 3

Time—25 Minutes
24 Questions

For each of the following questions, choose the best answer and darken the corresponding oval on the answer sheet.

Select the lettered word or set of words that best completes the sentence.

Example:

Today's small, portable computers contrast markedly with the earliest electronic computers, which were ----.

(A) effective
(B) invented
(C) useful
(D) destructive
(E) enormous

25. Even though there was much curiosity about their personal lives, the celebrities of earlier times were able to maintain a degree of ---- that today's celebrities ----.

(A) privacy . . . envy
(B) dignity . . . regret
(C) significance . . . mimic
(D) separation . . . mock
(E) regard . . . celebrate

26. Even in the most informal settings, Mrs. Davis always had the instinct to ---- and could not resist the urge to spread knowledge among her acquaintances.

(A) obscure
(B) evaluate
(C) educate
(D) speculate
(E) mediate

27. By frequently mentioning the titles of books he had read and quoting poems he had memorized, thus ---- his ----, John alienated many of his friends.

(A) enduring . . . success
(B) delivering . . . release
(C) praising . . . conviction
(D) flaunting . . . erudition
(E) degrading . . . achievement

28. Legends often celebrate characters whose actions, such as robbing the rich to give to the poor or defying ---- authority, are perceived as ----.

(A) unjust . . . unacceptable
(B) legitimate . . . incredible
(C) impotent . . . sufficient
(D) grandiose . . . insurmountable
(E) corrupt . . . commendable

GO ON TO THE NEXT PAGE

29. Many Swedish health experts claim that sitting in a hot sauna and then plunging into ice-cold water can have ---- effect that invigorates both the body and the spirit.

(A) a tonic
(B) an enfeebling
(C) a delirious
(D) an amorphous
(E) a soothing

30. *Pamela: or Virtue Rewarded* by Samuel Richardson can be classified as ---- novel, since it takes the form of a series of letters.

(A) a substantial
(B) an epistolary
(C) a popular
(D) an auspicious
(E) an eloquent

GO ON TO THE NEXT PAGE

Answer the questions below based on the information in the accompanying passages.

Questions 31–32 refer to the following passage.

Modern readers are often initially confused by the idea of honor held by the ancient Greeks. As described in the epic poem *The Iliad*, for example, honor can be attained in
(5) a tangible way, in the form of a reward for victory in battle. In that work, the transformation of the hero Achilles both illustrates this traditional conception and presages a more modern, less tangible connotation.
(10) Achilles feels himself gravely insulted and withdraws from the Trojan war when his war prize is confiscated by his confederate Agamemnon. Yet, when Agamemnon offers him an enormous reward for heroism later
(15) in the epic, Achilles refuses to accept it, protesting that material possessions cannot compensate for the friends lost in battle.

31. The word "gravely" in line 10 most nearly means

   (A) seriously
   (B) morbidly
   (C) impressively
   (D) catastrophically
   (E) gratuitously

32. Based on the passage, Achilles's conception of honor

   (A) came to exemplify the Homeric Greek ideal
   (B) was destroyed by Agamemnon's insult
   (C) was entirely based on heroism in battle
   (D) prompted a generous gift from Agamemnon
   (E) evolved to one more like a modern conception

GO ON TO THE NEXT PAGE

Questions 33–45 refer to the following passages.

The following passages discuss the use of dogs in law enforcement. Passage 1 is from an article that appeared in a popular science magazine. Passage 2 is adapted from a letter written by an expert in dog training that was published in a newspaper.

Passage 1

Although they are a relatively recent invention, canine (or K-9) units have gained widespread acceptance in police departments around the world. The use of dogs in police
(5) work has met with success for a number of reasons. First, dogs' phenomenal tracking instincts make them very valuable additions to searches, whether for suspects or missing persons. In addition, dogs' sense of smell
(10) makes searches more efficient than those carried out by humans alone. For example, while a crew of police officers might take a considerable amount of time to carefully search a large area for a suspect, a single
(15) police dog can make short work of the task. Furthermore, because odors can be detected in the dark and through the smallest crack under a door, a dog can work in dim areas and is undeterred by locks. Dogs can even
(20) apprehend suspects in a way that minimizes the chance of injury to the dogs, the suspects, and the dogs' handlers. Of course, all of these skills are not fully developed in the average canine—extensive training is needed
(25) to channel a dog's natural gifts to form an effective police dog.

The extraordinarily keen sense of smell that dogs possess—capable of perceiving even the faintest scent from a considerable
(30) distance—is the root of dogs' ability to track, which is the K-9 unit's most frequent assignment in police work. In exercising their sense of smell, dogs actually detect microscopic skin particles, known as skin
(35) rafts, that are continuously shed as people move through an environment. A tracking session begins with the introduction to the dog of a scent article, an item that bears the smell of the person being sought. A
(40) well-used item of clothing is ideal, but even something as far removed from a person as a clean cotton pad that has been exposed to the steering wheel in his or her car can suffice. K-9 dogs are trained to identify the
(45) odor from the scent article and then follow the trail of that scent. Although helpful at most times, dogs' tracking instincts and the needs of police work can come into conflict. An animal in the wild will gladly abandon
(50) the track of the person sought by police if the creature encounters another, fresher track. After all, why not pursue the prey that has passed by most recently? In a police investigation, however, it is essential that the
(55) dog stay focused on the trail of the original subject in spite of the myriad competing scents that the dog will encounter in a hunt through a crowded urban environment. Victory over a dog's instincts can only
(60) be achieved by extensive and continuing training.

Other forms of training are also vital for an effective K-9 unit. Seeing the muscled bodies and sharp teeth of a German Shepard
(65) striding alongside a police officer, many assume that the dog is likely to ferociously attack anyone who crosses its path. But in fact, the extensive process known as aggression training teaches the dogs to attack under
(70) only three circumstances: when commanded to do so by the handler, when the handler is attacked, and in order to protect the patrol

GO ON TO THE NEXT PAGE →

car. Under other circumstances, the dogs are
quite approachable and pose no threat to oth-
(75) ers. Rather than a dangerous weapon, then,
a well-trained dog is thus best considered a
highly selective tool.

Passage 2

A puppy learns and grows at an extraordinary rate in its first two years of life; even a
dog's capacity to learn later in life is shaped at
this point. During no other period will such
(5) massive transformations in structure and
capacity occur so quickly: A puppy grows
from complete dependence into a dog capable of exploring its surroundings, obeying
complicated commands, and even potentially
(10) surviving on its own. And, while dog owners the world over have long recognized a
puppy's fundamental need for protection,
nourishment, and nurturing, recent research
has revealed that owners and trainers play a
(15) far larger role than simply providing physical shelter and sustenance during these first
few years of a dog's life. Laboratory studies
have demonstrated conclusively that puppies
raised by attentive, stern owners or trainers in
(20) safe environments develop into better learn-
ers than do those raised in less secure environments with less attention and discipline.

While few would disagree that all young
dogs deserve nurturing and protection during
(25) their formative years, such treatment is
especially important for police dogs, which
will be required to secure public safety and
assist in crime prevention. Most state law
enforcement agencies provide sufficient time
(30) while the dogs are still young and malleable
to train their canine officers. These states
also ensure postnatal health care for their
law enforcement canines. In stark contrast,
our state has failed to provide adequately for
(35) either of these vital measures, an unfortunate
lapse in judgment that seriously compromises
the quality of our police dogs.

Our political leaders have shown a marked
interest in the safety and welfare of our state,
(40) including concerns about the state's police
dogs and the quality of our current canine
officer training program. However, simply
addressing the funding of our police dog
training alone is not the solution to the
(45) emerging police dog problem. We must also
consider the ages of dogs entering training.
We must mandate that units train younger
dogs, not the older, harder-to-teach canines
that are now being recruited for training.
(50) We must recognize the truth of that old saw,
"you can't teach an old dog new tricks"; a
young dog is highly trainable and can serve
as a valuable asset to our state police force.

33. The author of Passage 1 notes that a police dog
"can work in dim areas and is undeterred by
locks" (lines 18–19) to emphasize the fact that

(A) dogs are physically strong enough to
overcome such obstacles

(B) extensive training prepares the dogs for
such situations

(C) dogs work more quickly than their
human counterparts

(D) a dark area allows the dogs to concentrate more fully on tracking

(E) dogs rely on their sense of smell rather
than that of sight

34. As used in line 27 of Passage 1, "keen" most
nearly means

(A) acute

(B) willing

(C) eager

(D) aggressive

(E) instinctual

GO ON TO THE NEXT PAGE

35. Based on Passage 1, a clean cotton pad that has been exposed to the steering wheel of the subject of a hunt's car can serve as a scent article because

    (A) the cotton pad is familiar to the tracking dog

    (B) skin rafts were transferred from the wheel to the pad

    (C) it trains a dog to ignore competing scents

    (D) scent articles bear the smell of the person being tracked

    (E) a dog's instincts compel it to follow the freshest trail

36. The sentence in lines Passage 1, lines 52–53 ("After all,...recently?"), serves primarily to

    (A) exemplify dogs' ability to focus on a single scent

    (B) emphasize the need for dogs to ignore competing scents

    (C) question the effectiveness of dogs' instincts

    (D) illustrate the skill of dogs' tracking abilities

    (E) clarify the purpose of dogs' instinctual behavior

37. In the final paragraph of Passage 1, the author distinguishes between

    (A) the importance of tools and weapons

    (B) dangerous and well-trained dogs

    (C) aggression training and tracking training

    (D) popular perception and reality

    (E) the quality of dog training and the age at which it begins

38. The author of Passage 2 argues that the care and training of young dogs

    (A) is less important than providing shelter and sustenance

    (B) refines dogs' natural tracking ability

    (C) has a great impact on dogs' later ability to learn

    (D) has only recently been recognized as important

    (E) will ensure dogs' ability to survive on their own

39. In Passage 2, the phrase "these vital measures" (line 35) refers to

    (A) the nurturing and protection of young dogs

    (B) early training and postnatal care

    (C) dogs that are both young and malleable

    (D) tracking and aggression training

    (E) the training policies of the state in question and those of other states

GO ON TO THE NEXT PAGE

40. As used in Passage 2, line 38, "marked" most nearly means

    (A) evident
    (B) satisfactory
    (C) indicated
    (D) stained
    (E) correct

41. The author of Passage 2 notes that "simply addressing the funding of our police dog training alone is not the solution to the emerging police dog problem (lines 42–45)" because

    (A) many politicians are insufficiently informed about the true cause of this problem
    (B) police dogs are best viewed as tools rather than weapons
    (C) it is also essential to change the age at which dogs are trained
    (D) the present quality of training is woefully inadequate
    (E) training programs should concentrate of tracking skills rather than aggression training

42. The authors of Passage 1 and Passage 2 would most likely both agree that

    (A) training that occurs early in a police dog's life is most effective
    (B) training must continue throughout a police dog's life
    (C) tracking is the primary function of most police dogs
    (D) training is essential to the development of an effective police dog
    (E) politicians should work to ensure the success of K-9 programs

43. The author of Passage 2 would most likely agree with which of the following statements about lines 24–26 of Passage 1 ("extensive training…effective police dog")?

    (A) Such training is especially important to train police dogs to attack only under certain circumstances.
    (B) The care and nurturing of young dogs is more important than police-work training.
    (C) It is vital to instill both tracking and aggression skills.
    (D) The primary function of such training is to refine a dog's natural tracking skills.
    (E) Simply training extensively may not be sufficient to ensure the best possible police dog.

GO ON TO THE NEXT PAGE

44. Passage 1 and Passage 2 differ in that

(A) Passage 1 takes a historical perspective, while Passage 2 takes a scientific perspective

(B) Passage 1 describes a governmental policy, while Passage 2 explores the effects of that policy

(C) Passage 1 presents a position, while Passage 2 argues against that position

(D) Passage 1 seeks to inform, while Passage 2 seeks to persuade

(E) Passage 1 is written for the general public, while Passage 2 is aimed at experts

45. The author of Passage 2 most likely includes the well-known quote "you can't teach an old dog new tricks" in line 51 because

(A) he likes to use clichés

(B) in this case, the cliché is really true

(C) readers will recognize the cliché

(D) he thinks it is funny

(E) he doesn't like old dogs

GO ON TO THE NEXT PAGE

Questions 46–48 refer to the following passage.

The rate of human speech is approximately
180 words per minute. Although we have long
known that listeners can understand speech
at a far faster rate (one of at least 400 words
(5) per minute), in the past it was difficult to
accelerate a recording of speech without
raising the pitch of the voice, creating the
undesirable, if amusing, "chipmunk effect."
However, digital time compression, a new
(10) technology, offers a solution. Instead of
simply playing a recording more quickly,
this method uses a computer to shave
off silences and prolonged segments of
vowels. Recordings can thus be abbreviated
(15) considerably without sacrificing quality.

46. Which statement below is directly supported
by evidence in the passage?

(A) Any abbreviation of a sound recording
entails a loss of quality.

(B) Manipulating sound on a cassette deck
is usually the most effective method of
abbreviating recordings.

(C) The rate of human speech has not varied
significantly over time.

(D) There is a difference between the typical
rate of speech and that of speech
comprehension.

(E) Digital time compression, while
advantageous, may have unforeseen
disadvantages.

47. The author regards the "chipmunk effect"
(line 8) as

(A) a useful but costly outcome

(B) a tragic but unavoidable outcome

(C) a comical but vital effect

(D) an unfortunate but unforeseen result

(E) an amusing but unwelcome consequence

48. The word "prolonged" in line 13 most nearly
means

(A) unnecessary

(B) previous

(C) longer

(D) produced

(E) gigantic

IF YOU FINISH BEFORE TIME IS CALLED, YOU MAY CHECK YOUR WORK ON
THIS SECTION ONLY. DO NOT TURN TO ANY OTHER SECTION IN THE TEST. | **STOP**

SECTION 4

Time—25 Minutes
20 Questions

Solve each of the following problems, decide which is the best answer choice, and darken the corresponding oval on the answer sheet.

Notes:

(1) Calculator use is permitted.

(2) All numbers used are real numbers.

(3) Figures are provided for some problems. All figures are drawn to scale and lie in a plane UNLESS otherwise indicated.

(4) Unless otherwise specified, the domain of any function f is assumed to be the set of all real numbers x for which $f(x)$ is a real number.

Reference Information

$A = \frac{1}{2}bh$ $c^2 = a^2 + b^2$ Special right triangles $A = \pi r^2$ $C = 2\pi r$ $V = \ell wh$ $V = \pi r^2 h$ $A = \ell w$

The sum of the degree measures of the angles in a triangle is 180.
The number of degrees of arc in a circle is 360.
A straight angle has a degree measure of 180.

19. If $5a = 4$ and $\dfrac{b}{3} = 5$, then $ab =$

(A) 4
(B) 8
(C) 12
(D) 15
(E) 20

Figure I   Figure II   Figure III

20. In the figures above, Figure I is a triangle with exactly two equal sides, Figure II is a square, and Figure III is a regular hexagon. Which of the figures has more than three lines of symmetry?

(A) II only
(B) III only
(C) I and III
(D) II and III
(E) I, II, and III

GO ON TO THE NEXT PAGE

21. If $f(x) = 4^x - 5x$ what is the value of $f(2)$?

    (A)   3
    (B)   6
    (C) 10
    (D) 16
    (E) 18

22. If P is the set of all numbers between 0 and 10, inclusive, and Q is the set of all prime numbers, then the intersection of P and Q contains how many elements?

    (A) 0
    (B) 1
    (C) 2
    (D) 3
    (E) more than 3

23. The absolute value of a certain integer is greater than 7 and less than 12. Which of the following could NOT be the integer?

    (A) −11
    (B) −10
    (C) −8
    (D)   7
    (E)   8

24. A soccer team won X games, lost twice as many games as it won, and tied Y games. What fraction of the total number of games played was lost?

    (A) $\dfrac{2X}{X+Y}$

    (B) $\dfrac{2X}{3X+Y}$

    (C) $\dfrac{2X}{XY}$

    (D) $\dfrac{2X}{2X^2Y}$

    (E) $\dfrac{2X+Y}{X}$

25. In the figure above, the radius of circle O is 6. If $ST = 4$, what is the length of $\overline{SR}$?

    (A) 6
    (B) $2\sqrt{13}$
    (C) 8
    (D) $2\sqrt{17}$
    (E) 10

GO ON TO THE NEXT PAGE

26. If $a^n \neq 0$, $\dfrac{a^{m+n}}{a^n} =$

(A) a^m

(B) a^{m+2n}

(C) $\dfrac{1}{a^m}$

(D) $-a^m$

(E) a^{m+1}

28. How many three-digit integers greater than 500 contain only odd digits?

(A) 25

(B) 75

(C) 125

(D) 200

(E) 250

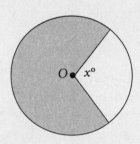

27. In the figure above, O is the center of the circle and the radius of the circle is 10. If the area of the shaded region is 70π, what is the value, in degrees, of x?

(A) 98

(B) 108

(C) 144

(D) 208

(E) 252

DIRECTIONS FOR STUDENT-PRODUCED RESPONSE QUESTIONS

For each of the questions below (29–38), solve the problem and indicate your answer by darkening the ovals in the special grid. For example:

Answer: 1.25 or $\frac{5}{4}$ or 5/4

Write answer →
in boxes.

Grid-in result. →

Fraction line
Decimal point

You may start your answers in any column, space permitting. Columns not needed should be left blank.

Either position is correct.

- It is recommended, though not required, that you write your answer in the boxes at the top of the columns. However, you will receive credit only for darkening the ovals correctly.

- Grid only one answer to a question, even though some problems have more than one correct answer.

- Darken no more than one oval in a column.

- No answers are negative.

- Mixed numbers cannot be gridded. For example: the number $1\frac{1}{4}$ must be gridded as 1.25 or 5/4.

  (If $\boxed{1\ |\ 1\ |\ /\ |\ 4}$ is gridded, it will be interpreted as $\frac{11}{4}$, not $1\frac{1}{4}$.)

- Decimal Accuracy: Decimal answers must be entered as accurately as possible. For example, if you obtain an answer such as 0.1666…, you should record the result as .166 or .167. **Less accurate values such as .16 or .17 are not acceptable.**

Acceptable ways to grid $\frac{1}{6}$ = .1666 …

29. Half a number is four more than one-third of the number. What is the number?

30. What is the 499th term of the sequence 1, 2, 3, 4, 5, 1, 2, 3, 4, 5, 1, 2, ... ?

GO ON TO THE NEXT PAGE →

31. The previous figure is a rectangle with an area of 48. What is the value of a?

33. If p is 20 percent of 140 and q is 25 percent of 56, what percent of p is q?

32. If $m^2 - n^2 = 15$ and $m - n = 3$, what is the value of $m + n$?

34. If $x > 0$ and $3\sqrt{x} - 7 = 20$, what is the value of x?

GO ON TO THE NEXT PAGE

35. How many identical cubes, each with edges of 2 inches, can fit in a box that measures 18 inches by 10 inches by 8 inches?

37. The product of two consecutive positive integers is 29 more than their sum. What is the larger of the two integers?

36. If y varies directly as x^2, and $y = 8$ when $x = 2$, what is the value of y when $x = 1$?

38. If $a > 0$ and $b < 0$, and both a and b satisfy the equation $x^2 - 5x - 24 = 0$, what is the value of $a - b$?

IF YOU FINISH BEFORE TIME IS CALLED, YOU MAY CHECK YOUR WORK ON THIS SECTION ONLY. DO NOT TURN TO ANY OTHER SECTION IN THE TEST.

STOP

SECTION 5

Time—25 Minutes
39 Questions

For each of the following questions, choose the best answer and darken the corresponding oval on the answer sheet.

Directions: The following sentences test your knowledge of grammar, usage, diction (choice of words), and idioms.

Some sentences are correct.

No sentence contains more than one error.

You will find that the error, if there is one, is underlined and lettered. Elements of the sentence that are not underlined will not be changed. In choosing answers, follow the requirements of standard written English.

If there is an error, select the <u>one underlined part</u> that must be changed to make the sentence correct, and fill in the corresponding oval on your answer sheet.

If there is no error, fill in answer oval (E).

1. <u>Realizing that</u> the community opera
      A
   company <u>did not have</u> sufficient revenue to
          B
   produce *La Traviata*, <u>its perennial favorite,</u>
                 C
   <u>the board members</u> began to raise money for
      D
   the performance. <u>No error</u>
             E

2. <u>One of the most</u> frequent types of injury
      A
   that baseball players <u>sustain is</u> a dislocated
             B
   <u>shoulder, another</u> that occurs <u>nearly as</u>
      C   D
   frequently is a strained hamstring. <u>No error</u>
                   E

3. The hot air balloonists <u>successfully traveled</u>
                A
   around the world, but they refused to take
   full credit either for the technology <u>they</u>
                     B
   <u>invented</u> for the flight <u>or for</u> their quick time,
    B   C
   because they <u>had received</u> a good deal of
             D
   help. <u>No error</u>
        E

4. <u>Although</u> she takes at least three singing
    A
   lessons a week, Mary is <u>almost as</u> poor a
               B
   singer <u>as she is</u> <u>a dancer.</u> <u>No error</u>
       C   D   E

GO ON TO THE NEXT PAGE →

5. <u>Examining</u> their differences, the novelist's
   A
and the reporter's <u>writing styles</u> are used
                B
<u>to portray</u> the same political situation in
  C
completely <u>different ways</u>. <u>No error</u>
          D   E

6. Many international vacationers <u>find</u>
                      A
airplane rides uncomfortable and <u>long, in</u>
                            B
<u>other respects</u> they enjoy <u>traveling to</u> foreign
  C   D
countries. <u>No error</u>
        E

7. The relationships between identical twins

<u>have a particular</u> fascination <u>for</u> many people
    A   B
<u>which</u> have maintained close relationships
  C
with <u>their</u> own siblings. <u>No error</u>
     D   E

8. <u>Exaggerating</u> <u>their</u> nutritional importance,
    A   B
<u>dietitians</u> overuse chocolate as an example
  C
of both a <u>beneficial and a harmful</u> food.
              D
<u>No error</u>
  E

9. The social consequences of France's

invasion of Russia in the 19th century

<u>had perhaps</u> <u>even more</u> of an impact on
   A   B
literature <u>than either</u> politics <u>or relations</u>
          C   D
between nations. <u>No error</u>
          E

10. Sam <u>liked</u> to read <u>novels,</u> of <u>which</u> he found
     A   B   C
mysteries <u>especially</u> gripping. <u>No error</u>
        D   E

11. Many <u>pieces of</u> music <u>composed by</u> 19th-
      A   B
century musicians in Europe, <u>in particular</u>
                    C
religious pieces, were <u>adaptations of</u> hymns
               D
sung in church. <u>No error</u>
        E

12. <u>Trained to</u> tense her muscles and breathe
   A
from the chest, <u>the dancer</u> had the <u>most</u>
           B   C
<u>difficulty</u> with <u>yoga's</u> loose and full breathing
  C   D
methods. <u>No error</u>
      E

GO ON TO THE NEXT PAGE

13. The <u>rapid spread</u> of infectious <u>diseases,</u>
        A   B
<u>frequently</u> compounded in certain regions
        B
<u>because</u> the methods for detection and
        C
prevention are not <u>well understood</u>. <u>No error</u>
                            D   E

14. Suzanne Farrell, a retired New York City

Ballet principal dancer <u>widely known</u> for her
                                    A

grace and elegance <u>onstage</u>, <u>conducts</u> the
                            B   C

<u>upcoming</u> workshop. <u>No error</u>
        D   E

Directions: The following sentences test correctness and effectiveness of expression. In choosing answers, follow the requirements of standard written English; that is, pay attention to grammar, choice of words, sentence construction, and punctuation.

In each of the following sentences, part of the sentence or the entire sentence is underlined. Beneath each sentence, you will find five ways of phrasing the underlined part. Choice (A) repeats the original; the other four are different.

Choose the answer that best expresses the meaning of the original sentence. If you think the original is better than any of the alternatives, choose it; otherwise, choose one of the others. Your choice should produce the most effective sentence—clear and precise, without awkwardness or ambiguity.

15. This season, the Raiders' football games were mostly losses, <u>but those that did feature</u> considerable athletic performances.

(A) but those that did feature

(B) but they did feature

(C) but that did feature

(D) however featuring

(E) however that does feature

16. Many of the students <u>studied relentless for passing</u> the test necessary to earn an A in the course.

(A) studied relentless for passing

(B) studied relentless to pass

(C) studied to pass relentlessly

(D) studied relentlessly for passing

(E) studied relentlessly to pass

17. The violinist was overly excited at the beginning of the concert, <u>having shown admirable calm once the violin sonata got</u> under way.

(A) having shown admirable calm once the violin sonata got

(B) but he showed admirable calm once the violin sonata got

(C) but showing admirable calm once the violin sonata got

(D) once he showed admirable calm when the violin sonata got

(E) however, he showed admirable calm when the violin sonata had been

18. The compositions of modern composers and their <u>predecessors, suggestive</u> of Bach's later work in that beat, instrumentation, and style combine to form a very rhythmic sound.

(A) predecessors, suggestive

(B) predecessors are suggesting

(C) predecessors are suggestive

(D) predecessors suggesting

(E) predecessors, suggestions

GO ON TO THE NEXT PAGE

19. Looking through the school's telescope on top of the science laboratory, <u>far above them a shooting star flew by</u>.

    (A) far above them a shooting star flew by

    (B) there was a shooting star flying above them

    (C) a shooting star flew by far above them

    (D) they saw a shooting star fly by far above them

    (E) they saw far above them a shooting star flew

20. The increase in available space has made it possible for our library to be entertaining <u>as well as educate</u>.

    (A) as well as educate

    (B) and being educational as well

    (C) as well as educational

    (D) and educates as well

    (E) as well as education

21. In the mid to late 1500s, Queen Elizabeth I ascended the English throne and surprised much of English <u>society; she wanted</u> strong rule over her people and so did not marry.

    (A) society; she wanted

    (B) society, which allowed her to want

    (C) society, their idea was to want

    (D) society, and so she could want

    (E) society; in this way leading to the wanted

22. Whether there is truth to the assertion that there is extraterrestrial life in the universe remains unknown, <u>and somehow</u> many people have seen unidentified flying objects (UFOs) in the sky.

    (A) and somehow

    (B) somehow

    (C) and that somehow

    (D) but somehow

    (E) that somehow

23. Home-team loyalty allows an athletic feat, no matter how many times previously accomplished, <u>to be proclaimed as staggering when attempted</u> and completed by a favorite athlete in a home game.

    (A) to be proclaimed as staggering when attempted

    (B) that is attempted as staggering to be proclaimed

    (C) to have been proclaimed as staggering when attempted

    (D) to be attempted as staggering when proclaimed

    (E) which once can proclaim as staggering when attempted

GO ON TO THE NEXT PAGE

24. Nervous about change and new people, <u>the deterioration of the society was brought about by its apprehensive leaders</u>.

   (A) the deterioration of the society was brought about by its apprehensive leaders
   (B) the deterioration of the society has been brought about by its apprehensive leaders
   (C) the society was apprehensive its leaders caused to collapse
   (D) the apprehensive leaders of that society have brought about their collapse
   (E) the apprehensive leaders of that society brought about its collapse

25. Because women buy approximately 80 percent of the ties sold in the United States, <u>they are often displayed</u> near the perfume or women's clothing departments.

   (A) they are often displayed
   (B) they are often in display
   (C) ties are often displayed
   (D) ties are often being displayed
   (E) they can often be found at or

26. Laval, the first bishop of Quebec, exemplified aristocratic vigor and concern, <u>on account of his giving up his substantial inheritance to become an ecclesiastic</u> and to help shape Canadian politics and education.

   (A) on account of his giving up his substantial inheritance to become an ecclesiastic
   (B) since he gave up his substantial inheritance to become an ecclesiastic
   (C) since giving up his substantial inheritance to become an ecclesiastic
   (D) because of his having given up his substantial inheritance for the purpose of becoming an ecclesiastic
   (E) as a result of becoming an ecclesiastic through giving up his substantial inheritance

27. Even though the senators on the committee <u>were reluctant to schedule</u> a formal inquiry, they went on record as favoring one.

   (A) were reluctant to schedule
   (B) were reluctant as far as scheduling
   (C) were reluctant in scheduling
   (D) have been reluctant at scheduling
   (E) have had reluctance to schedule

28. Having read the works of Hemingway, Fitzgerald, and Steinbeck, <u>Hemingway is definitely overrated as a writer</u>.

   (A) Hemingway is definitely overrated as a writer
   (B) Hemingway has definitely been overrated as a writer
   (C) I am convinced that Hemingway is overrated as a writer
   (D) the writing abilities of Hemingway are overrated, I am convinced
   (E) I am convinced as a writer that Hemingway is overrated

29. Her eyes shining with tears, Aunt Helga told us over and over again how much she appreciated <u>us coming to her</u> 90th birthday party.

   (A) us coming to her
   (B) our coming to her
   (C) us having come to her
   (D) that we come to her
   (E) us for the fact of our coming to her

GO ON TO THE NEXT PAGE

30. Many researchers contend that driving while talking on a cellular phone poses essentially the same risks <u>than if you drive</u> while intoxicated.

(A) than if you drive

(B) than to drive

(C) as if one drives

(D) as driving

(E) as it does when driving

31. Before 1988, the corporation's board of directors included 153 <u>members, none of the members were women</u>.

(A) members, none of the members were women

(B) members; and no women

(C) members, none of them women

(D) members, and of the members not one of them was a woman

(E) members; none of them being women

32. <u>The client was waiting for 15 minutes when</u> the receptionist suddenly looked up from her work, noticed him, and informed him that his appointment had been canceled.

(A) The client was waiting for 15 minutes when

(B) The client, having waited for 15 minutes, when

(C) Already the client was waiting for 15 minutes when

(D) When the client waited for 15 minutes,

(E) The client had been waiting for 15 minutes when

33. <u>Because the polar ice caps are melting, therefore many</u> scientists and environmentalists fear that several small island nations will be completely covered by water in only a few decades.

(A) Because the polar ice caps are melting, therefore many

(B) Because the polar ice caps are melting, many

(C) The polar ice caps are melting, therefore many

(D) Because the polar ice caps are melting; many

(E) The polar ice caps are melting; and many

34. One of the great literary artists of the 19th <u>century was Gustave Flaubert known for his obsession with the writer's craft</u>.

(A) century was Gustave Flaubert known for his obsession with the writer's craft

(B) century, Gustave Flaubert's obsession with the writer's craft was well known

(C) century, Gustave Flaubert was known for his obsession with the writer's craft

(D) century, Gustave Flaubert, known for his obsession with the writer's craft

(E) century was Gustave Flaubert: known for his obsession with the writer's craft

GO ON TO THE NEXT PAGE

Directions: The passage below is an early draft of an essay. Parts of the passage need to be rewritten.

Read the passage, and answer the questions that follow. Some questions are about individual sentences or parts of sentences; in these questions, you are asked to select the choice which will improve sentence structure and word choice. Other questions refer to parts of the essay or the entire essay and ask you to consider the organization and development. You should follow the conventions of standard written English in answering the questions. After you have chosen your answer, fill in the corresponding oval on your answer sheet.

Questions 35–39 are based on the following passage.

(1) One of the most important achievements after the American Revolution was the creation of the presidential office. (2) This was difficult because they feared popular leadership. (3) In the Founding Fathers' view, it was dangerous for the President to gain power from popularity.

(4) The Founders believed in the ignorance of the populace. (5) The office of the President needed to be independent of the popular will and the "common man."

(6) George Washington was a perfect example. (7) Just as the Founders wished, his heroics and regal bearing put him on a pedestal. (8) However, some of America's most famous presidents did not follow the Founders' ideals. (9) Andrew Jackson (nicknamed "Old Hickory") identified himself as a "common man" and used his popularity as a military hero to win the presidential election. (10) In other words, he makes the presidency what it is today: a popularity contest.

(11) Fourteen years later, Abraham Lincoln was virtually everything the Founders had not wanted in a leader. (12) He did not stand above popular opinion. (13) He courted public favor as "Honest Abe." (14) He had humble roots, a fact that he emphasized to gain public favor. (15) The Founders would have hated this.

(16) But many people think that Lincoln was one of our best Presidents. (17) This suggests maybe they were wrong.

35. Which of the following best replaces the word "they" in sentence 2 (reproduced below)?

    This was difficult because they feared popular leadership.

    (A) the revolutionaries
    (B) the complications
    (C) the Founding Fathers
    (D) the presidents
    (E) the populace

36. In context, which of the following words are the most logical to insert at the beginning of sentence 5 (reproduced below)?

    The office of the President needed to be independent of the popular will and the "common man."

    (A) I have found that
    (B) On the other hand,
    (C) And yet, for him
    (D) To them,
    (E) Resulting in,

GO ON TO THE NEXT PAGE

37. In context, which is the best way to combine sentences 6 and 7 (reproduced below)?

    George Washington was a perfect example. Just as the Founders wished, his heroics and regal bearing put him on a pedestal.

    (A) (As it is now.)

    (B) George Washington is a perfect example of what the Founders wanted although he was placed on a pedestal for his heroics and regal bearing.

    (C) Just like the Founders asked, George Washington's heroics and regal bearing put him on a pedestal.

    (D) George Washington is a perfect example of what the Founders wanted because his heroics and regal bearing put him on a pedestal.

    (E) George Washington is a perfect example of what they wanted, his heroics and regal bearing put him on a pedestal.

38. In context, which of the following revisions is necessary in sentence 10 (reproduced below)?

    In other words, he makes the presidency what it is today: a popularity contest.

    (A) Replace "he" with "Jackson"

    (B) Replace "the presidency" with "the President"

    (C) Replace "it is" with "it was"

    (D) Replace "makes" with "had made"

    (E) Replace "makes" with "made"

39. In context, which is the best way to combine sentences 16 and 17 (reproduced below)?

    But many people think that Lincoln was one of our best Presidents. This suggests maybe they were wrong.

    (A) They were wrong, many people suggested, thinking that Lincoln was one of our best Presidents.

    (B) Suggesting that they were wrong, many people think that Lincoln was one of our best Presidents.

    (C) But many people think that Lincoln was one of our best presidents, which suggests that maybe the Founders were wrong.

    (D) Furthermore, many people think that Lincoln was one of our best Presidents, suggesting that maybe the Founders were wrong.

    (E) Yet maybe the Founders were wrong, many people think that Lincoln was one of our best Presidents.

(Answers on the next page.)

PRACTICE TEST THREE: **ANSWER KEY**

SECTION 1

1. D	9. D	17. C
2. B	10. C	18. D
3. A	11. D	19. C
4. E	12. C	20. B
5. D	13. C	21. B
6. C	14. A	22. A
7. D	15. E	23. E
8. B	16. B	24. D

SECTION 2

1. A	8. D	15. D
2. D	9. A	16. B
3. B	10. A	17. A
4. C	11. E	18. E
5. B	12. C	
6. B	13. A	
7. A	14. A	

SECTION 3

25. A	33. E	41. C
26. C	34. A	42. D
27. D	35. B	43. E
28. E	36. E	44. D
29. A	37. D	45. B
30. B	38. C	46. D
31. A	39. B	47. E
32. E	40. A	48. C

SECTION 4

19. C	29. 24
20. D	30. 4
21. B	31. 4
22. E	32. 5
23. D	33. 50
24. B	34. 81
25. C	35. 180
26. A	36. 2
27. B	37. 7
28. B	38. 11

SECTION 5

1. E	14. C	27. A
2. C	15. B	28. C
3. B	16. E	29. B
4. E	17. B	30. D
5. A	18. C	31. C
6. B	19. D	32. E
7. C	20. C	33. B
8. B	21. A	34. C
9. C	22. D	35. C
10. C	23. A	36. D
11. E	24. E	37. D
12. E	25. C	38. E
13. B	26. B	39. C

PRACTICE TEST THREE: ASSESS YOUR STRENGTHS

Use the following tables to determine which question types you need to review most.

Question Type	Section and Question
Sentence Completion	Section 1, 1–7 Section 3, 25–30
Reading Comprehension	Section 1, 8–24 Section 3, 31–48
Regular Math	Section 2, 1–18 Section 4, 19–28
Grid-in Math	Section 4, 29–38
Identifying Sentence Errors	Section 5, 1–14
Improving Sentences	Section 5, 15–34
Improving Paragraphs	Section 5, 35–39

Question Type	Number of Questions on Test	Number Correct
Sentence Completion	13	
Reading Comprehension	35	
Regular Math	28	
Grid-in Math	10	
Identifying Sentence Errors	14	
Improving Sentences	20	
Improving Paragraphs	5	

ANSWERS AND EXPLANATIONS

SECTION 1

1. D

The students lost their sense of originality, so their paintings must have been similar to the teacher's. *Copied* is a good prediction. Choice (D) is a good match for that.

2. B

Don't overlook important clues in the sentence. Here, all the words could apply to the English Channel, but only one of them fits all the clues. If the athlete's body temperature dropped and she shivered uncontrollably, the English Channel must have been *very cold*. Choice (B) is a good match.

3. A

In this two-blank sentence completion, the first blank is a requirement for the second blank. (Only a dog that is *blank* can be trained to have *blank*.) All of the choices could make sense for the first blank, but fortunately the second blank gives you a clue: the quality the dogs need to have is described as "unwavering." Of the second blank choices, only *obedience* can be described in this way, so (A) is the correct choice. Even if you didn't know that *tractable* meant "easy to control," the second blank would have put you on the right track.

4. E

Start with the second blank. If the valley region of the state needs to be relieved of drought, the governor must be *recommending* or *implementing* water-saving measures. The first blank should be a word that can describe a valley. Choice (E) works for both blanks. Choice (B) can't be right, because although it would make sense for the governor to *encourage* water-saving measures, if the valley is suffering from drought, it can't be described as *sodden*, which means "soaked with liquid."

5. D

Here (A) and (B) make some sense, but don't fit the clues as well as the correct answer. The Phantom must have looked very different from the other cars, since some quality in its appearance was highlighted by those cars. The other cars looked awkward and boxy, so the Phantom must have looked quite *graceful*. Choice (D) is a good match. *Sleek* is the opposite of boxy and awkward.

6. C

Don't be tempted by a choice just because of a familiar context, such as *forecast* and *thunderstorm*. *Despite* indicates that there is a contrast in this sentence. The contrast is between a fast-approaching thunderstorm and what the workers did before they went indoors. In (C), you get the contrast you need in the second blank. *Diligent* means careful and conscientious effort in one's duties.

7. D

This sentence provides a definition; you need a word that refers to *plots and schemes*. Choice (D) is a good match.

LUNAR ECLIPSES PASSAGE

The first paragraph introduces the passage's topic— lunar eclipses. The author notes that, although lunar eclipses are less well-known than solar eclipses, they last longer, are more common, and are easier to observe. The second paragraph gets into details: lunar eclipses happen when the Earth comes in between the Sun and the Moon. Also they can be divided into three types: total, partial, and penumbral. The final paragraph explains that, unlike solar eclipses, lunar eclipses can be directly observed. It's important to note that this passage is purely informational; the author of this passage doesn't express a particular point of view, except perhaps an implication that lunar eclipses deserve more attention.

8. B

The author discusses several things in the passage, all of which contribute to the general discussion of lunar eclipses. Sometimes the simplest answer is the correct one.

9. D

The author says that lunar eclipses are spectacular and that they last a long time. So, the "stability" of lunar eclipses refers to the fact that they last a long time; they don't disappear quickly like solar eclipses. Choice (D) makes sense. The eclipses have a long duration.

10. C

The author discusses the types of lunar eclipses in paragraph 2, so go there for the answer. You learn that a partial eclipse occurs when a part of the Moon passes through part of the Earth's umbral shadow.

Choice (A) is a distortion; it describes a total eclipse. Choice (B) is a misused detail; it is the total number of *all types* of lunar eclipses per year.

11. D

It's difficult to make a prediction here, but you do know that the distinctions among penumbral, partial, and full eclipses appear only in paragraph 2. So the correct answer will come from information in that paragraph. Choice (D) fits. They are *brief and subtle* and are often *unobserved by all but astronomers and the most avid devotees*, while other lunar eclipses are *quite easy to see*.

12. C

The issue of safety is discussed in paragraph 3. There you learn that "the Moon's light is dissipated, reflected sunlight." The light is not dangerous

because it is not coming directly from the Sun, but is instead reflecting off of the Moon. Choice (C) is a good match.

FLYING MACHINE PASSAGE

This short passage looks at the idea that the concept of flying machines dates all the way back to ancient Greece. The author traces the concept back to Archimedes, mentions a couple of scientists and philosophers, and ends by mentioning Joseph and Etienne Montgolfier's hot air balloon.

13. C

The word *implies* should tip you off that you will need to put together clues from the passage. The passage concentrates on the principle of buoyancy in connection with flying machines, so search for an answer choice that establishes this connection. Choice (C) works. The passage states that the discovery of buoyancy led Archimedes and Bacon and Albertus Magnus to consider flying machines and that the principle of these machines was tested by the hot air balloon.

14. A

Like Archimedes may have done, the other scientists created or put forward designs for flying machines. Choice (A) is a good match. It makes sense to say that the scientists *proposed* designs.

MOVIE PASSAGES

These two short passages offer contrasting views on whether a movie is the result of one individual or a group of people. The writer of Passage 1 believes that a film is the result of one person, an *auteur*, who brings order to the film. The writer of Passage 2, on the other hand, says that a film is a collaborative effort in which many different artistic visions are responsible for the result.

15. E

A writer would most strongly disagree with a statement that conflicts with his or her central argument. Read each statement to see if it agrees or disagrees with the author's central argument—that the director is the *auteur* of a film. Remember that you're looking for the choice with which the author would *disagree*. Author 2 would agree with (E), but it is the opposite of the thesis for Passage 1. Because you're looking for something with which Author 1 would *disagree*, this is the correct answer. Choice (B) is tempting because it mentions *many kinds of artists*, but Author 1 doesn't dispute that many artists work on a film; he simply argues that the director is the most important one.

16. B

In the first sentence, the author states that *a film is a collaborative work*, and the rest of the passage emphasizes the importance of the individual contributions of the artists who create films. Choice (B) matches your prediction well.

17. C

The quote comes from Author 1, who thinks that films solely represent the vision of the director. Author 2, however, writes that *any sensitive viewer responds not to a single artistic vision in a film, but to dozens of such visions*. In other words, viewers respond to the input of many different contributors. Choice (C) makes sense. To say that people only respond to the director's vision is a *simplification*, since it ignores the influence of all the contributions that Author 2 writes about.

18. D

Passage 1 says that an *auteur* creates a film in the same way that an artist creates a painting. Passage 2, on the other hand, says that a movie is not like a painting because film is a collaborative effort. Choice (D) is a good match.

MOSCOW 1926 PASSAGE

Make sure to read the italicized introduction to get an idea of when and where the passage is talking about. There are two parts to this passage. The first is before the writer attends a performance. The writer frets over her tattered fur, her hair, and the possibility of danger. The second is after she attends the performance. The writer says she hadn't needed to worry about anything. She enjoyed the show, even though she realized too late that the actors had not come out on stage after the performance for the curtain call, so she had been applauding for dummies.

19. C

The author is commenting on her own nervousness when she says, *It's as if I've never been to a proper theater.* Of course, she had been to the theater quite often before, a *proper theater* before the war. Here, *proper* means the real deal. Choice (C) fits well with your prediction.

20. B

The author describes the play as *a rebellious act*, and asks, "Will we be putting ourselves in danger tonight? It's hard to believe we will not." So she thinks that fear of getting in trouble might keep people away. Choice (B) is a good match.

21. B

The author notes that some other attendees were even more tattered, *but people were not judged for the state of their clothing*. In other words, other aspects of the event were more important than what people looked like. Choice (B) fits your prediction.

22. A

The author writes that *the pace of the show was breathtaking. I found that I could scarcely keep up.* So the pace must have been quite *fast.* Choice (A) is a good match.

23. E

Because there's a lot of information about the play, it's tough to put it all together to make a prediction. You can at least say confidently that she enjoyed the play, so look for a positive choice. Choice (E) fits. In the first entry, you learn that she used to go to the theater frequently and later missed it. In the second entry, she's very excited to be at the play, so it makes sense to say that she's *elated to be in the theater again.*

24. D

Beware of half-right, half-wrong answers like (A). In the afternoon, the author is quite nervous: *I did not expect to be this nervous.* In the evening, she writes that *I was so overwhelmed with emotion, I found myself on my feet clapping.* She seems to be delighted to see the play. Choice (D) fits well.

SECTION 2

1. A

Most of your initial work here centers on finding x, but remember that you're asked to find $6x$.

$$7x - 2 = 12x + 13$$
$$-15 = 5x$$
$$-3 = x$$

Then solve for $6x$:

$$6x = 6(-3) = -18$$

2. D

You don't know the actual values of a, b, c, and d, but you don't need to. Focus on how the angles are related to one another.

(A) If two angles are vertical, then they are congruent. So c and d are congruent, and $2c$ must be equal to $2d$.

(B) If two angles form a straight line, then they are supplementary angles and their sum is 180°. So $a + d = 180°$ and $b + d = 180°$.

(C) $a - b = 0$ and $d - c = 0$.

(D) This statement could be true—if any of the angles were right, for example—but does not have to be true. For example, if a is 60°, $a + b = 120°$ and $c + d = 240°$.

(E) $a + c = 180°$ and $b + d = 180°$. Multiplying each sum by 2 does not undo the equality of the two sums.

3. B

Insert data from the question into the probability formula:

$$\text{Probability} = \frac{\text{Number of desired outcomes}}{\text{Number of possible outcomes}}$$

2 pennies

1 nickel

3 dimes

2 quarters
_____

8 coins

Dimes as a fraction of all coins are $\dfrac{3}{8}$.

4. C

Some questions test your ability to translate a word problem into a math problem.

$$x = \text{cost of one pencil}$$
$$y = \text{cost of one pen}$$

$$12x + 6y = 3.34$$
$$3x = 0.10$$

Solve for x:

$$x = \frac{0.10}{3}$$

Substitute the value of x into the first equation:

$$12\left(\frac{0.10}{3}\right) + 6y = 3.34$$
$$0.4 + 6y = 3.34$$
$$y = \$.49$$

5. B

Begin by thinking about the meaning of "$\overline{BD}$ bisects $\angle ABC$."

If $\angle ABD = 20$, $\angle CBD = 20$, so $\angle ABC = 40$.

The right angle at A, added to 40, is 130. Therefore, $180 - 130 = 50$.

6. B

Pick numbers. Say $a = 1$ and $b = 2$.

(A) $2(1) + (2) = 4$

(B) $3(1) + (2) = 5$

(C) $2[(1) + (2)] = 6$

(D) $\dfrac{(2)}{(1)} = 2$

(E) $1 + \dfrac{(2)}{(2)} = 2$

Because we must eliminate (A), (C), (D), and (E), the only possible answer is (B).

7. A

Manage the problem in two steps. First isolate x, then square it.

Solve for x:

$$x^{-3} = 8$$

$$\frac{1}{x^3} = 8$$

$$x^3 = \frac{1}{8}$$

$$x = \frac{1}{2}$$

Then solve for x^2:

$$x^2 = \frac{1}{4}$$

8. D

Begin a ratio question by making sure you are clear about the parts being compared. In this case, you want the shaded area to the unshaded area.

Area of entire figure $= \pi r^2 = \pi(6)^2 = 36\pi$

Area of small unshaded circle $= \pi(2)^2 = 4\pi$

Area of shaded region $= 36\pi - 4\pi = 32\pi$

Shaded:Unshaded $= 32\pi : 4\pi = 8:1$

9. A

Focus on how one piece of data sheds light on the next. You're asked for the number of sophomores, but the way to arrive at it is by first finding the number of freshmen.

Number of seniors $= 0.4 \times 60$ players $= 24$ seniors

Number of freshman $= 0.5 \times$ seniors $= 12$ freshman

Number of juniors $= 0.3 \times 60$ players $= 18$ juniors

$24 + 12 + 18 = 54$

Number of sophomores $= 60 - 54 = 6$ sophomores

10. A

In this question, our answer must be an inequality. It's often helpful to write an equation until you solve the problem. Then, go back and incorporate the inequality.

$$a + b + 60 = 180$$
$$b = 180 - 60 - a$$
$$b = 120 - a$$

If a were exactly 50, b would be exactly 70.

Since $a > 50°$, $b < 70°$.

11. E   ₁②₃

To maximize the value of a fraction in which top and bottom are positive numbers, maximize the top and minimize the bottom.

$$\frac{\max x}{\min y} = \frac{0.5}{0.25} = 2$$

12. C

Draw and label points as you work through the solution. This will help you to visualize the relationships among the points. Think of M as 0. Because $2\overline{MN} = 5\overline{MP}$, MN must be longer than MP. P will be located between M and N on the number line. You can choose convenient locations for P and N as long as you keep the ratio of lengths correct. The easiest way is to let $P = 2$, $N = 5$, so $2MN = 5MP$.

Now $PN = 3$, $MP = 2$, for a ratio of 3:2.

13. A

If you know that a line with a downward slant has a negative slope, you can immediately eliminate three choices.

Estimate the slope of a line drawn through the center of the points. It is closest to a line that drops down three units and over one unit, giving it a slope of -3.

14. A   ₁②₃

This question looks more complex than it actually is. Don't get sidetracked trying to solve for a. Once you substitute the given values of x and y, a will cancel out.

$$\begin{aligned} x - y &= (a - 5) - (a + 1) \\ &= a - 5 - a - 1 \\ &= -6 \end{aligned}$$

15. D

Use data you're given about $ABCD$ to draw conclusions about the smaller squares. The perimeter of a square is four times the measure of a side, so each side of $ABCD$ must be 2 units long.

Each side is divided into four sections, so each section is $\frac{2}{4} = \frac{1}{2}$ unit.

Each section is a square, so the lengths of the sides are identical. The perimeter of the individual squares is $4 \times \frac{1}{2}$ unit = 2 units.

16. B

"The average of x and y" means $\frac{x + y}{2}$. Manipulate the equation into this form:

$$\frac{5x + 5y = 20}{5}$$

$$x + y = 4$$

$$\frac{x + y}{2} = \frac{4}{2} = 2$$

17. A

If the operation denoted by the symbol is complex—as it is here—the numbers to which you'll apply the symbolic operation have to be relatively simple.

$$_2\triangle_6^4 = \frac{4 + 6}{2} - \frac{2 + 6}{4} - \frac{2 + 4}{6} = 5 - 2 - 1 = 2$$

18. E

Probably the easiest way to answer this question is to draw a coordinate grid and locate each of the points. Although it might take a few moments to set up the grid, doing so will save you time in the long run.

In a 45-45-90 or isosceles right triangle, the legs are equal, and perpendicular.

Each of the possibilities for triangle *DEF* above clearly has two perpendicular edges forming the legs of a right triangle. Now calculate the leg lengths of each triangle to see if they are equal. Because the legs are all vertical and horizontal lines, you don't need the distance formula to find their lengths. You can just subtract the *x*-coordinates of the endpoints to find the lengths of the horizontal legs and the *y*-coordinates of the endpoints to find the lengths of the vertical legs. Each possible triangle *DEF* has legs that are 6 units long, making each an isosceles right triangle. All three points could be the coordinates of point *F*.

SECTION 3

25. A

The sentence compares the past and present of an aspect of the lives of celebrities; the phrase *curiosity about their personal lives* tips you off that this aspect has to do privacy, and the words *even though* indicate a contrast between what the public wanted and what the stars maintained. *Privacy* is a good prediction for the first blank. It's tough to make a prediction for the second blank, so look for a word that makes sense. Choice (A) fits well.

26. C

Mrs. Davis liked to *spread knowledge*, so a good prediction for the first blank is *teach* or *inform*. Choice (C) is the best match.

27. D

Identify the positive or negative charge of a blank. Because John alienated his friends, the blanks must have a negative connotation. What has alienated John's friends? His habit of *mentioning titles of books he had read and quoting poems he had memorized*. While it's tough to make an exact prediction, *showing off* his *achievements* is one possibility. Choice (D) fits well.

28. E

Start by predicting a possible answer for the blank you find easier to deal with. In this question, that may be the second blank. Because the characters are celebrated in legends, actions such as *robbing the rich to give to the poor* must be perceived as *admirable*. For the first blank, predict a word that makes *defying...authority* a good thing, for example, if that authority is *corrupt* or *unjust*. Choice (E) works well for both blanks.

29. A

When a question involves a straightforward definition, you can often use a word from the sentence as your prediction.

Plunging into ice-cold water doesn't sound like much fun, but the author writes that it can *invigorate* the body and spirit. In fact, *invigorating* would be a good prediction here. Choice (A) is a good match. Choice (E) is tempting because it is the only other positive term, but *soothing* means relaxing, which is the opposite of *invigorating*.

30. B

The only thing you know about the novel is that it is made up of letters. Look for a word that has this definition. Choice (B) fits. Even if you didn't know the definition of this uncommon term, you could probably eliminate the other choices, which contain more familiar words.

GREEK HONOR PASSAGE

This short passage discusses the idea of honor in the epic poem *The Iliad*. The author says there are two kinds of honor. The first is tangible; the other evolved to the less tangible, modern concept.

31. A

Because Achilles withdrew from a war over an insult, he must have felt *very* insulted. Choice (A) fits.

32. E

Watch out for answer choices that are only partially correct. In a tough passage like this one, it's easy to get confused if you aren't clear on the author's main idea.

The paragraph says that Achilles's sense of honor changes. At the beginning, he is concerned with possessions won in battle. Later, however, Achilles thinks material possessions can't make up for lost friends. The author also says that this is more attuned to a modern conception of honor. Choice (E) is a good match.

CANINE POLICE PASSAGES

PASSAGE 1

Passage 1 provides a general overview of police dogs. In paragraph 1, the author describes why the dogs are useful: they have *phenomenal tracking instincts*, can search quickly, aren't deterred by darkness and locks, and can apprehend suspects in a way that minimizes the chance of injury. Paragraph 2 describes dogs' tracking abilities and how police use dogs for this purpose. It closes by noting that tracking success *can only be achieved only by extensive and continuing training*. Paragraph 3 emphasizes the importance of aggression training, which trains a dog to attack only under specific circumstances.

PASSAGE 2

Passage 2 presents an argument, although this is not apparent until the second paragraph. In paragraph 1, the author stresses the importance of the first two years of a dog's life. In paragraph 2, the author writes that early training is *especially important for police dogs*. Unlike other states, the author's state doesn't provide such training. In paragraph 3, the author argues that politicians who are concerned with the quality of police dog training should consider not only its funding but also the age at which the dogs are trained.

33. E

The referenced sentence continues *because odors can be detected in the dark and through the smallest crack under a door*. As long as a dog can use its sense of smell, it can search, unlike people who rely primarily on their sense of sight and need light and unobstructed views. Choice (E) is a good match.

34. A

Carefully read the sentence in which the subject of the question appears. Here, *keen* applies to the sense of smell, not the dog, so you can rule out choices like (B) and (D). The dogs obviously have a very *developed* sense of smell, so look for a choice that connotes this. Choice (A) is a good match.

35. B

This is an Inference question. The passage states that a scent article *bears the smell of the person being sought*. The cotton pad, therefore, must pick up the person's scent from the steering wheel. Choice (B) fits. The passage states that skin rafts are what the dogs track. So for the cotton pad to serve as a scent article, the skin rafts must have been transferred to the pad from the steering wheel.

36. E

The passage discusses the tendency of animals in the wild to abandon one trail for another, fresher one. The author indicates that this makes sense, because it allows the hunter to find prey that *passed by most recently*, and is therefore likely to be closer and easier to catch. Look for a choice that refers to this explanation of the dogs' behavior. Choice (E) is a good match.

37. D

When a question is limited to a specific part of the passage (such as the last paragraph of Passage 1 here), watch out for choices that don't focus on the same section. In the final paragraph, the author writes that *many assume that the dog is likely to ferociously attack*. The truth is that well-trained dogs attack only under specific circumstances. Choice (D) works. *Popular perception* refers to the perception of many who assume the dog will attack, while reality refers to the true nature of the well-trained dogs.

38. C

The main idea of the first paragraph of Passage 2 is that *a dog's capacity to learn later in life is shaped* in the first two years of a puppy's life. Choice (C) is a good match.

39. B

Backtrack from the sentence in question. The previous sentence mentions *postnatal health care*, while the *next* sentence back mentions *time while the dogs are still young…to train*. These must be the *vital measures*. Choice (B) is a good match.

40. A

What kind of interest have the politicians shown? They have *concerns about the state's police dogs and the quality of our current canine officer training programs*. That sounds like a fairly *great* interest. Choice (A) works, and makes sense with the word *marked*.

41. C

Right after the sentence in question, the author writes *We must also consider the ages of dogs entering training. We must mandate that units train younger dogs, not the older, harder-to-teach canines that are now being recruited for training*. So, funding is not as important as the age of the dogs in training. Choice (C) is a good match.

42. D

For questions about paired passages, mentally summarize the author's main ideas in a single sentence before you attack the answer choices. For example, Author 1 writes about the importance of training, and Author 2 writes about the importance of early training. The overlap is training, so that's probably a good thing to look for as you look through the choices. Both authors would agree with (D). Of course, Author 2 would also note that the timing of the training is important, but he certainly wouldn't deny the importance of training. The answer to a question asking what the authors of paired passages would *agree* on will usually be fairly general.

43. E

Consider the main idea of the passages when a question asks you to speculate about the reaction of one author to another. Author 2 agrees that training is important, but also feels that it must occur early in a dog's life. Choice (E) makes sense. Author 2 would state that the training must also take place at the right time in the dog's life.

44. D

There's not much to go on in the question stem, so dive right into the answer choices. Only (D) makes sense. Passage 1 provide lots of information about police dogs, while Passage 2 is intended to argue for a particular position, namely that police dogs should be trained earlier.

45. B

In order to find the correct answer, you need to read the text around the quote. The author specifically states, *We must recognize the truth of that old saw.* That means, even though it is a cliché, it is true.

CHIPMUNK EFFECT PASSAGE

This short passage says that people can hear at least 400 words per minute and looks at how technology has allowed people to hear recordings faster without having to speed them up and sacrifice sound quality.

46. D

There's no way to make a prediction here, so jump right into the answers. Choice (D) is a good match. The paragraph compares the rate of 180 words per minute for speaking versus the listening comprehension rate of 400 words per minute.

47. E

The author says that the *chipmunk effect* is *undesirable, if amusing.* Look for a choice that

matches the sense of this pairing. Choice (E) is a good match.

48. C

Even if the answer seems obvious, you should refer to the context in which the word is used. The passage is discussing making recordings shorter, without making them faster, so you should look for a word that refers to length. Although the prolonged segments may be unnecessary, the meaning of *prolonged* in this sentence is longer.

SECTION 4

 Picking Numbers

 Backsolving

 Eyeballing

19. C

Focus on moving quickly but meticulously.

$$a = \frac{4}{5}$$

$$b = 15$$

$$ab = \frac{4}{5}(15) = 12$$

20. D

Think of a line of symmetry simply as a line that creates a mirror image on either side.

Figure I   Figure II   Figure III

21. B

Substitute 2 for x in the equation:

$$f(2) = 4^2 - 5(2) = 16 - 10 = 6$$

22. E

The intersection of sets is the set of common elements of the sets being intersected. Think of the intersection as the overlap of sets. The symbol for the intersection of sets is $\cap$.

To be in $P \cap Q$—that is, the intersection of P and Q—a number would have to be between 0 and 10, inclusive, and it would have to be prime. There are four such numbers: 2, 3, 5, 7.

23. D

All the integers from 7 to 12, exclusive, and all the integers from -7 to -12, exclusive, are possible values for the number in question. Only (D) doesn't fall into either one of these ranges.

24. B

Focus on this fraction:

$$\frac{\text{lost}}{\text{lost} + \text{won} + \text{tied}}$$

Lost = $2X$

Won = X

Tied = Y

$$\frac{\text{lost}}{\text{lost} + \text{won} + \text{tied}} = \frac{2X}{2X + X + Y} = \frac{2X}{3X + Y}$$

25. C

Be on the lookout for Pythagorean triplets such as the 3-4-5 right triangle.

$OR = OT = 6$

$ST = 4$

$OS = 10$

So triangle ORS is a 3-4-5 right triangle in which the 3-4-5 ratio has been doubled to side lengths of 6, 8,

and 10. Had you not noticed this, you could have solved for $\overline{SR}$ using the Pythagorean theorem:

$$6^2 + x^2 = 10^2$$
$$36 + x^2 = 100$$
$$x^2 = 64$$
$$x = 8$$
$$SR = 8$$

26. A

In this question, picking numbers is a great alternative to the algebra below.

$$\frac{a^{m+n}}{a^n} = \frac{a^m a^n}{a^n} = a^m$$

27. B

Knowing the radius of the circle, you can determine its area, and then its unshaded area. The ratio of the unshaded area to the total area is the same as the ratio of x to 360.

Area of circle $= \pi r^2 = 100\pi$

Area of shaded portion $= 70\pi$

Area of unshaded portion $= 100\pi - 70\pi = 30\pi$

$$\frac{30\pi}{100\pi} = \frac{3}{10} = \frac{x}{360}$$
$$10x = 1,080$$
$$x = 108$$

28. B

Three-digit integers greater than 500 must be between 501 and 999. Eliminate groups that contain an even number of hundreds.

500s

~~600s~~

700s

~~800s~~

900s

Then eliminate groups that contain an even number of tens.

10s ~~20s~~ 30s ~~40s~~ 50s

~~60s~~ 70s ~~80s~~ 90s

Finally, eliminate groups that contain an even number of ones.

1 ~~2~~ 3 4 5

6 7 ~~8~~ 9

3 groups of hundreds $\times$ 5 groups of tens $\times$ 5 groups of ones = 75.

29. 24

Some questions test your ability to translate words into math. Once you complete the translation, most of these questions become straightforward algebra.

$$\frac{1}{2}x = 4 + \frac{1}{3}x$$

$$\frac{x}{2} - \frac{x}{3} = 4$$

$$\frac{3x}{6} - \frac{2x}{6} = 4$$

$$\frac{3x - 2x}{6} = 4$$

$$\frac{x}{6} = 4$$

$$x = 24$$

30. 4

Look for a pattern.

Every 5th term is 5. So the 500th term is 5. One term before the 500th is then 4.

31. 4

Though several key formulas—such as area of a rectangle is length times width—are provided, know them ahead of time. You'll then move through related questions more quickly and confidently.

$$3a \times a = 48$$

$$a^2 = 16$$

$$a = 4$$

32. 5

This question illustrates the payoff for recognizing certain classic factorables—such as the difference of two squares—on sight.

$$m^2 - n^2 = (m - n)(m + n) = 15$$

$$3(m + n) = 15$$

$$m + n = 5$$

33. 50

When percent questions take the form "… of a is b," put the *of* term on bottom and the *is* term on top. In this case, "… of p is q" becomes $\frac{q}{p}$.

$$p = 0.20(140) = 28$$

$$q = 0.25(56) = 14$$

$$\frac{q}{p} = \frac{14}{28} = 0.5 = 50\%$$

34. 81

Square both sides of an equation to get rid of a square root.

$$3\sqrt{x} - 7 = 20$$

$$3\sqrt{x} = 27$$

$$\sqrt{x} = 9$$

$$x = 81$$

35. 180

Notice that each dimension of one of the cubes fits evenly into each dimension of the box. Because of this, the answer to the question is simply the volume of the box divided by the volume of one of the cubes.

Volume of box: $18 \times 10 \times 8 = 1{,}440$ square inches

Volume of each cube: $2 \times 2 \times 2 = 8$ square inches

$1{,}440 \div 8 = 180$

36. 2

Don't let fancy wording intimidate you; this question only calls for a simple proportion and then some substitution.

"y varies directly with x^2" means $y = kx^2$. Substitute the given information:

$$8 = k(2)^2$$
$$8 = 4k$$
$$2 = k$$

Now substitute this value for k back into the original equation and solve for y when x is 1.

$$y = 2(1)^2$$
$$y = 2$$

37. 7

The consecutive integers can be expressed as x and $x + 1$. So:

$$x(x + 1) = 29 + [x + (x + 1)]$$
$$x^2 + x = 29 + 2x + 1$$
$$x^2 - x - 30 = 0$$
$$(x - 6)(x + 5) = 0$$
$$x = -5 \text{ or } 6$$

The question states that x is a positive integer, so eliminate -5.

If $x = 6$, $x + 1 = 7$.

38. 11

You're given $x^2 + 5x - 24 = 0$, which is a classic quadratic that you know how to factor. You're given that $a > 0$ and $b < 0$, which means simply that one root of the equation is positive and the other is negative. Finally, you're asked to identify the roots and then subtract the negative one from the positive one.

$$x^2 - 5x - 24 = 0$$
$$(x - 8)(x + 3) = 0$$
$$x = 8 \text{ or } -3$$

$a > 0$, so $a = 8$

$b < 0$, so $b = -3$

$$a - b = 8 - (-3) = 11$$

SECTION 5

1. E

The sentence is correct as written. Choices (A) and (B) use the correct verb tenses. Choice (C) clearly refers to *La Traviata* and the possessive pronoun *its* correctly refers to *the community opera company*. Choice (D) is the right subject to be modified by the long introductory clause.

2. C

This is an example of a run-on that uses a comma to connect two complete sentences. Choice (C) should use a semicolon instead of a comma. Choice (A) is idiomatically correct. In (B), the verbs *sustain* and *is* are correctly in the present tense. Choice (D) correctly compares the frequencies of dislocated shoulders and strained hamstrings.

3. B

Look closely at the sequence of events. The technology was invented before the successful trip around the world. Therefore *they invented* should be in the past perfect (*they had invented*). In (A), the adverb *successfully* correctly modifies the verb *traveled*. Choice (C) is the second part of *either…or*. Choice (D) is correctly in the past perfect, as they received help before the successful travel.

4. E

Don't forget that 20 percent of Identifying Sentence Errors questions are correct as written. The sentence is correct. Choice (A) correctly sets up the contrast between Mary taking many singing lessons and being a poor singer. Choices (B) and (C) correctly set up the comparison between Mary's singing and dancing. Choice (D) is in the same form as *a singer* and is thus a logical comparison.

5. A

The introductory phrase lacks a subject. Who is *examining their differences*? Choice (A) should state who is examining the differences (for example, *If you examine*). Choice (B) is plural because it refers to both the novelist's and the reporter's styles. The infinitive *to portray* (C) is used correctly. The adjective and noun pair *different ways* is correct.

6. B

When a comma divides two clauses, check whether they are both independent clauses. These are both independent clauses, making the sentence a run-on. The comma (B) should be a semicolon. Choice (A) is correctly in the present tense. Choices (C) and (D) are idiomatically correct.

7. C

The sentence uses the relative pronoun *which* to refer to people. The correct pronoun is *who*. Choices (A) and (B) are idiomatically correct. Choice (D) correctly refers to *many people*.

8. B

The plural pronoun *their* would be correct if it referred to the plural noun *dietitians*, but the nutritional importance of *chocolate*, not *dietitians*, is exaggerated. Choice (B) should use the singular possessive pronoun *its*. Choice (A) is the correct form for this modifying phrase. Choice (C) agrees with its verb *overuse*. In (D), the adjectives *beneficial* and *harmful*, although opposite in meaning, are used correctly.

9. C

The comparison between the impact of social consequences on literature and on politics or

relations between nations must be parallel. Choice (C) should read *than on either*. In (D), the other parallel structure here—*either...or*—is done correctly. Choice (A) is correctly in the past tense. Choice (B) correctly sets up the comparison.

10. C

The relative pronoun *which* is incorrect. We can't substitute *novels* for *which* (try it: *he found the mysteries of novels especially gripping* doesn't catch the meaning). The verb *liked* (A) correctly continues the past tense in *found*. The comma in (B) is fine as the sentence stands because the second clause is dependent. In (D), the adverb *especially* is used correctly to modify *gripping*.

11. E

This sentence is correct as written. Choice (A) is idiomatically correct. Choice (B) is correctly in the past tense. Choice (C) correctly introduces the intervening phrase, and (D) uses the correct preposition.

12. E

This sentence is complicated, so take it one part at a time. Choice (A) correctly refers to *the dancer*. Choice (B) is the correct noun to be placed directly after the introductory clause. Choice (C) is idiomatically correct. Choice (D) uses the possessive to refer to its *loose and full breathing methods*.

13. B

As written, this sentence is a fragment because there is no verb. Choice (B) can be changed to *diseases is frequently*, creating a full sentence. Choices (A) and (D) are idiomatically correct. Choice (C) correctly sets up a causal relationship.

14. C

The word *upcoming* indicates that the workshop is in the future, but the sentence is in the present tense. In (C), the verb *conducts* should be in the future tense (*will conduct*). Choices (A) and (B) are idiomatically correct. Choice (D) agrees with the noun *workshop*.

15. B

The two main clauses of the sentence are not parallel. The subject of the two clauses should be the same, linked by the comparison word *but*. The subject *football games* is parallel to the personal pronoun *they*. Choice (B) corrects this problem and correctly omits the relative pronoun *that*. Choice (D) removes the subject from the second clause altogether and also unnecessarily interchanges the transition words *however* and *but*. Choices (C) and (E) substitute the relative pronoun *that* for the correct personal pronoun *they*.

16. E

The word *relentless* modifies the verb *studied* and so should be an adverb. Choices (C), (D), and (E) correctly change *studied relentless* to *studied relentlessly*. Choices (C) and (E) also change *for passing* to the idiomatically correct *to pass*, but (C) changes the meaning by altering the word order so that *relentlessly* modifies the verb *pass* instead of *studied*. Choice (B) doesn't address the adverb issue.

17. B

The verb tenses should reflect the fact that the second clause happened after the first clause. Choices (B) and (E) correct the verb tense problem, but only (B) is correct idiomatically. Choice (E) incorrectly substitutes *had been* for *got*. Choice (C) incorrectly adds the gerund *showing*. Choice (D) changes the meaning by putting the word *once* in front.

18. C

This is a sentence fragment; there is no verb in an independent clause. The verb *combine* in the second clause is made subordinate by the conjunction *that*. Only (B) and (C) add the needed verb *are*, and only (C) retains the meaning. Choice (B) incorrectly states that the compositions themselves are actually suggesting. Choices (D) and (E) don't correct the original problem.

19. D

There is no noun for the introductory clause to modify. *They* were looking through the school's telescope, so *they* needs to begin the second clause. Choices (D) and (E) both do this but (E) incorrectly uses the past tense for *flew* (*they saw a star flew* should be *they saw a star fly*). Choice (B) doesn't add a noun, and (C) adds the wrong noun. The shooting star didn't look through the telescope.

20. C

The two phrases at the end of the sentence are not parallel: *entertaining* is an adjective; *educate* is a verb. Both phrases must either describe the library (adjective) or what the library does (verb). Choice (C) correctly changes the verb *educate* to the adjective *educational* so that the library is entertaining and educational. Choice (B) makes this change but adds *being* which is not parallel to *to be*. Choice (D) simply changes the plural verb *educate* to the singular verb *educates*. Choice (E) changes the verb *educate* to the noun *education*.

21. A

The sentence is correct as it is—two independent clauses joined by a semicolon. Choice (B) changes the sequence of events. Choices (C) and (D) change the meaning from the Queen wanting strong rule to English society wanting strong rule. Choice (C) also creates a run-on. Choice (E) incorrectly forms a dependent clause after the semicolon.

22. D

The sentence sets up a contrast: we don't know if there is other life in the universe, but people have seen UFOs. We need a contrast transition word. Only (D) adds *but* and so is the correct answer. Choice (C) keeps the transition word *and*. Choices (B) and (E) don't include a transition word.

23. A

This is a complicated sentence, but it is correct. Home-team loyalty (the sentence's first clause) allows all of the second clause to happen. Choices (B) and (D) state that the feat was attempted as staggering instead of proclaimed as staggering. Choice (C) illogically puts the second clause in the past tense. Choice (E) is a sentence fragment.

24. E

The introductory phrase incorrectly modifies *the deterioration*. The deterioration was not nervous, the leaders were. Choices (D) and (E) correct the modification problem, but only (E) uses the correct verb tense and pronoun. Choice (D) incorrectly uses the present perfect tense and the pronoun *their*, which would indicate the leaders' rather than society's collapse. Choices (B) and (C) don't correct the modification problem.

25. C

Who's *they*? The ties or the women? From a commonsense perspective, of course, it has to be the ties. But *they* has an unclear antecedent, and to make this sentence correct you need to find a choice that makes it clear that the sentence is referring to the ties. Both (C) and (D) begin with the noun *ties* and are good places to start. Since you didn't identify

any problem with the verb, (C), which maintains the original verb, looks like a good choice. Sure enough, when you check out (D), you see that it uses *being*. Be wary of any verb constructions that use *being*. On the PSAT, they are often incorrect.

26. B

Choice (B) is the clearest and most concise choice. All the other choices use overly wordy and imprecise constructions.

27. A

The original sentence is best. Choice (B) is confusingly wordy. The remaining choices are idiomatically incorrect, with (D) and (E) unnecessarily using the present perfect tense instead of the simple past.

28. C

Having read the works describes the speaker, so you know that the correct answer will have *I* as the first word (the way the sentence is written, it sounds as though *Hemingway* read the works, because his name is placed directly after the modifying phrase). Only (C) and (E) begin with *I*, but (E) introduces yet another misplaced modifier (it says the speaker is a writer, not Hemingway).

29. B

The key to this question is realizing what Aunt Helga appreciates: it's not *us*, but our act of coming to her birthday party. *Our coming* correctly phrases this idea; *coming* is a gerund (a verb form that acts as a noun), and *our* is a possessive pronoun. *Us coming* is a common mistake; it's wrong because the pronoun *us* is not in the possessive form. Choice (E) rephrases the sentence to makes *us* the correct object of Aunt Helga's appreciation, but it is unnecessarily wordy.

30. D

Idiomatically, *the same* should be followed by the preposition *as*, not *than*. There is also a problem of parallelism here: the two things being compared should be in the same grammatical form. Because *talking* is a gerund, the thing it's being compared to should also be a gerund: *driving*.

31. C

This run-on sentence is best corrected by (C), which is grammatically correct and doesn't include extra verbiage. Choices (B) and (E) use the semicolon improperly, and (D) is wordy.

32. E

The sentence is unclear because it doesn't use the correct sequence of tenses. Because the client had already been waiting for 15 minutes before the moment when the receptionist looked up, the first verb must be in the past perfect: *had been waiting*.

33. B

There is an error of subordination here. To express the causal relationship between melting ice caps and the flooding of islands, you need only one conjunction: *because* or *therefore*. To have both is redundant.

34. C

This sentence fragment is best corrected by moving the verb *was* and inserting a comma after the introductory phrase describing Flaubert.

THE PRESIDENTIAL OFFICE PASSAGE

35. C

There is no plural noun before *they* so we must read further. Sentence 3 states that the Founding Fathers considered it *dangerous* for the President to gain power from popularity. Therefore, it is the Founding Fathers who *feared popular leadership*, and (C) is correct. Choice (A) is out of scope; revolutionaries are never mentioned, just the Revolution itself. Choice (B) is illogical; complications cannot fear anything. Choices (D) and (E) pick up the wrong words from sentence 3.

36. D

Adding a phrase to the beginning of sentence 5 will probably set up its relationship to sentence 4. Sentence 5 makes a conclusion based on the Founders' idea in sentence 4. Choice (D) refers to the Founders and shows that sentence 5 definitely follows from sentence 4. Choice (A) uses the first person, although the author never refers to herself in the passage. Choices (B) and (C) incorrectly set up a contrast between sentences 5 and 4. Choice (C) also adds the pronoun *him*, which doesn't clearly refer to anyone. Choice (E) creates a sentence fragment.

37. D

We are given two short sentences and asked to combine them; we must determine their relationship to each other and the passage. Sentence 6 states that Washington is an example of the ideas in paragraph 2. Sentence 7 explains why he is a good example. Choice (D) combines the sentences and adds the causal word *because*. It also puts the first part of the sentence in present tense (he is an example) and changes *asked* to *wanted*. Choice (B) incorrectly uses the contrast transition word *although*. Choice (C) omits the idea that this is an example. Choice (E) uses the ambiguous pronoun *they* instead of *the Founders* and also is a run-on.

38. E

This sentence confuses tenses. Andrew Jackson acted in the past to make the presidency what it is in the present. Choice (E) correctly puts *makes* in the past tense. Choice (A) is incorrect because *he* is not ambiguous; *he* clearly refers to Andrew Jackson. Choice (B) is illogical; the president isn't a popularity contest, the presidency is. Choice (C) puts what is happening in the present into the past tense. Choice (D) changes to the past perfect tense, which would work only if a later action by Jackson was mentioned.

39. C

As written, the sentence states that *many people* may have been wrong. But the author's point is that the Founders may have been wrong. Choice (C) corrects that problem and substitutes *the Founders* for the ambiguous pronoun *they*. Choices (A) and (B) change the meaning to say that the people actively suggested that the Founders were wrong. Choice (D) uses the wrong transition word; it should be a word that indicates contrasts with sentence 15. Choice (E) is a run-on sentence with a comma splice.

CHAPTER 11: COMPUTE YOUR SCORE

These scores are intended to give you an approximate idea of your performance. There is no way to determine your exact score for the following reasons.

- Various statistical factors and formulas are taken into account on the real test.
- For each grade, the scaled score range changes from year to year.

The official score range for each subject of the PSAT will be 20–80. Taken together, the perfect total score becomes 240. The subject scores correspond to the SAT score range of 200–800.

STEP 1: FIGURE OUT YOUR RAW SCORE FOR THE DIAGNOSTIC TEST AND EACH PRACTICE TEST

First, check your answers against the answer keys on the previous pages, and count up the number of right and the number of wrong answers for each section (except for Grid-ins, where you do not lose points for wrong answers). Remember, do not count questions left blank as wrong. Round up to the nearest whole number.

DIAGNOSTIC TEST

	Number Right	Number Wrong	Raw Score

CRITICAL READING

Sections 1 & 3: ☐ − (.25 × ☐) = ☐

Critical Reading Raw Score = ☐

WRITING

Section 5: ☐ − (.25 × ☐) = ☐

Writing Raw Score = ☐

MATH

Section 2: ☐ − (.25 × ☐) = ☐

Section 4A:
(QUESTIONS 19–28) ☐ − (.25 × ☐) = ☐

Section 4B:
(QUESTIONS 29–38) ☐ (no wrong answer penalty) = ☐

Math Raw Score = ☐

PRACTICE TEST ONE

	Number Right		Number Wrong			Raw Score

CRITICAL READING

Sections 1 & 3: ☐ − (.25 × ☐) = ☐

Critical Reading Raw Score = ☐

WRITING

Section 5: ☐ − (.25 × ☐) = ☐

Writing Raw Score = ☐

MATH

Section 2: ☐ − (.25 × ☐) = ☐

Section 4A:
(QUESTIONS 19–28) ☐ − (.25 × ☐) = ☐

Section 4B:
(QUESTIONS 29–38) ☐ (no wrong answer penalty) = ☐

Math Raw Score = ☐

PRACTICE TEST TWO

	Number Right	Number Wrong	Raw Score

CRITICAL READING

Sections 1 & 3: ☐ − (.25 × ☐) = ☐

Critical Reading Raw Score = ☐

WRITING

Section 5: ☐ − (.25 × ☐) = ☐

Writing Raw Score = ☐

MATH

Section 2: ☐ − (.25 × ☐) = ☐

Section 4A:
(QUESTIONS 19–28) ☐ − (.25 × ☐) = ☐

Section 4B:
(QUESTIONS 29–38) ☐ (no wrong answer penalty) = ☐

Math Raw Score = ☐

PRACTICE TEST THREE

	Number Right	Number Wrong		Raw Score

CRITICAL READING

Sections 1 & 3: ☐ − (.25 × ☐) = ☐

Critical Reading Raw Score = ☐

WRITING

Section 5: ☐ − (.25 × ☐) = ☐

Writing Raw Score = ☐

MATH

Section 2: ☐ − (.25 × ☐) = ☐

Section 4A:
(QUESTIONS 19–28) ☐ − (.25 × ☐) = ☐

Section 4B:
(QUESTIONS 29–38) ☐ (no wrong answer penalty) = ☐

Math Raw Score = ☐

STEP 2: CONVERT YOUR RAW SCORE TO A SCALED SCORE

For each subject area in the Practice Test, convert your raw score to your scaled score using the table below.

RAW SCORE	SCALED SCORE* Critical Reading	Math	Writing
48	80		
47	80		
46	79		
45	78		
44	77		
43	76		
42	75		
41	74		
40	73		
39	72		80
38	71	80	80
37	70	80	79
36	69	78	78
35	68	76	77
34	67	74	76
33	66	73	74
32	65	72	73
31	64	71	72
30	63	70	70
29	62	69	69
28	61	68	68
27	60	66	67
26	59	65	66
25	58	64	64
24	57	63	63
23	56	62	62
22	55	60	60
21	54	59	59

RAW SCORE	SCALED SCORE* Critical Reading	Math	Writing
20	53	58	57
19	52	57	56
18	51	55	55
17	50	53	53
16	49	51	52
15	48	50	50
14	47	49	49
13	46	48	47
12	44	47	46
11	43	46	44
10	42	45	43
9	41	44	42
8	40	42	41
7	39	41	40
6	38	40	39
5	36	39	38
4	35	38	36
3	34	36	34
2	33	35	32
1	32	34	30
0	30	32	29
−1	29	30	28
−2	28	28	26
−3	27	26	25
−4	26	24	24
−5	24	22	23
−6	22	21	21
−7	20	20	20

*Unofficial scores; for guidance purposes only

| Part Five |

PSAT RESOURCES

SAT ESSAY PREVIEW

This section has nothing to do with your PSAT preparation. This section is only for the student who is using the PSAT to practice for the SAT or the student who plans to take the SAT next year. Is that you? If so, read on.

The PSAT does not have an essay, but the SAT does. You can consider this appendix your practice for the SAT's essay. (Of course our SAT book has lots more on the SAT essay, but we wanted to at least give you some advance warning in the PSAT book as well.)

The SAT Writing section is divided into three parts—an essay section and two multiple-choice sections. The multiple-choice sections are a lot like the PSAT's multiple-choice Writing section. The essay is totally different.

THE SAT ESSAY

For the essay portion of the test, your task is to write a short, *persuasive* essay on an assigned topic. The word *persuasive* is key. You can write the best essay ever on a meaningful experience or ways to become more involved in your community, but if you have not persuaded the reader to see things from a particular point of view, you won't earn a high score.

You are required to write about the topic you are given, but you don't need any specific knowledge to complete the SAT essay, and you do have a lot of freedom in what you actually write. Because the topic will be very broad in scope, you can write about what you know and are interested in.

ESSAY DIRECTIONS

The College Board has stated that the directions for the essay will look like the following:

The essay gives you an opportunity to show how effectively you can develop and express ideas. You should, therefore, take care to develop your point of view, present your ideas logically and clearly, and use language precisely.

Your essay must be written in your Answer Grid Booklet—you will receive no other paper on which to write. You will have enough space if you write on every line, avoid wide margins, and keep your handwriting to a reasonable size. Remember that people who are not familiar with your handwriting will read what you write. Try to write or print so that what you are writing is legible to those readers.

You have twenty-five minutes to write an essay on the topic assigned below. DO NOT WRITE ON ANOTHER TOPIC. AN OFF-TOPIC ESSAY WILL RECEIVE A SCORE OF ZERO.

Think carefully about the issue presented in the following excerpt and the assignment below.

> "The longer I live the more I see that I am never wrong about anything, and that all the pains I have so humbly taken to verify my notions have only wasted my time."
>
> —George Bernard Shaw

Assignment: Is a certain amount of arrogance a good human quality? In an essay, support your position by discussing an example (or examples) from literature, science and technology, the arts, current events, or your own experience or observation.

DO NOT WRITE YOUR ESSAY IN YOUR TEST BOOK.
You will receive credit only for what you write in your Answer Grid Booklet.

Essay Scoring

The essays will be scored quickly and *holistically* by two readers. *Holistically* means your essay gets a single score—a number—that indicates its overall quality. This number takes into account a variety of essay characteristics, including organization and development of ideas, sentence structure, vocabulary, and grammar and usage. Thus, a highly persuasive and eloquent essay that has several run-ons or other minor errors could still earn a top score because of its overall effectiveness and impact.

Each reader will assign your essay a score ranging from a high of 6 to a low of 1. These two scores are added together to get a total score ranging from a high of 12 to a low of 2. The essay score accounts for one-third of your final SAT Writing section score.

The following chart is a rubric that shows the main criteria that the graders use to score your essay.

THE ESSAY SCORING CHART

Score	Demonstrates	Organization	Language
6	clear and consistent competence, though it may have errors	is well organized and fully developed with supporting examples	displays consistent language facility, varied sentence structure, and range of vocabulary
5	reasonable competence, with occasional errors or lapses in quality	is generally organized and well developed with appropriate examples	displays language facility, with syntactic variety and a range of vocabulary
4	adequate competence, with occasional errors and lapses in quality	is organized and adequately developed with examples	displays adequate but inconsistent language facility
3	developing competence, with weaknesses	inadequate organization or development	many errors in grammar or diction; little variety
2	some incompetence, with one or more weaknesses	poor organization, thin development	frequent errors in grammar and diction; no variety
1	incompetence, with serious flaws	no organization, no development	severe grammar and diction errors obscure meaning

Here is what this means in plainer English:

6 OUTSTANDING ESSAY

Convincingly and insightfully fulfills the writing assignment; ideas are well developed, clearly presented, and logically organized; superior command of vocabulary, grammar, style, and accepted conventions of writing; a few minor flaws may occur.

5 SOLID ESSAY

Convincingly fulfills the writing assignment; ideas are adequately developed, clearly presented, and logically organized; strong command of vocabulary, grammar, style, and accepted conventions of writing; some minor flaws may occur.

4 ADEQUATE ESSAY

Fulfills the writing assignment; ideas are adequately developed, presented, and organized; satisfactory command of vocabulary, grammar, style, and accepted conventions of writing; some flaws may occur.

3 LIMITED ESSAY

Doesn't adequately fulfill the writing assignment; lacks adequate development and organization of ideas; unsatisfactory command of vocabulary, grammar, style, and accepted conventions of writing; contains many flaws.

2 FLAWED ESSAY

Doesn't fulfill the writing assignment; ideas are vague, poorly presented, and not logically organized; poor command of vocabulary, grammar, style, and accepted conventions of writing; contains numerous serious flaws.

1 DEFICIENT ESSAY

Doesn't fulfill the writing assignment; ideas are extremely vague, very poorly presented, and not logically organized; extremely poor command of vocabulary, grammar, style, and accepted conventions of writing; is so seriously flawed that basic meaning is obscured.

ESSAY STRATEGIES

To help you achieve a high-scoring SAT essay, Kaplan has developed an SAT essay-writing strategy called THINK-ORGANIZE-WRITE-FIX, otherwise known as TOWF. After you read your essay topic, you:

THINK about the topic (2 minutes)
ORGANIZE your ideas (5 minutes)
WRITE your essay (15 minutes)
FIX any mistakes (3 minutes)

Here's our minute-by-minute rundown of the TOWF method.

Minutes 1–2: Think

This step takes two minutes. That leaves you 23 minutes to organize, write, and fix your essay. We suggest that you wait to write anything down during these two minutes and just brainstorm. There's plenty of time for writing later. But if it helps you to jot notes down while you think, then go for it.

Let's say that you get the following quote:

> "A man walking down a crowded street noticed a dog lying by the side of the road that looked like it might be injured; but since everyone else just passed by, the man was satisfied to assume that the dog was fine. The next day he learned that the dog had been hit by a car and lay injured for two hours before a concerned man stopped and took it to the vet. The animal recovered, but the man never forgave himself for leaving it for someone else to help."
>
> —Narawhal Bherundi, *Autobiography*

Assignment: What is your view on individual responsibility in a situation in which many people could have reacted?

Then the assignment asks you to take a specific example from your personal experience, from current events, or from history, literature, or any other discipline and develop it to support your persuasive argument, using the quote as a guidepost.

Pick a Stance

In this essay, you must decide what your stance will be concerning individual responsibility. For example, if you believe that human beings do not have any obligation to help others, then you will want to build your argument around a particular story or experience explaining just that. Or you might believe that everyone is responsible for the welfare of others, even strangers, and thus you would write to persuade the reader of that. What's important is that you take a position and state how you feel. It is not important what other people might think, just what you think, so avoid statements such as "some people feel …" or "a lot of people think … " Get the picture?

Choose Your Examples

Once you have picked your stance, you must choose examples that back up your argument. Think up two to three specific examples that you can write about intelligently and passionately. You could use an example from history, such as Mother Teresa and her life's work of helping others. You could use the scenario of a

EXPERT TUTOR TIP

" Note that the actual essay question comes after the Assignment. Make sure you answer that and don't get lost in the quotation, which sometimes can take a very specific slant on the question. That doesn't mean that the quotation is useless, however. One effective strategy for building an introduction to your essay is to argue with the author of the quote. See if you can spin the author's words to your end or use them to spark some brainstorming. "

EXPERT TUTOR TIP

" Practice brainstorming essays. Take five to seven minutes and plot out a thesis, as much evidence as you can muster, an order for that evidence, linking transitions, and a conclusion. "

bystander witnessing a mugging. You could use an example from your life, like how you were stranded on the side of a road, and no one would stop to see if you needed help.

USE SPECIFIC EVIDENCE

You've got to cite evidence to support your examples. When you are thinking of your examples, also think about one piece of evidence for each of them. Remember, arguing your point of view without having a good reason is not convincing and won't get you your highest essay score. For instance, you could cite the many visits Mother Teresa made to impoverished countries as evidence for the before-mentioned example.

MINUTES 3–7: ORGANIZE

This step takes up to five minutes. That may seem like a lot of time to spend before you write a single essay sentence. But taking a few minutes to organize your essay is definitely worth the time. If you take a few minutes to organize what you want to write, the essay will be a lot easier to write once you start it.

So you have your argument, your examples, and your evidence in your head. It's time to plan your essay. Use the scratch paper that is provided for you. Here is one way that your essay paragraphs could be organized:

FIRST PARAGRAPH

Clearly state your argument.
Briefly mention the evidence that you're going to cite in support of that argument.

MIDDLE PARAGRAPHS (2–3 PARAGRAPHS)

Explore and explain your evidence in detail. These paragraphs explain how the evidence supports the argument.

LAST PARAGRAPH

Briefly summarize your argument.

Let's try it out. We'll go with humans having an obligation to help others.

- **P1.** Humans should take initiative to help/individual can have an effect.
- **P2.** Shirking responsibility/sister stuck on side of road/no one stopped/had to make a dangerous walk.
- **P3.** Personal experience/girl lost/walked her to class/made a new friend.
- **P4.** Everyone has a responsibility to help, even if others don't.

MINUTES 8–22: WRITE

The writing step of your essay should take about 15 minutes. That's plenty of time to write three to five solid paragraphs if you work from a prepared outline.

To write your strongest essay, follow your outline. You spent five minutes thinking about and organizing your essay, so stick to it! Don't panic and write from the opposing point of view. However, if you come up with the perfect example halfway through your essay, replace it in your outline, see how it works, then continue. But *try try try* not to erase and rewrite any big chunks of text. Trust yourself.

You also need to write clearly, write concisely, write complete sentences, and use proper grammar. If you do this on test day, your essay WILL be well written. But you only have 15 minutes. So write fast. Here is a quickly written essay (a draft version, you might say) about responsibility:

> An individual can have a major effect on another individual or situation. In the example above, an individual save a dog's life. A group of people ignored the situation but an individual man actually did something. He stepped out of the mob mentality. Everyone else conformed to each other and walked by. This man stopped and saved the dog.
>
> However, the primary man in the example did not do so. He conformed and walked by. He shirked his responsibility. This is like that one time my sister needed help and didn't get it. On her way home from college, she had car trouble and was stranded on the side of the road at night. Many cars passed by but no one stopped to see if they could give her a hand. After waiting for forever, she ended up having to walk to the nearest gas station two miles away, which is not safe for a young girl to do by herself. Here, no individual took responsibility to help her, and this refusal of responsibility could have led to more severe consequences.
>
> On a lighter but related note, I had personal experience with individual responsibility. At the beginning of last year, I was walking to first period science class when I noticed a confused, nervous girl standing in the hallway. She looked like she was about to cry as everyone rushed past her. She was obviously lost, but no one who knew the way took responsibility to help her. I felt badly so approached her and asked if I could help. It turned out that she had just moved from another part of the country and knew no one at my high school. She couldn't find her science class, which turned out to be my science class, and was too shy

EXPERT TUTOR TIP

" If you've thought and planned well, the production phase should be about style, not content—how best to express your ideas, not coming up with them on the fly. Trust your plan. You'll be surprised how much you can get down on paper in 15 long minutes. "

to ask for help. I walked with her to science class, made a new friend, and took the responsibility to help someone.

At the end of the day, everyone has the responsibility not to conform in a situation in which many people can react. Each person should be the individual who takes action and helps. No one should assume that someone else will take responsibility, because maybe no one will.

Minutes 23–25: Fix

This step takes three minutes. It involves proofreading and fixing your essay. Hopefully, all you'll need to do is fix minor grammatical or spelling errors, change a few words here and there, and maybe add a sentence or two for clarity's sake.

If you spend the bulk of the 25 minutes thinking about, organizing, and writing the essay, the repair step should entail nothing more than putting the finishing touches on an already strong essay.

Here is our fixed-up essay:

> An individual can have a major effect on another individual or situation. In the example above, an individual <u>saved</u> a dog's life. A group of people ignored the <u>situation, but</u> an individual man actually did something. He stepped out of the mob mentality. Everyone else conformed to each other and walked by. This man stopped and saved the dog.
>
> However, <u>the man</u> in the example did not do so. He conformed and walked by. He shirked his responsibility. <u>This relates to a situation that my sister experienced</u>. On her way home from college, she had car trouble and was stranded on the side of the road at night. Many cars passed <u>by, but</u> no one stopped to see if they could give her a hand. After waiting for <u>over an hour</u>, she ended up having to walk to the nearest gas station two miles away, which is not safe for a young girl to do by herself. Here, no individual took responsibility to help her, and this refusal of responsibility could have led to more severe consequences.
>
> On a lighter but related note, I <u>had a personal</u> experience with individual responsibility. At the beginning of last year, I was walking to first period science class when I noticed a confused, nervous girl standing in the hallway. She looked like she was about to cry as everyone rushed past her. She was obviously lost, but no one who knew the way took responsibility to help her. I felt <u>bad for her, so I approached</u> her and asked if I could help. It turned out that she had just moved from another part of the country

and knew no one at my high school. She couldn't find her science class, which turned out to be my science class, and was too shy to ask for help. I walked with her to science class, made a new friend, and took the responsibility to help someone.

At the end of the day, everyone has the responsibility not to conform in a situation in which many people can react. Each person should be the individual who takes action and helps. No one should assume that someone else will take responsibility, because maybe no one will.

SAMPLE ESSAYS AND GRADERS' COMMENTS

Here are three sample essays pertaining to the assignment below and how an SAT grader would probably grade them.

The essay gives you an opportunity to show how effectively you can develop and express ideas. You should, therefore, take care to develop your point of view, present your ideas logically and clearly, and use language precisely.

Your essay must be written in your Answer Grid Booklet—you will receive no other paper on which to write. You will have enough space if you write on every line, avoid wide margins, and keep your handwriting to a reasonable size. Remember that people who are not familiar with your handwriting will read what you write. Try to write or print so that what you are writing is legible to those readers.

You have twenty-five minutes to write an essay on the topic assigned below. DO NOT WRITE ON ANOTHER TOPIC. AN OFF-TOPIC ESSAY WILL RECEIVE A SCORE OF ZERO.

Think carefully about the issue presented in the following excerpt and the assignment below.

"Don't flatter yourself that friendship authorizes you to say disagreeable things to your intimates. The nearer you come into relation with a person, the more necessary do tact and courtesy become. Except in cases of necessity, which are rare, leave your friend to learn unpleasant things from his enemies; they are ready enough to tell them."

—Oliver Wendell Holmes,
The Autocrat of the Breakfast-Table

"A good friend can tell you what is the matter with you in a minute. He may not seem such a good friend after telling."

—Arthur Brisbane, *The Book of Today*

Assignment: Should friends be honest with each other, even if a truthful comment could be hurtful? In an essay, support your position by discussing an example (or examples) from literature, science and technology, the arts, current events, or your own experience or observation.

DO NOT WRITE YOUR ESSAY IN YOUR TEST BOOK.
You will receive credit only for what you write in your Answer Grid Booklet.

GRADE 6 ESSAY

One of the defining qualities of a good friendship is that both friends can be completely honest with each other. This does not mean that the two friends don't consider each others feelings or blurt out comments without thinking, but it does mean that each person can rely on the other to tell the truth, even if the truth can sometimes be awkward or hurtful.

My sister and I have always been close friends, even when we were younger. When my sister was in junior high school and I was in elementary school, she decided to get her hair permed because all of her friends were doing the same thing. Unfortunately, the treatment didn't work well on her hair and she ended up with a big, frizzy clump of curls that stuck out on the sides. Most of her friends didn't have the courage to tell her that it didn't look good. Instead, they just made fun of her behind her back. So it was up to me to tell her the truth. I was a bit scared to confront my older sister, because I knew that she would be upset. But I also knew that she would be more upset if no one dared to be honest with her. A few years earlier, we were in the opposite roles, and she had gently but firmly advised me against a choice that I later realized would have been embarrassing for me when I started school.

Although my sister was hurt when I told her that the perm didn't look good, she was more hurt to learn that some of her other friends had thought the same thing but hadn't said anything to her. She was angry with me at first for making a negative comment, but in the end she was glad I had told her so that she could go back to the hair

> **EXPERT TUTOR TIP**
>
> " Read editorials from highly regarded newspapers and magazines such as the *New York Times, Washington Post, Wall Street Journal, Time, Newsweek,* etc. Try to figure out how the authors are creating their arguments and then emulate their tactics. Imitation is the sincerest form of flattery after all! "

stylist to fix the problem. Since my sister was very concerned about her appearance and personal style at that time in her life, she appreciated my honesty because it helped her get through a tough situation and our friendship grew stronger as a result of this experience.

In the years since this incident, my sister and I have both continued to be honest and up front with each other, and we value this aspect of our relationship. After all, friendly honesty is far better than hostile honesty, so being a good friend involves telling the truth, no matter what the circumstances. Honesty truly is an essential component of a good friendship.

Grader's Comments: The author begins this essay with a clear statement based on the prompt, showing that she has clearly understood the topic. The remainder of the essay presents and develops an example to support her opinion. The example provided is relevant to multiple aspects of the prompt—the importance of honesty in friendship as well as the possibility that being honest can be difficult in certain situations.

The essay is well organized, with a clear narrative flow framed by a cohesive introduction and conclusion. The structure of the essay reflects that the author took time to plan before writing and carefully followed her plan as she composed her essay. Although the vocabulary used in the essay is not very sophisticated, the author's ideas are communicated effectively. Finally, there are few grammatical or spelling errors: *others* instead of *other's* in the first paragraph; a couple of sentences lacked commas in the second and third paragraphs. This author clearly managed her time effectively so that she could proofread her essay.

GRADE 4 ESSAY

Being honest is part of being a good friend. However, their are times when you shouldn't be completely honest because what you say might hurt your friend's feelings.

For example, imagine that your best friend tells you his parents are getting divorced. He is obviously upset by this even though you know his parents haven't been getting along well because he constantly complained about their fights and even joked about hoping they'd get a divorce so he wouldn't have to listen to them anymore. In this situation, reminding your friend of his earlier comments or pointing out that his parents will be happier apart isn't the right thing to do because at a time like this you're friend doesn't need you to tell him the harsh truth, he needs you to by sympathetic and supportive. It's pretty likely that he'll hear all about the negative things from other people or even from his parents, so your job as his best friend is to try not to say or do anything unpleasant.

Another example could be if you're friend has bought something that she's really excited about. You might not agree that she's made a good choice or you might not like what she bought, but you don't need to spoil her enthusiasm by making a negative comment. Again, this is a time when you should keep quiet about your own opinion so that your friend can be happy.

There are certain situations when it's okay not to tell the complete truth to your friends. You should never lie to your friends, but an important part of being a good friend is knowing when to be totally honest and when to keep silent because a truthful comment could do more harm than good.

Grader's Comments: The author introduces his essay with a clear statement of his opinion, showing that he has understood the prompt. His two examples provide decent support for the topic, but the second example is vague and not well developed. The author would have a stronger essay if he expanded upon the prompt and provided additional details for the first example rather than trying to include a weak second example. Having a clear plan could help to accomplish this change in structure.

The essay is fairly well organized, with several key words (*however*, *for example*, *another example*, *again*) that add structure to the author's argument. The weakest parts of this essay are some simplistic language and awkward sentences: in the second paragraph, the second sentence is long and wordy, and the third sentence is a run-on sentence and is very difficult to follow, so the author's meaning almost gets obscured by the effort it takes to decipher his thoughts. There are also a few usage/spelling errors: *their* instead of *they're* in the first paragraph; *you're* instead of *your* in the second and third paragraphs. The author needs to be more deliberate when writing the essay and needs to proofread to catch these spelling errors and prevent run-on sentences or awkward sentence structure.

GRADE 2 ESSAY

No matter what, friends should tell each other the truth. That's the whole point of having friends, so you have some people around you that you can trust and talk to and that you know will tell you everything.

Friends can tell you negative things in a kind way so you can here the truth even if its not so good. Enemies tell you the same negative things in a mean way because their trying to hurt you. But friends can accomplish this in a nicer way.

Its important to know and learn the truth even if its about yourself or its something you don't want to face. You need honest friends to tell you the truth, because they do it out of love not hate like enemies.

Grader's Comments: This author starts strongly with a clear statement of her opinion, which is directly related to the topic of the prompt. However, the author continues with a series of generalizations, none of which are specific examples to support her opinion. She needs to spend more time planning her essay to make sure that she's got at least one strong example to include to support her argument.

This essay does not follow an organized structure, and it lacks good transitions and key words. To improve this part of her writing, the author should make an outline during her planning stage and should focus on using several key words while she writes, which will give her essay a stronger and clearer structure.

The author's language is simplistic and repetitive. The essay contains several grammatical and spelling errors: *that* twice instead of *whom/who* when referring to people in the first paragraph; *here* and *their* are misused for *hear* and *they're* in the second paragraph; *its* is misused numerous times for *it's* in the second and third paragraphs. The author should study the SAT grammar materials to improve this aspect of her writing and should also be sure to proofread to avoid careless errors.

WORD FAMILIES

These lists group words with related meanings. Often, even simply knowing the general concept that a word is associated with will be enough to help you choose the correct answer on the Reading sections of the PSAT.

❑ **Talkative**

garrulous
glib
loquacious
raconteur
verbose
voluble

❑ **Secret/Hidden**

abscond
alias
arcane
clandestine
covert
cryptic
enigma
furtive
incognito
inconspicuous
lurk
obscure
skulk
subterranean
surreptitious

❑ **Not Talkative**

concise
curt
laconic
pithy
reticent
succinct
taciturn

❑ **Praise**

accolade
adulation
commend
eulogize
exalt
extol
laud
lionize
plaudit
revere

❑ **Criticize/Scold**

admonish
berate
castigate
censure
chastise
defame
denigrate
disdain
disparage
excoriate
malign
obloquy
rail
rebuke
reproach
reprimand
reprove
revile
upbraid
vilify

❑ **Stubborn**

intractable
mulish
obdurate
obstinate
pertinacious
recalcitrant
refractory
tenacious

❑ **Lazy/Lacking Energy**

indolent
lackadaisical
laggard
languid
lassitude
lethargic
listless
loiter
phlegmatic
sluggard
somnolent
torpid

❑ **Cowardly**

craven
diffident
pusillanimous
timid
timorous

❑ **Inexperienced**

callow
fledgling
infantile
ingenuous
neophyte
novice
tyro

❑ **Obedient**

amenable
assent
compliant
deferential
docile
pliant
submissive
tractable

❑ **Haughty/Pretentious**

affected
aloof
bombastic
grandiloquent
grandiose
magniloquent
mannered
ostentatious
pontificate
supercilious

❑ **Friendly**

affable
amiable
amicable
bonhomie
convivial
gregarious

❑ **Lucky**

auspicious
fortuitous
opportune
serendipity

❑ **Soothe**

allay
alleviate
anodyne
assuage
liniment
mitigate
mollify
pacify
palliate
placate

❑ **Hostility/Hatred**

abhor
anathema
animosity
antagonism
antipathy
aversion
contentious
deplore
odious
rancor

❑ **Stupid**

buffoon
dolt
dupe
fatuous
imbecile
inane
insipid
obtuse
simpleton
vacuous
vapid

❑ **Subservient**

fawn
grovel
obsequious
servile
subjection
sycophant
toady

❑ **Argumentative**

adversarial
bellicose
belligerent
fractious
irascible
obstreperous
pugnacious
quibble

❑ **Cautious**

chary
circumspect
discretion
leery
prudent
wary

❑ **Impermanent**

ephemeral
evanescent
fleeting
transient
transitory

❑ **Ability/Intelligence**

acumen
adept
adroit
agile
astute
cogent
deft
dexterous
erudite
literate
lucidity
sagacious
trenchant

❑ **Kind/Generous**

altruistic
beneficent
benevolent
bestow
largess
liberal
magnanimous
munificent
philanthropic

ROOT LIST

The following is a list of some common roots in English, with examples of words that contain them. Familiarity with these basic elements of words can help you decode tough test vocabulary in a pinch.

❑ A, AN—not, without

amoral, atrophy, asymmetrical, anarchy, anesthetic, anonymity, anomaly

❑ AB, A—from, away, apart

abnormal, abdicate, aberration, abhor, abject, abjure, ablution, abnegate, abortive, abrogate, abscond, absolve, abstemious, abstruse, annul, avert, aversion

❑ AC, ACR—sharp, sour

acid, acerbic, exacerbate, acute, acuity, acumen, acrid, acrimony

❑ AD, A—to, toward

adhere, adjacent, adjunct, admonish, adroit, adumbrate, advent, abet, accede, accretion, acquiesce, affluent, aggrandize, aggregate, alleviate, alliteration, allude, allure, ascribe, aspersion, aspire, assail, assonance, attest

❑ ALI, ALTR—another

alias, alienate, inalienable, altruism

❑ AM, AMI—love

amorous, amicable, amiable, amity

❑ AMBI, AMPHI—both

ambiguous, ambivalent, ambidextrous, amphibious

❑ AMBL, AMBUL—walk

amble, ambulatory, perambulator, somnambulist

❑ ANIM—mind, spirit, breath

animal, animosity, unanimous, magnanimous

❑ ANN, ENN—year

annual, annuity, superannuated, biennial, perennial

❑ ANTE, ANT—before

antecedent, antediluvian, antebellum, antepenultimate, anterior, antiquity, antiquated, anticipate

❑ ANTHROP—human

anthropology, anthropomorphic, misanthrope, philanthropy

❑ ANTI, ANT—against, opposite

antidote, antipathy, antithesis, antacid, antagonist, antonym

❑ AUD—hear

audio, audience, audition, auditory, audible

❑ AUTO—self

autobiography, autocrat, autonomous

❑ BELLI, BELL—war

belligerent, bellicose, antebellum, rebellion

❑ BENE, BEN—good

benevolent, benefactor, beneficent, benign

❑ BI—two

bicycle, bisect, bilateral, bilingual, biped

❑ BIBLIO—book

Bible, bibliography, bibliophile

❑ BIO—life

biography, biology, amphibious, symbiotic,
macrobiotic

❑ BURS—money, purse

reimburse, disburse, bursar

❑ CAD, CAS, CID—happen, fall

accident, cadence, cascade, deciduous

❑ CAP, CAPT, CEPT, CIP—take, hold, seize

capable, capacious, captivate, deception, intercept,
precept, inception, anticipate, emancipation,
incipient, percipient

❑ CAP, CIP—head

captain, decapitate, capitulate, precipitous,
precipitate, recapitulate

❑ CARN—flesh

carnal, carnage, carnival, carnivorous, incarnate

❑ CED, CESS—yield, go

cease, cessation, incessant, cede, precede, accede,
recede, antecedent, intercede, secede, cession

❑ CHROM—color

chrome, chromatic, monochrome

❑ CHRON—time

chronology, chronic, anachronism

❑ CIDE—murder

suicide, homicide, infanticide, regicide, patricide

❑ CIRCUM—around

circumference, circumlocution, circumnavigate,
circumscribe, circumspect, circumvent

❑ CLIN, CLIV—slope

incline, inclination, declivity, proclivity

❑ CLUD, CLUS, CLAUS, CLOIS—shut, close

conclude, reclusive, claustrophobia, cloister, preclude,
occlude

❑ CO, COM, CON—with, together

coeducation, coagulate, coalesce, coerce,
cogent, cognate, collateral, colloquial, colloquy,
commensurate, commodious, compassion,
compatriot, complacent, compliant, complicity,
compunction, concerto, conciliatory, concord,
concur, condone, conflagration, congeal, congenial,
congenital, conglomerate, conjugal, conjure,
conscientious, consecrate, consensus, consonant,
constrained, contentious, contrite, contusion,
convalescence, convene, convivial, convoke,
convoluted, congress

❑ COGN, GNO—know

recognize, cognition, cognizance, incognito,
diagnosis, agnostic, prognosis, gnostic, ignorant

❑ CONTRA—against

controversy, incontrovertible, contravene

❑ CORP—body

corpse, corporeal, corpulence

❑ COSMO, COSM—world

cosmopolitan, cosmos, microcosm, macrocosm

❑ CRAC, CRAT—rule, power

democracy, bureaucracy, theocracy, autocrat, aristocrat, technocrat

❑ CRED—trust, believe

incredible, credulous, credence

❑ CRESC, CRET—grow

crescent, crescendo, accretion

❑ CULP—blame, fault

culprit, culpable, inculpate, exculpate

❑ CURR, CURS—run

current, concur, cursory, precursor, incursion

❑ DE—down, out, apart

depart, debase, debilitate, declivity, decry, deface, defamatory, defunct, delegate, delete, demarcation, demean, demur, deplete, deplore, depravity, deprecate, deride, derivative, desist, detest, devoid

❑ DEC—ten, tenth

decade, decimal, decathlon, decimate

❑ DEMO, DEM—people

democrat, demographics, demagogue, epidemic, pandemic, endemic

❑ DI, DIURN—day

diary, quotidian, diurnal

❑ DIA—across

diagonal, diatribe, diaphanous

❑ DIC, DICT—speak

abdicate, diction, interdict, predict, indict, verdict

❑ DIS, DIF, DI—not, apart, away

disaffected, disband, disbar, disburse, discern, discordant, discredit, discursive, disheveled, disparage, disparate, dispassionate, dispirit, dissemble, disseminate, dissension, dissipate, dissonant, dissuade, distend, differentiate, diffidence, diffuse, digress, divert

❑ DOC, DOCT—teach

docile, doctrine, doctrinaire

❑ DOL—pain

condolence, doleful, dolorous, indolent

❑ DUC, DUCT—lead

seduce, induce, conduct, viaduct, induct

❑ EGO—self

ego, egoist, egocentric

❑ EN, EM—in, into

enter, entice, encumber, endemic, ensconce, enthrall, entreat, embellish, embezzle, embroil, empathy

❑ ERR—wander

erratic, aberration, errant

❑ EU—well, good

eulogy, euphemism, euphony, euphoria, eurythmics, euthanasia

❑ EX, E—out, out of

exit, exacerbate, excerpt, excommunicate, exculpate, execrable, exhume, exonerate, exorbitant, exorcise, expatriate, expedient, expiate, expunge, expurgate, extenuate, extort, extremity, extricate, extrinsic, exult, evoke, evict, evince, elicit, egress, egregious

❑ FAC, FIC, FECT, FY, FEA—make, do

factory, facility, benefactor, malefactor, fiction, fictive, beneficent, affect, confection, refectory, magnify, unify, rectify, vilify, feasible

❑ FAL, FALS—deceive

infallible, fallacious, false

❑ FERV—boil

fervent, fervid, effervescent

❑ FID—faith, trust

confident, diffidence, perfidious, fidelity

❑ FLU, FLUX—flow

fluent, affluent, confluence, effluvia, superfluous, flux

❑ FORE—before

forecast, foreboding, forestall

❑ FRAG, FRAC—break

fragment, fracture, diffract, fractious, refract

❑ FUS—pour

profuse, infusion, effusive, diffuse

❑ GEN—birth, class, kin

generation, congenital, homogeneous, heterogeneous, ingenious, engender, progenitor, progeny

❑ GRAD, GRESS—step

graduate, gradual, retrograde, centigrade, degrade, gradation, gradient, progress, congress, digress, transgress, ingress, egress

❑ GRAPH, GRAM—writing

biography, bibliography, epigraph, grammar, epigram

❑ GRAT—pleasing

grateful, gratitude, gratis, ingrate, congratulate, gratuitous, gratuity

❑ GRAV, GRIEV—heavy

grave, gravity, aggravate, grieve, aggrieve, grievous

❑ GREG—crowd, flock

segregate, gregarious, egregious, congregate, aggregate

❑ HABIT, HIBIT—have, hold

habit, cohabit, habitat, inhibit

❑ HAP—by chance

happen, haphazard, hapless, mishap

❑ HELIO, HELI—sun

heliocentric, heliotrope, aphelion, perihelion, helium

❑ HETERO—other

heterosexual, heterogeneous, heterodox

❑ HOL—whole

holocaust, catholic, holistic

❑ HOMO—same

homosexual, homogenize, homogeneous, homonym

❑ HOMO—man

homo sapiens, homicide, bonhomie

❑ HYDR—water

hydrant, hydrate, dehydration

❑ HYPER—too much, excess

hyperactive, hyperbole, hyperventilate

❑ HYPO—too little, under

hypodermic, hypothermia, hypochondria,
hypothesis, hypothetical

❑ IN, IG, IL, IM, IR—not

incorrigible, indefatigable, indelible, indubitable,
inept, inert, inexorable, insatiable, insentient,
insolvent, insomnia, interminable, intractable,
incessant, inextricable, infallible, infamy,
innumerable, inoperable, insipid, intemperate,
intrepid, inviolable, ignorant, ignominious, ignoble,
illicit, illimitable, immaculate, immutable, impasse,
impeccable, impecunious, impertinent, implacable,
impotent, impregnable, improvident, impassioned,
impervious, irregular

❑ IN, IL, IM, IR—in, on, into

invade, inaugurate, incandescent, incarcerate,
incense, indenture, induct, ingratiate, introvert,
incarnate, inception, incisive, infer, infusion, ingress,
innate, inquest, inscribe, insinuate, inter, illustrate,
imbue, immerse, implicate, irrigate, irritate

❑ INTER—between, among

intercede, intercept, interdiction, interject,
interlocutor, interloper, intermediary, intermittent,
interpolate, interpose, interregnum, interrogate,
intersect, intervene

❑ INTRA, INTR—within

intrastate, intravenous, intramural, intrinsic

❑ IT, ITER—between, among

transit, itinerant, transitory, reiterate

❑ JECT, JET—throw

eject, interject, abject, trajectory, jettison

❑ JOUR—day

journal, adjourn, sojourn

❑ JUD—judge

judge, judicious, prejudice, adjudicate

❑ JUNCT, JUG—join

junction, adjunct, injunction, conjugal, subjugate

❑ JUR—swear, law

jury, abjure, adjure, conjure, perjure, jurisprudence

❑ LAT—side

lateral, collateral, unilateral, bilateral, quadrilateral

❑ LAV, LAU, LU—wash

lavatory, laundry, ablution, antediluvian

❑ LEG, LEC, LEX—read, speak

legible, lecture, lexicon

❑ LEV—light

elevate, levitate, levity, alleviate

❑ LIBER—free

liberty, liberal, libertarian, libertine

❑ LIG, LECT—choose, gather
eligible, elect, select

❑ LIG, LI, LY—bind
ligament, oblige, religion, liable, liaison, lien, ally

❑ LING, LANG—tongue
lingo, language, linguistics, bilingual

❑ LITER—letter
literate, alliteration, literal

❑ LITH—stone
monolith, lithograph, megalith

❑ LOQU, LOC, LOG—speech, thought
eloquent, loquacious, colloquial, colloquy, soliloquy, circumlocution, interlocutor, monologue, dialogue, eulogy, philology, neologism

❑ LUC, LUM—light
lucid, elucidate, pellucid, translucent, illuminate

❑ LUD, LUS—play
ludicrous, allude, delusion, allusion, illusory

❑ MACRO—great
macrocosm, macrobiotics

❑ MAG, MAJ, MAS, MAX—great
magnify, magnanimous, magnate, magnitude, majesty, master, maximum

❑ MAL—bad
malady, maladroit, malevolent, malodorous

❑ MAN—hand
manual, manuscript, emancipate, manifest, manumission

❑ MAR—sea
submarine, marine, maritime

❑ MATER, MATR—mother
maternal, matron, matrilineal

❑ MEDI—middle
intermediary, medieval, mediate

❑ MEGA—great
megaphone, megalomania, megaton, megalith

❑ MEM, MIN—remember
memory, memento, memorabilia, reminisce

❑ METER, METR, MENS—measure
meter, thermometer, perimeter, metronome, commensurate

❑ MICRO—small
microscope, microorganism, microcosm, microbe

❑ MIS—wrong, bad, hate
misunderstand, misanthrope, misapprehension, misconstrue, misnomer, mishap

❑ MIT, MISS—send
transmit, emit, missive

❑ MOLL—soft
mollify, emollient, mollusk

❑ MON, MONIT—warn

admonish, monitor, premonition

❑ MONO—one

monologue, monotonous, monogamy, monolith, monochrome

❑ MOR—custom, manner

moral, mores, morose

❑ MOR, MORT—dead

morbid, moribund, mortal, amortize

❑ MORPH—shape

amorphous, anthropomorphic, metamorphosis, morphology

❑ MOV, MOT, MOB, MOM—move

remove, motion, mobile, momentum, momentous

❑ MUT—change

mutate, mutability, immutable, commute

❑ NAT, NASC—born

native, nativity, natal, neonate, innate, cognate, nascent, renascent, renaissance

❑ NAU, NAV—ship, sailor

nautical, nauseous, navy, circumnavigate

❑ NEG—not, deny

negative, abnegate, renege

❑ NEO—new

neoclassical, neophyte, neologism, neonate

❑ NIHIL—none, nothing

annihilation, nihilism

❑ NOM, NYM—name

nominate, nomenclature, nominal, cognomen, misnomer, ignominious, antonym, homonym, pseudonym, synonym, anonymity

❑ NOV—new

novelty, innovation, novitiate

❑ NOX, NIC, NEC, NOC—harm

obnoxious, noxious, pernicious, internecine, innocuous

❑ NUMER—number

numeral, numerous, innumerable, enumerate

❑ OB—against

obstruct, obdurate, obfuscate, obnoxious, obsequious, obstinate, obstreperous, obtrusive

❑ OMNI—all

omnipresent, omnipotent, omniscient, omnivorous

❑ ONER—burden

onerous, exonerate

❑ OPER—work

operate, cooperate, inoperable

❑ PAC—peace

pacify, pacifist, pacific

❑ PALP—feel

palpable, palpitation

❏ PAN—all

panorama, panacea, panegyric, pandemic, panoply

❏ PATER, PATR—father

paternal, paternity, patriot, compatriot, expatriate, patrimony, patricide, patrician

❏ PATH, PASS—feel, suffer

sympathy, antipathy, empathy, apathy, pathos, impassioned

❏ PEC—money

pecuniary, impecunious, peculation

❏ PED, POD—foot

pedestrian, pediment, expedient, biped, quadruped, tripod

❏ PEL, PULS—drive

compel, compelling, expel, propel, compulsion

❏ PEN—almost

peninsula, penultimate, penumbra

❏ PEND, PENS—hang

depend, pendant, pendulous, compendium, suspense, propensity

❏ PER—against, destruction

perfidious, pernicious, perjure

❏ PER—through, by, for, throughout

perambulator, percipient, perfunctory, permeable, perspicacious, pertinacious, perturbation, perusal, perennial, peregrinate

❏ PERI—around

perimeter, periphery, perihelion, peripatetic

❏ PET—seek, go toward

petition, impetus, impetuous, petulant, centripetal

❏ PHIL—love

philosopher, philanderer, philanthropy, bibliophile, philology

❏ PHOB—fear

phobia, claustrophobia, xenophobia

❏ PHON—sound

phonograph, megaphone, euphony, phonetics, phonics

❏ PLAC—calm, please

placate, implacable, placid, complacent

❏ PON, POS—put, place

postpone, proponent, exponent, preposition, posit, interpose, juxtaposition, depose

❏ PORT—carry

portable, deportment, rapport

❏ POT—drink

potion, potable

❏ POT—power

potential, potent, impotent, potentate, omnipotence

❏ PRE—before

precede, precipitate, preclude, precocious, precursor, predilection, predisposition, preponderance, prepossessing, presage, prescient, prejudice, predict, premonition, preposition

❏ PRIM, PRI—first

prime, primary, primal, primeval, primordial, pristine

❑ PRO—ahead, forth

proceed, proclivity, procrastinator, profane, profuse, progenitor, progeny, prognosis, prologue, promontory, propel, proponent, propose, proscribe, protestation, provoke

❑ PROTO—first

prototype, protagonist, protocol

❑ PROX, PROP—near

approximate, propinquity, proximity

❑ PSEUDO—false

pseudoscientific, pseudonym

❑ PYR—fire

pyre, pyrotechnics, pyromania

❑ QUAD, QUAR, QUAT—four

quadrilateral, quadrant, quadruped, quarter, quarantine, quaternary

❑ QUES, QUER, QUIS, QUIR—question

quest, inquest, query, querulous, inquisitive, inquiry

❑ QUIE—quiet

disquiet, acquiesce, quiescent, requiem

❑ QUINT, QUIN—five

quintuplets, quintessence

❑ RADI, RAMI—branch

radius, radiate, radiant, eradicate, ramification

❑ RECT, REG—straight, rule

rectangle, rectitude, rectify, regular

❑ REG—king, rule

regal, regent, interregnum

❑ RETRO—backward

retrospective, retroactive, retrograde

❑ RID, RIS—laugh

ridiculous, deride, derision

❑ ROG—ask

interrogate, derogatory, abrogate, arrogate, arrogant

❑ RUD—rough, crude

rude, erudite, rudimentary

❑ RUPT—break

disrupt, interrupt, rupture

❑ SACR, SANCT—holy

sacred, sacrilege, consecrate, sanctify, sanction, sacrosanct

❑ SCRIB, SCRIPT, SCRIV—write

scribe, ascribe, circumscribe, inscribe, proscribe, script, manuscript, scrivener

❑ SE—apart, away

separate, segregate, secede, sedition

❑ SEC, SECT, SEG—cut

sector, dissect, bisect, intersect, segment, secant

❑ SED, SID—sit

sedate, sedentary, supersede, reside, residence, assiduous, insidious

❏ SEM—seed, sow

seminar, seminal, disseminate

❏ SEN—old

senior, senile, senescent

❏ SENT, SENS—feel, think

sentiment, nonsense, assent, sentient, consensus, sensual

❏ SEQU, SECU—follow

sequence, sequel, subsequent, obsequious, obsequy, non sequitur, consecutive

❏ SIGN—mark, sign

signal, designation, assignation

❏ SIM, SEM—similar, same

similar, verisimilitude, semblance, dissemble

❏ SIN—curve

sine curve, sinuous, insinuate

❏ SOL—alone

solo, solitude, soliloquy, solipsism

❏ SOL—sun

solar, parasol, solarium, solstice

❏ SOMN—sleep

insomnia, somnolent, somnambulist

❏ SON—sound

sonic, consonance, dissonance, assonance, sonorous, resonate

❏ SOPH—wisdom

philosopher, sophistry, sophisticated, sophomoric

❏ SPEC, SPIC—see, look

spectator, circumspect, retrospective, perspective, perspicacious, perspicuous

❏ SPER—hope

prosper, prosperous, despair, desperate

❏ SPERS, SPAR—scatter

disperse, sparse, aspersion, disparate

❏ SPIR—breathe

respire, inspire, spiritual, aspire, transpire

❏ STRICT, STRING—bind

strict, stricture, constrict, stringent, astringent

❏ STRUCT, STRU—build

structure, obstruct, construe

❏ SUB—under

subconscious, subjugate, subliminal, subpoena, subsequent, subterranean, subvert

❏ SUMM—highest

summit, summary, consummate

❏ SUPER, SUR—above

supervise, supercilious, supersede, superannuated, superfluous, insurmountable, surfeit

❏ SURGE, SURRECT—rise

surge, resurgent, insurgent, insurrection

❏ SYN, SYM—together

synthesis, sympathy, synonym, syncopation, synopsis, symposium, symbiosis

❏ TACIT, TIC—silent

tacit, taciturn, reticent

❏ TACT, TAG, TANG—touch

tact, tactile, contagious, tangent, tangential, tangible

❏ TEN, TIN, TAIN—hold, twist

detention, tenable, tenacious, pertinacious, retinue, retain

❏ TEND, TENS, TENT—stretch

intend, distend, tension, tensile, ostensible, contentious

❏ TERM—end

terminal, terminus, terminate, interminable

❏ TERR—earth, land

terrain, terrestrial, extraterrestrial, subterranean

❏ TEST—witness

testify, attest, testimonial, testament, detest, protestation

❏ THE—god

atheist, theology, apotheosis, theocracy

❏ THERM—heat

thermometer, thermal, thermonuclear, hypothermia

❏ TIM—fear, frightened

timid, intimidate, timorous

❏ TOP—place

topic, topography, utopia

❏ TORP—stiff, numb

torpedo, torpid, torpor

❏ TORT—twist

distort, extort, tortuous

❏ TOX—poison

toxic, toxin, intoxication

❏ TRACT—draw

tractor, intractable, protract

❏ TRANS—across, over, through, beyond

transport, transgress, transient, transitory, translucent, transmutation

❏ TREM, TREP—shake

tremble, tremor, tremulous, trepidation, intrepid

❏ TURB—shake

disturb, turbulent, perturbation

❏ UMBR—shadow

umbrella, umbrage, adumbrate, penumbra

❏ UNI, UN—one

unify, unilateral, unanimous

❏ URB—city

urban, suburban, urbane

❏ VAC—empty

vacant, evacuate, vacuous

❏ VAL, VAIL—value, strength

valid, valor, ambivalent, convalescence, avail, prevail, countervail

❏ VEN, VENT—come

convene, contravene, intervene, venue, convention, circumvent, advent, adventitious

❑ VER—true

verify, verity, verisimilitude, veracious, aver, verdict

❑ VERB—word

verbal, verbose, verbiage, verbatim

❑ VERT, VERS—turn

avert, convert, revert, incontrovertible, divert, subvert, versatile, aversion

❑ VICT, VINC—conquer

victory, conviction, evict, evince, invincible

❑ VID, VIS—see

evident, vision, visage, supervise

❑ VIL—base, mean

vile, vilify, revile

❑ VIV, VIT—life

vivid, vital, convivial, vivacious

❑ VOC, VOK, VOW—call, voice

vocal, equivocate, vociferous, convoke, evoke, invoke, avow

❑ VOL—wish

voluntary, malevolent, benevolent, volition

❑ VOLV, VOLUT—turn, roll

revolve, evolve, convoluted

❑ VOR—eat

devour, carnivore, omnivorous, voracious

WRITING SKILLS

PUNCTUATION REVIEW

COMMAS

USE COMMAS TO SEPARATE ITEMS IN A SERIES

If more than two items are listed in a series, they should be separated by commas. The final comma—the one that precedes the word *and*—may be omitted. An omitted final comma would not be considered an error on the PSAT.

> Example: My recipe for buttermilk biscuits includes flour, baking soda, salt, shortening, and buttermilk.

> ALSO RIGHT: My recipe for buttermilk biscuits includes flour, baking soda, salt, shortening and buttermilk.

Be watchful for commas placed **before** the first element of a series **or after** the last element.

> WRONG: My recipe for chocolate cake includes, flour, baking soda, sugar, eggs, milk and chocolate.

> WRONG: Flour, baking soda, sugar, eggs, milk and chocolate, are the ingredients in my chocolate cake.

USE COMMAS TO SEPARATE TWO OR MORE ADJECTIVES BEFORE A NOUN

> Example: I can't believe you sat through that long, dull movie three times in a row.

It is **incorrect** to place a comma **after** the last adjective in a series.

> WRONG: The manatee is a blubbery, bewhiskered, creature.

USE COMMAS TO SET OFF PARENTHETICAL CLAUSES AND PHRASES

If a phrase or clause is not necessary to the main idea expressed by a sentence, it should be set off by commas.

> Example: Phillip, who never had any formal chef's training, bakes excellent cheesecake.

The main idea here is that Phillip bakes an excellent cheesecake. The intervening clause merely serves to further describe Phillip; it should therefore be enclosed in commas.

USE COMMAS AFTER INTRODUCTORY PHRASES

Example: Having watered his petunias every day during the drought, Harold was disappointed when his garden was destroyed by aphids.

Example: After the banquet, Harold and Melissa went dancing.

USE COMMAS TO SEPARATE INDEPENDENT CLAUSES

Use a comma before a conjunction (*and*, *but*, *nor*, *yet*, etc.) that connects two independent clauses.

Example: Marta is good at basketball, but she's better at soccer.

SEMICOLONS

Like commas, semicolons can be used to separate independent clauses. As we saw above, two related independent clauses that are connected by a conjunction such as *and*, *but*, *nor*, or *yet* should be punctuated by a comma. If the words *and*, *but*, *nor*, or *yet* aren't used, the clauses should be separated by a semicolon.

Example: Whooping cranes are an endangered species; there are only 50 of them alive today.

Example: Whooping cranes are an endangered species, and they are unlikely to survive if we continue to pollute their habitat.

Semicolons may also be used between independent clauses connected by words like *therefore*, *nevertheless*, and *moreover*. For more on this topic, see the section on "Sentence Structure" in this Appendix.

COLONS

In standard written English, the colon is used only as a means of signaling that what follows is a list, definition, explanation, or restatement of what has gone before. A word or phrase such as *like the following*, *as follows*, *namely*, or *this* is often used along with the colon to make it clear that a list, summary, or explanation is coming up.

Example: This is what I found in her refrigerator: a moldy lime and a jar of peanut butter.

Example: Your instructions are as follows: read the passage carefully, answer the questions, and turn over your answer sheet.

THE DASH

The dash has two uses. One is to indicate an abrupt break in thought.

Example: The alligator, unlike the crocodile, will usually not attack humans—unless, that is, she feels that her young are in danger.

The dash can also be used to set off a parenthetical expression from the rest of the sentence.

Example: At 32° Fahrenheit—which is zero on the Celsius scale—water will freeze.

THE APOSTROPHE

The apostrophe has two distinct functions. It is used with contracted verb forms to indicate that one or more letters have been eliminated:

Example: The **boy's** an expert at chess. (The boy is an expert at chess.)

Example: The **boy's** left for the day. (The boy has left for the day.)

The apostrophe is also used to indicate the possessive form of a noun.

Example: The **boy's** face was covered with mosquito bites after a day in the swamp.

GRAMMAR REVIEW

SUBJECT-VERB AGREEMENT

The form of a verb must match, or agree with, its subject in two ways: person and number.

1. AGREEMENT OF PERSON

When we talk about *person*, we're talking about whether the subject and verb of a sentence show that the author is making a statement about himself (first person), the person he is speaking to (second person), or some other person, place, or thing (third person).

First Person Subjects: I, we

Example: **I am** going to Paris. **We are** going to Rome.

Second Person Subject: you

Example: **Are you** sure you weren't imagining that flying saucer?

Third Person Subjects: he, she, they, it, and names of people, places, and things

Example: **He is driving** me crazy.

2. AGREEMENT OF NUMBER

When we talk about number, we're talking about whether the subject and verb show that one thing is being discussed (singular) or that more than one thing is being discussed (plural).

HINT: Subjects and verbs must agree in number. Subjects and verbs that don't agree in number appear very frequently on the PSAT.

WRONG: The **children catches** the school bus every morning.

RIGHT: The **children catch** the school bus every morning.

Be especially careful of subject-verb agreement when the subject and verb are separated by a long string of words.

WRONG: **Wild animals** in jungles all over the world **is** endangered.

RIGHT: **Wild animals** in jungles all over the world **are** endangered.

PRONOUNS

A pronoun is a word that is used in place of a noun. The antecedent of a pronoun is the word to which the pronoun refers.

Example: <u>Mary</u> was late for work because <u>she</u>
      ANTECEDENT   PRONOUN

forgot to set the alarm.

Occasionally, an antecedent will appear in a sentence *after* the pronoun.

Example: Because <u>he</u> sneezes so often, <u>Arthur</u>
       PRONOUN   ANTECEDENT

always thinks <u>he</u> might have the flu.
       PRONOUN

PRONOUNS AND AGREEMENT

In clear, grammatical writing, a pronoun must clearly refer to, and agree with, its antecedent.

Number agreement of pronouns is more frequently tested on the PSAT than person agreement, although you may see a question that tests person agreement.

NUMBER AND PERSON

	Singular	Plural
First Person	I, me	we, us
	my, mine	our, ours
Second Person	you	you
	your, yours	your, yours
Third Person	he, him	they, them
	she, her	
	it	
	one	
	his	their, theirs
	her, hers	
	its	
	one's	

Number Agreement

Pronouns must agree in number with their antecedents. A singular pronoun should stand in for a singular antecedent. A plural pronoun should stand in for a plural antecedent. Here's a typical PSAT pronoun error.

> WRONG: The bank turned Harry down when he applied for a loan because **their** credit department discovered that he didn't have a job.

What does the plural possessive *their* refer to? The singular noun *bank*. The singular possessive *its* is what we need here.

> RIGHT: The bank turned Harry down for a loan because **its** credit department discovered that he didn't have a job.

Person Agreement

Pronouns must agree with their antecedents in person too. A first-person pronoun should stand in for a first-person antecedent, and so on. One more thing to remember about which pronoun to use with which antecedent: never use the relative pronoun *which* to refer to a human being. The pronouns *who* or *whom* are used to refer to people; depending on the context, the pronoun *that* can refer to either things or people.

> WRONG: The woman **which** is standing at the piano is my sister.

> RIGHT: The woman **who** is standing at the piano is my sister.

PRONOUNS AND CASE

A more subtle type of pronoun problem is one in which the pronoun is in the wrong case. Look at the following chart:

CASE	Subjective	Objective
First Person	I	me
	we	us
Second Person	you	you
Third Person	he	him
	she	her
	it	it
	they	them
	one	one

Relative Pronouns   who   whom
                      that   that
                      which   which

When to Use Subjective Case Pronouns

Use the subjective case for the subject of a sentence.

    Example: **She** is falling asleep.

    WRONG: Nancy, Claire, and **me** are going to the ballet.

    RIGHT: Nancy, Claire, and **I** are going to the ballet.

Use the subjective case after a linking verb like *to be*.

    Example: It is **I**.

Use the subjective case in comparisons between the subject of verbs that are not stated but understood.

    Example: Gary is taller than **they** (are).

When to Use Objective Case Pronouns

Use the objective case for the object of a verb.

    Example: I called **her**.

Use the objective case for the object of a preposition.

    Example: I laughed at **him**.

Use the objective case after infinitives and gerunds.

    Example: Asking **him** to go was a big mistake.

    Example: To give **him** the scare of his life, we all jumped out of his closet.

Use the objective case in comparisons between objects of verbs that are not stated but understood.

    Example: She calls you more than (she calls) **me**.

WHO AND WHOM

Another thing you'll need to know is when to use the relative pronoun *who* (subjective case) and when to use the relative pronoun *whom* (objective case: *whom* goes with *him* and *them*). The following method is very helpful when you're deciding which one to use.

    Example: Sylvester, (*who* or *whom*?) is afraid of the dark, sleeps with a Donald Duck night-light on.

Look only at the relative pronoun in its clause. Ignore the rest of the sentence.

    (*Who* or *whom*?) is afraid of the dark.

Turn the clause into a question. Ask yourself:

    Who or *whom* is afraid of the dark?

Answer the question with an ordinary personal pronoun.

    He is.

If you've answered the question with a subjective case pronoun (as you have here), you need the subjective case *who* in the relative clause.

    Sylvester, **who** is afraid of the dark, sleeps with a Donald Duck night-light on.

If you answer the question with an objective case pronoun, you need the objective case *whom* in the relative clause.

    HINT: Try answering the question with *he* or *him*. *Who* goes with *he* (subjective case) and *whom* goes with *him* (objective case).

SENTENCE STRUCTURE

A **sentence** is a group of words that can stand alone because it expresses a complete thought. To express a complete thought, it must contain a subject, about which something is said, and a verb, which says something about the subject.

Example: Dogs bark.

Example: The explorers slept in yak-hide tents.

Example: Looking out of the window, John saw a flying saucer.

Every sentence consists of at least one clause. Many sentences contain more than one clause (and phrases, too).

A **clause** is a group of words that contains a subject and a verb. *Dogs bark, The explorers slept in a yak-hide tent,* and *John saw a flying saucer* are all clauses.

A **phrase** is a group of words that does not have both a subject and a verb. *Looking out of the window* is a phrase.

SENTENCE FRAGMENTS

On the PSAT, some of those innocent-looking groups of words beginning with capital letters and ending with periods are only masquerading as sentences. In reality, they're sentence fragments.

A sentence fragment is a group of words that seems to be a sentence but which is *grammatically* incomplete because it lacks a subject or a verb **or** which is *logically* incomplete because other elements necessary for it to express a complete thought are missing.

WRONG: Eggs and fresh vegetables on sale at the farmers' market.

This is not a complete sentence because there's no verb to say something about the subject, *eggs and fresh vegetables*.

WRONG: Because Richard likes hippopotamuses.

Even though this contains a subject (*Richard*) and a verb (*likes*), it's not a complete sentence because it doesn't express a complete thought. We don't know what's true "*because* Richard likes hippopotamuses."

WRONG: Martha dreams about dinosaurs although.

This isn't a complete sentence because it doesn't express a complete thought. What makes Martha's dreaming about dinosaurs in need of qualification or explanation?

RUN-ON SENTENCES

Just as unacceptable as an incomplete sentence is a "too-complete" sentence, a run-on sentence.

A run-on sentence is actually two complete sentences stuck together either with just a comma or with no punctuation at all.

WRONG: The children had been playing in the park, they were covered with mud.

WRONG: The children had been playing in the park they were covered with mud.

There are a number of ways to fix this kind of problem. They all involve a punctuation mark or a connecting word that can properly connect two clauses.

Join the clauses with a semicolon.

RIGHT: The children had been playing in the park; they were covered with mud.

Join the clauses with a coordinating conjunction (*and, but, for, nor, or, so, yet*) and a comma.

> RIGHT: The children had been playing in the park, and they were covered with mud.

Join the clauses with a subordinating conjunction (*after, although, if, since, while*).

> RIGHT: Because the children had been playing in the park, they were covered with mud.

> OR

> RIGHT: The children were covered with mud because they had been playing in the park.

And, of course, the two halves of a run-on sentence can be written as two separate, complete sentences.

> RIGHT: The children had been playing in the park. They were covered with mud.

VERBS

On the PSAT, you'll find items that are wrong because a verb is in the wrong tense. To spot this kind of problem, you need to be familiar both with the way each tense is used **and** with the ways the tenses are used together. English has six tenses, and each has a simple form and a progressive form.

	Simple	Progressive
Present	I work	I am working
Past	I worked	I was working
Future	I will work	I will be working
Present Perfect	I have worked	I have been working
Past Perfect	I had worked	I had been working
Future Perfect	I will have worked	I will have been working

USING THE PRESENT TENSE

Use the present tense to describe a state or action occurring in the present time.

> Example: I **am** a student.

> Example: They **are studying** the Holy Roman Empire.

Use the present tense to describe habitual action.

> Example: They **eat** at Joe's Diner every night.

> Example: My father never **drinks** coffee.

Use the present tense to describe things that are always true.

> Example: The earth **is** round.

> Example: Grass **is** green.

USING THE PAST TENSE

Use the simple past tense to describe an event or state that took place at a specific time in the past and is now over and done with.

> Example: Norman **broke** his toe when he tripped over his son's tricycle.

USING THE FUTURE TENSE

Use the future tense for actions expected in the future.

> Example: I **will call** you on Wednesday.

We often express future actions with the expression *to be going to*.

> Example: I **am going to move** to another apartment soon.

USING THE PRESENT PERFECT TENSE

Use the present perfect tense for actions and states that started in the past and continue up to and into the present time.

> Example: I **have been living** here for the last two years.

Use the present perfect for actions and states that happened a number of times in the past and may happen again in the future.

> Example: I **have heard** that song several times on the radio.

Use the present perfect for something that happened at an unspecified time in the past.

> Example: Anna **has seen** that movie already.

USING THE PAST PERFECT TENSE

The past perfect tense is used to represent past actions or states that were completed before other past actions or states. The more recent past event is expressed in the simple past, and the earlier past event is expressed in the past perfect.

> Example: When I turned my computer on this morning, I realized that I **had quit** the program yesterday without saving my work.

USING THE FUTURE PERFECT TENSE

Use the future perfect tense for a future state or event that will take place before another future event.

> Example: By the end of the week, I **will have worked** four hours of overtime.

USING THE PROPER PAST PARTICIPLE FORM

If you use the present, past, or future perfect tense, make sure that you use the past participle and not the simple past tense.

> WRONG: I have **swam** in that pool every day this week.

> RIGHT: I have **swum** in that pool every day this week.

Irregular verbs have two different forms for simple past and past participle tenses. The following are some of the most common irregular verbs.

IRREGULAR VERBS

Infinitive	Simple Past	Past Participle
arise	arose	arisen
become	became	become
begin	began	begun
blow	blew	blown
break	broke	broken
come	came	come
do	did	done
draw	drew	drawn
drink	drank	drunk
drive	drove	driven
eat	ate	eaten
fall	fell	fallen
fly	flew	flown
freeze	froze	frozen
give	gave	given
grow	grew	grown
know	knew	known
ride	rode	ridden
rise	rose	risen
run	ran	run
see	saw	seen
shake	shook	shaken
shrink	shrank	shrunk
sing	sang	sung
speak	spoke	spoken
take	took	taken
throw	threw	thrown

ADJECTIVES AND ADVERBS

On the PSAT, you may find an occasional item that's wrong because it uses an adjective where an adverb is called for, or vice versa.

An adjective modifies, or describes, a noun or pronoun.

> Example: A woman in a **white** dress stood next to the **old** tree.

> Example: The boat, **leaky** and **dirty**, hadn't been used in years.

An adverb modifies a verb, an adjective, or another adverb. Most, but not all, adverbs end in *-ly*. (Don't forget that some **adjectives**—*friendly*, *lovely*—also end in *-ly*.)

> Example: The interviewer looked *approvingly* at the *neatly* dressed applicant.

PARALLEL STRUCTURE

On the PSAT, matching constructions must be expressed in parallel form. Make sure that when a sentence contains a **list** or makes a **comparison**, the items being listed or compared exhibit parallel structure.

ITEMS IN A LIST

WRONG: I love **skipping, jumping**, and **to play** tiddlywinks.

WRONG: I love **to skip, jump**, and **to play** tiddlywinks.

RIGHT: I love to **skip, jump**, and **play** tiddlywinks.

ALSO RIGHT: I love **to skip, to jump**, and **to play** tiddlywinks.

ALSO RIGHT: I love **skipping, jumping**, and **playing** tiddlywinks.

ITEMS IN A COMPARISON

Comparisons must do more than just exhibit parallel structure. Most faulty comparisons relate to the notion that you can't compare apples and oranges. You don't merely want comparisons to be grammatically similar; they must be logically similar as well.

WRONG: **To visualize** success is not the same as **achieving** it.

RIGHT: **To visualize** success is not the same as **to achieve** it.

ALSO RIGHT: **Visualizing** success is not the same as **achieving** it.

WRONG: **The rules of chess** are more complex than **checkers**.

RIGHT: **The rules of chess** are more complex than **those of checkers**.

ALSO RIGHT: **Chess** is more complex than **checkers**.

STYLE REVIEW

PRONOUNS AND REFERENCE

When we talk about pronouns and their antecedents, we say pronouns refer to or refer back to their antecedents. We noted earlier that pronouns must agree in person and number with their antecedents. But a different kind of pronoun reference problem exists when a pronoun either doesn't refer to any antecedent at all or doesn't refer clearly to one, and only one, antecedent.

Sometimes an incorrectly used pronoun has no antecedent.

> POOR: Joe doesn't like what **they play** on this radio station.

Who are *they*? We can't tell because there is no antecedent for *they*. On the PSAT, this sort of usage is an error.

> RIGHT: Joe doesn't like what **the disc jockeys play** on this radio station.

Don't use pronouns without antecedents when doing so makes a sentence unclear. Sometimes a pronoun seems to have an antecedent until you look closely and see that the word that appears to be the antecedent is not a noun, but an adjective, a possessive form, or a verb. The antecedent of a pronoun must be a noun.

> WRONG: When you are painting, make sure you don't get **it** on the floor.

> RIGHT: When you are painting, make sure you don't get **paint** on the floor.

Other examples of pronoun reference problems:

> WRONG: I've always been interested in astronomy and finally have decided to become **one**.

> RIGHT: I've always been interested in astronomy and finally have decided to become an **astronomer**.

Don't use pronouns with remote references. A pronoun that is too far away from what it refers to is said to have a remote antecedent.

> WRONG: Jane quit smoking and, as a result, temporarily put on a lot of weight. **It** was very bad for her health.

> RIGHT: Jane quit smoking because **it** was very bad for her health, and, as a result, she temporarily gained a lot of weight.

Don't use pronouns with faulty broad reference. A pronoun with broad reference is one that refers to a whole idea instead of to a single noun.

> WRONG: He built a fence to stop people from looking into his backyard. **That's** not easy.

> RIGHT: He built a fence to stop people from looking into his backyard. **The fence was not easy to build.**

REDUNDANCY

This type of style error is sometimes tested on the PSAT. Words or phrases are redundant when they have basically the same meaning as something already stated in the sentence. Don't use two phrases when one is sufficient.

> WRONG: The school was **established and founded** in 1906.

> RIGHT: The school was **established** in 1906.

VERBOSITY

Sometimes having extra words in a sentence results in a style problem. Conciseness is something that is valued on the PSAT.

> WORDY: The supply of **musical instruments that are antique** is limited, so they become more valuable each year.

> BETTER: The supply of **antique musical instruments** is limited, so they become more valuable each year.

> WORDY: We **were in agreement with each other** that Max was an unsuspecting old fool.

> BETTER: We **agreed** that Max was an unsuspecting old fool.

COMMONLY MISUSED WORDS

accept/except

Don't confuse the two. To *accept* means "to receive or agree to something," whereas *except* is usually a preposition meaning "excluding," although it can also mean "to leave out."

> WRONG: Can you **except** my apology?

> RIGHT: Can you **accept** my apology?

affect/effect

These are easy to confuse. To *affect* means to have an *effect* on something. When the word is being used as a verb, the proper word to use is almost always *affect*; when it's being used as a noun, the proper word to use is almost always *effect*. (It should be noted that *effect* can also be a verb, meaning "to bring about or cause to happen.")

> WRONG: His affectations **effected** me to no good **affect**.

> RIGHT: His affectations **affected** me to no good **effect**.

among/between

In most cases, you should use *between* for two items and *among* for more than two.

> Example: The competition **between** Anne and Michael has grown more intense.

> Example: He is always at his best **among** strangers.

But use common sense. Sometimes *among* is not appropriate.

> Example: Plant the trees in the area **between** the road, the wall, and the fence.

amount/number

Amount should be used to refer to a uncountable quantity. *Number* should refer to a countable quantity.

> Example: The **amount** of food he threw away would feed a substantial **number** of people.

as/like

Like is a preposition; it takes a noun object. *As*, when functioning as a conjunction, introduces a subordinate clause. Remember, a clause is a part of a sentence containing a subject and verb.

> Example: He sings **like** an angel.

> Example: He sings **as** an angel sings.

as . . . as . . .

The idiom is *as . . . as . . .*, **not** *as . . . than . . .*

> WRONG: That suit is **as** expensive **than** this one.

> RIGHT: That suit is **as** expensive **as** this one.

fewer/less

Use *fewer* before a plural noun; use *less* before a singular one.

> Example: There are **fewer** apples on this tree than there were last year.

> Example: He makes **less** money than she does.

neither . . . nor . . .

The correlative conjunction is *neither . . . nor . . .*, not *neither . . . or . . .*

> Example: He is **neither** strong **nor** flexible.

> Avoid the redundancy caused by using *nor* following a negative.

> WRONG: Alice's departure was **not** noticed by Debby **nor** Sue.

> RIGHT: Alice's departure was **not** noticed by Debby **or** Sue.

its/it's

Many people confuse *its* and *it's*. *Its* is possessive; *it's* is a contraction of *it is*:

> Example: The cat licked **its** paws.

> Example: **It's** raining cats and dogs.

their/they're/there

Many people confuse *their*, *there*, and *they're*. *Their* is possessive; *they're* is a contraction of *they are*:

> Example: The girls rode **their** bikes home.

> Example: **They're** training for the big race.

There has two uses: it can indicate place, and it can be used as an expletive—a word that doesn't do anything in a sentence except delay the subject.

> Example: Put the book over **there**.

> Example: **There** will be 15 runners competing for the prize.

COMMONLY TESTED IDIOMS

Some phrases are wrong simply because that's just not the way we say it in English. This is especially true of verb-preposition word combinations. For instance:

> WRONG: The fashion police **frown at** wearing hats adorned with flowers.

> RIGHT: The fashion police **frown upon** wearing hats adorned with flowers.

The first sentence is only wrong because *frown at* is not the correct idiomatic expression. Either your ear will recognize the correct idiom or it won't. Can you trust your ear on the following commonly tested idioms?

Commonly Tested Idioms

associate *with*	different *from*
accuse *of*	discriminate *against*
apologize *for*	distinguish *from*
arrive *at*	dream *about/of*
believe *in*	forbid *to*
believe *to be*	frown *upon*
apologize *for*	object *to*
attribute *to*	prohibit *from*
continue *to*	substitute *for*
contrast *with*	target *at*
credit *with*	use *as*
decide *to*	view *as*
define *as*	worry *about*

WORD LIST

PSAT EMERGENCY

" If you're short on time, you may want to just skim through these words to familiarize yourself with the type of vocabulary the PSAT often tests. "

A

ABANDON (n.)—total lack of inhibition

ABASE—to humble; disgrace

ABATE—to decrease, reduce

ABDICATE—to give up a position, right, or power

ABERRATION—something different from the usual

ABET—to aid; act as accomplice

ABHOR—to loathe, detest

ABJECT—miserable, pitiful

ABORTIVE—interrupted while incomplete

ABRIDGE—to condense, shorten

ABROGATE—to put an end to, abolish by authority

ABSCOND—to depart secretly

ABSOLVE—to forgive, free from blame

ABSTAIN—to choose not to do something

ACCOLADE—praise, distinction

ACCRUE—to accumulate, grow by additions

ACERBIC—bitter, sharp in taste or temper

ACME—highest point; summit

ACQUIESCE—to agree; comply quietly

ACRID—harsh, bitter

ACRIMONY—bitterness, animosity

ACUITY—sharpness

ACUMEN—sharpness of insight

ADAGE—old saying or proverb

ADAMANT—uncompromising, unyielding

ADAPT—to accommodate; adjust

ADHERE—to cling; follow without deviation

ADJACENT—next to

ADMONISH—to caution or reprimand

ADROIT—skillful, accomplished, highly competent

ADULATION—high praise

ADUMBRATE—to sketch, outline in a shadowy way

ADVERSARIAL—antagonistic, competitive

AERIE—nook or nest built high in the air

AESTHETIC—pertaining to beauty or art

AFFABLE—friendly, easy to approach

AFFECTED (adj.)—pretentious, phony

AFFLUENT—rich, wealthy

AFFRONT (n.)—personal offense, insult

AGENDA—plan, schedule

AGILE—well coordinated, nimble

AGITATION—commotion, excitement; uneasiness

AGRARIAN—relating to farming or rural matters

ALACRITY—cheerful willingness, eagerness; speed

ALIAS—assumed name

ALIENATED—distanced, estranged

ALLEGORY—symbolic representation

ALLEVIATE—to relieve, improve partially

ALLURE (v.)—to entice by charm; attract

ALLUSION—indirect reference

ALOOF—detached, indifferent

ALTRUISM—unselfish concern for others' welfare

AMBIGUOUS—uncertain; subject to multiple interpretations

AMBIVALENCE—attitude of uncertainty; conflicting emotions

AMELIORATE—to make better, improve

AMENABLE—agreeable, cooperative

AMEND—to improve or correct flaws in

AMENITY—pleasantness; something increasing comfort

AMIABLE—friendly, pleasant, likable

AMICABLE—friendly, agreeable

AMORAL—unprincipled, unethical

AMORPHOUS—having no definite form

AMPHIBIAN—creature equally at home on land or in water

AMPLE—abundant, plentiful

AMULET—ornament worn as a charm against evil spirits

ANACHRONISTIC—outdated; inappropriate for its time period

ANARCHY—absence of government or law; chaos

ANIMATION—enthusiasm, excitement

ANIMOSITY—hatred, hostility

ANNUL—to cancel, nullify, declare void, or make legally invalid

ANOMALY—irregularity or deviation from the norm

ANONYMITY—condition of having no name or an unknown name

ANTAGONIST—foe, opponent, adversary

ANTECEDENT (adj.)—coming before in place or time

ANTHOLOGY—collection of literary works

ANTIPATHY—dislike, hostility; extreme opposition or aversion

ANTIQUATED—outdated, obsolete

ANTIQUITY—ancient times; the quality of being old

ANTITHESIS—exact opposite or direct contrast

APATHY—lack of interest or concern

APHORISM—old saying or short, pithy statement

APOCRYPHAL—not genuine; fictional

APPEASE—to satisfy, placate, calm, pacify

APPROBATION—praise; official approval

APPROPRIATE (v.)—to take possession of

ARABLE—suitable for cultivation

ARBITRARY—depending solely on individual will; inconsistent

ARBOREAL—relating to trees; living in trees

ARCANE—secret, obscure, known only to a few

ARCHAIC—antiquated, from an earlier time; outdated

ARCHIPELAGO—large group of islands

ARDENT—passionate, enthusiastic, fervent

ARDUOUS—extremely difficult, laborious

ARID—extremely dry; deathly boring

ARSENAL—ammunition storehouse

ARTICULATE (adj.)—well spoken, expressing oneself clearly

ARTISAN—craftsperson; expert

ASCEND—to rise or climb

ASCETIC—self-denying, abstinent, austere

ASHEN—resembling ashes; pale

ASKEW—crooked, tilted

ASPERSION—false rumor, damaging report, slander

ASPIRE—to have great hopes; to aim at a goal

ASSAIL—to attack, assault

ASSIDUOUS—diligent, persistent, hardworking

ASSUAGE—to make less severe, ease, relieve

ASTRINGENT (adj.)—harsh, severe, stern

ASTUTE—having good judgment; shrewd

ATONE—to make amends for a wrong

ATROCIOUS—monstrous, shockingly bad

ATTAIN—to accomplish, gain

ATTENUATE—to make thin or slender; weaken

AUDACIOUS—bold, daring, fearless

AUDIBLE—capable of being heard

AUGMENT—to expand, extend

AUGUST (adj.)—dignified, awe inspiring, venerable

AUSPICIOUS—having favorable prospects, promising

AUSTERE—stern, strict, unadorned

AUTHORITARIAN—extremely strict, bossy

AUTOCRAT—dictator

AVARICE—greed

AVENGE—to retaliate, take revenge for an injury or crime

AVER—to declare to be true, affirm

AVERSION—intense dislike

AVERT—to turn something away; prevent, hinder

AVIARY—large enclosure housing birds

AWRY—crooked, askew, amiss

B

BALEFUL—harmful, threatening

BALLAD—folk song, narrative poem

BALM—soothing, healing influence

BANAL—trite, overly common

BANE—something causing death, destruction, or ruin

BANTER—playful conversation

BASTION—fortification, stronghold

BAY (v.)—to bark, especially in a deep, prolonged way

BEGUILE—to deceive, mislead; charm

BEHEMOTH—huge creature; something enormous

BELABOR—to insist repeatedly or harp on

BELIE—to misrepresent; expose as false

BELLIGERENT—hostile, tending to fight

BENEFACTOR—someone giving aid or money

BENEFICENT—kindly, charitable; producing good effects

BENIGHTED—unenlightened, ignorant

BENIGN—kindly, gentle, or harmless

BEQUEATH—to give or leave through a will; to hand down

BERATE—to scold harshly

BESEECH—to beg, plead, implore

BESTIAL—beastly, animal-like

BIAS—prejudice, slant

BIBLIOGRAPHY—list of books

BISECT—to cut into two (usually equal) parts

BLANCH—to pale; take the color out of

BLANDISH—to coax with flattery

BLASPHEMOUS—cursing, profane, irreverent

BLATANT—glaring, obvious, showy

BLIGHT (v.)—to afflict, destroy

BOISTEROUS—rowdy, loud, unrestrained

BOMBASTIC—using high-sounding but meaningless language

BOOR—crude person, one lacking manners or taste

BOTANIST—scientist who studies plants

BOVINE—cowlike; relating to cows

BRAZEN—bold, shameless, impudent; of or like brass

BROACH (v.)—to mention or suggest for the first time

BURGEON—to sprout or flourish

BURNISH—to polish, make smooth and bright

BUTTRESS (v.)—to reinforce or support

C

CACOPHONY—jarring, unpleasant noise

CAJOLE—to flatter, coax, persuade

CALLOUS—thick-skinned, insensitive

CALLOW—immature, lacking sophistication

CANDOR—honesty of expression

CANNY—smart; founded on common sense

CAPITULATE—to submit completely, surrender

CAPRICIOUS—impulsive, whimsical, without much thought

CARICATURE—exaggerated portrait, cartoon

CARTOGRAPHY—science or art of making maps

CASTIGATE—to punish, chastise, criticize severely

CATALYST—something causing change without being changed

CATHOLIC (adj.)—universal; broad and comprehensive

CAUCUS—smaller group within an organization; a meeting of such a group

CAUSTIC—biting, sarcastic; corrosive

CEDE—to surrender possession of something

CENSORIOUS—severely critical

CESSATION—temporary or complete halt

CHAGRIN—shame, embarrassment, humiliation

CHAMPION (v.)—to defend or support

CHAOTIC—extremely disorderly

CHARLATAN—quack, fake

CHARY—watchful, cautious, extremely shy

CHASTISE—to punish, discipline, scold

CHIDE—to scold, express disapproval

CHROMATIC—relating to color

CIRCUITOUS—roundabout

CIRCUMFERENCE—boundary or distance around a circle or sphere

CIRCUMSCRIBE—to encircle; set limits on, confine

CIRCUMSPECT—cautious, wary

CITADEL—fortress or stronghold

CIVIL—polite; relating to citizens

CLAIRVOYANT (adj.)—having ESP, psychic

CLAMOR (v.)—to make a noisy outcry

CLANDESTINE—secretive

CLEMENCY—merciful leniency

CLOISTER (v.)—to confine, seclude

COALESCE—to grow together or cause to unite as one

CODDLE—to baby, treat indulgently

COERCE—to compel by force or intimidation

COGENT—logically forceful, compelling, convincing

COHERENT—intelligible, lucid, understandable

COLLATERAL (adj.)—accompanying, secondary

COLLOQUIAL—characteristic of informal speech

COLLUSION—collaboration, complicity, conspiracy

COMMENSURATE—proportional

COMMODIOUS—roomy, spacious

COMMUNICABLE—transmittable

COMMUTE—to change a penalty to a less severe one

COMPENSATE—to repay or reimburse

COMPLACENT—self-satisfied, smug

COMPLEMENT—to complete, perfect

COMPLIANT—submissive and yielding

COMPLICITY—knowing partnership in wrongdoing

COMPUNCTION—feeling of uneasiness caused by guilt or regret

CONCAVE—curving inward

CONCEDE—to yield, admit

CONCILIATORY—appeasing or disarming

CONCUR—to agree

CONDONE—to pardon or forgive; overlook, justify, or excuse a fault

CONDUIT—tube, pipe, or similar passage

CONFLAGRATION—big, destructive fire

CONFOUND—to baffle, perplex

CONGEAL—to become thick or solid, as a liquid freezing

CONGENIAL—similar in tastes and habits

CONGLOMERATE (n.)—collected group of varied things; large corporation

CONJECTURE (n.)—speculation, prediction

CONSCIENTIOUS—governed by conscience; careful and thorough

CONSECRATE—to declare sacred; dedicate to a goal

CONSENSUS—unanimity, agreement of opinion or attitude

CONSOLATION—something providing comfort or solace for a loss or hardship

CONSOLIDATE—to combine, incorporate

CONSTRAINED—forced, compelled; confined, restrained

CONSTRUE—to explain or interpret

CONTENTIOUS—quarrelsome, disagreeable, belligerent

CONTINENCE—self-control, self-restraint

CONTRAVENE—to contradict, deny, act contrary to

CONTRITE—deeply sorrowful and repentant for a wrong

CONUNDRUM—riddle, puzzle or problem with no solution

CONVALESCENCE—gradual recovery after an illness

CONVENE—to meet, come together, assemble

CONVENTIONAL—typical, customary, commonplace

CONVEX—curved outward

CONVOLUTED—twisted, complicated, involved

COPIOUS—abundant, plentiful

CORROBORATE—to confirm, verify

COSMETIC (adj.)—relating to beauty; affecting the appearance of something

COSMOPOLITAN—sophisticated, free from local prejudices

COTERIE—small group of persons with a similar purpose

COVERT—hidden; secret

COVET—to desire strongly something possessed by another

CRASS—crude, unrefined

CRAVEN—cowardly

CREDENCE—acceptance of something as true or real

CREDULOUS—gullible, trusting

CREED—statement of belief or principle

CRYPTIC—puzzling

CUISINE—characteristic style of cooking

CULMINATION—climax, final stage

CULPABLE—guilty, deserving of blame

CUPIDITY—greed

CURMUDGEON—cranky person

CURSORY—hastily done, superficial

CURT—abrupt, blunt

CURTAIL—to shorten

CYNIC—person who distrusts the motives of others

D

DAUNT—to discourage, intimidate

DEARTH—lack, scarcity, insufficiency

DEBASE—to degrade or lower in quality or stature

DEBILITATE—to weaken, enfeeble

DEBUNK—to discredit, disprove

DECIDUOUS—shed seasonally; short-lived, temporary

DECORUM—proper behavior, etiquette

DECRY—to condemn, denounce

DEFACE—to mar the appearance of, vandalize

DEFAMATORY—slanderous, injurious to the reputation

DEFERENTIAL—respectful and polite in a submissive way

DEFLATION—decrease, depreciation

DEFUNCT—no longer existing, extinct

DELECTABLE—appetizing, delicious

DELEGATE (v.)—to give powers to another

DELETERIOUS—harmful, destructive, detrimental

DELUGE—flood

DEMAGOGUE—leader, rabble-rouser, usually using appeals to emotion or prejudice

DEMEAN—to degrade, humiliate, humble

DEMOGRAPHICS—data relating to study of human population

DEMOTE—to reduce to a lower grade or rank

DEMUR—to express doubts or objections

DENIGRATE—to slur someone's reputation

DEPLETE—to use up, exhaust

DEPLORE—to express or feel disapproval of; regret strongly

DEPLOY—to spread out strategically over an area; put into action

DEPRAVITY—sinfulness, moral corruption

DEPRECATE—to belittle, disparage

DEPRECIATE—to lose value gradually

DERIDE—to mock, ridicule, make fun of

DERIVATIVE—copied or adapted; not original

DESICCATE—to dry completely, dehydrate

DESIST—to stop doing something

DESPONDENT—feeling discouraged and dejected

DESPOT—tyrannical ruler

DESULTORY—rambling, unmethodical; half-hearted

DETER—to discourage; prevent from happening

DEVIATE—to stray, wander

DEXTEROUS—skilled physically or mentally

DIALECT—regional style of speaking

DIAPHANOUS—allowing light to show through; delicate

DIATRIBE—bitter verbal attack

DICTUM—authoritative statement; popular saying

DIDACTIC—excessively instructive

DIFFIDENCE—shyness, lack of confidence

DIFFUSE—widely spread out

DIGRESS—to turn aside; to stray from the main point

DILAPIDATED—in disrepair, run-down, neglected

DILATE—to enlarge, swell, extend

DILATORY—slow, tending to delay

DIPLOMACY—discretion, tact; negotiations

DIRGE—funeral hymn

DISARRAY—clutter, disorder

DISBURSE—to pay out

DISCERN—to perceive something obscure

DISCONCERTING—bewildering, perplexing, slightly disturbing

DISCORDANT—harsh-sounding, badly out of tune

DISCREDIT—to dishonor or disgrace

DISCREPANCY—difference between

DISDAIN—to regard with scorn and contempt

DISGORGE—to vomit, discharge violently

DISHEVELED—untidy, disarranged, unkempt

DISPARAGE—to belittle, speak disrespectfully about

DISPARATE—dissimilar, different in kind

DISPASSIONATE—free from emotion; impartial, unbiased

DISPEL—to drive out or scatter

DISPENSE—to distribute, administer

DISPERSE—to break up, scatter

DISPIRIT—to dishearten, make dejected

DISREPUTE—disgrace, dishonor

DISSEMBLE—to pretend, disguise one's motives

DISSEMINATE—to spread far and wide

DISSIPATE—to scatter; to pursue pleasure to excess

DISSUADE—to persuade someone to alter original intentions

DISTRAUGHT—very worried and distressed

DITHER—to move or act confusedly or without clear purpose

DIURNAL—daily

DIVINE (v.)—to foretell or know by inspiration

DIVISIVE—creating disunity or conflict

DOCILE—tame, willing to be taught

DOCTRINAIRE—rigidly devoted to theories

DOGMATIC—rigidly fixed in opinion, opinionated

DOLEFUL—sad, mournful

DORMANT—at rest, inactive, in suspended animation

DOTING—excessively fond, loving to excess

DOUR—sullen and gloomy; stern and severe

DRIVEL—stupid talk; slobber

DROLL—amusing in a wry, subtle way

DULCET—pleasant sounding, soothing to the ear

DUPE (v.)—to deceive, trick

DUPLICITY—deception, dishonesty, double-dealing

DYSPEPTIC—suffering from indigestion; gloomy and irritable

E

EBB—to fade away, recede

EBULLIENT—exhilarated, full of enthusiasm and high spirits

ECLECTIC—selecting from various sources, diverse

ECSTATIC—joyful

EDICT—law, command, official public order

EDIFICE—building

EDIFY—to instruct morally and spiritually

EFFACE—to erase or make illegible

EFFERVESCENT—bubbly, lively

EFFIGY—stuffed doll; likeness of a person

EFFRONTERY—impudent boldness, audacity

EFFULGENT—brilliantly shining

EFFUSIVE—expressing emotion without restraint

EGOCENTRIC—acting as if things are centered around oneself

EGREGIOUS—conspicuously bad

ELATION—exhilaration, joy

ELEGY—mournful poem

ELICIT—to draw out, provoke

ELOQUENCE—fluent and effective speech

EMACIATED—skinny, scrawny, gaunt, especially from hunger

EMANCIPATE—to set free, liberate

EMBELLISH—to ornament; make attractive with decoration or details; add details
          to a statement

EMBEZZLE—to steal money in violation of a trust

EMINENT—celebrated, distinguished; outstanding

EMOLLIENT—having soothing qualities, especially for skin

EMPATHY—identification with another's feelings

EMULATE—to copy, imitate

ENDEMIC—belonging to a particular area, inherent

ENERVATE—to weaken, sap strength from

ENGENDER—to produce, cause, bring about

ENIGMATIC—puzzling, inexplicable

ENJOIN—to urge, order, command; forbid or prohibit, as by judicial order

ENMITY—hostility, antagonism, ill-will

ENNUI—boredom, lack of interest and energy

ENORMITY—state of being gigantic or terrible

ENSCONCE—to settle comfortably into a place

ENTHRALL—to captivate, enchant, enslave

ENTREAT—to plead, beg

ENUNCIATE—to pronounce clearly

EPHEMERAL—momentary, transient, fleeting

EPICURE—person with refined taste in food and wine

EPIGRAM—short, witty saying or poem

EPILOGUE—concluding section of a literary work

EPITOME—perfect example of something summary

EQUANIMITY—calmness, composure

EQUINE—relating to horses

EQUIVOCAL—ambiguous, open to more than one interpretation

EQUIVOCATE—to use vague or ambiguous language intentionally

ERADICATE—to erase or get rid of

ERRANT—straying, mistaken, roving

ERUDITE—learned, scholarly

ESCHEW—to abstain from, avoid

ESOTERIC—understood by only a learned few

ESPOUSE—to support or advocate; to marry

ESTRANGE—to alienate, keep at a distance

ETHEREAL—not earthly, spiritual, delicate

EULOGY—high praise, often in a public speech

EUPHEMISM—use of an inoffensive word or phrase in place of a more
distasteful one

EUPHONY—pleasant, harmonious sound

EUPHORIA—feeling of well-being or happiness

EVADE—to avoid, dodge

EVANESCENT—momentary, transitory, short-lived

EVICT—to put out or force out

EXACERBATE—to aggravate, intensify the bad qualities of

EXASPERATION—irritation

EXCERPT (n.)—selection from a book or play

EXCRUCIATING—agonizing, intensely painful

EXCULPATE—to clear of blame or fault, vindicate

EXECRABLE—utterly detestable, abhorrent

EXHILARATION—state of being energetic or filled with happiness

EXHORT—to urge or incite by strong appeals

EXONERATE—to clear of blame, absolve

EXORBITANT—extravagant, unreasonably high in price

EXPEDIENT (adj.)—convenient, efficient, practical

EXPIATE—to atone for, make amends for

EXPLICIT—clearly defined, specific; forthright in expression

EXPONENT—one who champions or advocates

EXPOUND—to elaborate; to expand or increase

EXPUNGE—to erase, eliminate completely

EXPURGATE—to censor

EXTEMPORANEOUS—unrehearsed, on the spur of the moment

EXTENUATE—to lessen the seriousness, strength, or effect of

EXTOL—to praise

EXTRICATE—to free from, disentangle

EXTRINSIC—not inherent or essential, coming from without

EXUBERANT—lively, happy, and full of good spirits

EXUDE—to give off, ooze

EXULT—to rejoice

F

FABRICATE—to make or devise; construct

FACADE—face, front; mask, superficial appearance

FACILE—very easy; simplistic

FALLACIOUS—wrong, unsound, illogical

FALLOW—uncultivated, unused

FANATICISM—extreme devotion to a cause

FARCICAL—absurd, ludicrous

FASTIDIOUS—careful with details

FATHOM (v.)—to understand, gauge

FATUOUS—stupid; foolishly self-satisfied

FAWN (v.)—to flatter excessively, seek the favor of

FAZE—to bother, upset, or disconcert

FECKLESS—ineffective, careless, irresponsible

FEIGN—to pretend, give a false impression; to invent falsely

FELICITOUS—suitable, appropriate; well-spoken

FELL (v.)—to chop, cut down

FERVID—passionate, intense, zealous

FETID—foul-smelling, putrid

FIASCO—disaster, utter failure

FIDELITY—loyalty

FINICKY—fussy, difficult to please

FLACCID—limp, flabby, weak

FLAGRANT—outrageous, shameless

FLAMBOYANT—flashy, garish; exciting, dazzling

FLAUNT—to show off

FLORA—plants

FLORID—gaudy, extremely ornate; ruddy, flushed

FLOUNDER—to falter, waver; to muddle, struggle

FLOUT—to treat contemptuously, scorn

FLUCTUATE—to alternate, waver

FOIBLE—minor weakness or character flaw

FOIL (v.)—to defeat, frustrate

FOMENT—to arouse or incite

FORD (v.)—to cross a body of water at a shallow place

FOREBODING—dark sense of evil to come

FORESTALL—to prevent, delay; anticipate

FORETHOUGHT—anticipation, foresight

FORGO—to go without, refrain from

FORLORN—dreary, deserted; unhappy, hopeless, despairing

FORSWEAR—to repudiate, renounce, disclaim, reject

FORTE—strong point, something a person does well

FORTUITOUS—happening by luck, fortunate

FOSTER—to nourish, cultivate, promote

FOUNDER (v.)—to fall helplessly; sink; fail

FRACAS—noisy dispute

FRACTIOUS—unruly, rebellious

FRAUDULENT—deceitful, dishonest, unethical

FRAUGHT—full of, accompanied by; anxious

FRENETIC—wildly frantic, frenzied, hectic

FULSOME—sickeningly excessive; repulsive

FUNEREAL—mournful, appropriate to a funeral

FURTIVE—secret, stealthy

G

GARGANTUAN—giant, tremendous

GARNER—to gather, collect

GARRULOUS—very talkative

GAUNT—thin and bony

GENRE—type, class, category

GERMINATE—to begin to grow (as with a seed or idea)

GESTATION—growth process from conception to birth

GIBE—to make heckling, taunting remarks

GIRTH—distance around something

GLIB—fluent in an insincere manner; offhand, casual

GLUTTONY—eating and drinking to excess

GOAD—to prod or urge; to provoke

GRANDILOQUENCE—pompous talk, fancy but meaningless language

GRANDIOSE—magnificent and imposing; exaggerated and pretentious

GRATIS—free, costing nothing

GRATUITOUS—free, voluntary; unnecessary and unjustified

GREGARIOUS—outgoing, sociable

GRIEVOUS—causing grief or sorrow; serious and distressing

GRIMACE—facial expression showing pain or disgust

GROVEL—to humble oneself in a demeaning way

GUILE—trickery, deception

GULLIBLE—easily deceived

GUSTATORY—relating to the sense of taste

H

HABITAT—dwelling place

HACKNEYED—worn out by overuse; unoriginal

HAPLESS—unfortunate, having bad luck

HARBINGER—precursor, sign of something to come

HARDY—robust, vigorous

HAUGHTY—arrogant and condescending

HEDONISM—pursuit of pleasure

HEGEMONY—leadership, domination, usually by a country

HEINOUS—shocking, wicked, terrible

HEMORRHAGE (n.)—heavy bleeding

HETEROGENEOUS—composed of unlike parts, different, diverse

HEW—to cut with an ax

HIATUS—break, interruption, vacation

HOMAGE—public honor and respect

HOMOGENEOUS—composed of identical parts

HONE—to sharpen

HUSBAND (v.)—to farm; manage carefully and thriftily

HUTCH—pen or coop for animals

HYGIENIC—clean, sanitary

HYPERBOLE—purposeful exaggeration for effect

HYPOCHONDRIA—unfounded belief that one is often ill

HYPOCRITE—person claiming beliefs or virtues he or she doesn't really possess

HYPOTHESIS—assumption subject to proof

I

ICONOCLAST—one who attacks traditional beliefs

IDEALISM—pursuit of noble goals

IDIOSYNCRASY—peculiarity of temperament, eccentricity

IGNOMINIOUS—disgraceful and dishonorable

ILLICIT—illegal, improper

ILLUSORY—unreal, deceptive

ILLUSTRIOUS—famous, renowned

IMMACULATE—spotless; free from error

IMMERSE—to bathe, dip; to engross, preoccupy

IMMUNE—exempt; protected from harm or disease; unresponsive

IMMUTABLE—unchangeable, invariable

IMPAIR—to damage, injure

IMPASSE—blocked path, dilemma with no solution

IMPASSIVE—showing no emotion

IMPEACH—to charge with misdeeds in public office; accuse

IMPECCABLE—flawless, without fault

IMPECUNIOUS—poor, having no money

IMPEDIMENT—barrier, obstacle; speech disorder

IMPERIOUS—arrogantly self-assured, domineering, overbearing

IMPERTINENT—rude

IMPERVIOUS—impossible to penetrate; incapable of being affected

IMPETUOUS—quick to act without thinking

IMPLACABLE—inflexible, incapable of being pleased

IMPLICATE—to involve in a crime, incriminate

IMPLICIT—implied, not directly expressed

IMPORTUNE—to ask repeatedly, beg

IMPOTENT—powerless, ineffective, lacking strength

IMPOVERISH—to make poor or bankrupt

IMPRECATION—curse

IMPREGNABLE—totally safe from attack, able to resist defeat

IMPUDENT—arrogant, audacious

IMPUGN—to call into question, attack verbally

INANE—foolish, silly, lacking significance

INAUGURATE—to begin or start officially; to induct into office

INCANDESCENT—shining brightly

INCARCERATE—to put in jail; to confine

INCENDIARY—combustible, flammable, burning easily

INCENSE (v.)—to infuriate, enrage

INCEPTION—beginning

INCESSANT—continuous, never ceasing

INCHOATE—imperfectly formed or formulated

INCIPIENT—beginning to exist or appear; in an initial stage

INCISIVE—perceptive, penetrating

INCOGNITO—in disguise, concealing one's identity

INCONTROVERTIBLE—unquestionable, beyond dispute

INCORRIGIBLE—incapable of being corrected

INCREDULOUS—skeptical, doubtful

INCULCATE—to teach, impress in the mind

INDEFATIGABLE—never tired

INDELIBLE—permanent, not erasable

INDIGENOUS—native, occurring naturally in an area

INDIGENT—very poor

INDIGNANT—angry, incensed, offended

INDOLENT—habitually lazy, idle

INDOMITABLE—fearless, unconquerable

INDUBITABLE—unquestionable

INDUCE—to persuade; bring about

INEPT—clumsy, awkward

INERT—unable to move, tending to inactivity

INEVITABLE—certain, unavoidable

INEXORABLE—inflexible, unyielding; unstoppable

INFAMY—reputation for bad deeds

INFER—to conclude, deduce

INFINITESIMAL—extremely tiny

INFIRMITY—disease, ailment

INGENIOUS—original, clever, inventive

INGENUOUS—straightforward, open; naive and unsophisticated

INGRATE—ungrateful person

INGRATIATE—to bring oneself purposely into another's good graces

INHIBIT—to hold back, prevent, restrain

INIMICAL—hostile, unfriendly

INJUNCTION—command, order

INNATE—natural, inborn

INNOCUOUS—harmless; inoffensive

INNOVATE—to invent, modernize, revolutionize

INNUENDO—indirect and subtle criticism, insinuation

INSATIABLE—never satisfied

INSCRUTABLE—impossible to understand fully

INSIDIOUS—sly, treacherous, devious

INSINUATE—to suggest, say indirectly, imply

INSIPID—bland, lacking flavor; lacking excitement

INSOLENT—insulting and arrogant

INSTIGATE—to incite, urge, agitate

INSULAR—isolated, detached

INSURGENT (adj.)—rebellious, insubordinate

INSURRECTION—rebellion

INTEGRAL—central, indispensable

INTEGRITY—decency, honesty; wholeness

INTEMPERATE—showing no sign of being under control; immoderate

INTER—to bury

INTERLOPER—trespasser; meddler in others' affairs

INTERMITTENT—starting and stopping; sporadic

INTERROGATE—to question formally

INTIMATION—clue, suggestion

INTRACTABLE—not easily managed

INTRANSIGENT—uncompromising, refusing to be reconciled

INTREPID—fearless

INTRINSIC—inherent, internal

INTROSPECTIVE—contemplating one's own thoughts and feelings

INTROVERT—someone given to self-analysis

INUNDATE—to cover with water; overwhelm

INURE—to harden; accustom; become used to

INVECTIVE—verbal abuse

INVETERATE—confirmed, long-standing, deeply rooted

INVIDIOUS—obnoxious, unpleasant; unfair

INVINCIBLE—invulnerable, unbeatable

IOTA—very tiny amount

IRASCIBLE—easily angered

IRIDESCENT—showing many colors

ITINERANT—wandering from place to place, unsettled

ITINERARY—route of a traveler's journey

J

JADED—tired by excess or overuse; slightly cynical

JARGON—nonsensical talk; specialized language

JETTISON—to cast off, throw cargo overboard

JINGOISM—belligerent support of one's country

JOCULAR—jovial, playful, humorous

JUNCTURE—point where two things are joined

K

KERNEL—innermost, essential part; seed grain, often in a shell

KINETIC—relating to motion; characterized by movement

KNELL—sound of a funeral bell

KUDOS—fame, glory, honor

L

LABYRINTH—maze

LACHRYMOSE—tearful

LACKADAISICAL—idle, lazy; apathetic, indifferent

LACONIC—using few words

LAGGARD—dawdler, loafer, lazy person

LAMENT (v.)—to deplore, grieve

LAMPOON—to attack with satire, mock harshly

LANGUID—lacking energy, indifferent; slow, leisurely

LARDER—place where food is stored

LARGESS—generosity; gift

LASSITUDE—lethargy, sluggishness

LATENT—present but hidden; potential

LAUDABLE—deserving of praise

LAXITY—carelessness

LEGERDEMAIN—trickery

LEGIBLE—readable

LENIENT—easygoing, permissive

LETHARGY—indifferent inactivity

LEVITATE—to rise in the air or cause to rise

LEVITY—humor, frivolity, gaiety

LEXICON—dictionary, list of words

LIBERAL—tolerant, broad-minded; generous, lavish

LIBERTINE—one without moral restraint

LICENTIOUS—immoral; unrestrained by society

LIMPID—clear, transparent

LIONIZE—to treat as a celebrity

LISSOME—easily flexed, limber, agile

LISTLESS—lacking energy and enthusiasm

LITERATE—able to read and write; well-read and educated

LITHE—moving and bending with ease; graceful

LIVID—discolored from a bruise; reddened with anger

LOITER—to stand around idly

LOQUACIOUS—talkative

LUCID—clear and easily understood

LUDICROUS—laughable, ridiculous

LUGUBRIOUS—sorrowful, mournful; dismal

LUMBER (v.)—to move slowly and awkwardly

LUMINOUS—bright, brilliant, glowing

LURID—harshly shocking, sensational; glowing

LUXURIANCE—lavishness, lushness

LYRICAL—suitable for poetry and song; expressing feeling

M

MAELSTROM—whirlpool; turmoil; agitated state of mind

MAGNANIMOUS—generous, noble in spirit

MAGNATE—powerful or influential person

MALADY—illness

MALAPROPISM—humorous misuse of a word

MALCONTENT—discontented person, one who holds a grudge

MALEFACTOR—evil-doer; culprit

MALEVOLENT—ill-willed; causing evil or harm to others

MALICE—animosity, spite, hatred

MALINGER—to evade responsibility by pretending to be ill

MANDATORY—necessary, required

MANNERED—artificial or stilted in character

MAR—to damage, deface; spoil

MARITIME—relating to the sea or sailing

MARTIAL—warlike, pertaining to the military

MARTINET—strict disciplinarian, one who rigidly follows rules

MARTYR—person dying for his or her beliefs

MAUDLIN—overly sentimental

MAWKISH—sickeningly sentimental

MEDIEVAL—relating to the Middle Ages (about A.D. 500–1500)

MELANCHOLY—sadness, depression

MENAGERIE—various animals kept together for exhibition

MENDACIOUS—dishonest

MENDICANT—beggar

MENTOR—experienced teacher and wise adviser

MERCURIAL—quick, shrewd, and unpredictable

MERETRICIOUS—gaudy, falsely attractive

MERITORIOUS—deserving reward or praise

METAMORPHOSIS—change, transformation

METAPHOR—figure of speech comparing two different things

METICULOUS—extremely careful, fastidious, painstaking

METTLE—courageousness; endurance

MILITATE—to operate against, work against

MISANTHROPE—person who hates human beings

MISCONSTRUE—to misunderstand, misinterpret

MISERLINESS—extreme stinginess

MISNOMER—an incorrect name or designation

MISSIVE—note or letter

MITIGATE—to soften, make milder

MNEMONIC—relating to memory; designed to assist memory

MOLLIFY—to calm or make less severe

MOLT—to shed hair, skin, or an outer layer periodically

MONASTIC—characteristic of monks or a monastery; extremely plain or secluded

MONOLOGUE—dramatic speech performed by one actor

MONTAGE—composite picture

MOOT—debatable; purely academic, deprived of practical significance

MORBID—gruesome; relating to disease; abnormally gloomy

MORIBUND—dying, decaying

MOROSE—gloomy, sullen, or surly

MORSEL—small bit of food

MOTE—small particle, speck

MOTLEY—many colored; composed of diverse parts

MOTTLE—to mark with spots

MUNDANE—commonplace; dull

MUNIFICENT—generous

MUTABILITY—changeability

MYRIAD—immense number; multitude

N

NADIR—lowest point

NASCENT—starting to develop, coming into existence

NEBULOUS—vague, cloudy

NEOPHYTE—novice, beginner

NETTLE (v.)—to irritate

NICHE—recess in a wall; best position for something

NIHILISM—belief that existence and all traditional values are meaningless

NOCTURNAL—pertaining to night; active at night

NOISOME—stinking, putrid

NOMADIC—moving from place to place

NOMINAL—existing in name only; negligible

NOTORIETY—unfavorable fame

NOVICE—apprentice, beginner

NOXIOUS—harmful, unwholesome

NUANCE—shade of meaning

NULLIFY—to make legally invalid; to counteract the effect of

O

OBDURATE—stubborn

OBFUSCATE—to confuse, obscure

OBLIQUE—indirect, evasive; misleading, devious

OBLIVIOUS—unaware, inattentive

OBSEQUIOUS—overly submissive, brownnosing

OBSOLETE—no longer in use

OBSTINATE—stubborn

OBSTREPEROUS—troublesome, boisterous, unruly

OBVIATE—to make unnecessary; to anticipate and prevent

OCCLUDE—to shut, block

ODIOUS—hateful, contemptible

OFFICIOUS—too helpful, meddlesome

OMINOUS—menacing, threatening, indicating misfortune

OMNISCIENT—having infinite knowledge, all-seeing

ONEROUS—burdensome

OPAQUE—impervious to light; difficult to understand

OPINE—to express an opinion

OPPORTUNE—appropriate, fitting

OPPROBRIOUS—disgraceful, contemptuous

OPULENCE—wealth

ORATION—lecture, formal speech

OSCILLATE—to move back and forth

OSSIFY—to turn to bone; to become rigid

OSTENTATIOUS—showy

OSTRACISM—exclusion, temporary banishment

OUSTER—expulsion, ejection

OVERWROUGHT—agitated, overdone

P

PACIFY—to restore calm, bring peace

PALATIAL—like a palace, magnificent

PALAVER—idle talk

PALL (n.)—covering that darkens or obscures; cloth draped over a coffin

PALL (v.)—to lose strength or interest

PALLIATE—to make less serious, ease

PALLID—lacking color or liveliness

PALPABLE—obvious, real, tangible

PALTRY—pitifully small or worthless

PANACEA—cure-all

PANACHE—flamboyance, verve

PANDEMIC (adj.)—spread over a whole area or country

PANEGYRIC—elaborate praise; formal hymn of praise

PANORAMA—broad view; comprehensive picture

PARADIGM—ideal example, model

PARADOX—contradiction, incongruity; dilemma, puzzle

PARAGON—model of excellence or perfection

PARAMOUNT—supreme, dominant, primary

PARAPHRASE—to reword, usually in simpler terms

PARASITE—person or animal that lives at another's expense

PARCH—to dry or shrivel

PARIAH—outcast

PARITY—equality

PAROCHIAL—of limited scope or outlook, provincial

PARODY—humorous imitation

PARRY—to ward off or deflect

PARSIMONY—stinginess

PARTISAN—strong supporter; biased in favor of

PASTICHE—piece of literature or music imitating other works

PATHOS—pity, compassion

PATRICIAN—aristocrat

PATRONIZE—to condescend to, disparage; to buy from

PAUCITY—scarcity, lack

PAUPER—very poor person

PEDAGOGUE—teacher

PEDANT—boring academic; nitpicker

PEDESTRIAN (adj.)—commonplace

PEER (n.)—contemporary, equal, match

PEERLESS—unequaled

PENCHANT—inclination

PENSIVE—thoughtful

PENURY—extreme poverty

PERENNIAL—present throughout the years; persistent

PERFIDIOUS—faithless, disloyal, untrustworthy

PERFUNCTORY—done in a routine way; indifferent

PERIPATETIC—moving from place to place

PERJURE—to tell a lie under oath

PERMEABLE—penetrable

PERNICIOUS—very harmful

PERPETUAL—endless, lasting

PERTINENT—applicable, appropriate

PERUSAL—close examination

PESTILENCE—epidemic, plague

PETULANCE—rudeness, peevishness

PHALANX—massed group of soldiers, people, or things

PHILANDERER—pursuer of casual love affairs

PHILANTHROPY—love of humanity; generosity to worthy causes

PHILISTINE—narrow-minded person, someone lacking appreciation for art or culture

PHLEGMATIC—calm in temperament; sluggish

PHOBIA—exaggerated, illogical fear

PIETY—devoutness, religiousness

PILFER—to steal

PINNACLE—peak, highest point of development

PIQUE (n.)—fleeting feeling of hurt pride

PITHY—profound, substantial; concise, succinct, to the point

PLACATE—to soothe or pacify

PLACID—calm

PLAGIARIST—one who steals words or ideas

PLAINTIFF—injured person in a lawsuit

PLATITUDE—stale, overused expression

PLENITUDE—abundance, plenty

PLETHORA—excess, overabundance

PLIANT—pliable, yielding

PLUCKY—courageous, spunky

PLUMMET—to fall, plunge

PLY (v.)—to use a tool or engage in a trade; to provide with food or drink

POIGNANT—emotionally moving

POLEMIC—controversy, argument; verbal attack

POLYGLOT—speaker of many languages

PONTIFICATE—to speak in a pretentious manner

PORE (v.)—to study closely or meditatively

POROUS—full of holes, permeable to liquids

PORTENT—omen

POSTERITY—future generations; all of a person's descendants

POTABLE—drinkable

PRAGMATIC—practical; moved by facts rather than abstract ideals

PRATTLE (n.)—meaningless, foolish talk

PRECARIOUS—uncertain, unsteady

PRECIPICE—edge, steep overhang

PRECIPITOUS—hasty, quickly, with too little caution

PRECLUDE—to rule out

PRECOCIOUS—unusually advanced at an early age

PRECURSOR—forerunner, predecessor

PREDILECTION—preference, liking

PREFACE (n.)—introduction to a book; introductory remarks to a speech

PREMEDITATE—to consider, plan beforehand

PREPOSSESSING—attractive, engaging, appealing

PREPOSTEROUS—absurd, illogical

PRESAGE—to foretell, indicate in advance

PRESCIENT—having foresight

PRESUMPTUOUS—rude, improperly bold

PRETEXT—excuse, pretended reason

PREVALENT—widespread

PREVARICATE—to lie, evade the truth

PRISTINE—untouched, uncorrupted

PRIVATION—lack of usual necessities or comforts

PROBITY—honesty, high-mindedness

PROCLIVITY—tendency, inclination

PROCRASTINATOR—one who continually and unjustifiably postpones

PRODIGAL—wasteful, extravagant, lavish

PRODIGIOUS—vast, enormous, extraordinary

PROFICIENT—expert, skilled in a certain subject

PROFUSE—lavish, extravagant

PROGENITOR—originator, forefather, ancestor in a direct line

PROGENY—offspring, children

PROGNOSIS—prediction of disease outcome; any prediction

PROLIFIC—productive

PROLOGUE—introductory section of a literary work or play

PROMONTORY—piece of land or rock higher than its surroundings

PROMULGATE—to make known publicly

PROPENSITY—inclination, tendency

PROPITIOUS—favorable, advantageous

PROPONENT—advocate, defender, supporter

PROSAIC—relating to prose; dull, commonplace

PROSCRIBE—to condemn; to forbid, outlaw

PROSTRATE—lying face downward, lying flat on ground

PROTAGONIST—main character in a play or story, hero

PROTEAN—readily assuming different forms or characters

PROTOCOL—ceremony and manners observed by diplomats

PROVINCIAL—rustic, unsophisticated, limited in scope

PROWESS—bravery, skill

PROXIMITY—nearness

PRUDENT—careful, cautious

PRY—to intrude into; force open

PSEUDONYM—pen name; fictitious or borrowed name

PUERILE—childish, immature, silly

PUGNACIOUS—quarrelsome, eager, and ready to fight

PULCHRITUDE—beauty

PUNCTILIOUS—careful in observing rules of behavior or ceremony

PUNGENT—strong or sharp in smell or taste

PUNITIVE—having to do with punishment

PURGE—to cleanse or free from impurities

Q

QUAGMIRE—marsh; difficult situation

QUANDARY—dilemma, difficulty

QUARANTINE—isolation to prevent spread of disease

QUELL—to crush or subdue

QUERULOUS—inclined to complain, irritable

QUIBBLE—to argue about insignificant and irrelevant details

QUIESCENCE—inactivity, stillness

QUINTESSENCE—most typical example

QUIXOTIC—overly idealistic, impractical

QUOTIDIAN—occurring daily; commonplace

R

RACONTEUR—witty, skillful storyteller

RAIL (v.)—to scold with bitter or abusive language

RAMBLE—to roam, wander; to babble, digress

RAMIFICATION—an implication, outgrowth, or consequence

RANCOR—bitter hatred

RANT—to harangue, rave, forcefully scold

RAPPORT—relationship of trust and respect

RAPT—deeply absorbed

RAREFIED—distant from ordinary concerns, refined

RASH (adj.)—careless, hasty, reckless

RAUCOUS—harsh sounding; boisterous

RAVAGE—to destroy, devastate

RAVENOUS—extremely hungry

RAZE—to tear down, demolish

REACTIONARY—marked by extreme conservatism, especially in politics

REBUFF (n.)—blunt rejection

REBUKE—to reprimand, scold

REBUT—to refute by evidence or argument

RECALCITRANT—resisting authority or control

RECANT—to retract a statement, opinion, etc.

RECLUSIVE—shut off from the world

RECONDITE—relating to obscure learning; known to only a few

RECOUNT—to describe facts or events

REDRESS (n.)—relief from wrong or injury

REDUNDANCY—unnecessary repetition

REFRACT—to deflect sound or light

REFUGE—escape, shelter

REGIMEN—systematic plan

REJOINDER—response

RELINQUISH—to renounce or surrender something

RELISH (v.)—to enjoy greatly

REMUNERATION—pay or reward for work, trouble, etc.

RENASCENT—reborn, revived

RENEGADE—traitor, person abandoning a cause

RENEGE—to go back on one's word

RENOWN—fame, widespread acclaim

REPAST—meal or mealtime

REPEAL—to revoke or formally withdraw (often a law)

REPENTANT—apologetic, guilty, remorseful

REPLETE—abundantly supplied

REPOSE—relaxation, leisure

REPREHENSIBLE—blameworthy, disreputable

REPROACH—to find fault with; blame

REPROBATE—morally unprincipled person

REPROVE—to criticize or correct

REQUITE—to return or repay

RESCIND—to repeal, cancel

RESIDUE—remainder, leftover, remnant

RESILIENT—able to recover quickly after illness or bad luck; able to bounce back to shape

RESOLUTE—determined; with a clear purpose

RESPITE—interval of relief

RESPLENDENT—splendid, brilliant

RESTIVE—impatient, uneasy, restless

RETICENT—not speaking freely; reserved

RETORT (n.)—cutting response

RETROSPECTIVE—review of the past

REVELRY—boisterous festivity

REVERE—to worship, regard with awe

REVERT—to backslide, regress

REVILE—to criticize with harsh language, verbally abuse

RHETORIC—persuasive use of language

RIBALD—humorous in a vulgar way

RIDDLE (v.)—to make many holes in; permeate

RIFE—widespread, prevalent; abundant

RISQUÉ —bordering on being inappropriate or indecent

ROBUST—strong and healthy; hardy

ROTUND—round in shape; fat

RUE—to regret

RUMINATE—to contemplate, reflect upon

RUSTIC—rural

S

SACCHARINE—excessively sweet or sentimental

SAGACIOUS—shrewd

SALIENT—prominent or conspicuous

SALLOW—sickly yellow in color

SALUBRIOUS—healthful

SALUTATION—greeting

SANCTION (n.)—permission, support; law; penalty

SANCTUARY—haven, retreat

SANGUINE—cheerfully optimistic

SARDONIC—cynical, scornfully mocking

SATIATE—to satisfy

SAUNTER—to amble; walk in a leisurely manner

SAVANT—learned person

SAVORY—agreeable in taste or smell

SCALE (v.)—to climb to the top of

SCINTILLA—trace amount

SCINTILLATE—to sparkle, flash

SCOFF—to deride, ridicule

SCORE (n.)—notation for a musical composition

SCORE (v.)—to make a notch or scratch

SCRUPULOUS—restrained; honest; careful and precise

SCRUTINY—careful observation

SCURRILOUS—scandalous, insulting

SECULAR—not religious

SEDENTARY—inactive, stationary; sluggish

SEMINAL—influential, groundbreaking

SENESCENT—aging, growing old

SENTIENT—aware, conscious, able to perceive

SEQUESTER—to remove or set apart; put into seclusion

SERAPHIC—angelic, pure, sublime

SERPENTINE—serpentlike; twisting, winding

SERVILE—submissive, obedient

SHARD—piece of broken glass or pottery

SHIRK—to avoid a task due to laziness or fear

SIMPER—to smirk, smile foolishly

SINECURE—well-paying job or office that requires little or no work

SINGE—to burn slightly, scorch

SINUOUS—winding; intricate, complex

SKEPTICAL—doubtful, questioning

SKULK—to move in a stealthy or cautious manner; sneak

SLIGHT (v.)—to treat as unimportant; insult

SLOTH—sluggishness, laziness

SLOUGH—to discard or shed

SLOVENLY—untidy, messy

SOBRIETY—seriousness, soberness

SODDEN—thoroughly soaked; saturated

SOJOURN—visit, stay

SOLACE—comfort in distress; consolation

SOLICITOUS—concerned, attentive; eager

SOLILOQUY—literary or dramatic speech by one character, not addressed to others

SOLUBLE—capable of being solved or dissolved

SOMBER—dark and gloomy; melancholy, dismal

SOMNOLENT—drowsy, sleepy; inducing sleep

SONOROUS—producing a full, rich sound

SOPHISTRY—deceptive reasoning or argumentation

SOPHOMORIC—immature and overconfident

SOPORIFIC—sleepy or tending to cause sleep

SORDID—filthy; contemptible and corrupt

SOVEREIGN (adj.)—having supreme power, independently governed

SPARTAN—austere, severe, grave; simple, bare

SPONTANEOUS—on the spur of the moment, impulsive

SPORADIC—infrequent, irregular

SPURIOUS—lacking authenticity; counterfeit, false

SPURN—to reject or refuse contemptuously; scorn

SQUALID—filthy; morally repulsive

SQUANDER—to waste

STACCATO—marked by abrupt, clear-cut sounds

STAID—self-restrained to the point of dullness

STAND (n.)—group of trees

STARK—bare, empty, vacant

STIFLE—to smother or suffocate; suppress

STIPEND—allowance; fixed amount of money paid regularly

STOIC—indifferent to or unaffected by emotions

STOLID—having or showing little emotion

STRIDENT—loud, harsh, unpleasantly noisy

STRINGENT—imposing severe, rigorous standards

STUPEFY—to dull the senses of; stun, astonish

STYMIE—to block or thwart

SUAVE—smoothly gracious or polite; blandly ingratiating

SUBJUGATE—to conquer, subdue; enslave

SUBLIME—awe-inspiring; of high spiritual or moral value

SUBLIMINAL—subconscious; imperceptible

SUBTERFUGE—trick or tactic used to avoid something

SUBTERRANEAN—hidden, secret; underground

SUBTLE—hard to detect or describe; perceptive

SUBVERT—to undermine or corrupt

SUCCINCT—terse, brief, concise

SUCCULENT—juicy; full of vitality or freshness

SULLEN—brooding, gloomy

SULLY—to soil, stain, tarnish, taint

SUPERCILIOUS—arrogant, haughty, overbearing, condescending

SUPERFICIAL—shallow, trivial, not thorough

SUPERFLUOUS—extra, more than necessary

SUPERSEDE—to take the place of; replace

SUPPLICANT—one who asks humbly and earnestly

SURFEIT—excessive amount

SURLY—rude and bad-tempered

SURMISE—to make an educated guess

SURMOUNT—to conquer, overcome

SURREPTITIOUS—characterized by secrecy

SUSCEPTIBLE—vulnerable, unprotected

SYBARITE—person devoted to pleasure and luxury

SYCOPHANT—self-serving flatterer, yes-man

SYLLABUS—outline of a course

SYMBIOSIS—cooperation, mutual helpfulness

SYNOPSIS—plot summary

SYNTHESIS—blend, combination

T

TACIT—silently understood or implied

TACITURN—uncommunicative, not inclined to speak much

TACTILE—relating to the sense of touch

TAINT—to spoil or infect; to dishonor

TALON—claw of an animal, especially a bird of prey

TANG—sharp flavor or odor

TANGENTIAL—digressing, diverting; not directly related

TANGIBLE—able to be sensed, perceptible, measurable

TAWDRY—gaudy, cheap, showy

TEMPERANCE—restraint, self-control, moderation

TEMPERED—moderated, restrained

TEMPESTUOUS—stormy, raging, furious

TENABLE—defensible, reasonable

TENACIOUS—stubborn, holding firm

TENET—belief, doctrine

TENUOUS—weak, insubstantial

TEPID—lukewarm; showing little enthusiasm

TERSE—concise, brief, free of extra words

TESTAMENT—statement of belief; will

TETHER—to bind, tie

THEOCRACY—government by priests representing a god

THESAURUS—book of synonyms and antonyms

TIMOROUS—timid, shy, full of apprehension

TIRADE—long, violent speech; verbal assault

TOADY—flatterer, hanger-on, yes-man

TOME—book, usually large and academic

TORPID—lethargic; unable to move; dormant

TORTUOUS—having many twists and turns; highly complex

TOXIN—poison

TRACTABLE—obedient, yielding

TRANSCEND—to rise above, go beyond

TRANSIENT (adj.)—temporary, short-lived, fleeting

TRANSITORY—short-lived, impermanent

TRANSLUCENT—partially transparent

TRAVESTY—parody, exaggerated imitation, caricature

TREMULOUS—trembling, quivering; fearful, timid

TRENCHANT—acute, sharp, incisive; forceful, effective

TREPIDATION—fear and anxiety

TRIFLING—of slight worth, trivial, insignificant

TRITE—shallow, superficial

TRUNCATE—to cut off, shorten by cutting

TUNDRA—treeless plain found in arctic or subarctic regions

TURGID—swollen, bloated

TURPITUDE—inherent vileness, foulness, depravity

TYRO—beginner, novice

U

UBIQUITOUS—being everywhere simultaneously

UMBRAGE—offense, resentment

UNADULTERATED—absolutely pure

UNANIMITY—state of total agreement or unity

UNCONSCIONABLE—unscrupulous; shockingly unfair or unjust

UNCTUOUS—greasy, oily; smug and falsely earnest

UNDULATING—moving in waves

UNEQUIVOCAL—absolute, certain

UNIFORM (adj.)—consistent and unchanging; identical

UNIMPEACHABLE—beyond question

UNSCRUPULOUS—dishonest

UPBRAID—to scold sharply

UPROARIOUS—loud and forceful

URBANE—courteous, refined, suave

USURP—to seize by force

USURY—practice of lending money at exorbitant rates

UTOPIA—perfect place

V

VACILLATE—to waver, show indecision

VAGRANT—person with no home and no means of support

VANQUISH—to conquer, defeat

VAPID—uninteresting, dull

VARIEGATED—varied; marked with different colors

VAUNTED—boasted about, bragged about

VEHEMENT—strong, urgent

VENDETTA—prolonged feud marked by bitter hostility

VENERABLE—respected because of age

VENT (v.)—to express, say out loud

VERACITY—accuracy, truth

VERBATIM—word for word

VERBOSE—wordy

VERITY—truthfulness; belief viewed as true and enduring

VERMIN—small creatures offensive to humans

VERNACULAR—everyday language used by ordinary people

VERNAL—related to spring

VERSATILE—adaptable, all-purpose

VESTIGE—trace, remnant

VEX—to irritate, annoy; confuse, puzzle

VIABLE—workable, able to succeed or grow

VICARIOUS—enjoyed through imagined participation in another's experience

VIE—to compete, contend

VIGILANT—attentive, watchful

VILIFY—to slander, defame

VIM—energy, enthusiasm

VINDICATE—to clear of blame; support a claim

VINDICTIVE—spiteful, vengeful, unforgiving

VIRTUOSO—someone with masterly skill; expert musician

VIRULENT—extremely poisonous; malignant; hateful

VISCOUS—thick, syrupy, and sticky

VITRIOLIC—burning, caustic; bitterly critical

VITUPERATE—to abuse verbally

VIVACIOUS—lively, spirited

VOCIFEROUS—loud, vocal, and noisy

VOLITION—free choice, free will; act of choosing

VOLUBLE—speaking much and easily, talkative; glib

VORACIOUS—having a great appetite

VULNERABLE—defenseless, unprotected; innocent, naive

W

WAIVE—to refrain from enforcing a rule; to give up a legal right

WAN—sickly pale

WANTON—undisciplined, unrestrained, reckless

WARY—careful, cautious

WHET—to sharpen, stimulate

WHIMSICAL—playful or fanciful

WRY—amusing, ironic

X

XENOPHOBIA—fear or hatred of foreigners or strangers

Y

YOKE (v.)—to join together

Z

ZENITH—highest point, summit

ZEPHYR—gentle breeze

ZOOLOGIST—scientist who studies animals

100 ESSENTIAL MATH CONCEPTS

The math on the PSAT covers a lot of ground—from arithmetic to algebra to geometry.

Don't let yourself be intimidated. We've highlighted the 100 most important concepts that you'll need for PSAT Math and listed them in this chapter.

Use this list to remind yourself of the key concepts you'll need to know. Do four concepts a day, and you'll be ready within a month. If a concept continually causes you trouble, circle it and refer back to it as you try to do the questions.

You've probably been taught most of these concepts in school already, so this list is a great way to refresh your memory.

NUMBER PROPERTIES

1. NUMBER CATEGORIES

Integers are whole numbers; they include positive and negative numbers and zero, but not fractions or decimals.

A **rational number** is a number that can be expressed as a **ratio of two integers. Irrational numbers** are real numbers—they have locations on the number line—but they **can't be expressed precisely as a fraction or decimal.** For the purposes of the PSAT, the most important **irrational numbers** are $\sqrt{2}$, $\sqrt{3}$, and π.

2. ADDING/SUBTRACTING SIGNED NUMBERS

To **add a positive and a negative,** first ignore the signs and find the positive difference between the number parts. Then attach the sign of the original number with the larger number part. For example, to add 23 and −34, first ignore the minus sign and find the positive difference between 23 and 34—that's 11. Then attach the sign of the number with the larger number part—in this case it's the minus sign from the −34. So, 23 + (−34) = −11.

Make **subtraction** situations simpler by turning them into addition. For example, you can think of −17 − (−21) as −17 + (+21).

To **add or subtract a string of positives and negatives,** first turn everything into addition. Then combine the positives and negatives so that the string is reduced to the sum of a single positive number and a single negative number.

3. MULTIPLYING/DIVIDING SIGNED NUMBERS

To multiply and/or divide positives and negatives, treat the number parts as usual and **attach a minus sign** if there were originally an odd number of **negatives.** For example, to multiply −2, −3, and −5, first multiply the number parts: $2 \times 3 \times 5 = 30$. Then go back and note that there were **three**—an **odd** number—negatives, so the product is negative: $(−2) \times (−3) \times (−5) = −30$.

4. PEMDAS

When performing multiple operations, remember to perform them in the right order: **PEMDAS,** which means **Parentheses** first, then **Exponents,** then **Multiplication** and **Division** (left to right), and lastly **Addition** and **Subtraction** (left to right). In the expression $9 − 2 \times (5 − 3)^2 + 6 \div 3$, begin with the parentheses: $(5 − 3) = 2$. Then do the exponent: $2^2 = 4$. Now the expression is: $9 − 2 \times 4 + 6 \div 3$. Next do the multiplication and division to get: $9 − 8 + 2$, which equals 3. If you have difficulty remembering PEMDAS, use this sentence to recall it: **P**lease **E**xcuse **M**y **D**ear **A**unt **S**ally.

5. COUNTING CONSECUTIVE INTEGERS

To count consecutive integers, **subtract the smallest from the largest and add 1.** To count the number of integers from 13 through 31, subtract: $31 − 13 = 18$. Then add 1: $18 + 1 = 19$.

NUMBER OPERATIONS AND CONCEPTS

6. EXPONENTIAL GROWTH

If r is the ratio between consecutive terms, a_1 is the first term, a_n is the nth term, and S_n is the sum of the first n terms, then $a_n = a_1 r^{n-1}$ and $S_n \frac{a_1 - a_1 r^n}{1 - r}$.

7. UNION AND INTERSECTION OF SETS

The things in a set are called elements or members. The union of Set A and Set B, sometimes expressed as $A \cup B$, is the set of elements that are in either or both of Set A and Set B. If Set $A = \{1, 2\}$ and Set $B = \{3, 4\}$, then $A \cup B = \{1, 2, 3, 4\}$. The intersection of Set A and Set B, sometimes expressed as $A \cap B$, is the set of elements common to both Set A and Set B. If Set $A = \{1, 2, 3\}$ and Set $B = \{3, 4, 5\}$, then $A \cap B = \{3\}$.

DIVISIBILITY

8. FACTOR/MULTIPLE

The **factors** of integer n are the positive integers that divide into n with no remainder. The **multiples** of n are the integers that n divides into with no remainder. For example, 6 is a factor of 12, and 24 is a multiple of 12. Therefore, 12 is both a factor and a multiple of itself, since $12 \times 1 = 12$ and $12 \div 1 = 12$.

9. PRIME FACTORIZATION

To find the prime factorization of an integer, continue factoring until **all the factors are prime.** For example, to factor 36: $36 = 4 \times 9 = 2 \times 2 \times 3 \times 3$.

10. RELATIVE PRIMES

Relative primes are integers that have no common factor other than 1. To determine whether two integers are relative primes, break them both down to their prime factorizations. For example: $35 = 5 \times 7$ and $54 = 2 \times 3 \times 3 \times 3$. They have **no prime factors in common,** so 35 and 54 are relative primes.

11. COMMON MULTIPLE

A common multiple is a number that is a multiple of two or more integers. You can always get a common multiple of two integers by **multiplying** them, but unless the two numbers are relative primes, the product will not be the *least* common multiple. For example, to find a common multiple for 12 and 15, you could just multiply: $12 \times 15 = 180$.

To find the **least common multiple (LCM),** check out the **multiples of the larger integer** until you find one that's **also a multiple of the smaller.** To find the LCM of 12 and 15, begin by taking the multiples of 15: 15 is not divisible by 12, nor are 30 or 45. But the next multiple of 15, 60, *is* divisible by 12, so it's the LCM.

12. GREATEST COMMON FACTOR (GCF)

To find the greatest common factor, break down the integers into their prime factorizations and multiply **all the prime factors they have in common.** For example, $36 = 2 \times 2 \times 3 \times 3$ and $48 = 2 \times 2 \times 2 \times 2 \times 3$. These integers have a 2×2 and a 3 in common, so the GCF is $2 \times 2 \times 3 = 12$.

13. EVEN/ODD

To predict whether a sum, difference, or product will be even or odd, just **take simple numbers such as 1 and 2 and see what happens.** There are rules—"odd times even is even," for example—but there's no need to memorize them. What happens with one set of numbers generally happens with all similar sets.

14. MULTIPLES OF 2 AND 4

An integer is divisible by 2 (even) if the **last digit is even.** An integer is divisible by 4 if the **last two digits form a multiple of 4.** The last digit of 562 is 2, which is even, so 562 is a multiple of 2. The last two digits form 62, which is *not* divisible by 4, so 562 is not a multiple of 4. The integer 512, however, is divisible by 4 because the last two digits form 12, which is a multiple of 4.

15. MULTIPLES OF 3 AND 9

An integer is divisible by 3 if the **sum of its digits is divisible by 3.** An integer is divisible by 9 if the **sum of its digits is divisible by 9.** The sum of the digits in 957 is 21, which is divisible by 3 but not by 9, so 957 is divisible by 3 but not by 9.

16. MULTIPLES OF 5 AND 10

An integer is divisible by 5 if the **last digit is 5 or 0.** An integer is divisible by 10 if the **last digit is 0.** The last digit of 665 is 5, so 665 is a multiple of 5 but *not* a multiple of 10.

17. REMAINDERS

The remainder is the **whole number left over after division.** For example, 487 is 2 more than 485, which is a multiple of 5, so when 487 is divided by 5, the remainder is 2.

FRACTIONS AND DECIMALS

18. REDUCING FRACTIONS

To reduce a fraction to lowest terms, **factor out and cancel** all factors the numerator and denominator have in common.

$$\frac{28}{36} = \frac{4 \times 7}{4 \times 9} = \frac{7}{9}$$

19. ADDING/SUBTRACTING FRACTIONS

To add or subtract fractions, first find a **common denominator,** then add or subtract the numerators.

$$\frac{2}{15} + \frac{3}{10} = \frac{4}{30} + \frac{9}{30} = \frac{4+9}{30} = \frac{13}{30}$$

20. MULTIPLYING FRACTIONS

To multiply fractions, **multiply** the numerators and **multiply** the denominators.

$$\frac{5}{7} \times \frac{3}{4} = \frac{5 \times 3}{7 \times 4} = \frac{15}{28}$$

21. DIVIDING FRACTIONS

To divide fractions, **invert** the second one and **multiply.**

$$\frac{1}{2} \div \frac{3}{5} = \frac{1}{2} \times \frac{5}{3} = \frac{1 \times 5}{2 \times 3} = \frac{5}{6}$$

22. MIXED NUMBERS AND IMPROPER FRACTIONS

To convert a mixed number to an improper fraction, **multiply** the whole number part by the denominator, then **add** the numerator. The result is the new numerator (over the same denominator). To convert $7\frac{1}{3}$, first multiply 7 by 3, then add 1, to get the new numerator of 22. Put that over the same denominator, 3, to get $\frac{22}{3}$.

To convert an improper fraction to a mixed number, divide the denominator into the numerator to get a **whole number quotient with a remainder.** The quotient becomes the whole number part of the mixed number, and the remainder becomes the new numerator—with the same denominator. For example, to convert $\frac{108}{5}$, first divide 5 into 108, which yields 21 with a remainder of 3. Therefore, $\frac{108}{5} = 21\frac{3}{5}$.

23. RECIPROCAL

To find the reciprocal of a fraction, **switch the numerator and the denominator.** The reciprocal of $\frac{3}{7}$ is $\frac{7}{3}$. The reciprocal of 5 is $\frac{1}{5}$. The product of reciprocals is 1.

24. COMPARING FRACTIONS

One way to compare fractions is to **reexpress them with a common denominator.** For example, $\frac{3}{4} = \frac{21}{28}$ and $\frac{5}{7} = \frac{20}{28}$. Now, $\frac{21}{28}$ is greater than $\frac{20}{28}$, so $\frac{3}{4}$ is greater than $\frac{5}{7}$. Another method is to **convert them both to decimals.** For example, $\frac{3}{4}$ converts to 0.75 , and $\frac{5}{7}$ converts to approximately 0.714.

25. CONVERTING FRACTIONS AND DECIMALS

To convert a fraction to a decimal, **divide the bottom into the top.** To convert $\frac{5}{8}$, divide 8 into 5, yielding 0.625.

To convert a decimal to a fraction, set the decimal over 1 and **multiply the numerator and denominator by 10** raised to the number of digits which are to the right of the decimal point.

To convert 0.625 to a fraction, you would multiply $\frac{0.625}{1}$ by $\frac{10^3}{10^3}$ or $\frac{1,000}{1,000}$.

Then simplify: $\frac{625}{100} = \frac{5 \times 125}{8 \times 125} = \frac{5}{8}$.

26. REPEATING DECIMAL

To find a particular digit in a repeating decimal, note the **number of digits in the cluster that repeats.** If there are 2 digits in that cluster, then every second digit is the same. If there are 3 digits in that cluster, then every third digit is the same. And so on.

For example, the decimal equivalent of $\frac{1}{27}$ is 0.037037037…, which is best written $0.\overline{037}$. There are 3 digits in the repeating cluster, so every 3rd digit is the same: 7. To find the 50th digit, look for the multiple of 3 just less than 50—that's 48. The 48th digit is 7, and with the 49th digit the pattern repeats with 0. The 50th digit is 3.

27. IDENTIFYING THE PARTS AND THE WHOLE

The key to solving most fraction and percent word problems is to identify the part and the whole. Usually you'll find the **part** associated with the verb *is/are* and the **whole** associated with the word *of.* In the sentence, "Half of the boys are blonds," the whole is the boys (*of* the boys), and the part is the blonds (*are* blonds).

PERCENTS

28. PERCENT FORMULA

Whether you need to find the part, the whole, or the percent, use the same formula:

Part = Percent × Whole

Example:	What is 12 percent of 25?
Setup:	Part = 0.12 × 25
Example:	15 is 3 percent of what number?
Setup:	15 = 0.03 × Whole
Example:	45 is what percent of 9?
Setup:	45 = Percent × 9

29. PERCENT INCREASE AND DECREASE

To increase a number by a percent, **add the percent to 100 percent,** convert to a decimal, and multiply. To increase 40 by 25 percent, add 25 percent to 100 percent, convert 125 percent to 1.25, and multiply by 40:

$$1.25 \times 40 = 50$$

30. FINDING THE ORIGINAL WHOLE

To find the **original whole before a percent increase or decrease,** set up an equation. Think of the result of a 15 percent increase over x as $1.15x$.

Example: After a 5 percent increase, the population was 59,346. What was the population before the increase?

Setup: $1.05x = 59,346$

31. COMBINED PERCENT INCREASE AND DECREASE

To determine the combined effect of multiple percent increases and/or decreases, **start with 100 and see what happens.**

Example: A price went up 10 percent one year, and the new price went up 20 percent the next year. What was the combined percent increase?

Setup: First year: 100 + (10 percent of 100) = 110. Second year: 110 + (20 percent of 110) = 132. That's a combined 32 percent increase.

AVERAGES

32. AVERAGE FORMULA

To find the average of a set of numbers, **add them and divide by the number of numbers.**

$$\text{Average} = \frac{\text{Sum of the terms}}{\text{Number of terms}}$$

To find the average of the five numbers 12, 15, 23, 40, and 40, first add them: $12 + 15 + 23 + 40 + 40 = 130$. Then divide the sum by 5: $130 \div 5 = 26$.

33. AVERAGE OF EVENLY SPACED NUMBERS

To find the average of evenly spaced numbers, just **average the smallest and the largest.** The average of all the integers from 13 through 77 is the same as the average of 13 and 77:

$$\frac{13 + 77}{2} = \frac{90}{2} = 45$$

34. USING THE AVERAGE TO FIND THE SUM

Sum = (Average) × (Number of terms)

If the average of ten numbers is 50, then they add up to 10×50, or 500.

35. FINDING THE MISSING NUMBER

To find a missing number when you're given the average, **use the sum.** If the average of four numbers is 7, then the sum of those four numbers is 4×7, or 28. Suppose that three of the numbers are 3, 5, and 8. These three numbers add up to 16 of that 28, which leaves 12 for the fourth number.

36. MEDIAN AND MODE

The median of a set of numbers is the **value that falls in the middle of the ordered set.** If you have five test scores, and they are 88, 86, 57, 94, and 73, you must first list the scores in increasing or decreasing order: 57, 73, 86, 88, 94.

The median is the middle number, or 86. If there is an even number of values in a set (six test scores, for instance), simply take the average of the two middle numbers.

The mode of a set of numbers is the **value that appears most often.** If your test scores were 88, 57, 68, 85, 99, 93, 93, 84, and 81, the mode of the scores would be 93 because it appears more often than any other score. If there is a tie for the most common value in a set, the set has more than one mode.

RATIOS, PROPORTIONS, AND RATES

37. SETTING UP A RATIO

To find a ratio, put the number associated with the word *of* **on top** and the quantity associated with the word *to* **on the bottom** and reduce. The ratio of 20 oranges to 12 apples is $\dfrac{20}{12}$, which reduces to $\dfrac{5}{3}$.

38. PART-TO-PART RATIOS AND PART-TO-WHOLE RATIOS

If the parts add up to the whole, a part-to-part ratio can be turned into two part-to-whole ratios by putting **each number in the original ratio over the sum of the numbers.** If the ratio of males to females is 1 to 2, then the males-to-people ratio is $\dfrac{1}{1+2} = \dfrac{1}{3}$ and the females-to-people ratio is $\dfrac{2}{1+2} = \dfrac{2}{3}$. In other words, $\dfrac{2}{3}$ of all the people are female.

39. SOLVING A PROPORTION

To solve a proportion, **cross-multiply:**

$$\frac{x}{5} = \frac{3}{4}$$
$$4x = 3 \times 5$$
$$x = \frac{15}{4} = 3.75$$

40. RATE

To solve a rate problem, **use the units** to keep things straight.

Example: If snow is falling at the rate of one foot every four hours, how many inches of snow will fall in seven hours?

Setup: $\dfrac{1 \text{ foot}}{4 \text{ hours}} = \dfrac{x \text{ inches}}{7 \text{ hours}}$

$\dfrac{12 \text{ inches}}{4 \text{ hours}} = \dfrac{x \text{ inches}}{7 \text{ hours}}$

$4x = 12 \times 7$

$x = 21$

41. AVERAGE RATE

Average rate is *not* simply the average of the rates.

$$\text{Average } A \text{ per } B = \frac{\text{Total } A}{\text{Total } B}$$
$$\text{Average speed} = \frac{\text{Total distance}}{\text{Total time}}$$

To find the average speed for 120 miles at 40 mph and 120 miles at 60 mph, **don't just average the two speeds.** First figure out the total distance and the total time. The total distance is 120 + 120 = 240 miles. The times are three hours for the first leg and two hours for the second leg, or five hours total. The average speed, then, is $\dfrac{240}{5} = 48$ miles per hour.

POSSIBILITIES AND PROBABILITY

42. COUNTING THE POSSIBILITIES

The fundamental counting principle: if there are *m* **ways** one event can happen and *n* **ways** a second event can happen, then there are $m \times n$ **ways** for the two events to happen. For example, with five shirts and seven pairs of pants to choose from, you can have $5 \times 7 = 35$ different outfits.

43. PROBABILITY

$$\text{Probability} = \frac{\text{Favorable outcomes}}{\text{Total possible outcomes}}$$

For example, if you have 12 shirts in a drawer and 9 of them are white, the probability of picking a white shirt at random is $\frac{9}{12} = \frac{3}{4}$. This probability can also be expressed as 0.75 or 75%.

POWERS AND ROOTS

44. MULTIPLYING AND DIVIDING POWERS

To multiply powers with the same base, **add the exponents and keep the same base:**

$$x^3 \times x^4 = x^{3+4} = x^7$$

To divide powers with the same base, **subtract the exponents and keep the same base:**

$$y^{13} \div y^8 = y^{13-8} = y^5$$

45. RAISING POWERS TO POWERS

To raise a power to a power, **multiply the exponents:**

$$(x^3)^4 = x^{3 \times 4} = x^{12}$$

46. SIMPLIFYING SQUARE ROOTS

To simplify a square root, **factor out the perfect squares** under the radical, unsquare them, and put the result in front.

$$\sqrt{12} = \sqrt{4 \times 3} = \sqrt{4} \times \sqrt{3} = 2\sqrt{3}$$

47. ADDING AND SUBTRACTING ROOTS

You can add or subtract radical expressions **when the part under the radicals is the same:**

$$2\sqrt{3} + 3\sqrt{3} = 5\sqrt{3}$$

Don't try to add or subtract when the radical parts are different. There's not much you can do with an expression like:

$$3\sqrt{5} + 3\sqrt{7}$$

48. MULTIPLYING AND DIVIDING ROOTS

The product of square roots is equal to the **square root of the product:**

$$\sqrt{3} \times \sqrt{5} = \sqrt{3 \times 5} = \sqrt{15}$$

The quotient of square roots is equal to the **square root of the quotient:**

$$\frac{\sqrt{6}}{\sqrt{3}} = \sqrt{\frac{6}{3}} = \sqrt{2}$$

49. NEGATIVE EXPONENTS AND RATIONAL EXPONENTS

To find the value of a number raised to a negative exponent, simply rewrite the number, without the negative sign, as the bottom of a fraction with 1 as the numerator of the fraction: $3^{-2} = \frac{1}{3^2} = \frac{1}{9}$. If x is a positive number and a is a nonzero number, then $x^{\frac{1}{a}} = a\sqrt{x}$. So $4^{\frac{1}{2}} = 2\sqrt{4} = 2$. If p and q are integers, then $x^{\frac{p}{q}} = \sqrt[q]{x^p}$. So $4^{\frac{3}{2}} = \sqrt[2]{4^3} = \sqrt{64} = 8$.

ABSOLUTE VALUE

50. DETERMINING ABSOLUTE VALUE

The absolute value of a number is the distance of the number from zero on the number line. Because absolute value is a distance, it is always positive. The absolute value of 7 is 7; this is expressed $|7| = 7$. Similarly, the absolute value of -7 is 7: $|-7| = 7$. Every positive number is the absolute value of two numbers: itself and its negative.

ALGEBRAIC EXPRESSIONS

51. EVALUATING AN EXPRESSION

To evaluate an algebraic expression, **plug in** the given values for the unknowns and calculate according to **PEMDAS.** To find the value of $x^2 + 5x - 6$ when $x = -2$, plug in -2 for x:

$(-2)^2 + 5(-2) - 6 = -12$

52. ADDING AND SUBTRACTING MONOMIALS

To combine like terms, **keep the variable part unchanged while adding or subtracting the coefficients:**

$2a + 3a = (2 + 3)a = 5a$

53. ADDING AND SUBTRACTING POLYNOMIALS

To add or subtract polynomials, **combine like terms:**

$$(3x^2 + 5x - 7) - (x^2 + 12) =$$
$$(3x^2 - x^2) + 5x + (-7 - 12) =$$
$$2x^2 + 5x - 19$$

54. MULTIPLYING MONOMIALS

To multiply monomials, **multiply the coefficients and the variables separately:**

$2a \times 3a = (2 \times 3)(a \times a) = 6a^2$

55. MULTIPLYING BINOMIALS—FOIL

To multiply binomials, use **FOIL.** To multiply $(x + 3)$ by $(x + 4)$, first multiply the **F**irst terms: $x \times x = x^2$. Next the **O**uter terms: $x \times 4 = 4x$. Then the **I**nner terms: $3 \times x = 3x$. And finally the **L**ast terms: $3 \times 4 = 12$. Then add and combine like terms:

$$x^2 + 4x + 3x + 12 = x^2 + 7x + 12$$

56. MULTIPLYING OTHER POLYNOMIALS

FOIL works only when you want to multiply two binomials. If you want to multiply polynomials with more than two terms, make sure you **multiply each term in the first polynomial by each term in the second:**

$$(x^2 + 3x + 4)(x + 5) =$$
$$x^2(x + 5) + 3x(x + 5) + 4(x + 5) =$$
$$x^3 + 5x^2 + 3x^2 + 15x + 4x + 20 =$$
$$x^3 + 8x^2 + 19x + 20$$

After multiplying two polynomials together, the number of terms in your expression before simplifying should equal the number of terms in one polynomial multiplied by the number of terms in the second. In the example, you should have $3 \times 2 = 6$ terms in the product before you simplify like terms.

FACTORING ALGEBRAIC EXPRESSIONS

57. FACTORING OUT A COMMON DIVISOR

A factor common to all terms of a polynomial can be **factored out.** All three terms in the polynomial $3x^3 + 12x^2 - 6x$ contain a factor of $3x$. Pulling out the common factor yields $3x(x^2 + 4x - 2)$.

58. FACTORING THE DIFFERENCE OF SQUARES

One of the test maker's favorite factorables is the **difference of squares.**

$$a^2 - b^2 = (a - b)\ (a + b)$$

$x^2 - 9$, for example, factors to $(x - 3)(x + 3)$.

59. FACTORING THE SQUARE OF A BINOMIAL

Recognize polynomials that are squares of binomials:

$$a^2 + 2ab + b^2 = (a + b)^2$$

$$a^2 - 2ab + b^2 = (a - b)^2$$

For example, $4x^2 + 12x + 9$ factors to $(2x + 3)^2$, and $n^2 - 10n + 25$ factors to $(n - 5)^2$.

60. FACTORING OTHER POLYNOMIALS— FOIL IN REVERSE

To factor a quadratic expression, **think about what binomials you could use FOIL on to get that quadratic expression.** To factor $x^2 - 5x + 6$, think about what First terms will produce x^2, what Last terms will produce $+6$, and what Outer and Inner terms will produce $-5x$. Some common sense—and a little trial and error—lead you to $(x - 2)(x - 3)$.

61. SIMPLIFYING AN ALGEBRAIC FRACTION

Simplifying an algebraic fraction is a lot like simplifying a numerical fraction. The general idea is to **find factors common to the numerator and denominator and cancel them.** Thus, simplifying an algebraic fraction begins with factoring.

For example, to simplify $\dfrac{x^2 - x - 12}{x^2 - 9}$, first factor the numerator and denominator:

$$\frac{x^2 - x - 12}{x^2 - 9} = \frac{(x - 4)(x + 3)}{(x - 3)(x + 3)}$$

Canceling $x + 3$ from the numerator and denominator leaves you with $\dfrac{x - 4}{x - 3}$.

SOLVING EQUATIONS

62. SOLVING A LINEAR EQUATION

To solve an equation, do whatever is necessary to both sides to **isolate the variable.** To solve the equation $5x - 12 = -2x + 9$, first get all the xs on one side by adding $2x$ to both sides: $7x - 12 = 9$. Then add 12 to both sides: $7x = 21$. Then divide both sides by 7: $x = 3$.

63. SOLVING "IN TERMS OF"

To solve an equation for one variable **in terms of** another means to **isolate the one variable on one side of the equation,** leaving an expression containing the other variable on the other side of the equation. To solve the equation $3x - 10y = -5x + 6y$ for x in terms of y, isolate x:

$$3x - 10y = -5x + 6y$$

$$3x + 5x = 6y + 10y$$

$$8x = 16y$$

$$x = 2y$$

64. TRANSLATING FROM ENGLISH INTO ALGEBRA

To translate from English into algebra, look for the key words and systematically turn phrases into algebraic expressions and sentences into equations. Be careful about order, especially when subtraction is called for.

Example: Celine and Remi play tennis. Last year, Celine won 3 more than twice the number of matches that Remi won. If Celine won 11 more matches than Remi, how many matches did Celine win?

Setup: You are given two sets of information. One way to solve this is to write a system of equations—one equation for each set of information. Use variables that relate well with what they represent. For example, use r to represent Remi's winning matches. Use c to represent Celine's winning matches. The phrase "Celine won 3 more than twice. . . Remi" can be written as:

$$c = 2r + 3$$

The phrase "Celine won 11 more matches than Remi" can be written as:

$$c = r + 11$$

65. Solving a Quadratic Equation

To solve a quadratic equation, put it in the "$ax^2 + bx + c = 0$" form, **factor** the left side (if you can), and set each factor equal to 0 separately to get the two solutions. To solve $x^2 + 12 = 7x$, first rewrite it as $x^2 - 7x + 12 = 0$. Then factor the left side:

$$(x - 3)(x - 4) = 0$$
$$x - 3 = 0 \text{ or } x - 4 = 0$$
$$x = 3 \text{ or } 4$$

66. Solving a System of Equations

You can solve for two variables only if you have two distinct equations. Two forms of the same equation will not be adequate. **Combine the equations** in such a way that **one of the variables cancels out.** To solve the two equations $4x + 3y = 8$ and $x + y = 3$, multiply both sides of the second equation by -3 to get: $-3x - 3y = -9$. Now add the two equations; the $3y$ and the $-3y$ cancel out, leaving: $x = -1$. Plug that back into either one of the original equations and you'll find that $y = 4$.

A second way to solve for two variables is to use substitution. This is especially useful if one of the variables has a coefficient of 1 or is already solved for. For example, to solve the two equations $5x + 2y = 12$ and $y = x - 1$, we can directly substitute from the second equation into the first one. This gives us $5x + 2(x - 1) = 12$, which becomes $5x + 2x - 2 = 12$. This is simplified to $7x = 14$, or $x = 2$. Now that we know x, we plug it back into the equations to find $y = 1$.

67. Solving an Inequality

To solve an inequality, do whatever is necessary to both sides to **isolate the variable.** Just remember that when you **multiply or divide both sides by a negative number,** you must **reverse the sign.** To solve $-5x + 7 < -3$, subtract 7 from both sides to get: $-5x < -10$. Now divide both sides by -5, remembering to reverse the sign: $x > 2$.

68. Radical Equations

A radical equation contains at least one radical expression. Solve radical equations by using standard rules of algebra. If $5\sqrt{x} - 2 = 13$, then $5\sqrt{x} = 15$ and $\sqrt{x} = 3$, so $x = 9$.

FUNCTIONS

69. Function Notation and Evaluation

Standard function notation is written $f(x)$ and read "f of 4." To evaluate the function $f(x) = 2x + 3$ for $f(4)$, replace x with 4 and simplify: $f(4) = 2(4) + 3 = 11$.

70. Direct and Inverse Variation

In direct variation, $y = kx$, where k is a nonzero constant. In direct variation, the variable y changes directly as x does. If a unit of Currency A is worth 2 units of Currency B, then $A = 2B$. If the number of units of B were to double, the number of units of A would double, and so on for halving, tripling, etc. In inverse variation, $xy = k$, where x and y are variables and k is a constant. A famous inverse relationship is *rate × time = distance*, where distance is constant. Imagine having to cover a distance of 24 miles. If you were to travel at 12 miles per hour, you'd need two hours. But if you were to halve your rate, you would have to double your time. This is just another way of saying that rate and time vary inversely.

71. DOMAIN AND RANGE OF A FUNCTION

The domain of a function is the set of values for which the function is defined. For example, the domain of $f(x) = \dfrac{1}{1-x^2}$ is all values of x except 1 and −1, because for those values the denominator has a value of 0 and is therefore undefined. The range of a function is the set of outputs or results of the function. For example, the range of $f(x) = x^2$ is all numbers greater than or equal to zero, because x^2 cannot be negative.

COORDINATE GEOMETRY

72. FINDING THE DISTANCE BETWEEN TWO POINTS

To find the distance between points, **use the Pythagorean theorem** or **special right triangles.** The difference between the xs is one leg and the difference between the ys is the other.

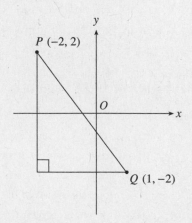

In the figure, PQ is the hypotenuse of a 3-4-5 triangle, so $PQ = 5$.

You can also use the **distance formula:**

$$d = \sqrt{(x_1 - x_2)^2 + (y_1 - y_2)^2}$$

To find the distance between $R(3, 6)$ and $S(5, -2)$:

$$d = \sqrt{(3-5)^2 + [6-(-2)]^2}$$
$$= \sqrt{(-2)^2 + (8)^2}$$
$$= \sqrt{68} = 2\sqrt{17}$$

73. USING TWO POINTS TO FIND THE SLOPE

$$\text{Slope} = \frac{\text{Change in } y}{\text{Change in } x} = \frac{\text{Rise}}{\text{Run}}$$

The slope of the line that contains the points $A(2, 3)$ and $B(0, -1)$ is:

$$\frac{y_A - y_B}{x_A - x_B} = \frac{3-(-1)}{2-0} = \frac{4}{2} = 2$$

74. USING AN EQUATION TO FIND THE SLOPE

To find the slope of a line from an equation, put the equation into the **slope-intercept** form:

$$y = mx + b$$

The **slope is m.** To find the slope of the equation $3x + 2y = 4$, rearrange it:

$$3x + 2y = 4$$
$$2y = -3x + 4$$
$$y = -\frac{3}{2}x + 2$$

The slope is $-\dfrac{3}{2}$.

75. USING AN EQUATION TO FIND AN INTERCEPT

To find the y-intercept, you can either put the equation into $y = mx + b$ **(slope-intercept)** form—

in which case *b* **is the *y*-intercept**—or you can just **plug *x* = 0** into the equation and **solve for *y*.** To find the *x*-intercept, **plug *y* = 0** into the equation and **solve for *x*.**

LINES AND ANGLES

76. INTERSECTING LINES

When two lines intersect, **adjacent angles are supplementary and vertical angles are equal.**

In the figure above, the angles marked $a°$ and $b°$ are adjacent and supplementary, so $a + b = 180$. Furthermore, the angles marked $a°$ and $60°$ are vertical and equal, so $a = 60$.

77. PARALLEL LINES AND TRANSVERSALS

A transversal across parallel lines forms **four equal acute angles and four equal obtuse angles.** If the transversal meets the lines at a right angle, then all eight angles are right angles.

In the figure above, line 1 is parallel to line 2. Angles *a, c, e,* and *g* are obtuse, so they are all equal. Angles *b, d, f,* and *h* are acute, so they are all equal.

Furthermore, **any of the acute angles is supplementary to any of the obtuse angles.** Angles *a* and *h* are supplementary, as are *b* and *e, c* and *f,* and so on.

TRIANGLES—GENERAL

78. INTERIOR AND EXTERIOR ANGLES OF A TRIANGLE

The three angles of any triangle **add up to 180 degrees.**

In the figure above, $x + 50 + 100 = 180$, so $x = 30$.

An exterior angle of a triangle is equal to the **sum of the remote interior angles.**

In the figure above, the exterior angle labeled $x°$ is equal to the sum of the remote angles:

$$x = 50 + 100 = 150$$

The three exterior angles of a triangle add up to 360 degrees.

In the figure above, $a + b + c = 360$.

79. SIMILAR TRIANGLES

Similar triangles have the same shape: **corresponding angles are equal and corresponding sides are proportional.**

The triangles above are similar because they have the same angles. The 3 corresponds to the 4, and the 6 corresponds to the s.

$$\frac{3}{4} = \frac{6}{s}$$
$$3s = 24$$
$$s = 8$$

80. AREA OF A TRIANGLE

Area of Triangle $= \frac{1}{2}$(base)(height)

The height is the perpendicular distance between the side that's chosen as the base and the opposite vertex.

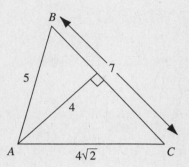

In the triangle above, 4 is the height when the 7 is chosen as the base.

$$\text{Area} = \frac{1}{2}bh = \frac{1}{2}(7)(4) = 14$$

81. TRIANGLE INEQUALITY THEOREM

The length of one side of a triangle must be **greater than the difference and less than the sum** of the lengths of the other two sides. For example, if it is given that the length of one side is 3 and the length of another side is 7, then you know that the length of the third side must be greater than $7 - 3 = 4$ and less than $7 + 3 = 10$.

82. ISOSCELES AND EQUILATERAL TRIANGLES

An isosceles triangle is a triangle that has **two equal sides.** Not only are two sides equal, but the angles opposite the equal sides, called **base angles,** are also equal.

Equilateral triangles are triangles in which **all three sides are equal.** Since all the sides are equal, all the angles are also equal. All three angles in an equilateral triangle measure 60 degrees, regardless of the lengths of sides.

RIGHT TRIANGLES

83. PYTHAGOREAN THEOREM

For all right triangles:

$$(\text{leg}_1)^2 + (\text{leg}_2)^2 = (\text{hypotenuse})^2$$

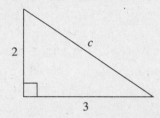

If one leg is 2 and the other leg is 3, then:

$$2^2 + 3^2 = c^2$$
$$c^2 = 4 + 9$$
$$c = \sqrt{13}$$

84. THE 3-4-5 TRIANGLE

If a right triangle's leg-to-leg ratio is 3:4, or if the leg-to-hypotenuse ratio is 3:5 or 4:5, it's a 3-4-5 triangle and you don't need to use the Pythagorean theorem to find the third side. Just figure out what multiple of 3-4-5 it is.

In the right triangle shown, one leg is 30 and the hypotenuse is 50. This is 10 times 3-4-5. The other leg is 40.

85. THE 5-12-13 TRIANGLE

If a right triangle's leg-to-leg ratio is 5:12, or if the leg-to-hypotenuse ratio is 5:13 or 12:13, then it's a 5-12-13 triangle and you don't need to use the Pythagorean theorem to find the third side. Just figure out what multiple of 5-12-13 it is.

Here one leg is 36 and the hypotenuse is 39. This is 3 times 5-12-13. The other leg is 15.

86. THE 30-60-90 TRIANGLE

The sides of a 30-60-90 triangle are in a ratio of $x : x\sqrt{3} : 2x$. You don't need the Pythagorean theorem.

If the hypotenuse is 6, then the shorter leg is half that, or 3; and then the longer leg is equal to the short leg times $\sqrt{3}$, or $3\sqrt{3}$.

87. THE 45-45-90 TRIANGLE

The sides of a 45-45-90 triangle are in a ratio of $x : x : x\sqrt{2}$.

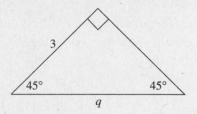

If one leg is 3, then the other leg is also 3, and the hypotenuse is equal to a leg times $\sqrt{2}$, or $3\sqrt{2}$.

OTHER POLYGONS

88. CHARACTERISTICS OF A RECTANGLE

A rectangle is a **four-sided figure with four right angles.** Opposite sides are equal. Diagonals are equal.

Quadrilateral *ABCD* above is shown to have three right angles. The fourth angle therefore also measures 90 degrees, and *ABCD* is a rectangle. The perimeter of a rectangle is equal to the sum of the lengths of the four sides, which is equivalent to 2(length + width).

Area of Rectangle = length × width

The area of a 7-by-3 rectangle is $7 \times 3 = 21$.

89. CHARACTERISTICS OF A PARALLELOGRAM

A parallelogram has **two pairs of parallel sides.** Opposite sides are equal. Opposite angles are equal. Consecutive angles add up to 180 degrees.

In the previous figure, *s* is the length of the side opposite the 3, so $s = 3$.

Area of Parallelogram = base × height

In parallelogram *KLMN* above, 4 is the height when *LM* or *KN* is used as the base. Base × height = $6 \times 4 = 24$.

90. CHARACTERISTICS OF A SQUARE

A square is a **rectangle with four equal sides.**

If *PQRS* is a square, all sides are the same length as *QR*. The perimeter of a square is equal to four times the length of one side.

Area of Square = (side)²

The square above, with sides of length 5, has an area of $5^2 = 25$.

91. INTERIOR ANGLES OF A POLYGON

The **sum of the measures of the interior angles of a polygon** $= (n - 2) \times 180$**,** where n is the number of sides.

$$\text{Sum of the Angles} = (n - 2) \times 180$$

The eight angles of an octagon, for example, add up to $(8 - 2) \times 180 = 1{,}080$.

CIRCLES

92. CIRCUMFERENCE OF A CIRCLE

$$\text{Circumference} = 2\pi r$$

In the circle above, the radius is 3, and so the circumference is $2\pi(3) = 6\pi$.

93. LENGTH OF AN ARC

An **arc** is a piece of the circumference. If n is the degree measure of the arc's central angle, then the formula is:

$$\text{Length of an Arc} = \left(\frac{n}{360}\right)(2\pi r)$$

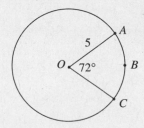

In the previous figure, the radius is 5 and the measure of the central angle is 72 degrees. The arc length is $\frac{72}{360}$ or $\frac{1}{5}$ of the circumference:

$$\left(\frac{72}{360}\right)(2\pi)(5) = \left(\frac{1}{5}\right)(10\pi) = 2\pi$$

94. AREA OF A CIRCLE

$$\text{Area of a Circle} = \pi r^2$$

The area of the circle is $\pi(4)^2 = 16\pi$.

95. AREA OF A SECTOR

A **sector** is a piece of the area of a circle. If n is the degree measure of the sector's central angle, then the formula is:

$$\text{Area of a Sector} = \left(\frac{n}{360}\right)(\pi r^2)$$

In the figure above, the radius is 6 and the measure of the sector's central angle is 30 degrees. The sector has $\frac{30}{360}$ or $\frac{1}{12}$ of the area of the circle:

$$\left(\frac{30}{360}\right)(\pi)(6^2) = \left(\frac{1}{12}\right)(36\pi) = 3\pi$$

96. TANGENCY

When a line is tangent to a circle, the radius of the circle is perpendicular to the line at the point of contact.

SOLIDS

97. SURFACE AREA OF A RECTANGULAR SOLID

The surface of a rectangular solid consists of three pairs of identical faces. To find the surface area, find the area of each face and add them up. If the length is l, the width is w, and the height is h, the formula is:

Surface Area = $2lw + 2wh + 2lh$

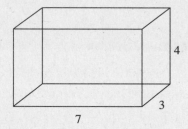

The surface area of the box above is:
$2(7 \times 3) + 2(3 \times 4) + 2(7 \times 4) = 42 + 24 + 56 = 122$

98. VOLUME OF A RECTANGULAR SOLID

Volume of a Rectangular Solid = lwh

The volume of a 4-by-5-by-6 box is:
$4 \times 5 \times 6 = 120$

A cube is a rectangular solid with length, width, and height all equal. If e is the length of an edge of a cube, the volume formula is:

Volume of a Cube = e^3

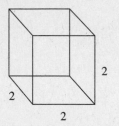

The volume of this cube is $2^3 = 8$.

99. VOLUME OF A CYLINDER

Volume of a Cylinder = $\pi r^2 h$

In the cylinder above, $r = 2$, $h = 5$, so:

Volume $= \pi(2^2)(5) = 20\pi$

100. FINDING THE MIDPOINT

The midpoint of two points on a line segment is the average of the x-coordinates of the endpoints and the average of the y-coordinates of the endpoints. If the endpoints are (x_1, y_1) and (x_2, y_2), the midpoint is $\left(\dfrac{x_1 + x_2}{2}, \dfrac{y_1 + y_2}{2} \right)$. The midpoint of $(3, 5)$ and $(9, 1)$ is $\left(\dfrac{3+9}{2}, \dfrac{5+1}{2} \right)$.